Redescribing God

Princeton Theological Monograph Series

K. C. Hanson, Charles M. Collier, D. Christopher Spinks,
and Robin Parry, Series Editors

Recent volumes in the series:

Myk Habets
Trinitarian Theology after Barth

Jens Zimmermann
*Being Human, Becoming Human: Dietrich Bonhoeffer
and Social Thought*

Friedrich-Wilhelm Marquardt
Theological Audacities: Selected Essays

Randall W. Reed
*A Clash of Ideologies: Marxism, Liberation Theology,
and Apocalypticism in New Testament Studies*

Neal J. Anthony
*Cross Narratives: Martin Luther's Christology and the Location
of Redemption*

Hermann Peiter
*Christliche Ethik bei Schleiermacher—Christian Ethics according to
Schleiermacher: Gesammelte Aufsätze und Besprechungen—
Collected Essays and Reviews*

Myk Habets
The Anointed Son: A Trinitarian Spirit Christology

Christopher L. Fisher
*Human Significance in Theology and the Natural Sciences: An
Ecumenical Perspective with Reference to Pannenberg, Rahner,
and Zizioulas*

William J. Meyer
*Metaphysics and the Future of Theology: The Voice of Theology
in Public Life*

Redescribing God

The Roles of Scripture, Tradition, and Reason in Karl Barth's Doctrines of Divine Unity, Constancy, and Eternity

TODD B. POKRIFKA

☙PICKWICK *Publications* • Eugene, Oregon

REDESCRIBING GOD
The Roles of Scripture, Tradition, and Reason in Karl Barth's Doctrines of Divine Unity, Constancy, and Eternity

Princeton Theological Monograph Series 121

Copyright © 2010 Todd B. Pokrifka. All rights reserved. Except for brief quotations in critical publications or reviews, no part of this book may be reproduced in any manner without prior written permission from the publisher. Write: Permissions, Wipf and Stock Publishers, 199 W. 8th Ave., Suite 3, Eugene, OR 97401.

New Revised Standard Version Bible, copyright © 1989, Division of Christian Education of the National Council of the Churches of Christ in the United States of America. Used by permission. All rights reserved.

Pickwick Publications
An imprint of Wipf and Stock Publishers
199 W. 8th Ave., Suite 3
Eugene, OR 97401

www.wipfandstock.com

ISBN 13: 978-1-60608-198-3

Cataloguing-in-Publication data:

Pokrifka, Todd B.

    Redescribing God : the roles of scripture, tradition, and reason in Karl Barth's doctrines of divine unity, constancy, and eternity / Todd B. Pokrifka.

    x + 318 p. ; 23 cm. — Includes bibliographical references and index.

    Princeton Theological Monograph Series 121

    ISBN 13: 978-1-60608-198-3

    1. Barth, Karl, 1886–1968. I. Title. II. Series.

BX4827.B3 P65 2010

Manufactured in the U.S.A.

For Junia

Contents

Acknowledgments / ix

1. Recent Scholarship and the Argument of the Book / 1
2. A Conceptual Framework for the Exposition of Barth's Theological Method in *Church Dogmatics* / 45
3. Scripture, Tradition, and Reason within Barth's Doctrine of God / 110
4. Barth's Doctrine of Divine Unity / 159
5. Barth's Doctrine of Divine Constancy / 197
6. Barth's Doctrine of Divine Eternity / 248
7. Conclusion / 294

Appendix: The Shared Formal Structure of Barth's Doctrines of Divine Unity, Constancy, and Eternity / 303

Bibliography / 307

Index of Names / 315

Acknowledgments

THIS BOOK IS A SLIGHTLY REVISED VERSION OF THE DOCTORAL THESIS that I wrote from 1998–2002 and that was approved in early 2003 by the Faculty of Divinity at the University of St. Andrews in St. Andrews, Scotland. Various commitments in the home, church, and academy delayed the publication of this thesis, but my interest in the subject matter did not wane. Therefore, I am deeply grateful to the staff of Wipf and Stock Publishers, especially editor Charlie Collier, for the opportunity to share my work on Karl Barth's theological method with a wider group of potential readers.

I am also grateful to those who first sparked my interest in Karl Barth. I am thankful for Kurt Richardson, who first introduced me to Barth by inviting me to participate in a Barth reading group in the last year of my MDiv studies at Gordon-Conwell Seminary. We read volume II/1 of Barth's *Church Dogmatics* in that group, which captivated me with its combination of theological reverence, grandeur and insight. I am also grateful to Serene Jones of Yale Divinity School, who required her students to read volume II/1 for a seminar on Calvin and Barth. This second reading of II/1 at Yale was enough to convince me that, if I were to do doctoral studies in Theology, it would be on Barth and probably specifically on aspects of what I found so captivating in *CD* II/1. That is exactly what I was able to do at the University of St. Andrews beginning in the Fall of 1998.

With sincere gratitude, I wish to acknowledge a number of people who made the writing of my doctoral thesis on Barth possible. To begin, I thank my supervisor Trevor Hart, for his advice and guidance throughout the entire project. I acknowledge several theologians, who gave of their time through personal conversation with me between 1999 and 2001: John Webster, Neil MacDonald, Andreas Loos, Christopher Seitz, Alan Torrance, George Hunsinger, and Stanley Hauerwas. These conversations helped me to sharpen and develop my thinking about subjects covered in the thesis. I thank Harry M. Hine of the University of St. Andrews for providing the vast majority of the English translations of Latin passages cited in this thesis. I thank Michael Partridge for reading drafts of chapters 4 and 5 and providing helpful feedback on them. Especially hearty thanks go to my proof-readers: to Roy McGregor, for correcting drafts of chapters 5–6, to my father, Rev. John Pokrifka, for proofing the entire thesis before its submission to my doctoral examiners, and to Joanna Kimball and Eliza Stuart for proofreading the whole work again as I prepared it for publication.

Last but not least, I wish to thank my dear wife, Junia, for her constant support and forbearance throughout the long process of writing my doctoral thesis and then of bringing it to publication years later. I am grateful to her not only for encouraging me to publish this thesis, but for offering much practical help—especially editing and proofreading—to help make it happen. I dedicate this book to her.

1

Recent Scholarship and the Argument of the Book

OUR MAIN TASKS IN THIS CHAPTER ARE TO SURVEY THE SCHOLARSHIP on Karl Barth relevant to this book, to identify the contributions and deficiencies of that scholarship, and to state the central contentions of the book against the backdrop of this survey of scholarship. As such, this chapter will give the reader an idea of the main argument of the book and of its significance in relation to recent studies of Barth's Theology. The secondary literature that will be surveyed is broad and extensive, because this book involves the intersection of several specialized areas of research.

The way the chapter is organized is attuned to the specific demands of our argument in this book—an argument that leads us to consider Barth's theological method by means of a study of Barth's use of Scripture, tradition, and reason within his doctrine of divine perfections. Thus, we will sub-divide our treatment of the relevant Barth scholarship into five sub-categories: (1) scholarship that deals with Barth's theological method on a general level, (2) scholarship on the role of Scripture in Barth's theology, (3) scholarship on the role of tradition, (4) scholarship on the role of reason, and (5) scholarship on Barth's doctrine of divine perfections. Then, in the concluding section, we will state the thesis we aim to defend and our method of defending it.

Barth's Theological Method

Introduction to the Study of Barth's Theological Method

In referring to Barth's theological method, we refer to the way in which he handles theological questions, the approach, or procedure by which he does theology. This can be distinguished, though not separated, from Barth's particular material conclusions on various theological loci. Put differently, Barth's method is the set of practices and procedures that he uses to reach those conclusions. Within the vast amount of scholarship that has been done on Barth's theology, relatively few studies have focused exclusively or even primarily on Barth's theological method in his *Church Dogmatics*.[1]

There are at least two possible reasons for this lacuna. First, even in his prolegomena (*CD* I/1 and I/2), Barth did not spell out a comprehensive methodology in the sense in which this is usually understood or expected in modern theology. This will be evident as we unfold what Barth's method actually does involve. Second, Barth's theological practice demonstrates an unusually thorough integration of theological method and theological content, an integration that makes it difficult to speak of Barth's "theological method" on its own, abstracted from material theological content.

These two reasons also indicate why certain ways of approaching this question of Barth's method are less adequate than other ways. If Barth's method is his distinctive way of doing theology, then studies that focus primarily on Barth's incomplete and ad hoc theoretical comments about method (in I/1 and I/2) are bound to miss aspects of what emerges in Barth's actual theological practice. Furthermore, studies that for any other reason neglect the concrete material contours of Barth's theological practice (i.e., what and how he argues about various theological topics) are likely to have an incomplete or distorted understanding of the complex method that Barth actually (and perhaps sometimes unconsciously) employs.

Our own way of discerning the nature of Barth's method—the method by which we understand Barth's theological method—is an

---

1. Some books that concentrate on of Barth's method are G. H. Clark, *Karl Barth's Theological Method*; Sykes, *Karl Barth: Studies of His Theological Method*; and Ramm *After Fundamentalism: The Future of Evangelical Theology*. Clark's book clarifies aspects of how reason functions for Barth (see below) but is coloured by some significant misunderstandings of Barth's work. Sykes's volume is a collection of essays, some of which are very helpful (e.g., see our comments on Ford's essay below); however, as a collection, it fails to offer an adequately comprehensive and integrated interpretation of Barth's method. Ramm's book is also helpful but again fails to be adequately comprehensive (it focuses on Barth's way of responding to the Enlightenment). Crawford's article, "The Theological Method of Karl Barth," is relatively comprehensive in scope, but very brief.

expository analysis of Barth's method as it appears in his treatment of specific doctrinal issues. This, we believe, is a promising way of coming to grips with Barth's distinctive theological method in his *Church Dogmatics* that avoids the problems noted above.[2]

Some Studies Pertaining to Barth's Theological Method

Despite the general lack of studies specifically on Barth's method, many of the best general treatments or introductions to Karl Barth have gone some way toward clarifying Barth's theological method. Two recent studies are particularly helpful. The first is George Hunsinger's well-known *How to Read Karl Barth* (1991), an excellent treatment of Barth's theology in terms of six patterns or motifs that mark his theology. Some of the six motifs Hunsinger expounds upon are significantly methodological in character (e.g., particularism and rationalism) and nearly all of them have methodological implications (that Hunsinger does not always delineate). In this book, we will highlight and draw from the methodological significance of Hunsinger's work. Accordingly, we will return to an exposition of relevant aspects of Hunsinger's work later in this chapter (see the section below on the "Role of reason") and occasionally in later chapters.

A second helpful study is Gary Dorrien's *The Barthian Revolt in Modern Theology* (2000), which stresses Barth's distinctive methodological approach to theology and places it in historical context. Thus, he regards Barth's theology as a "Herrmannian,"[3] "new-Reformationist"[4] theology centered in the "exegesis of the Spirit-illumined Word."[5] The

---

2. In this book, we concentrate primarily on the English translation of *Die kirchliche Dogmatik* (*KD*), the *Church Dogmatics* (*CD*). This, rather than the German original, is the "final canonical form" that has been received in the English speaking world and that has prompted most of the secondary literature with which we will interact. Accordingly, we will devote our attention primarily to the English secondary literature that comments on this English translation. Our main argument does not depend on detailed matters of wording or translation. However, we do consult Barth's German original frequently when doing close reading of his work in order to increase our understanding of Barth. In addition, we consult German secondary literature that is pertinent to the matters discussed in the thesis—matters that were generally more abundantly discussed in English scholarly literature.

3. This adjective refers to Barth's adherence in certain respects to the approach of Wilhelm Herrmann (see Dorrien, *Barthian Revolt*, 15ff., 168ff., and passim).

4. Dorrien, *Barthian Revolt*, 2.

5. Ibid., 3; cf. 192ff.

three aspects of Dorrien's characterization of Barth's theology correspond roughly to the three aspects of his method on which we will focus in this study, namely, the roles of reason, tradition, and Scripture, respectively. That is, Barth's appropriation of the modern, post-Kantian intellectual heritage mediated to him by Herrmann (and others) involves a specific theological use of reason; Barth's appropriation of the theological tradition of the Reformation is a clear instance of his use of theological tradition, and Barth's distinctive theological exegesis of the Word attested in Scripture is a crucial manifestation of the central role of Scripture in his theology.

In addition to the methodological contributions of these comprehensive interpretations of Barth's theology, a great deal of scholarship has been devoted to several specific discussions of aspects of Barth's theology that bear directly or indirectly on his methodology. Many of these will be treated in the remainder of the chapter under the rubric of the functions of Scripture, tradition, and reason.

The Strategy of This Book in Relation to Previous Studies

In this book, we will variously complement, develop, and improve upon previous studies of Barth's theological method. Stated in general terms, we will do so by offering a "framework" that allows for a more comprehensive and accurate understanding of Barth's theological method than has been available thus far. An understanding of how Scripture, tradition, and reason function and interrelate within Barth's theology provides this framework. Hence, even as Hunsinger provided a kind of "map" of the shape of Barth's overall theology (in *CD*) by means of an analysis of six motifs,[6] we will provide a kind of map of Barth's theological method in *CD* by tracing three aspects of Barth's way of doing theology. Drawing from the terminology of the Anglican tradition (especially the seventeenth century Anglican divine Richard Hooker and his followers), we will refer to these three aspects of theological method as the "threefold cord."

In Barth's theology, the three strands of this cord stand in a complex ordered interrelationship to each other. As a Reformed theologian, Barth gives priority to Scripture over tradition and reason in his theology. This priority is expressed in the way that the theological function or

---

6. Hunsinger, *Disruptive Grace*, ix–x.

use of Scripture is the central and foundational feature of his theological method (see the next section of this chapter on "the Role of Scripture" and the book statement in the concluding section below). The roles of tradition and reason in Barth's theology are largely incorporated into and qualified by the decisive role that Scripture plays in that theology.

The claims we will defend in relation to the threefold cord in Barth's theology constitute a relatively comprehensive interpretation of Barth's theological method, at least as compared with previous scholarship. Previous studies treating Barth's method tended to focus on only one or perhaps two of the three "strands" of this three-fold cord or some sub-aspect of them. Our more comprehensive account has the advantage of being able to place the various main aspects of Barth's theological method together and in proper proportion to one other. Hence, the function of Scripture is understood in relation to the complementary and subordinate function of tradition, forms of reasoning like "dialectic" are understood in relation to Barth's effort to use Scripture and tradition properly. Indeed, the full significance of Barth's use of any one of the three strands or factors is best understood when one sees how that strand is interwoven with the others to produce his overall theological method. This is true even with respect to the primary role of Scripture, which cannot be separated from Barth's use of tradition or reason.

In keeping with the scope of our book indicated in its title, we treat Barth's method as it appears in a specific section of his *Church Dogmatics* (*CD*): his treatment of divine unity, constancy, and eternity in *CD* II/1. Studies of his theoretical statements about proper theological method (found largely in his prolegomena in *CD* I/1 and I/2) shed some light on Barth's actual method.[7] However, Barth's theological method is best grasped by an examination of Barth's actual theological practice—i.e., the way he does theology with respect to the particular loci he treats after his prolegomena (see our comments on our method of research in the concluding section of this chapter).

We believe that an intensive examination of Barth's theological method in a specific section of his work (selections of II/1, chapter VI) proves more fruitful in understanding his approach than does a relatively shallow and general examination of a larger scope of his work. If

---

7. Some studies on Barth's theoretical doctrine of Scripture and tradition are: Dean, "Relation between Scripture and Tradition," and R. M. Brown, *Scripture and Tradition in the Theology of Karl Barth*.

we are to attend carefully to how the method is displayed in relation to detailed material content, then this limits how much of Barth's work we can examine.

In addition, there are several specific reasons that we chose to treat Barth's account of "The Reality of God" in II/1, chapter VI for our study. First, there is good reason to think that this is the first chapter of *CD* to implement the final shift in his thinking to the more intensely Christocentric theology of the "mature Barth."[8] Second, the subject matter of the doctrine of God is a crucial testing ground for Barth's distinctive revelational theology, since this is a doctrine in which philosophical or "natural theology" had been predominant in the work of many previous theologians. If Barth's method can be shown to be "revelational" and "scriptural" even here, then it almost goes without saying that it will be so in the later volumes of *CD* where the material content of the doctrines tends to be more directly related to the biblical witness to the economy of salvation and revelation. Third, Barth's translator (and interpreter) T. F. Torrance, regarded volume II/1 (and especially chapter VI) as the "high point" of *CD*, a view that Barth himself apparently shared.[9] If we give this assessment the benefit of the doubt, then this section of *CD* should be fruitful for understanding the method of Barth at his best. Finally, there has been no extensive treatment of Barth's theological method within his doctrine of God (II/1, chapter VI).[10]

We may conclude this subsection with two further comments on the strategy of this book. Firstly, despite our emphasis on the integration and interrelationship between Scripture, tradition, and reason in Barth's work, we often will treat these three aspects of his method individually for the purpose of clarifying and analyzing them. Thus, much of this chapter and the next will follow a Scripture-tradition-reason organization. Secondly, while our account of Barth's method will be adequately

---

8. McCormack, *Karl Barth's Critically Realistic Dialectic Theology*, 461.

9. Torrance, *Karl Barth: Biblical and Evangelical Theologian*, 124, 133. Torrance states that "Barth himself agreed that the high point has been reached in Volume II," as opposed to Volume IV (133).

10. See Baxter, "Movement from Exegesis to Dogmatics"; Ford, *Barth and God's Story*; and McGlasson, *Jesus and Judas*. Each of these have offered brief comments on Barth's use of Scripture in this section of *CD*, but these are incomplete even with respect to the use of Scripture, let alone the use of tradition or reason (see below).

comprehensive, there are aspects of his method that we will not treat extensively, such as the roles of imagination or experience.[11]

The Role of Scripture in Barth's Theology

Introduction

Barth scholars are increasingly recognizing the significance of the function of Scripture for understanding Barth's theological method and his theology as a whole. In referring to the *function of Scripture* in Barth's *CD*, we refer not only to his exegetical excursuses or explicit references to Scripture, but to the more subtle ways that Barth's lifelong engagement with Scripture shaped his theology.[12] We are not concerned so much with hermeneutics or exegesis in the narrow sense—with how Barth interpreted or read the Bible—but with the related but distinct question of how he *employed* his biblical interpretations in the theology, i.e., in the critique and construction of theological proposals.[13] That is, we are concerned with the question of how Barth's exegesis and other forms of Scripture-usage are *integrated into* his dogmatic theology. This is what we have in mind when we refer to the use or function of Scripture in his theology.

There are already many scholarly studies treating Barth's relationship to Scripture and they appear to be proliferating. But none has yet covered the *full variety* of functions that Scripture has in his theology

---

11. These are certainly areas for further exploration with respect to Barth's method, even if (in our view) they are not as significant as those that we designate by Scripture, tradition, and reason. One reason we do not comment extensively on the role of "experience" (the addition to the threefold cord that constitutes the Wesleyan Quadrilateral) within Barth's theological method is partly because our category of reason already allows us to focus on the intellectual aspects of experience that are most pertinent to Barth's theology (see *CD* I/1, 198–227). Also, we will not comment on imagination as a separate category, but will treat it occasionally within our broad conception of the role of "reason" (see Clark's *Divine Revelation and Human Practice*, esp. 197–222, for helpful reflections on how Barth's views of divine revelation can be related to imagination, when imagination is rightly understood).

12. The phrases "function of Scripture" and "role of Scripture" are able to include even sub-conscious influences of Scripture on Barth's work, as the phrase "use of Scripture" cannot. However, for our purposes in this book, we will use "function," "role," and "use" more or less interchangeably. This is because we will tend to assume that the main "scriptural" features of Barth's work were intentional, as his own comments in his prolegomena would suggest.

13. Kelsey, *Proving Doctrine*, xiv.

and sometimes the lacunae are significant and misleading. This leaves us with a problem of reductionism in studies of Barth's multifaceted use of Scripture, a problem that only exacerbates the related problem of the absence of an adequately comprehensive and multifaceted treatment of Barth's overall theological method. This is evidence that more needs to be said on the overall matter of Barth as a reader and user of Scripture.

In keeping with our chosen method in this book, the most significant resources for our argument regarding the place of Scripture in Barth's theology are those which examine Barth's theological practice in *CD*, rather than (as with many studies) his theoretical comments on theological hermeneutics[14] or historical criticism.[15] Our comments in the remainder of this section on the role of Scripture will therefore concentrate primarily on studies that are concerned with Barth's use of Scripture in his practice of doctrinal or dogmatic theology.[16]

Furthermore, there is no extensive treatment of Barth's use of Scripture in *CD* II/1, chapter VI, the "material" focus of this book. One reason for this lacuna is that scholars concerned with the role of Scripture in Barth's theology have, quite naturally, concentrated their attention on the later volumes of *CD* in which the exegetical component is more obvious (II/2, III, and IV). For this reason, to argue for a decisive role for Scripture and its interpretation within Barth's doctrine of divine perfections in II/1, a section of *CD* in which Barth does relatively little exegesis in the usual sense of the word, is significantly more difficult than it would be for other aspects of Barth's corpus. This is *particularly* true of the three "perfections of divine freedom" on which we will focus: unity, constancy, and eternity—divine attributes that traditionally have been given a highly philosophical rather than biblical treatment. But the choice of II/1 (chapter VI) is strategic. *If Scripture is a decisive basis for Barth's doctrinal criticism and construction even in his doctrines of unity, constancy, and eternity,* then (by means of a simple *a fortiori* argument) this is *surely* the case with

---

14. For some fine studies of Barth's hermeneutics, see Provence, "Hermeneutics of Karl Barth"; Jüngel, *Karl Barth*, 70–82; Wallace, *Second Naïveté*; and Hunsinger, *Disruptive Grace*, 210–27 [reprint of an 1987 article].

15. The question of Barth's relationship to higher-criticism has been the primary preoccupation of much earlier (largely German-speaking) scholarship on Barth's use of the Bible (see Smend, "Nachkritische Schriftauslegung" and Marquardt, "Exegese und Dogmatik").

16. See our definitions of "exegesis" and "dogmatics" in chapter 2.

respect to the vast majority of remaining doctrines where exegesis figures more prominently. Thus, although it would need confirmation in further studies, the argument of this book has significance for understanding Barth's mature theology throughout *CD*.

A few studies of Barth's theology have indicated in general terms how Barth's use of Scripture is related to his theological approach or theology as a whole. For example, Herbert Hartwell recognizes that "in Barth's view, the task of theology is the expository presentation of that revelation [i.e., God's self-revelation in Jesus Christ] on the basis of a theological exegesis of the content of the Bible."[17] Hartwell rightly sees that such exegesis is typically the temporally and logically prior *ground* of the claims made in the large print of *CD*. But the wide scope of Hartwell's introduction to Barth's theology does not allow him to show in detail *how* this is the case. In addition, an essay by Francis Watson[18] makes a brief, but compelling case for the significance of Scripture in Barth's overall *CD*. In his words, "From beginning to end, Barth's *Church Dogmatics* is nothing other than a sustained meditation on the texts of Holy Scripture . . . Barth's biblical interpretation is . . . the foundation and principle of coherence of his entire project."[19] Although this claim may be somewhat overstated, Watson does point towards the great importance of Scripture in Barth's dogmatic project. But again, the limited scope of his essay does not allow him to support this position in detail. One of the burdens of this book is to do just that with respect to our chosen section of *CD*.[20]

We will now give a brief description of the work of a number of the most important scholars for our purposes from the last three decades. We will group these scholars thematically, but in a way that happens to follow a roughly chronological order.

---

17. Hartwell, *Theology of Karl Barth*, 15, cf. 42ff. For similar ways of understanding Barth, see, Ramm, *After Fundamentalism*, 33ff., Cobb, *Living Options*, 177ff. and Dorrian, *Barthian Revolt*: 3, 181, 192ff., and Watson, "The Bible."

18. Watson, "The Bible."

19. Ibid., 57.

20. Ibid.

The Indirect Function of Scripture in Barth's Theology

In this subsection, we will examine two important studies in the 1970's, one German and one American, that have explicitly or implicitly raised the issue of the function of Scripture in Barth's Theology in the *Church Dogmatics*, as opposed to the narrower question of how Barth's interprets the Bible (his theological exegesis or hermeneutics). More specifically, both studies have argued, quite significantly, that the relationship of Scripture to Barth's theological proposals is largely indirect in character. As such, these studies treat the often tacit, but always significant function that Scripture has in Barth's *CD*—even when he is not doing exegesis in a narrow sense.

The first study is Wolfhart Schlichting's *Biblische Denkform in der Dogmatik: Die Vorbildlichkeit des biblischen Denkens für die Methode der Kirchlichen Dogmatik Karl Barths* (1971). Schlichting's primary concern is to understand how "biblical thought forms" function as paradigms or exemplars for Barth's theological method or dogmatic thinking.[21] In making this point, Schlichting aims to follow Barth's own characterisation of aspects of the biblical witness as a normative prototype or exemplar (*Vorbild*) for dogmatics as a function of the Church that hears and teaches the Word of God.[22] Schlichting draws out the implications of Barth's view that although dogmatics is biblical, it is something more than exegesis.[23] Schlichting goes some way toward expounding this something more—this indirect role of Scripture in Barth's theology. This is an important point that our own study will develop in its own way.

That said, there are significant respects in which Schlichting's work is underdeveloped and can be complemented by our work in this book. Most importantly, Schlichting demonstrates his thesis about the paradigmatic function of the Bible and biblical thought forms primarily on the basis of Barth's theoretical comments in his prolegomena volumes (*CD* I/1 and I/2) and only secondarily (and typically very briefly) on the basis of his dogmatic practice. Our study supports a similar thesis to Schlichting's about the function of the Bible in Barth's dogmatic method, but by means of roughly the reverse strategy of textual support.

---

21. Schlichting, *Biblische Denkform in der Dogmatik*, 42ff.

22. *CD* I/2, 816ff.

23. See Schlichting's lengthy chapter entitled "Die indirekte Vorbildlichkeit des biblischen Denkens für das dogmatische Denken" (*Biblische Denkform in der Dogmatik*, 133–252).

That is, we will concentrate primarily on Barth's dogmatic practice—specifically his doctrine of divine perfections[24]—and only secondarily give attention to relevant comments in his prolegomena in *CD*, vol. I. Not only does this complement (rather than reproduce) the work done by Schlichting, but it offers what we believe is a superior method to discerning the heart of Barth's actual theological method (see the final section of this chapter).[25]

David Kelsey is a second theologian who has drawn attention to the dimension of the "indirect authorization" of theological proposals by Scripture in Barth's work. In his helpful book *Proving Doctrine: The Uses of Scripture in Modern Theology* (1999; the revised edition of his 1975 work *The Uses of Scripture in Modern Theology*),[26] Kelsey comments on the "indirect authority" of Scripture in the practice of several modern theologians, including Barth. In a section on "Direct and Indirect Authority"[27] Kelsey notes how difficult it would be for theologians to authorize their theological proposals by means of a direct use of Scripture. More often, Kelsey thinks, theologians let Scripture bear upon their theology in indirect ways. This it true even of Barth's highly biblically-oriented style of theology. For example, in an insightful exposition of Barth's treatment of Jesus Christ as the "Royal Man" in *CD* IV/2, Kelsey points out that Scripture often bears upon Barth's theological proposals by rendering Jesus Christ as a particular agent, with a specific identity and character.[28] For Barth, theology learns what Jesus Christ is like, not primarily by means of direct translations of the conceptual content of various biblical statements about Christ, but by appealing to the various patterns and structures evident in the narra-

---

24. Schlichting only devotes a page to Barth's account of God's perfections (*Biblische Denkform in der Dogmatik*, 105f.).

25. Balthasar had earlier referred to the "thought-form" or "thought-forms" of Barth's work in his 1951 study of Barth's theology (*Karl Barth: Darstellung und Deutung seiner Theologie*, which was translated into English in 1971 under the title *Theology of Karl Barth*). Yet von Balthasar understood Barth's thought forms to be more Hegelian than biblical. Van Niekerk ("The Biblical Conceptual Form") refers to the "biblical conceptual form" of Barth's work, but does not cite Schlichting's work and develops the idea in a different direction than Schlichting. James Barr regards Schlichting as "almost slavishly uncritical" of Barth in regard to his success in adhering to biblical thought forms (Barr, *Biblical Faith and Natural Theology*, 140).

26. Kelsey, *Proving Doctrine*.

27. Ibid., 139ff.

28. Ibid., 39–50; cf. *CD* IV/2, 155–377.

tives of the Gospels and parts of Old Testament. In such ways, Kelsey's work is helpful in clarifying how Scripture functions in Barth's work.

However, two factors limit the value of Kelsey's work for our purposes. First, Kelsey's comments with respect to Barth are brief and highly selective. Thus, Kelsey is aware that he does not do justice to the "inventiveness and variety of the ways [Barth] uses the Bible."[29] We will need to probe this inventiveness and variety more deeply in an effort to discern how Kelsey's analysis applies to the functions of the Bible found in II/1, chapter VI.[30] Second, Kelsey's view of how Scripture functions authoritatively in theology (whether in direct or indirect ways) does not sufficiently allow for what Brevard Childs calls the "coercion or pressure of the biblical text itself" over the theologian and her theology[31]— something that Barth held to be important in the faithful theological use of Scripture.[32] That is, by placing undue weight on the theologian's (or her community's) independent imaginative construal of Christianity and thus of Scripture, Kelsey downplays the capacity of Scripture to shape theological readers.[33] It is true Kelsey recognizes that there are scriptural patterns or features that do impose controls on what a theologian may say about various theological topics; he does not believe the theologian is free to make Scripture say anything she wants.[34] But in the end, Kelsey believes that Scripture and the results of the study of Scripture are only "relevant . . . but not decisive" to the ways theologians construe Scripture and bring it to bear on theology.[35] At this point we can simply say that Scripture sometimes (though not always) seems to function for Barth in a way that is "decisive" in the determination of his theological proposals. When this is the case, contra Kelsey, it is primarily Scripture, not Barth's prior imaginative judgment, which determines

---

29. Ibid., 39.

30. Specifically, we will need to ask in what sense Scripture is functioning directly and in what sense indirectly. We as we will see that Barth does not primarily appeal to the "narrative" genre of Scripture in II/1 as he does in volumes like IV/2, and this has implications for the character of the indirect authorisation that is present in II/1.

31. Childs, "Toward Recovering Theological Exegesis," 17.

32. For similar critiques of Kelsey, see Vanhoozer, "Voice and the Actor," 74, and Work, *Living and Active*, 125ff.

33. For Kelsey's emphasis on the theologian's imaginative construal, see his *Proving Doctrine*, 160ff, 192ff.

34. Ibid., 196f.

35. Ibid., 201; cf. 197–201.

to which patterns in Scripture the theologian will appeal and to which uses he will put them.³⁶

This book will suggest that the indirect dimension of the authoritative function of Scripture that Schlichting and Kelsey highlight may on the whole be *more* crucial than exegesis of specific texts for understanding Barth's treatments of divine simplicity, constancy, and eternity. To clarify this indirect function of Scripture in Barth's theology is a significant goal of this study and has important implications for discerning Barth's distinctive theological method.³⁷

Comprehensive Analyses of the Role of Exegesis in Church Dogmatics

We now turn to the work of three scholars that, at least in terms of the scope of the texts they treat in Barth's corpus, are significantly more comprehensive than those treated above. We will focus exclusively on their commentary on Barth's *CD*.

We begin with the work of the British theologian Christina Baxter, as found in her University of Durham doctoral thesis entitled: "The Movement from Exegesis to Dogmatics in the Theology of Karl Barth, with Special Reference to Romans, Philippians, and *Church Dogmatics*" (1981).³⁸ The textual basis of Baxter's thesis is remarkably comprehensive, based on an analysis and classification of every single reference to Scripture in the entire *CD* (in addition to Barth's use of Scripture in two of his commentaries).³⁹ As the title indicates, Baxter construes Barth's work in terms of a movement from exegesis to dogmatics. Specifically,

36. Ibid., 201. Consider what Barth says about his reconstruction of the doctrine of predestination: "As I let the Bible itself speak to me ... I was driven irresistibly to reconstruction" (*CD* II/2, x). Furthermore, imaginative judgements made about Scripture or its use can themselves be shaped by reverent engagement with Scripture (see Greene-McCreight, *Ad Litteram*, 248f.).

37. The notion of the indirect but significant relationship of Scripture to theological proposals relates closely to what Vanhoozer calls a "higher form of interpretation" ("Voice and the Actor," 65) and what patristic writers like Athanasius referred to as the "mind" or "scope" of Scripture (see Young, *Biblical Exegesis*, 29–45 and Torrance, *Karl Barth*, 229–88).

38. Baxter has also published a shorter piece drawing on this thesis called "Nature and Place of Scripture."

39. Baxter, "Movement from Exegesis to Dogmatics," introduction. Her method is to deal with typical cases in the main text, to offer further parallels in the endnotes, and to supplement these methods with statistical analysis.

she discerns two distinct movements or procedures in *CD*, which together form his method of using Scripture in his theology: (1) a *simple* movement from the extended exegesis of a single passage to dogmatics and (2) a *complex* movement from collections of selected portions of Scripture to dogmatics.[40]

Baxter's study is distinctive, not only in its comprehensiveness, but also in its methodology. She claims to be the first to base her conclusions about Barth's method primarily on the basis of a descriptive analysis of how he actually works, rather than by considerations of his account of his theological method.[41] This promising methodology leads to insightful research results. For example, Baxter correctly discerns how Barth's interpretation and use of Scripture in *CD* is "form-sensitive," i.e., shaped by the various forms or genres of the biblical literary phenomena upon which he draws (concepts, themes, stories, etc.).[42] In such ways, Baxter's work shows a helpful awareness of the diversity and complexity of Barth's engagement with Scripture.

Baxter's work, despite its obvious contributions, is also marked by certain inadequacies that our present work aims to address. First of all, although Baxter's dissertation is marked by unprecedented comprehensiveness in some respects, it is not adequately comprehensive in others. By attending almost exclusively to the explicit citations of Scripture in *CD*, it largely neglects the crucial *indirect* relationship between Scripture and dogmatics that Schlichting and Kelsey have noted. Secondly, Baxter's dominant construal of Barth's method of engagement with Scripture in dogmatics in terms of a linear movement from exegesis to dogmatics is problematic.[43] It is not clear that this is the best way of understanding

---

40. Ibid., 1. In Baxter's statistical analysis of Barth's fine-print excursuses, the simple movement accounts for 25 percent of his use of Scripture and the complex movement 75% (126 n. 1).

41. Ibid., 6. This does not appear to be accurate, since Ford, whose 1979 work Baxter is aware of, had also aimed to describe and analyze Barth's practice rather than his theoretical proposals.

42. Ibid., 126ff.

43. Baxter sometimes qualifies this construal—claiming that the direction of the movement can be reversed or that there is a kind of circular relationship between dogmatics and exegesis (112, 120, 122). However, the metaphor of a linear movement remains predominant. Indeed, Baxter critiques Barth whenever he appears to stray from the linear model—i.e., a model that moves from pure, historical exegesis to theology. For a recent critique of such linear hermeneutics, see Joel Green's "Scripture and Theology."

or evaluating Barth's distinctively theological use of Scripture. In fact, Barth's way of understanding what he called "theological exegesis" resists domestication under Baxter's model. Our own study treats Barth's direct and indirect ways of relating Scripture to dogmatics in a way that avoids entrapment within a strictly linear model of the relationship of exegesis to theology. Thirdly, our detailed, in-depth analysis of a small portion of text in *CD* allows us to explore, in a way that Baxter could not, the detailed relations of Barth's method of using Scripture to his concrete material conclusions.

A second scholar who takes up a relatively comprehensive interpretation of Barth's use of Scripture is David Ford.[44] In an article called "Barth's Interpretation of Scripture" (1979) and in a book called *Barth and God's Story: Biblical Narrative and the Theological Method of Karl Barth in the "Church Dogmatics"* (1981), Ford argues that biblical narrative and narrative interpretation have pride of place within Barth's theological use of Scripture. He states this thesis as follows:

> Barth's exegesis covers the whole Bible and displays a great variety of hermeneutical skills and principles, but my thesis ... is that he uses one dominant approach that provides the structure of argument and much of the content of his whole theology. This is his interpretation of certain biblical narratives, notably the Gospels but also the creation stories and those Old Testament texts to which he appeals in support of his doctrine of election.[45]

Like Baxter, Ford claims to draw such conclusions based upon an analysis of Barth's theological practice, rather than his theoretical proposals. That said, Ford tends to lay greater emphasis than Baxter on providing a "depth-interpretation" of Barth that goes beyond a mere description—an interpretation that gets at Barth's "implicit principles." Specifically, Ford's interpretative proposal is that Barth's actual method of biblical interpretation has much in common with the method employed by Erich Auerbach and Peter Stern in their literary criticism of the genre of realistic narrative.[46] According to Ford, Barth "recognized that it is

---

44. Ford considers the role of Scripture within all the major doctrines of *CD* (doctrine of God, election, creation, and reconciliation) but does not aim to take into account every single reference to Scripture as Baxter does.

45. Ford, "Barth's Interpretation of the Bible," 56.

46. Ibid., 76–82. In drawing such parallels, Ford admits that he is offering a theoreti-

chiefly through stories that the Bible conveys its understanding of reality," i.e., its theology.[47] Also, Ford believes that Barth "went further in insisting that this way of rendering reality is one in which form and content are inseparable."[48]

Commentators such as Baxter have provided helpful critiques of Ford's work. Without rehearsing these critiques in detail here, we need only to point out that Baxter makes a strong case that, in many cases in Barth's theology, scriptural narratives are considered theologically mute without the theological statements of Scripture that interpret the narratives.[49] Our argument will suggest that there are insights on both sides of this Ford-Baxter debate and that the debate cannot be resolved by making general categorical statements about the priority of either theological statements or narratives (or any other literary form) within Barth's theology as a whole. Instead, assessments about the priority of theological statements or narratives must be made with respect to particular purposes within particular aspects of Barth's complex engagement with Scripture. We will see that narrative is not nearly as important in Barth's theological method in *CD* II/1 (chapter VI) as it is in later volumes of *CD*[50] and that the theological statements of the Bible play a more significant role in this context. However, because of the interrelatedness of Barth's theology, later volumes sometimes provide what we could call the "narrative grounds" for statements about the

---

cal account of hermeneutics that Barth himself does not offer, but he believes that he is doing so in a manner faithful to Barth's practice (Ford, *Barth and God's Story*, 48). In fact, Ford finds many of Barth's own descriptions of his method in the prolegomena volumes of *CD* to be relatively unhelpful in elucidating what emerges in his interpretative practice in later volumes of *CD* (*Barth and God's Story*, 23f.). For further support of the view that Barth interprets the Bible like a realistic novel, see Kelsey, *Proving Doctrine*, 43; cf. Frei, *Types of Christian Theology*, 90.

47. Ford, "Barth's Interpretation of the Bible," 77.

48. Ibid.

49. Baxter, "The Movement from Exegesis to Dogmatics," 165ff. More generally, Baxter believes that the Bible's "theological statements" have priority over other biblical "forms" within Barth's theology. Thus, she calls Barth's appeal to the theological statements of the Bible "the formative and definitive" method in *CD* (165; cf. 165ff., 173ff.; cf. Baxter's later work, "Nature and Place of Scripture," 49f.).

50. Ford states that in volume II/2 and following, the "mediation of the *story* become more pervasive" in Barth account of the scriptural witness to revelation (Ford, *Barth and God's Story*, 24). Indeed, story becomes "the *chief* source of support for his Theology" (56). In this view of Barth's theological development, Ford appears to take a cue from Frei (see *Eclipse of Biblical Narrative*, viii).

doctrine of God made in II/1. As such, Ford's work, while often not directly relevant to the main argument of this book, is also not in conflict with it. Accordingly, Ford offers insights into the nature of Barth's work that we will occasionally draw on in this book. At the same time, we will confirm the point that it is not adequate to regard Barth's engagement with Scripture as primarily "narrative interpretation" without any further qualification.

A third scholar in the 1980's to offer a relatively detailed and comprehensive study of Barth's use of Scripture in *CD* is Otto Bächli in his *Das Alte Testament in der kirchlichen Dogmatik von Karl Barth* (1987). The only respect in which Bächli's study is not comprehensive is that, when he considers Barth's exegetical-theological practice, he focuses on Barth's interpretation of the Old Testament, rather than the whole canon. However, in several other respects it is more comprehensive than either Baxter or Ford. For example, Bächli's book treats in detail, not only Barth's practice, but his theory of biblical interpretation (especially in I/2). There are three main contributions of Bächli that are relevant to our work in this book.

First, Bächli offers a particular view of how to characterize the exegesis[51] that Barth does within *CD*, specifically in his exegetical excursuses. As part of the task of dogmatic theology, he calls such exegesis "*Lokalexegese*" ("loci-exegesis"), exegesis of biblical texts in relation to particular dogmatic loci.[52] In contrast to his exegesis in his commentaries (e.g., *The Epistle to the Romans*), Barth's exegesis in *CD* treats Scripture selectively and topically, choosing to employ only those texts that illuminate or ground a particular doctrine. Bächli thinks that the overall structure of dogmatics, its arrangement into various loci, is largely determined by doctrinal tradition, not exegesis itself.[53] Yet he thinks that what Barth says with respect to the various loci (i.e., the material conclusions he reaches) is shaped strongly by Scripture, both directly in exegetical excursuses and also indirectly in other ways. Even the selection of biblical foundations (texts, themes, and patterns) for a

---

51. By "exegesis" Bächli refers to his citation of and engagement with particular texts, which is only a part, the "direct" part, of the total function of Scripture within *CD*. Bächli is also attentive to the other indirect aspects of Barth's use of Scripture (see Bächli's comments on *biblische Denkform*).

52. Bächli, *Das Alte Testament in der kirchlichen Dogmatik*, 136.

53. Ibid., 136.

particular dogmatic locus occurs "*im Rahmen der biblichen Denkform*" ("within the frame of a biblical form of thinking").[54] The exegesis of the excursuses and the dogmatic questions and framework stand in a reciprocal or mutual relation to each other. "The weight sometimes lies on the side of dogmatics, sometimes on the side of exegesis."[55]

Second, Bächli recognises that Barth's dogmatic *Lokalexegese* is multifaceted. To begin with, it involves at least the following three tasks: (1) exposition of a single biblical sentence [*Satz*],[56] (2) philological explanation of Hebrew (and Greek) vocabulary,[57] and (3) the stringing together of Scripture citations, with or without commentary as an expression of the Reformation principle that "Scripture interprets Scripture."[58] Barth takes up these various tasks of exegesis either in the context of "thematic exegesis,"[59] in which biblical passages and words are examined with respect to particular theological themes (as is typical of the passages we will treat in II/1), or in the context of "exegesis as theological commentary," as in parts of Barth's doctrine of creation.[60]

Third, Bächli further illuminates the discussion initiated by Schlichting and others about what Barth called the "biblical thought-form" of dogmatics (see our discussion above under "The Indirect Function of Scripture in Barth's Theology"). Bächli points out that Barth only once defined what he meant by this phrase (or similar phrases), and even there it is not very sharply defined.[61] Bächli rightly believes that it should be interpreted as an oppositional or polemical concept or term [*Oppositionsbegriff*] in which Barth opposes a biblical form of thinking to a "thinking schematism" [*Denkschematismus*] that is "anchored in

---

54. Ibid. The translations of Bächli, both here and below, are mine, with help from Andreas Loos.

55. Ibid., 142.

56. Ibid., 142–47.

57. Ibid., 147–54.

58. Ibid., 154–64.

59. Ibid., 167–224.

60. Ibid., 227–66.

61. Ibid., 141; cf. 139. The passage is found in *KD* IV/3, 102. As Bächli points out, even this definition of *biblische Denkform* is found in a very late formulation that cannot be claimed as applying to the whole *CD*. Especially in the earlier volumes of the dogmatics, the biblical form of thinking (*Denkform*) or attitude (*Haltung*) refers to a wide framework within which Barth moves, and is not filled with much concrete content.

philosophy and its theological offshoots." For Barth, such philosophical thought schemes "cannot be avoided even in theology; yet the theologian must be willing to let his thought schemes be broken and shattered and their place be taken by the biblical form of thinking."[62]

In these three ways and others, Bächli's fine study contributes to our understanding not only of the role of Scripture in Barth's theological method, but also to the role of tradition and reason as they relate to the function of Scripture. Even so, Bächli leaves much unresolved with respect to the specific tasks of this book. Most significantly, in keeping with the scope of his work, he does not treat the role of the New Testament in Barth's practice. Nor does he comment extensively on the role of Scripture within the passages that we will be treating in Barth's doctrine of God—where the indirect pressure of the "biblical thought-form" or other biblical elements are often more significant in shaping Barth's thought than the exegesis of specific texts. In fact, Bächli generally neglects to role of such indirect (non-exegetical) uses of Scripture in Barth's theological practice, although he appears to be aware of such uses in Barth's theory.

Specialized Studies of Barth's Theological Exegesis

In the period from 1990 to the present, it seems that the main studies related to Barth's use of Scripture are more specialized, rather than comprehensive. Two studies related to Barth's exegesis in select portions of *CD* are worthy of comment, both of which are based upon doctoral dissertations at Yale University.

Paul McGlasson's monograph, *Jesus and Judas: Biblical Exegesis in Barth* (1991)[63] examines Barth's biblical exegesis—especially in his exegetical excursuses—in volumes I and II of *CD*. Apparently unaware of Baxter's work, McGlasson knows of no "large scale work devoted to Barth' biblical exegesis."[64] McGlasson's work, like Baxter's, is based upon an examination of Barth's actual interpretation of Scripture, rather than his occasional theoretical comments about how to interpret Scripture.

---

62. Ibid., 141.

63. This is a published version of his Yale PhD thesis: "Karl Barth and the Scriptures: A Study of the Biblical Exegesis in *Church Dogmatics* I and II." The subtitle of the book is more accurate than the title (*Jesus and Judas*), since McGlasson treats Jesus and Judas only in one section dealing with one of Barth's excursuses in II/2 (135–47).

64. McGlasson, *Jesus and Judas*, 4.

Perhaps the main contribution of McGlasson's work is found in the insightful scheme of classification and analysis that he provides for describing and understanding Barth's exegesis, which could profitably be applied to *CD* as a whole.[65] For example, McGlasson distinguishes between "conceptual analysis"[66] and "narrative exegesis."[67] McGlasson rightly believes the former—"exegesis as the definition and clarification of biblical and theological concepts"[68]—represents the majority of the cases of Barth's exegesis in *CD* volumes I and II, and probably in *CD* as a whole. As such, McGlasson joins Baxter in critiquing Ford's narrative-priority view.[69] He shows ably how both of these two forms of exegesis (the concept-oriented and the narrative-oriented) relate to each other[70] and to the wider contours of Barth's theological method.[71]

McGlasson also makes several helpful material or substantial points in his interpretation of Barth. (1) McGlasson reinforces a point made independently by Baxter and Bächli, namely, that Barth's exegesis is marked by "enormous variety" and an irreducible methodological pluralism.[72] (2) Yet, despite this stress on methodological variety, McGlasson, also rightly, sees an order and unity in Barth's exegesis. This is provided by Barth's consistent construal and use of the Bible as a "witness" to the (Christological) Word of God.[73] (3) McGlasson also emphasizes and clarifies the way in which, for Barth, the text and its content should shape the reader (i.e., exegesis) rather than the reader

---

65. Ibid., 3. McGlasson distinguishes this "descriptive and analytical language" from a "systematic hermeneutic" (*Jesus and Judas*, 2).

66. Ibid., 117–23; cf. 81–113. Cf. Hans Frei (from whom McGlasson draws) on Barth's conceptual analysis or conceptual redescription of Scripture (see chapter 2).

67. McGlasson, *Jesus and Judas*, 123–32.

68. Ibid., 154.

69. Ibid., 117, 132ff.; cf. 6–9. McGlasson also shows how even with respect to *narrative* exegesis itself, Ford's reduces Barth's complex work to only one form of narrative interpretation (*Barth and God's Story*, 123–32).

70. Ibid., 132–35.

71. For example, we will examine McGlasson's comments below on the role of tradition and conceptual analysis (a form of the theological use of reason).

72. Ibid., 47–48. Again, this stands against Ford's reductionistic construal of Barth's interpretation of Scripture under the single rubric of narrative interpretation

73. Ibid., chapter 1 ("The Bible as Witness") and chapter 2 ("Christ and the Bible"). While Barth construes all Scripture as witness to the Word of God, he does so in a flexible and varied manner. This is partly owing to the fact that "not every strand of the biblical literature is straightforwardly witness" (20; cf. 20ff.).

the text (i.e., eisegesis)—even if Barth's work is not always successful in allowing this to take place.[74]

Despite these contributions of McGlasson, two main features of his work are deficient and require supplementation. First, like Baxter, McGlasson restricts his treatment of Barth's use of Scripture to Barth's *exegesis*—and thus deals almost exclusively with Barth's exegetical excursuses. But again, Barth's use of Scripture involves more than exegesis and, as such, it indirectly shapes the large-print sections of his work (where no texts are usually cited). Second, McGlasson often does not treat even Barth's exegesis with sufficient attention to detail, instead summarizing and surveying broad trends in Barth's work. Accordingly, he rarely quotes Barth, with the effect that we cannot easily hear Barth's voice coming through in his exposition.

A second special study of note in the decade of the 1990's is Mary K. Cunningham's *What is Theological Exegesis? Interpretation and Use of Scripture in Barth's Doctrine of Election* (1995). This work is brief (95 pages) and is significantly more narrow in scope than any of the studies we have examined so far. Cunningham focuses primarily on Barth's interpretation and use of one New Testament text about predestination (Eph 1:4f.) within Barth's doctrine of election in *CD* II/2. Like Ford, Baxter, and McGlasson, Cunningham is concerned with Barth's actual exegetical and theological practice rather than his theoretical hermeneutical comments.[75] Specifically, she is concerned to explicate the "internal logic" of Barth's approach under the rubric of theological exegesis.[76] She compares Barth's exegesis of Eph 1:4f (and other related texts, like John 1:1ff.) with the standard historical-critical exegesis of scholars like Bultmann.[77]

For our purposes in this book, Cunningham's most important contribution lies in her self-described effort to "illumine the relationship between Scripture and theology in [Barth's] thought by exploring how Barth interweaves biblical interpretation and theological claims in

---

74. Ibid., 34ff. His chapter 3 on "The Bible and Theology" speaks of Barth's presence as a theologian in his exegesis, which may sometimes involve Barth in "eisegesis."

75. Cunningham, *What is Theological Exegesis?*, 13f. Cunningham here gives several good reasons why it is methodologically superior to concentrate on Barth's practice rather than his theory; cf. McGlasson, *Jesus and Judas*, 6.

76. Cunningham, *What is Theological Exegesis?*, 9.

77. Ibid., 50–67.

developing the doctrine of election."[78] Cunningham's narrow focus on a particular doctrine and biblical text helps her to examine the contours of this symbiotic relationship more concretely and more accurately than others. She shows the specific ways that Barth's exegesis of Eph 1:4 and related texts shapes and grounds his doctrine of election and how his wider theological reflections affect his exegesis. Our treatment of Barth's use of Scripture in his treatments of divine unity, constancy, and eternity takes up a similar task.

Yet Cunningham's study can be complemented and corrected by our own. First, while her conception of theological exegesis is a step in the right direction, a still more comprehensive account of the relationship between Scripture and theology in Barth's work is needed.[79] Theological exegesis is not suited to include all the Bible's various influences over the basic themes and structures of Barth's thought. To do so would involve employing terms, such as use of Scripture, functions of Scripture, hermeneutical theology, or biblically-based dogmatic theology. As such, Cunningham too fails to adequately recognize the indirect authorization of dogmatics by Scripture. There is definitely a need to explore further how Barth's distinctive theological exegesis affects his theological method as a whole.

Concluding Comments

This concludes our survey of the main secondary literature in the last several decades of relevance to understanding the function of Scripture in Barth's theological method. Several other studies could be mentioned here,[80] but the studies selected are sufficient to provide a background

---

78. Ibid., 14; cf. 78–86.

79. In *Credo*, Barth himself defines "theological exegesis" broadly as "exposition of Holy Scripture" that occurs "within the pale of the Church" and that asks the question "To what extent is there given to us, here in this text, witness to God's Word?' (*Credo*, 177). Taken in a certain way, this may include the indirect use of Scripture, but this is not typical of the term "exegesis" in Barth's usage (see the treatment of the function of Scripture in chapter 2).

80. The following studies are worthy of mention:

(1) Wharton, "Karl Barth as an Exegete": This article examines Barth's "confessional exegesis" with a particular emphasis on his influence on biblical interpretation and his relationship to higher-criticism; as such, this work includes assessment of the earlier work on such subjects by Smend, "Nachkritische Schriftauslegung" and Marquardt, "Exegese und Dogmatik."

(2) Trowitzsch, *Karl Barths Schriftauslegung*: This German volume, edited by Michael Trowitzsch, contains the proceedings of a symposium held in October 1995

for understanding our contribution to the question of Barth's use of Scripture in the book.

As we have indicated throughout this section of the chapter on Barth's use of Scripture, our thesis aims to challenge and overcome the unduly narrow or reductionistic views of the theological function of Scripture that have often prevailed in Barth scholarship. More specifically, our contribution regarding Barth's use of Scripture involves four main elements: (1) uncovering new data—i.e., examining a section of *CD* for which Barth's use of Scripture has not yet been treated in detail, (2) clarifying the function of Scripture in this section of *CD* by placing it in relation to the functions of tradition and reason, (3) emphasizing the indirect relationship that often exists between Scripture and theology within Barth's theological practice, and (4) developing the claim that the great creativity and variety of Barth's use of Scripture is nonetheless ordered or disciplined by certain implicit hermeneutical rules and principles and even by the pressure of the text itself.

---

in Jena on Barth's interpretation of Scripture. It includes papers by Wolf Krötke, Walter Schmithals, Rudolf Smend, and Trowitzsch. A recurring theme of the papers is the connection between exegesis and dogmatics in Barth's work.

(3) Demson, *Hans Frei and Karl Barth*: This short book compares Barth and Frei concentrating on their treatments (in *CD* IV and *The Identity of Jesus* Christ, respectively) of the strand of gospel narrative that relates the events of Jesus' life, death, and resurrection to the calling and ministry of the twelve apostles. This study treats virtually no secondary literature on either thinker.

(4) Kirchstein, *Der souveräne Gott und die Heilige Schrift*: This German book provides an introduction to Barth's biblical hermeneutic. It is the published form of the author's 1991 doctoral thesis at Tübingen.

(5) Greene-McCreight, *Ad Litteram*: This expository and comparative study treats Augustine, Calvin, and Barth's readings of the "plain sense" of Genesis 1-3. This study provides a helpful analysis of the relationship between plain or literal sense as (a) verbal sense and as (b) ecclesial "ruled reading" (5-19; passim). Greene-McCreight's fine exposition of Barth employs a helpful distinction between "macro-exegesis" (174-206) and "micro-exegesis" (206-21) and clarifies what it means to speak of Barth's exegesis as "literal" (221-26). The relevance of this study to our own is limited, however, since its primary textual basis is Barth's extended treatment of a narrative text in Barth's Doctrine of Creation that is only very indirectly related to Barth's varied use of mainly non-narrative texts in II/1.

(6) Büttner, *Das Alte Testament als erster Teil der christlichen Bibel*: This German monograph, a revision of the author's 2000 doctoral thesis at Erlangen-Nüremberg, focuses on the role of the Old Testament in Barth's theological interpretation of Scripture.

The Role of Theological Tradition in Barth's Theology

Introductory Remarks About the Role of Tradition

The function of theological tradition is an important lacuna in the field of Barth scholarship. In contrast to the large number of full-length studies related to Barth's exegesis or use of Scripture, there are hardly any such studies treating the function of theological tradition (or traditions) in Barth's actual practice. In fact, no one has treated the function of tradition[81] comprehensively even with respect to a single section or chapter in *CD*. This is significant, since Barth spends as much time and space in *CD* interacting with theological tradition as he does interacting with Scripture.

Despite this general lacuna in scholarship about the role of theological tradition in Barth's work, there are several studies that shed light indirectly on specific aspects of his complex relationship to Christian theological tradition. In what follows, we will survey such studies under two main topical sub-divisions. We will concentrate on studies of Barth's relationship to pre-modern theological tradition, since this is the aspect of theological tradition with which Barth interacts most frequently in II/1.[82] We will generally not attend to treatments of his relationship to individual thinkers, but will pay more attention to his reference to and engagement with certain broader tendencies or groupings within theological tradition that are represented by large numbers of individual thinkers.[83]

---

81. When we refer to "tradition" in this book, we mean "*theological* tradition" unless otherwise stated.

82. Other scholars have already stated with adequate comprehensiveness and accuracy the nature of Barth's relationship to modern theology (e.g., McCormack, *Karl Barth's Critically Realistic Dialectic Theology*, and Dorrian, *Barthian Revolt*). The claims of this book fill out our understanding of Barth in a way that is largely complementary to the work of such scholars. In addition to Barth having "a very strong foot in the Nineteenth century" (McCormack, *Karl Barth's Critically Realistic Dialectic Theology*, 466), we add that Barth still has a "strong foot" in the pre-modern western exegetical-theological tradition (notably in the Fourth century and the Sixteenth century) and in the still earlier "world of Scripture."

83. Barth scholars have already done fairly extensive studies of Barth's relationship to individual theologians. For example, there are a number of studies on Barth's relationship to and interpretation of Anselm (Watson, "Karl Barth and St Anselm's Theological Programme," and Pugh, *Anselmic Shift*, both of whom respond to Barth's *Fides Quaerens Intellectum*). Also, for two illuminating, but somewhat differing, views on what Barth's theological method draws from Anselm, see Gunton (*Becoming and Being*, 117–27)

Barth's Critique of Tradition: Classical or Scholastic Views of God

"Classical" or "scholastic" views of God constitute what is probably the most significant sub-category of theological tradition that Barth interacts with in his treatment of divine perfections. We place the adjectives "classical" and "scholastic" in quotation marks in this subsection, since they are terms that tend to be used in a wide variety of ways in the field of theology. For this reason we will need to qualify carefully our use of these terms later (in chapter 2). At this time, we only need to indicate that in our usage, "classical" theology and "scholastic" theology both refer to theologies in the Christian West that involve a synthesis of Hellenistic philosophical conceptions of God and the biblical portrayal of God.

In his *Becoming and Being: The Doctrine of God in Charles Hartshorne and Karl Barth*, 1978, Colin Gunton offers one of very few detailed discussions of Barth's relationship to "classical theism."[84] Gunton defines classical theism in terms of an interpretation of Thomas Aquinas as its great exemplar.[85] As such, the classical tradition refers both to a particular view of God and to a theological method that tends to be associated with it. Gunton rightly judges Barth's view of God to depart significantly from the classical understanding and approach (at least as Gunton characterises it), but also to have retained certain traces of this classical paradigm.

---

and McCormack (*Karl Barth's Critically Realistic Dialectic Theology*, 421-48). Rogers (*Thomas Aquinas and Barth*) offers a comparison of Barth and Aquinas concentrating on the question of natural knowledge of God. For Barth's relationship to individual modern philosophers and theologians see the sources cited below in the subsection "Barth and Philosophy."

84. Several scholars have alluded to Barth's relationship with the classical theism, although few discuss it in detail. Welker ("Barth's Theology and Process Theology") explores this question briefly in the context of Barth's relationship to Process Theology. Like Gunton, Welker judges Barth to be largely critical of classical theism. Moltmann judges Barth to be more positively related to classical theism (that he calls simply theism or monotheism), both with respect to what he judges to be Barth's inadequately Trinitarian view of God (*Crucified God* and *Trinity and the Kingdom*; see our chapter 3) and with respect to Barth's allegedly Platonic understanding of God's eternity (*Coming of God*, 13-16, 18; see our chapter 6). Gunton's concern to emphasise Barth's critique of classical concepts of God has roots in the creative exposition of Barth provided by Robert Jenson in *God After God* in 1969.

85. Gunton, *Becoming and Being*, 1-7.

We will draw from Gunton's insightful work at several points in our exposition throughout this book, especially in terms of how it sheds light on Barth's distinctive theological method. However, Gunton does not specifically explore (as we will do) the significance of Barth's critical response to the classical approach in terms of the broader role of *theological tradition* in his theological method. This is something our book will need to do in the course of examining Barth's doctrine of God and especially certain perfections of divine freedom.

Thomas F. Torrance's *Karl Barth: Biblical and Evangelical Theologian* treats Barth's relationship to "scholasticism," in both its medieval and Protestant forms. Torrance uses the term "scholasticism" rather negatively to refer to a particular approach to theological method. The roots of this approach are found in the "Latin" tradition exemplified by Tertullian and Augustine, which he contrasts with the Greek patristic tradition exemplified above all by Athanasius.[86] Torrance regards Barth as marked by certain exemplary characteristics of this Greek tradition and as avoiding the negative characteristics of the Latin-scholastic tradition.[87] In addition, Torrance regards Barth as recapturing the insights of the Reformers after the theological decline represented by both the Protestant orthodox scholastics and the modern liberal theologians after Schleiermacher. Whether or not we agree with Torrance's reading of theological history,[88] his comments on the characteristics of Barth's theology and his employment of tradition (both as an object of critique and as a positive guide) are often insightful and always provocative. That said, their substantiation calls for a more sufficiently detailed exposition of Barth than Torrance provides. Some detailed exposition is supplied by the scholarship we will mention in the next subsection, and more will be provided by our book.

---

86. Clearly, our use of Greek here is to be contrasted with our earlier use of "Hellenistic" to refer to the earlier non-Christian Greek philosophical theological tradition (Plato and Aristotle, and so on).

87. T. Torrance goes as far as to refer to the "Latin Heresy" (*Karl Barth: Biblical and Evangelical Theologian*, 113ff.).

88. The accuracy of any given account of theological history is not our concern in this book. We are concerned with such historical accounts (whether by Barth or his interpreters) only as they bear on the interpretation of Barth's method.

Barth's Positive Use of Tradition: Trinitarian and Christological Doctrines

There are several relevant studies that relate to the methodological role of the ancient Trinitarian and Christological doctrines in Barth's theology. The most extensive and significant work in this category is Meijering's 1993 study, *Von Den Kirchenvatern zu Karl Barth*.[89] This masterful study of Barth's relationship to the Church Fathers shows in detail how Barth's *CD* is thoroughly permeated by the Trinitarian and Christological dogmas of the Church Fathers, as they are expressed in the Nicene Creed and Chalcedonian formulation. Meijering shows how Barth uses the Trinitarian and Christological dogmas in relation to each of the main doctrines of *CD*, including the doctrine of God.[90] In particular, he shows how Barth's use of these traditional Christian doctrines forms the basis for Barth's critique of other traditional patristic doctrines of God that have been influenced by forms of natural theology. As such, we see that Barth's interpretation and use of theological tradition allows him to employ some teachings of the fathers against others. In this book we will regard this two-fold (negative and positive) role of tradition to be a methodological pattern rooted largely in the scriptural critique of tradition (see below).[91] Meijering's work is useful to us, because it begins to clarify certain patterns in Barth's use of patristic tradition that are significant for understanding Barth's use of theological tradition as a whole within his theological method.

Another work showing the methodological significance of tradition, specifically the doctrine of the Trinity, in Barth's theology is Benjamin C. Leslie's *Trinitarian Hermeneutics: The Hermeneutical Significance of Karl Barth's Doctrine of the Trinity*, 1991. As the title indicates, Leslie is concerned specifically with the hermeneutical significance of the Trinitarian doctrine, that is, to show how the doctrine

---

89. On Barth's relationship to the Church Fathers (especially Athanasius), see also T. Torrance's *Karl Barth: Biblical and Evangelical Theologian*, 182–212.

90. Meijering, *Von Den Kirchenvatern zu Karl Barth*, 159–238.

91. Meijering avoids extensive consideration of the role of the Bible in Barth's work, restricting his attention to some important principles within his Bible-usage (*Von Den Kirchenvatern zu Karl Barth*, 3). However, he grants that the role of the Bible is to some extent inseparable from his consideration of the role of patristic tradition in Barth's work. For example, Meijering states that for Barth the "God of the Bible is the Triune God and the Triune God is the God of the Bible" (3; my translation).

of the Trinity functions pervasively in Barth's *CD* (he works directly with *KD*) to direct the "interpretation of Scripture, the formulation of language about God, and an understanding of the human self."[92]

Chapter 4 of Leslie's book focuses specifically on "the role of the tradition in the Trinitarian hermeneutic."[93] Leslie begins this chapter with a section on Barth's theoretical "model for relating Scripture and tradition" (drawing mainly from Barth's comments in I/2). He then turns to "concrete instances in which Barth uses tradition,"[94] especially in his development of the doctrine of the Trinity in I/1. Leslie argues correctly that Barth's use of tradition involves a "creative appropriation of traditional formulations."[95] This can be seen, for example, in Barth's controversial choice of the term *Seinsweise* or "mode of being" (the Western tradition's minority view) over the usual term "persons."[96] Despite such creativity, Leslie critiques Barth for often remaining overly concerned to retain the precise conceptual and linguistic form of the doctrine reached in the fourth century or in later Western developments of it (including the *filioque*). Such a conservative tendency, Leslie thinks, stands in tension with Barth's own theoretical affirmations of the historically relative and provisional character of all theological statements.[97]

---

92. Leslie, *Trinitarian Hermeneutics*, 1. We could also note that Barth himself appeared to regard the Trinity as a "critical principle" (or perhaps a "hermeneutical key") useful in the critique of modern (and perhaps earlier) theology (Barth in Godsey, *Karl Barth's Table Talk*, 48f.).

93. Ibid., 125–75.

94. Ibid., 143.

95. Ibid., 164.

96. See ibid., 149ff. Sympathetic to Barth's own self-understanding of his use of *Seinsweise*, Leslie states, "In challenging the tradition he is in effect championing the tradition" (*Trinitarian Hermeneutics*, 150). This relates to Barth's frequent methodological tendency to critique one part of tradition on the basis of another part that he regards a truer to Scripture and to the calling of the Church.

97. Ibid., 165f. This would appear to one of the legitimate points underlying the PhD thesis of Haupert ("Faith in Search of Certainty"). However, Haupert's interpretation of Barth is extreme and marked by serious flaws. For example, he believes that Barth is marked by a "creedal fundamentalism" (377ff.) that assumes that "creedal Tradition is an infallible articulation of revelation" and even a "fourth form" of "the Word of God" (xi, 339–76).

Responding to the Scholarly Situation Regarding Barth's Use of Tradition

As the studies surveyed above would suggest, Barth is marked by a dialectical relationship to pre-modern theological tradition, a relationship involving both affirmation and critique. On this general point, most commentators would probably agree, although they might disagree about whether affirmation or critique (or perhaps a subsequent synthesis) has the priority. But few scholars (including those cited above) have developed this point in any detail, as we will do in this study.

More specifically, our examination of the role of tradition in parts of *CD* II/1, chapter VI offers an interpretation of *why* Barth responds to the tradition as he does. Our claim is that the primary basis of Barth's evaluation of theological tradition is whether it proves faithful to Scripture. Thus, Barth's use of tradition is controlled by his interpretation and use of Scripture.[98]

The Role of Reason in Barth's Theology

Introduction to the Role of Reason

In turning to the question of the role of reason in Barth, we turn to a different order of inquiry than we did in considering the roles of Scripture and theological tradition. There are several reasons for this. (1) "Reason" can be defined as a faculty or capacity (even if that is not all that reason is), as neither Scripture nor tradition can. (2) Unlike Christian Scripture and theological tradition, reason (unless it is radically qualified) does not lie within the specific domain of the Church or of Christian faith. (3) While nearly all Barth scholars have recognized at some level the important roles of Scripture and tradition in his work, they have often not recognized the importance of the role of reason in his theology. In fact, Barth has been accused of being either a "fideist" or an "irrationalist."[99] Such charges, of course, involve a certain view of

---

98. There is also a sense in which the reverse is true. For example, Barth interprets Scripture in light of tradition and has a strong aversion to "Biblicism"—the notion that the theologian has direct interpretative contact with Scripture that can and should bypass the Church of both past and present (see I/1, 607f. and Barth, *Credo*, 155ff.).

99. These charges have perhaps been most vociferously voiced by some conservative evangelical theologians who believe firmly in a role for reason in the articulation and defence of the Christian faith (Clark, *Karl Barth's Theological Method*; Holder, "Karl

what faith and reason are or should be, often one quite different from that which is proposed by or operative in Barth.[100]

For such reasons, it will be helpful to consider some studies that have clarified how Barth construes and uses reason. We will see that Barth's construal and use of reason is complex and cannot be reduced to a simple perspective.

General Treatments of the Nature and Role of Reason in Barth's Theology

Two scholars that have been particularly helpful in clarifying the role of reason in Barth's work are Steven G. Smith and George Hunsinger.[101] Smith's relevant work is his article "Karl Barth and Fideism: A Reconsideration," to which we now turn.

The first point of relevance is that, according to Smith, Barth believes that faith transcends reason only in a specific sense of "reason." Barth consistently maintained that "the obedience of faith transcends reason (*Vernunft*)."[102] However, in such contexts "*Vernunft* means only the human individual's faculty of reason." While faith and its object in revelation transcend such *individual* reason, they do not transcend or contradict rationality or reason in any ultimate sense (i.e., God's "reason"). In fact, "revelation is described in the first volume of *Church Dogmatics* as a thoroughly rational event of the divine reason speaking to the human reason."[103]

Second, Smith makes the related point that Barth uses "reason" (*Vernunft* and related words) in different ways. (1) Sometimes Barth uses reason in what we might call a pragmatic or instrumental sense: as our created capacity to know "that two and two equals four instead of

---

Barth and the Legitimacy of Natural Theology"; see McDowell, "Response to Rodney Holder" for a critique of Holder). But such charges have also been voiced by non-conservative scholars that regard Barth as an obscurantist who devalues reason (Macquarrie, *Principles of Christian Theology*, 333ff., and Roberts, "Karl Barth's Doctrine of Time").

100. The majority of Barth scholars, however, do recognize Barth's efforts to be rational and to avoid mere fideism—as will be evident in the scholars cited below.

101. Other scholars giving helpful, but generally less extensive, comments on this general issue are Hartwell, *Theology of Karl Barth*, 42–48; Gunton, *Becoming and Being*, 218ff.; and Torrance, *Karl Barth: Biblical and Evangelical Theologian*, 45f.

102. Smith, "Karl Barth and Fideism," 69.

103. Ibid., 69; he cites I/1, 135.

five."[104] As such, reason is an innocent, even neutral, faculty that can be used for good or for ill. (2) At other times, by contrast, Barth uses reason to refer to a network of powers and aspirations in humanity that rebels against God and is thus in conflict with faith and God's revelation.[105] (3) Again, Barth also uses reason or rationality to refer to the capacity, given by God in the event of revelation/reconciliation, to conform one's thinking to God as the object of one's knowledge.[106] As such, right theological reasoning requires a decision of faith in God and a related openness and submission to God's Word.[107] In this book, we will need to be aware of all three meanings for "reason"—which we may call the neutral, the negative, and the positive senses of reason respectively.

Third, Smith distinguishes between two main functions of reason in theology: a constraining (or critical) function and an "enabling or freeing" (or constructive) function.[108] Barth's *CD* appears to employ reason in both of these functions, but gives priority to the latter function.[109] The former, constraining function of reason "disciplines our discourse by keeping it off the wrong paths"—and for Barth that includes any path that attempts to get to God from a basis in fallen humanity rather than revelation (i.e., natural theology).[110] The latter, freeing function of reason is the use of our minds as grounded in the obedience of faith.

In these ways, Smith begins to clarify how Barth construes and uses reason in *CD*, showing that Barth should not be classed as a "fideist." However, Smith does not adequately spell out the concrete manifestations of reason's role in any section of *CD*. Neither does Smith develop

---

104. Barth from *Table Talk*, as quoted in Smith, "Karl Barth and Fideism," 69.

105. Smith, "Karl Barth and Fideism," 69f.

106. Ibid., 70ff. This link between rationality and objectivity is an issue to which T. F. Torrance has given great emphasis (see his Barth studies in 1962 and 1996, following Barth's own emphasis on it in his book on Anselm, which was originally published in 1931.

107. Ibid., 75f.

108. Ibid., 75. Although the first function is negative in force, both functions are in the service of the positive or constructive theological end of the obedience of faith. As such both functions can be classified under the third "positive" (or legitimate) sense of reason mentioned in the preceding paragraph.

109. In Barth's earlier work (e.g., *Epistle to the Romans*), his priorities are reversed in this respect.

110. Smith, "Karl Barth and Fideism," 75.

the significance of the role of reason for understanding Barth's overall method (in relation to Scripture and tradition).

George Hunsinger, in his acclaimed book *How to Read Karl Barth: The Shape of his Theology*, not only makes a significant contribution towards our understanding of the role of reason in *CD*, but shows how the role of reason relates to larger trends in Barth's theological method. Hunsinger identifies "rationalism" as one of six motifs that pervade Barth's *CD*.[111] Hunsinger is quick to clarify that, when he uses the term "rationalism" to describe Barth's theology, he is using it in a highly distinctive sense. As he puts it, "The rationalism peculiar to Barth's theology, being internal and not external to faith, might instead by called 'reason within the limits of revelation alone.'"[112] Accordingly, Barth's theology is, like Anselm's, a project of "faith seeking understanding."

Hunsinger organizes his treatment of Barth's rationalism, under two complementary headings: "no knowledge without faith"[113] and "no faith without knowledge."[114] The former suggests the critical limits of the "knowledge of faith," i.e., knowledge based upon faith in God's self-revelation. Specifically, Barth allows for the following limits: no neutrality, no speculation, no apologetics, and no system.[115] The latter phrase, "no faith without knowledge" indicates how faith is intrinsically (though not exclusively) rational, marked by cognitive content that may be developed by means of various logical and cognitive operations. Barth's theological method involves five specific rational procedures: (1) *deriving* doctrines from the content of faith, (2) *grounding* the events that Scripture refers to in their conditions of possibility, (3) *ordering* the relation of parts to the whole, (4) *testing* each doctrine according to its relation to faith in Christ and its adequacy as an interpretation of Scripture, (5) and *assimilating* extra-biblical concepts in a way that transforms them so that they can fulfill their proper theological roles.[116]

---

111. We will briefly comment on the other motifs in chapter 2.

112. Hunsinger, *How to Read Karl Barth*, 49.

113 Ibid., 49–54. This corresponds to some extent to Smith's reference to the "constraining function" of reason ("Karl Barth and Fideism," 75; see above).

114. Ibid., 54–64. This corresponds roughly to Smith's "freeing function of reason" ("Karl Barth and Fideism," 75; see above).

115. Each of these limits on reason involves the relationship of rationalism to one or more of the other constitutive motifs that Hunsinger has identified in Barth's theology.

116. Ibid., 55–63.

Hunsinger's analysis of Barth's theology, in terms of these rational procedures and the limits of reason under the constraint and guidance of faith, provides a fairly comprehensive guide to the main ways that reason functions in CD. This includes some indication of how reason functions in relation to Scripture and (to a lesser extent) to tradition (see the procedures of deriving and assimilating in particular). However, Hunsinger's treatment is relatively brief and schematic. Our work in this thesis will fill out and test his account of Barth's rationalism within the accounts of God's unity, constancy and eternity in II/1.

Barth and Philosophy

Barth is often known for his explicit resistance to the *systematic* use of philosophy in theology, i.e., a use of philosophy in which a given philosophy is considered to be the necessary pre-understanding or worldview for interpreting revelation and doing theology.[117] However, most Barth scholars recognize Barth's indebtedness to "philosophy" in some form, especially modern philosophy, even though they do not agree about how one should assess the nature and degree of this indebtedness. Clearly, an understanding of the distinctive nature of Barth's way of thinking and reasoning requires discernment with respect to how the Western philosophical tradition was received by Barth, an endeavor that inevitably overlaps with the investigation of the role of theological tradition in his work.[118]

There have been many studies that deal with Barth's explicit or implicit relationship with various modern thinkers, both theological

---

117. This is perhaps most clear in his long-running debate with Bultmann and others over the question of a systematic (existentialist) philosophical pre-understanding for biblical interpretation. See the comments of Christoph Schwöbel on the general relationship in his essay on Barth's view of "Theology" ("Theology," 26ff.). For Barth's own theoretical comments on how reason and especially philosophy should function in biblical interpretation, see I/2, 727–36, on which we will comment further in chapter 2.

118. We could have considered the question of philosophy under the category of tradition (that we have decided to restrict to theological tradition) rather than reason. Following the work of Alastair MacIntyre, we tend to assume in this book that what counts as "reason" is to a large extent particular to social and historical contexts or traditions (see MacIntyre, *Whose Justice? Which Rationality?* and *Three Rival Traditions*). Given the general appropriateness of MacIntyre's conceptions of "tradition" and "traditioned rationality," then, Barth can be seen as a member and developer of a certain Christocentric-Reformed tradition of *theological rationality*.

and philosophical.[119] Barth clearly interacts extensively with modern thinkers in his theological work, giving a mixture of positive and negative evaluations of them.[120] What is less clear is the nature of the subtle implicit influences that modern thinkers or modern intellectual trends have had on Barth's theology.

In addition, scholars have raised questions about the role of ancient or pre-modern philosophy in Barth's thought. For example, some interpreters have characterized Barth as Platonic or Neo-Platonic,[121] a suggestion that, if true, would limit the decisiveness of Barth's critique of the classical (and often specifically Neo-Platonic) conception of God (see above).

A basic question in the interpretation of Barth's theology relates to the nature of the role or influence of philosophy in *CD*—philosophy that might be variously (neo-) Platonic, (neo-) Kantian, Hegelian, or existentialist in character. Virtually all interpreters recognize the presence of philosophical terminology or conceptuality in Barth's work: e.g., the Platonic distinctions between the eternal and the temporal or the Kantian subject-object or analytic-synthetic distinctions. The crucial question is how the presence of such terminology, or perhaps more substantive instances of philosophical thinking, is to be interpreted when it is found in Barth's work.

---

119. The following secondary sources are most important for tracing the relation of the Barth (especially the Barth of *CD*) to modern thinkers: Duke and Streetman (*Barth and Schleiermacher*); Jersild ("Natural Theology and the Doctrine of God"); Hendry ("Transcendental Method"); McCormack (*Karl Barth's Critically Realistic Dialectic Theology*) on Kant; Sherman ("Isaak August Dorner on Divine Immutability") and Gockel ("On the Way from Schleiermacher to Barth") on Dorner (see the concluding section of chapter 5 below); Dorrien (*Barthian Revolt*) on Herrmann, and Clark (*Divine Revelation and Human Practice*) on Polanyi. Various writers have commented on Barth's alleged Hegelianism, such as Balthasar (*Theology of Karl Barth*), Hendry ("Freedom of God"), Welker ("Barth's Theology and Process Theology"), and Bradshaw (*Trinity and Ontology*).

120. E.g., Barth's *Protestant Theology in the 19th Century* and various excursuses on modern philosophers in *CD* (see the list of these in Hartwell, *Theology of Karl Barth*, 16f.).

121. See especially the work of Moltmann, who regards Barth's conception of time and eternity and his related eschatology as "Platonic" (although also "idealistic in other respects"), a characteristic that he ascribes to the influence of Barth's brother Heinrich, a Plato scholar (Moltmann, *Coming of God*, 13–16, 18). See also the work of Regin Prenter and other scholars (cited by Leslie, *Trinitarian Hermeneutics*, 109f., 122, and Gunton, *Becoming and Being*, 183f.).

Barth scholars can be divided into two basic camps on this question. On the one hand, there are those who see the presence of philosophy as simply formal[122] or terminological and those who believe that Barth consistently transforms such philosophical forms or terms as needed to make them usable in a theology controlled by revelation.[123] As such, philosophy has little or no influence on the material content of Barth's theology. On the other hand, there are those who regard the influence of philosophy (usually modern philosophy) to be deep and pervasive in Barth's theology, significantly shaping his material claims. In this book, we will argue that it is impossible to frame this question in such general terms and that the nature of the influence of philosophy hovers between these two options depending on the specific part of Barth's work in question. In the parts of *CD* our investigation emphasizes, the first perspective is most often more accurate. That said, philosophy sometimes exercises some influence on the material content of Barth's doctrine of God. This is true in part because it is impossible to fully separate the formal and material aspects of a philosophy or a theology, as Barth himself indicated on many occasions. Accordingly, some scholars argue that Barth should have been more explicit about and critical of the philosophical influences shaping his theology.[124]

A Tool of Theological Reason: Dialectic

When asked by one student what reason meant for his theology, Barth replied, "I use it."[125] Barth's use of this "instrumental" sense of reason (see above) encourages us to explore the rational or conceptual tools that Barth uses within his theological method. Scholars have typically identified "dialectic" as the primary tool of this sort in Barth's work, although they have not always interpreted it correctly, especially in relation to "analogy." Since there has been much confusion and controversy over how to understand the role of dialectic in Barth's mature work in *CD*, we will use this subsection largely to summarize the

122. See Frei, *Types of Christian Theology*, 40f.

123. See Hunsinger on the procedure of "assimilation" (*How to Read Karl Barth*, 61ff.; see above).

124. For a similar position to ours on the philosophical influences affecting Barth's theology, especially his trinitarian doctrine, see Leslie, *Trinitarian Hermeneutics*, 87–123.

125. Bromiley, *Late Friendship*, 43.

contributions that the recent work of Bruce McCormack has made in clarifying this issue.

In his masterful study, *Karl Barth's Critically Realistic Dialectic Theology* (1995), McCormack has offered a compelling argument in favor of an alternative to the traditional two-stage, dialectic-to-analogy view of Barth's intellectual development. In the course of this argument, McCormack sheds light on the nature of dialectic and analogy and how they actually function in Barth's theology.

McCormack first clarifies how there are several kinds of dialectic in Barth's theology. For our purposes, the two main categories of dialectic are: (1) noetic dialectic, a dialectical method or form of thought (*Denkform*) that structures Barth's theological thought and speech and (2) an "ontic dialectic" (*Realdialektik*) that is descriptive of objective relations in reality (e.g., the relationship between time and eternity or between God's acts of veiling and unveiling).[126] Although McCormack regards Barth's *Realdialektik* as more basic and important than his "noetic dialectic" or "dialectical method," we will concentrate primarily on the former as a function (or tool) of Barth's distinctive theological reasoning.[127] McCormack understands Barth's dialectical method as "a method that calls for every theological statement to be placed over against a counter-statement, without allowing the dialectical tension between the two to be resolved in a higher synthesis."[128]

McCormack provides evidence that Barth continues to use this dialectical method in his later work in *CD*,[129] and does so in a way that

---

126. See McCormack, *Karl Barth's Critically Realistic Dialectic Theology*, 11f., where he is summarising four kinds of dialectic discerned by Michael Beintker in Barth's early theology. The term "ontic dialectic" is ours.

127. Ibid., 18. That said, we are inclined to join McCormack in seeing Barth's material convictions about the *Realdialectik* to be prior to and determinative of his dialectical method. Further, we wish to stress more generally how Barth's theological method is closely interrelated to and often inseparable from the material content of his thought, at least in its broad outlines.

128. Ibid., 11. As such, he understands Barth's dialectical *method* similarly to Balthasar, *Theology of Karl Barth* (see McCormack, *Karl Barth's Critically Realistic Dialectic Theology*, 7 n. 19), despite his other differences with Balthasar.

129. McCormack, *Karl Barth's Critically Realistic Dialectic Theology*, 16ff.; 346; 455ff. McCormack draws from the Princeton doctoral thesis of Terry Cross ("Use of Dialectic in Karl Barth's Doctrine of God") to support his view that dialectic is strongly present in *CD*, volume II. We will also make occasional appeal to Cross's work in this study. Also, McGlasson notes how "dialectic patterns of presentation and analysis" are often present even in Barth's exegesis within volume I and II of *CD* (*Jesus and Judas*, 89f.; see above).

harmoniously coexists with his use of "analogy."[130] For example, Barth's doctrine of God in II/1 is governed by the dialectical interplay between God's love and freedom (see chapter 3). In this book, we will show with greater concreteness than McCormack how such dialectic actually functions within Barth's accounts of divine unity, constancy, and eternity. We will see that dialectic is a mode of reasoning that allows the major aspects of the biblical witness to God to be heard without prematurely reducing one aspect to another.

Conclusion: Responding to Studies of the Role of Reason in Barth

We have seen how diverse studies of different aspects of Barth's theology have illuminated the role of reason in his theology. We have seen how this is the case with respect to some general studies of the role of reason, as well as specific studies pertaining to the role of philosophy or of dialectic within Barth's work. We have also seen some limitations of these studies that can be met by our present study. What will emerge is a conception of theological reason that is subordinate to and receptive of revelation. In the task of interpreting God's self-revelation attested in Scripture, reason functions in a variety of ad hoc ways. Instead of proposing the use of a systematic philosophical pre-understanding (as Bultmann did), Barth believes that the object known in revelation needs to determine the appropriate ways of being known, including the methodological functions of reason.[131] We now turn directly to Barth's understanding of the nature of the divine object that is known in revelation, the unique self-revealing God who is marked by certain perfections.

---

130. McCormack does not believe that analogy, at least Barth's dominant concept of *analogia fidei*, is a method at all (*Karl Barth's Critically Realistic Dialectic Theology*, 18f.). Instead, it is an actualistic conception of an ontic analogy created by God's gracious acts—that in the later Barth was understood Christocentrically. That said, McCormack concedes that there are "methodological implications" of the "analogy of faith" (19).

131. On Barth's "objectivism," see T. F. Torrance (*Karl Barth: Biblical and Evangelical Theologian*, 52–60) and Hunsinger (*How to Read Karl Barth*, 35–39). In *Divine Revelation and Human Practice*, 197–222, Tony Clark makes the related point that even creative human imagination should not be construed in an essentially constructivist mode when it is participating in and receiving scripturally witnessed divine revelation (see the concluding subsection of chapter 2 on the "creative" nature of Barth's theological use of Scripture).

Barth's Doctrine of the Perfections of Divine Freedom and Its Context

Introduction to Scholarship on Barth's Doctrine of God

As stated before, while this book is primarily concerned with Barth's theological method, we believe that his method cannot be abstracted from Barth's theological content. This conviction is implied by our overall strategic aim: to discern the nature of Barth's theological method primarily from his practice, rather than his theoretical comments about proper method. Since Barth's practice is always concerned with arguing for specific material conclusions, we cannot escape some consideration of these conclusions. In our case, we need to be concerned with the content of Barth's doctrine of "the reality [*Wirklichkeit*] of God."[132] Barth's doctrine of the "reality of God" is his "doctrine of God proper," a sub-set within a larger body of inquiry that forms the doctrine of God in a larger sense.[133] Much of this doctrine of the "reality of God" is concerned with the divine perfections, which Barth divides into the perfections of divine loving and the perfections of divine freedom (see chapter 3).

Before we turn to some studies on the "Doctrine of the Reality of God" we should note a number of studies of aspects of Barth's theology in *CD* that form part of the essential background or context necessary for understanding this portion of his work. These studies fall into two main categories. First, there are studies of Barth's doctrine of the Trinity, both his detailed treatment of the doctrine in *CD* I/1 and the significance of it in his overall theology.[134] To understand the doctrine of the

---

132. We remind our readers that well-known interpreters of Barth have regarded II/1 and especially chapter 6 as either a "high point" (T. F. Torrance, *Karl Barth: Biblical and Evangelical Theologian*, 124, 133) or a turning point (McCormack, *Karl Barth's Critically Realistic Dialectic Theology*, 22, 461) in Barth's theological work.

133. In the broad sense in which Barth used the term, "Doctrine of God" includes "Knowledge of God" (II/1, V) along with the doctrine of election and the ethics that flowed from it (II/2), but only II/1, chapter VI would fit the traditional definition of the term.

134. The most important works in both regards are Jüngel (*Doctrine of the Trinity*), Rowan Williams ("Barth on the Triune God" in Steven Sykes, *Karl Barth*), and Alan Torrance (*Persons in Communion* and "The Trinity"). In addition, the following are also helpful, especially for showing the significance of the Trinity in Barth's overall theology: Jenson (*God after God* and "Karl Barth"), Gunton (*Becoming and Being*; see subsection "Barth's critique of tradition" above), Bradshaw (*Trinity and Ontology*), and Leslie (*Trinitarian Hermeneutics*).

Trinity is foundational to understanding Barth's thoroughly Trinitarian doctrine of divine perfections. Second, studies of Barth's doctrine of election (in II/2, chapter VII) also provide part of the relevant context for understanding Barth doctrine of the "Reality of God," even though it was written later.[135] We will summarize our own conclusions pertaining to Barth's doctrine of the Trinity in the first part of chapter 3 and will comment on the role of election occasionally throughout the course of the book.

Studies of Barth's Doctrine of "The Reality of God"

The relatively few existing treatments of Barth's doctrine of the "Reality of God," in *CD* II/1, chapter VI, tend to fall into two categories. First, there are several "overviews," studies that are comprehensive in scope, but that are relatively brief and lacking in detail.[136] Second, there are detailed studies of individual divine perfections, such as divine power (or omnipotence)[137] or eternity.[138] We will draw on resources from both of these categories of study in our consideration of Barth in this book.

One treatment of Barth's doctrine of God that transcends these two categories, being both relatively comprehensive and relatively detailed, is the University of Edinburgh doctoral thesis of Thomas Currie (1976), entitled "Being in Act: Ontology and Epistemology in Karl Barth's Doctrine of God."[139] As the title indicates, Currie's focus is on Barth's unique answer to the Western intellectual problem of how to

---

135. On election, see Gunton "Karl Barth's Doctrine of Election" and McCormack "Grace and Being" (and the sources cited by him on page 110). Election is relevant to II/1, partly because Barth had a Christocentric doctrine of election in mind similar to that developed in II/2 even before he wrote about the being and perfections of God in II/1 (McCormack, *Karl Barth's Critically Realistic Dialectic Theology*, 453–63).

136. Some of the best of these overviews of Barth's doctrine of God are found the relevant portions of the following works: Camfield (*Reformation Old and New*), Gunton (*Becoming and Being*), Webster (*Barth's Ethics*), and Johnson (*Mystery of God*).

137. See the book by Patricia Greeve Daveney (*Divine Power*).

138. The best treatment of Barth's account of eternity in II/1 is in Hunsinger's *Disruptive Grace*, 186–209. Of the three perfections we have chosen to treat in this book, only "Eternity" has been treated in any detail by other scholars, but with a confusing array of contradictory interpretations and evaluations (see chapter 6). Unity and constancy are among the majority of Barth's "perfections" to have received only brief treatments by Barth scholars in the course of treating Barth's doctrine of God as a whole.

139. See also Currie, "Being in Act."

relate divine being and the human act of knowing. Barth's answer is found in his theological concept of God's "being in act"—a concept that Barth unfolds in the opening section of the "Reality of God" (§ 28.1). Currie's manner of grasping the nature and significance of Barth's distinctive concept of God's being-in-act leads him far beyond II/1, chapter IV, which he expounds upon in detail in only one of seven chapters of his thesis.[140] Nonetheless, Currie's treatment of Barth's chapter on the "Reality of God" remains one of the most helpful expositions available, especially with respect to the ontological and epistemological implications of Barth's distinctive theological view. The epistemological implications in particular shed light on the distinctive theological method that Barth employs (especially with respect to the "obedient" use of reason) in coming to know and speak of God's acts and being in II/1.

However, there are certain limitations to Currie's work that require supplementation in this book. His treatments of individual divine perfections (among the perfections of divine freedom, he treats God's eternity and glory in more detail[141]), while longer than those given in the "overviews" mentioned above, are not detailed enough to discern certain significant features of Barth's thought that we will take up in this book. For example, the role of Scripture as an important basis for Barth's viewpoints is virtually ignored in Currie's exposition, despite its taking up a significant portion of Barth's work in II/1.

In keeping with our primary focus on Barth's concrete theological practice and the method that is evident in it, the priorities of our expository analysis of Barth's doctrine of God are roughly the opposite of Currie's. That is, while Currie gives extended attention to the distinctive concept of being and knowing that Barth employs in his doctrine of God as a whole (God's "being in act"), as well as its significance in Barth's overall theology and in the history of Western thought, we will summarize Barth's use of this conceptuality only briefly (in chapter 3). Conversely, while Currie summarizes Barth's lengthy treatment of individual divine perfections relatively briefly, we will spend three chapters of our work doing extended expository analyses of three specific divine perfections of freedom (chapters 4 to 6). Our opposite emphasis will allow us to complement Currie's thesis and take up a fresh approach to grasping the content of Barth's doctrine of God. Furthermore, while

---

140. Ibid., 428–513.
141. Ibid., 490–508.

Currie gives a balanced treatment of the love and freedom sides of God's identity, our concern with how Barth responds to classical theological tradition and with the indirect scriptural authorization leads us to concentrate our attention on the perfections of divine freedom where this response is more evident.

A Need for Further Study on Barth's Treatment of the Divine Perfections

As may be obvious from the above, the main reason that there is a need for further study in Barth's account of the divine perfections is that there has simply been so little extensive work done on this area of his theology. Another reason is that there is a need to study Barth's accounts of divine perfections from a fresh angle, which, in our case, is provided by examining these accounts with a focus on the theological method they presuppose.

In addition, by beginning to fill in the lacuna in scholarly exposition of Barth's doctrine of perfections, we aim to arrive at a clearer understanding of Barth's doctrine of God as a whole, and in turn, his theology as a whole. The various aspects of Barth's total doctrine of God (including doctrines of the Trinity, Incarnation, and Election) exist in an interrelated and symbiotic relation to each other. Therefore, the present lacuna in regard to the doctrine of perfections leads to an impoverished understanding of Barth's doctrine of God as a whole. Such a better understanding of Barth's Doctrine of God ought to lead to a better understanding of Barth's theology in *CD* as a whole. As Robert Jenson has insightfully remarked, Barth's theology "is really *one vast doctrine of God*."[142]

The Thesis Statement and the Method for its Defense

The Thesis Statement

We can summarize the main point we want to defend in the following thesis statement: *In Barth's doctrines of God's unity, constancy, and eternity, Scripture functions as the authoritative source and basis for theological critique and construction, and tradition and reason are functionally subordinate to Scripture. Yet, in this process of redescribing the biblical*

---

142. Jenson, *God after God*, 72. Cf. Barth, *CD* II/1, 257.

testimony to God, Barth employs a predominantly indirect way of relating Scripture and theological proposals, a way that allows tradition and reason to play important mediatory roles.

In chapter 7, we will reflect on this thesis statement further as a way of summarizing the main argument of this book.

The Method of Interpretation and Argument

The primary method by which we will communicate and defend our interpretation of Barth's method could be called an analytical description or expository analysis. At times, we may straightforwardly describe what the text tells us about how Barth's arrives at his theological proposals. But we do not have direct access to Barth's method of arriving at his theological proposals, for he often does not spell out the way in which he arrives at those proposals. Therefore, much of our exposition will require discernment of Barth's often hidden method, on the basis of an examination of the results of his method, i.e., the material content of his theological proposals. However, we will also pay special attention to the fine print excursuses in which Barth interacts with Scripture and tradition, and thus more clearly displays the methodological grounds for the main doctrinal conclusions he states in the main text. By means of this expository analysis of Barth's treatment of the divine perfections of unity, constancy, and eternity—as understood in the context of Barth's doctrines of the Trinity and of election—we will come to a clear understanding of the roles of Scripture, tradition, and reason in Barth's treatment of divine perfections.

This method of interpreting Barth presupposes and emphasizes two kinds of "integration" in Barth's theology. First, Barth's theology is marked by integration between his method (how he arrives at proposals) and content (the proposals themselves). Second, there is integration between the various aspects of Barth's method, specifically, between the roles or functions of Scripture, tradition, and reason. We will now explain these two forms of integration more fully.

First, this study assumes and confirms the inseparability and inter-relationship of Barth's method and his substantive theological conclusions. That the material content of Barth's view of God as the unique Subject and object of revelation is correlated with his distinctive theological method is not a novel point,[143] but it is often not given its due in accounts of Barth's theology. This method-content integration is an expression of Barth's belief that the way in which we do theology (our knowledge of God itself and our way of rationally articulating it) must be grounded in who God is and what God has done to reveal himself. Otherwise, Barth thinks, theological thinking and speaking is vain speculation and anthropological projection. Again, in our desire to interpret Barth in a way that is sensitive to his own convictions, we will not make the mistake of passing quickly over the material content of these doctrines so as to arrive at some allegedly independent method. Barth's methods of arriving at theological truth are specifically tailored to the aspects of theological truth Barth is aiming to elucidate—in this case, the perfections of God. Specifically, Barth's concrete conception of God as a unique self-revealing sovereign Subject who has made himself known in Christ leads Barth towards certain appropriate ways of responding to God and to coming to know this God better, such as reverent meditation on Scripture in openness to God's dynamic Word.[144]

Second, our method of interpreting Barth assumes and expresses the internal integration of Barth's method in the form of the interrelationship of Scripture, tradition, and reason in his practice. One cannot properly understand the nature and significance of Barth's distinctive theological method and its central concern to be biblical without understanding this inter-relation between Scripture, tradition, and reason within Barth's theological practice. In addition to recognizing the "threeness" of the threefold cord, we need also to recognize its unity; it is one cord, one method. Yet previous studies have largely failed to do this and this has yielded somewhat one-sided and problematic portrayals of Barth's method. The method of "close reading" (i.e., expository analysis) employed in this study, combined with the relatively narrow

143. For example, T. F. Torrance has stressed this point in relation to his understanding of Barth's "scientific" theological rationality (*Karl Barth: Biblical and Evangelical Theologian*, 45–82).

144. That said, it does seem appropriate to speak of Barth's method in *some* abstraction from his specific material conclusions, as we will often do in this book. In fact, understanding Barth's theology in terms of its distinctive way of relating Scripture, tradition, and reason in its practice is a promising way of being faithful to the distinctive nature of Barth's theology. Barth's theology, even in his own self-understanding, is not a finished system that calls for the repetition of his particular dogmatic conclusions, but a distinctive approach to how theology should be done. See Gerhard Sauter's comments to this effect (*Eschatological Rationality*, 124–31).

textual scope to which it is applied, has the advantage of allowing us to pursue the primary function of Scripture in Barth's theology in relation to the functions of theological tradition and of reason in his theology.

2

A Conceptual Framework for the Exposition of Barth's Theological Method in *Church Dogmatics*

IN THIS CHAPTER WE WILL PROVIDE A "CONCEPTUAL FRAMEWORK" that will aid us in the expository analysis of selections of Barth's *Church Dogmatics* (*CD*) that we will take up in the remainder of the book. By "conceptual framework" we mean a network of interrelated and clearly-defined categories or conceptual tools. Grasping this framework will afford maximum clarity and comprehension of the distinctive ways in which we will employ various terms and concepts in the remainder of the book. Some of these categories we will draw from Barth's own (theoretical) comments on the nature of theology and theological method,[1] and others we will draw from our own reflections on Barth's theological practice. While we will give provisional evidence for the appropriateness of this conceptual framework in this chapter, the actual exposition in the remainder of the book will provide its fuller justification.

Categories Related to Barth's "Dogmatics"

Barth's Description of the Role of Dogmatics within the Task of Theology

The first volume (I/1 and I/2) of Barth's *Church Dogmatics* (*CD*) provides the "prolegomena" to his dogmatics, which, as part of dogmatics itself, takes the form of "The Doctrine of the Word of God." As Barth explains in §4, the Word of God takes three forms: the Word of God proclaimed (church proclamation), the Word of God written (Scripture) and the

---

1. We assume that Barth's theoretical comments about theological method are helpful for understanding his own theological practice, unless we encounter strong evidence that shows that they are not so.

Word of God revealed (Jesus Christ). Dogmatics is a form of obedient response to this three-fold Word of God.

Barth summarizes "the task of Dogmatics" (*CD* I/1, §1) as follows: "As a theological discipline, dogmatics is the scientific self-examination of the Christian Church with respect to the content of its distinctive talk about God."[2] Dogmatics is one discipline of scientific theology.[3] All forms of scientific theology put the truth-question to the Church's God-talk, i.e., they ask "the question as to *the agreement between the Church's distinctive talk about God with the being of the Church*."[4] The "being of the Church"—the criterion of the Church's God-talk—is Jesus Christ, that is, "God in His gracious revealing and reconciling address to man."

There are three forms or disciplines of scientific theology, each of which raises the question of the truth of the Church's God-language in a specific way. (1) Firstly, there is "biblical theology." This discipline asks the question of the *basis* of the Christian church's distinctive speech: i.e., "Does Christian utterance *derive from* Him [i.e., Jesus Christ] ?"[5] (2) Secondly, there is "practical theology," which asks the question of *goal* or aim: i.e., Does Christian utterance "lead to Him"? (3) Thirdly, there is dogmatics, or dogmatic theology. It asks "the question of the *content* of the distinctive utterance of the Church": i.e., "Is it conformable to him"? None of these three questions "can be put apart [i.e., from the others], but each must be put independently and with all possible force." This points to a mutual interdependence between these three main kinds of scientific theology.[6]

In this book we will be especially concerned with the relationship of mutual dependence between dogmatic theology and biblical theol-

---

2. I/1, 3.

3. Ibid., 3f. As a science, dogmatics pursues answers to its own questions in an orderly way. Being independent or autonomous in relation to other sciences, it does not operate under general criteria for what counts as "scientific" (I/1, 5–11.) See Barth's response to the general criteria outlined by H. Scholz (I/1, 8ff.) and Gordon Clark's critical exposition (*Karl Barth's Theological Method*, 51–75). Cf. T. F. Torrance's account of Barth's "scientific" dogmatics (*Karl Barth: Biblical and Evangelical Theologian*, 60–77).

4. I/1, 4.

5. Ibid., 4.

6. Ibid., 4f. Cf. I/2, 766f.; cf. I/1, 121. The distinction-in-unity of the three theological disciplines corresponds to the three "phases" of interpretation of Scripture that Barth explains in § 21.2 (I/2, 766).

ogy, i.e., with the relationship between the question of the content of theology and the question of its basis. The method of dogmatics, while distinct from that of biblical theology, is also thoroughly biblical in its own way, as both Barth's theory and practice testify.

Dogmatics also stands in relationship to other disciplines besides biblical or exegetical theology. Among these, two disciplines are important for our purposes in this book: church history and apologetic theology. Barth does not regard church history as an independent *theological* science, but rather an "auxiliary science indispensable to exegetical, dogmatic, and practical theology."[7] Specifically, church history is directly relevant in relating dogmatics to theological tradition or traditions, although dogmatics itself determines what it will select from history for its own purposes. Unlike the relationship of dogmatics to biblical theology or church history, the relationship of dogmatics to apologetics or polemics is largely negative, at least if one considers apologetics or polemics to be a theological discipline independent from dogmatics. In other words, Barth's believes that the apologetic task of opposing unbelief is best understood as an ongoing ad hoc task within dogmatics. Otherwise, apologetic theology is in danger of becoming an instance of natural theology that is quite opposed to dogmatics. Barth thus resisted all "independently-ventured" and planned programs or systems of apologetics or polemics.[8] This point is an aspect of the broader question of Barth's use of reason or rationality (e.g., philosophy or historical-critical method) in his theological method (see below).

The Method of Dogmatics: Some of Barth's Theoretical Comments

We will now summarize Barth's "theoretical" comments on the proper method for dogmatics. Before we turn to this summary, a few preliminary comments are in order. First, Barth's comments pertinent to theological method are scattered throughout his prolegomena (*CD* I/1 and I/2) and occasionally in later volumes. Barth does not offer an integrated and comprehensive statement of theological method. Second, none of Barth's comments constitute a detailed program of theological method even with respect to a single aspect of dogmatics. Rather, Barth's meth-

---

7. I/1, 5.
8. Ibid., 30f.

odological comments tend to be general, relatively abstract, principles about how one ought to *conceive of* dogmatics or dogmatic method. Any guidelines that are explicit or implicit in these comments allow for great freedom in how one might express or apply them in practice. Therefore, Barth's theoretical comments about dogmatic method, while they provide some basic concepts that we may employ in our exposition, cannot replace an examination of the actual methodological path that Barth decided to take in his dogmatic practice.

Some of Barth's most salient methodological comments in *CD* occur in the latter part of his prolegomena in his treatments of "The Dogmatic Norm" in § 23.2 and "The Dogmatic Method" (I/2, § 24.2) respectively. The absolute and objective norm of dogmatics, of course, is the Word of God—the self-revelation of God attested in Scripture and proclaimed in the Church.[9] Barth speaks of three concrete requirements for dogmatics that flow out of the reverent and obedient hearing of the objective norm of the Word of God. Dogmatics must be marked by three "attitudes" of hearing: (1) a *biblical attitude*, in which it listens to and follows the example of the biblical witnesses,[10] (2) a *confessional attitude*, in which it reverently listens to the creeds and confessions of the Church's tradition, both ecumenical and specifically Evangelical or Reformed,[11] and (3) a *churchly attitude*, in which it listens to the Church of today and its situation.[12] Together these three requirements constitute the kind of disposition or attitude that the dogmatic theologian ought to have in relation to the Word of God, the norm that constitutes the *objective possibility* of true and pure doctrine in the Church.

With this in mind we may turn to Barth's explicit treatment of method in *CD* § 24.2, on "The Dogmatic Method." The presupposition of this treatment is this: if dogmatics calls the Church to hear and obey the Word as a norm, it also calls it to teach the Word as a specific "content" or "object."[13] The method of dogmatics is to offer an "exemplary performance" to the Church of how such positive teaching can be done,

---

9. See I/2, 815f., where Barth speaks of the theonomy or the Word of God and the heteronomy of the relative norms that mediate it.
  10. I/2, 816–22. This relates directly to the role of Scripture in Barth's method.
  11. Ibid., 822–39. This relates directly to the role of tradition in Barth's method.
  12. Ibid., 339–43.
  13. See ibid., §24, section 1, "The material task of dogmatics" (see esp. I/2, 850).

A Conceptual Framework for the Exposition of Barth's Theological Method 49

of how to take the daring step from hearing to teaching.[14] Dogmatic method is "the procedure which dogmatics must adopt if it is successfully to handle its material task, i.e., the unfolding and presentation of the content of the Word of God."[15]

Dogmatic method is marked by a dialectical tension between constraint and freedom. On the one hand, dogmatic method is constrained by the Word of God. Thus, the dogmatician is not free to take up any method. He must be governed and shaped by God's ongoing work of revelation. As an effective, sacramental sign of the Word of God, dogmatics aims to be "wholly claimed by the object of church doctrine."[16] It is to be "characterized as a type of human thinking and speaking occupied and filled with the revelation attested in Holy Scripture."[17] Insofar as dogmatics is occupied and filled with this unique object—i.e., revelation—this object or content "prescribes its way and method."[18]

Yet dogmatic method is also freely chosen. The dogmatic theologian is not given a concrete external law that spells out his course in detail and ahead of time. Rather, the concrete direction of the dogmatician's method is a matter of his *free* obedience to revelation. In this sense dogmatic method is arbitrary, while still being responsible.[19] This free and responsible decision to take up a method that is fully appropriate to the nature of the content of dogmatics is the subjective possibility of pure doctrine. In obedience to the "spirit of the Word," dogmatics "receives what we call its method."[20] Because of the very nature of Barth's conception of method being a matter of free decision, he does not go on to offer systematic instructions about how one should relate and prioritize various proximate norms and sources for theology, such as Scripture, tradition, reason or experience.

---

14. Ibid., 854.
15. Ibid., 853.
16. Ibid., 855.
17. Ibid..
18. Ibid., 856.
19. Barth qualifies the traditional principle *methodus est arbitraria* in a helpful excursus (ibid., 860f.). Barth speaks of the freedom of dogmatic method in terms of the theologian's autonomy—an "autonomy of the Holy Spirit" (884) that corresponds to God's "theonomy."
20. Ibid., 858.

In keeping with the dialectical character of dogmatic method, Barth shows that "systems" are inappropriate for a dogmatics that aims to be obedient to the Word of God. Barth understands a "system" as a comprehensive scheme of thought marked by a two-fold structure of (a) a basic or foundational principle or set of principles (a "basic view") and (b) their non-basic consequences or implications.[21] Barth's primary concern with such a "foundationalist" system is that it allows a "basic view" constituted by a priori principles to replace the proper center and foundation of dogmatics, namely, the living Word of God. Further, the Word of God cannot be reduced to a basic viewpoint or a stable set of propositions. The Word of God (or revelation) has a dynamic (personalistic and actualistic) character in Barth's thought that resists conceptual closure and complete coherence.[22] The Word of God continues to authenticate itself in different situations, and thus *repeatedly* becomes the foundation of dogmatics in various concrete doctrinal contexts. Accordingly, all theology is provisional, ever open to the critical and constructive capacity of God's ongoing acts of revelation.

Barth does accept that dogmatics ought to be "systematic" in the sense of offering an "orderly and thoughtful organization of material" or by being "exhaustive in its interest."[23] In addition, as Colin Gunton rightly points out: "Karl Barth is a systematic theologian in the sense

---

21. Barth defines such a system as "a structure of principles and their consequences, founded on the presupposition of a basic view of things, constructed with the help of various sources of knowledge and axioms and self-contained and complete in itself" (I/2, 861; cf. I/2, 861ff.; cf. Godsey, *Karl Barth's Table Talk*, 23f.). This is one of the passages that other scholars have pointed to as evidence of Barth's non-foundationalism (Johnson, *Mystery of God*, 3f., 31ff.; cf. Dorrien, *Barthian Revolt*, 11ff. and Alan Torrance, *Persons in Communion*, chapter 1). To a large extent such scholars are correct. That said, Barth is not entirely opposed to a non-systematic, "weak foundationalism" (as opposed to the "strong foundationalism" described above), which can be defined simply as a structure of belief in which some beliefs are considered more basic than others. On various senses of foundationalism, see Plantinga and Wolterstorff (*Faith and Rationality*, 1–3). Barth's approach to epistemology can also be characterized as "Anselmian" or "weak coherentism" (see our comments on Barth's use of reason below).

22. E.g., I/2, 862, 872. The open and provisional character of Barth's conception of dogmatic method is evident in Barth's response to Balthasar's influential account of his thought. Barth objected that his own method cannot be reduced to a guiding "thought form" [*Denkform*], but that it employs a dynamic "movement of thought" or "way of thinking" [*Denkbewegung*] (Barth, as cited in Johnson, *Mystery of God*, 192 n. 14).

23. Godsey, *Karl Barth's Table Talk*, 23f. Barth goes on to say that "the Bible affords the only criterion for judging whether or not my theology is a system" (24), a clear statement of the importance of Scripture for Barth.

that nothing is written in one place without implicit or explicit reference to other theological themes."[24] This orderly interconnectedness is an obvious feature of Barth's dogmatic method in his practice in *CD*.

To summarize Barth's view, dogmatic method is essentially *a posture of reverent obedience before the revealed Word of God and an unrelenting attempt to be faithful to its content* (see our comments on "reverence" in the concluding section of this chapter). No specific method is given in the sense of a detailed explanation of the kind of practices he will engage in to determine his dogmatic answers. Barth's method in this more concrete sense will need to be uncovered by an examination of his actual dogmatic practice.

Natural Theology and its Dogmatic Remedies: The Two Criteria of Dogmatics

One helpful way to clarify the nature of Barth's dogmatic method is to understand his way of contrasting dogmatics with natural theology.[25] We begin with the definition of natural theology that Barth gave (in his piece entitled "Nein!") in his debate with Emil Brunner:

> By "natural theology" I mean every (positive *or* negative) *formulation of a system* which claims to be theological, i.e., to interpret divine revelation, whose *subject*, however, differs fundamentally from the revelation in Jesus Christ and whose *method* therefore differs equally from the exposition of Holy Scripture.[26]

There are several respects in which natural theology differs from dogmatics. First, natural theology is the "formulation of a system," which in itself is inappropriate to dogmatics, as we saw above. Second, while natural theology *claims* to be theological, i.e., to interpret divine revelation, *in fact* it has a fundamentally different *subject* (or content) than revelation. Barth's dogmatics, by contrast, is theological, because it has God's revelation in Jesus Christ as its only subject. Third, though natural theology claims to interpret revelation, it has a fundamentally different

---

24. Gunton, "Salvation," 143. See also Leslie, *Trinitarian Hermeneutics*, 67–71, on the question of the "systematic" character of Barth's theology.

25. For scholarly discussion of natural theology, see Hartwell, *Theology of Karl Barth*, 48–55, Torrance, *Karl Barth: Biblical and Evangelical Theologian*, 136–59; Barr, *Biblical Faith and Natural Theology*; and Hart, *Regarding Karl Barth*, 139–72.

26. Barth and Brunner, *Natural Theology*, 74f.

method than that of the exposition of Scripture. By contrast, the method of dogmatics is genuinely theological because its method is centrally preoccupied with the exposition of Scripture (i.e., the Word of God written).

Although these three aspects of the distinction between dogmatics and natural theology are relatively distinct from each other, they are also interrelated. It is because of the unique subject matter or content of dogmatics (the revealed Word of God) that it cannot be formulated into a system in which some other "basic view" becomes its central content. Likewise, since Barth believes the definitive witness to the subject of theology (the revelation in Jesus Christ) is found in the Scriptures, the exposition of Scripture is the fundamental theological method.

In light of the analysis we have given of it, Barth's definition of natural theology implies a two-sided remedy for the "theological disease" of natural theology. This remedy is to vigorously maintain (1) the proper subject or content of theology and (2) the proper method of theology.[27] While we are ultimately most concerned with the second, methodological part of this remedy in this book, both parts are of crucial significance and should be understood in connection to each other. We will comment on these two remedies in turn.

(1) Barth's concern over the proper subject matter or content of theology results in what we will call his "*material* criterion" or rule for theology. This criterion states that theology, if it is not to be natural theology, must have "the revelation of Jesus Christ" as its fundamental *content*. This criterion is closely related to the pervasive "Christocentrism" or "Christological concentration" of Barth's theology, which both Barth and his interpreters have identified as of crucial significance to understanding his theology. Bruce McCormack defines Barth's Christocentrism "the attempt (which characterized his mature theology) to understand every doctrine from a center in God's self-revelation in Jesus Christ."[28] Barth's dogmatics is *Christocentric in content*.[29]

---

27. While the two-fold scheme does not assign an explicit, independent role to Barth's concern to avoid a system, this concern is preserved in Barth's concern over the proper content and method of theology, as will be evident.

28. McCormack, *Karl Barth's Critically Realistic Dialectic Theology*, 454.

29. The phrase "in content" does not preclude "in method." In fact, McCormack says that Barth's Christocentrism is "a methodological rule, not an a priori principle" (ibid., 454).

(2) Barth's concern over proper method results in what we could call his *"methodological* criterion" for theology. According to this criterion, theology, if it is not to be natural theology, is to be fundamentally the exposition of Holy Scripture. This criterion or rule corresponds to Barth's emphasis on the "theological exegesis" of the "verbal sense" of Scripture. By verbal sense we mean the straightforward grammatical meaning of biblical sentences, understood in their literary contexts.[30] Readings of Scripture, including the macro-reading constituted by Barth's dogmatics as a whole, must have the "constraint of the verbal sense" as one of its crucial criteria.[31] In such ways, Barth's dogmatics is textually- based or *biblical in method.*

While they usually peacefully coexist in Barth's theology, a dialectical tension obtains between these two criteria that enables them to act as checks and balances in relation to each other. The material criterion keeps the methodological criterion from turning dogmatics into a disunited and disorderly collection of disparate exegetical-theological comments on various biblical passages. Alternatively, the methodological criterion keeps the material criterion from turning dogmatics into a static Christocentric system, in which there is no real openness to the dynamic Word of God as it is attested in diverse ways in Scripture. In the remaining sections of this chapter, we will include comments on how these two criteria relate to the respective roles of Scripture, tradition, and reason in Barth's theology.

Concepts Related to Scripture and its Theological Functions

There are three main categories for concepts related to the function of Scripture: the construal of Scripture, the interpretation of Scripture, and

---

30. In our usage, then, the verbal sense of the biblical text is an aspect of its "literal," "plain," or "natural" sense. I use the specific term "verbal sense," because the other terms in the last sentence can also include reference to a "communal construal," which we do not have in mind here (see Greene-McCreight, *Ad Litteram*, 21f.; cf. Watson, *Text, Church, and World*, 223–31, and Frei, "Literal Reading"). The sense of traditional or "communal construal" is more appropriate in referring to the Christocentric way of reading Scripture that is associated with Barth's "material criterion." The sense of the community and a text's relation to the center of Scripture (cf. Watson, *Text and Truth*, 123f.) can be seen as other aspects of the "literal sense" of Scripture that are distinct from, but potentially complementary to, Scripture's verbal sense.

31. Greene-McCreight, *Ad Litteram*, 21f.

the use of Scripture in dogmatics. There is a degree of overlap between these three categories, but they do provide a helpful way of organizing our analysis below. After treating these three conceptual categories, we will comment on the relationship between Barth's two criteria for dogmatics (treated above) and the function of Scripture.

Concepts Related to Barth's Construal of Scripture

The Construal of Scripture as a Whole

In this first subsection, we will lay out a series of concepts pertaining to how Barth construes Scripture as a whole, which may be called his "canonical construal."[32]

Barth's own doctrine of Scripture, given in his prolegomena to CD, is helpful in providing the concepts by which he refers to Scripture as a whole. The two most important are "Word of God" and "Witness to Revelation."[33] Since others have written on Barth's understanding of these concepts extensively, we only need to summarize briefly what Barth means by them. The concepts of Scripture as the "Word of God" and as "Witness to Revelation" stand in what we could call a "perichoretic" relationship to each other. They are distinct, complementary concepts, but they are inseparably united to each other.

In their distinctness, Word of God and Witness to Revelation each emphasize important, complementary aspects of Barth's dialectical view of Scripture. To refer to Scripture as the "Word of God written" (one of his three forms of the Word of God) emphasizes how God can speak through Scripture such that it becomes the very Word or Revelation of God.[34] In this way Scripture in some sense mediates a *divine* speech act, speech that comes from God and is directed to humanity.[35] Conversely,

---

32. See Wood, *Formation of Christian Understanding*; Kelsey, *Proving Doctrine*, 103–8. For Barth's own statements on the nature and unity of the canon, see especially I/2, 473–85; 597–603.

33. The following summary is based upon I/2, chapter 3 on "Holy Scripture," especially §19.

34. I/1, 99–111. As a form of the Word of God, Scripture is marked by a pattern that is found in all three forms of the Word: namely, that God reveals *himself* in his Word, but does so in indirect, mediated and human forms.

35. See Wolterstorff, *Divine Discourse*, 63–74 for a careful analysis that shows how Barth does not appear to allow for the *literal* ascription of speech acts to God in Scripture.

to refer to Scripture as the decisive witness of divine revelation[36] emphasizes that Scripture in and of itself is a collection of *human* speech-acts that attest to the revelation of God in Jesus Christ through expectation (Old Testament) or recollection (New Testament).

For our purposes, five significant claims are implicit in Barth's referring to the Bible as the "Word of God" and as "witness to revelation." First, the relationship of identity between the witness of Scripture and God's revelation (God's Word revealed) is *indirect*. The words point beyond themselves to the Word, Jesus Christ, who in turn reveals God *in se*.[37] Second, both "Word of God" and "witness" nevertheless emphasize the Bible's divinely authorized *uniqueness*, that we may know and expect that God speaks through this book in a way that he does not through others. As the first and only direct witness to the revelation of Jesus Christ, Scripture uniquely mediates that revelation to the Church. Third, both terms emphasize that, for Barth, the Bible is primarily "*kerygmatic*" in character; it is literature of preaching and proclamation.[38] Fourth, by referring to Scripture as a whole as "Word" or "Witness" in the singular, Barth emphasizes the *unity* of the Bible. Fifth, the audience and purpose of Scripture is *ecclesial*, in that it is the "Word of God for the Church"[39] and the witness of the apostles and prophets for the Church. These five claims in Barth's theological construal of the Bible offer some limited insights into how we might expect Barth to use Scripture in general, assuming (as we have been) that his practice is consistent with his theory.

The dual human-divine character of the Bible also has implications for how we interpret it. As a human book, the Bible ought to be read in an effort to discern the verbal sense of the text and the author; this is exegesis.[40] Yet, we must not become "stuck" in the words them-

---

36. Barth's more distinctive term for Scripture is "witness to revelation." *CD* I/2, 457. G. W. Bromiley notes that the English translation of the subsection "Scripture as a Witness to Divine Revelation" is misleading, since the German original has no article before the word for witness [*bezeugen*] (*Introduction to Karl Barth*, 34).

37. Thus Barth departs from the traditional static conception of verbal inspiration in which God's revelation is identified with the words of the text as such (*CD* I/2, 508–26).

38. See Barth's comments on this point in a helpful essay on the doctrine of revelation (Barth, "The Christian Understanding of Revelation," 220f.).

39. This is the title of *CD* § 19 (I/2, 457ff.).

40. I/2, 463f.

selves. Rather, the Bible also ought to be read theologically in an effort to grasp its referent, or that about which it is speaking; this is *theological exegesis*.[41] Indeed, Barth argues elsewhere that true understanding of Scripture requires a divine act by which the text's subject matter (the dynamic Word of God) confronts us and enables us to perceive it.

Barth's Construal of Scripture according to Its Various Parts

We have seen how Barth construes Scripture as a whole in a certain way. Barth also construes various parts of Scripture in a certain way. A proper description of the way that Scripture functions in *CD* requires attention to the specific aspect of Scripture that is being used in a particular case and to the way that Barth construes that aspect of Scripture. This is an important affirmation, since some influential studies of Barth's interpretation of Scripture have spoken in overly general or reductive terms about how Barth uses Scripture. We will employ two main categories to refer to the parts or aspect of Scripture: (1) the forms (or genres) of scripture and (2) its patterns. Our book will indicate that Barth's engagement with Scripture is (or at least aims to be) "contextual" and is thus "form-sensitive" and "pattern-sensitive."

When we refer to biblical forms or genres we have in mind primarily the main literary types that characterize the various books of the Bible (e.g., law, narrative, epistle, etc.) or its contents (e.g., hymn, psalm, saga, etc.). As we saw in chapter 1, some of Barth's interpreters have regarded a single genre or form as having central importance in his interpretation of Scripture (e.g., the role of narrative[42] or the role of "theological statements" in Scripture[43]).

Christina Baxter discusses seven specific biblical "forms" as particularly significant for understanding Barth's approach in *CD*, arguing that his interpretation and use of Scripture, instead of treating Scripture in a uniform or monolithic manner, is form-sensitive.[44] The seven forms are: (1) concept, (2) theme, (3) theological statement, (4) story, (5) typol-

---

41. I/2, 464f.; cf. 466ff.

42. See especially Ford, "Barth's Interpretation of the Bible," 56, and *Barth and God's Story*, 12, 56.

43. See especially Baxter, "Movement from Exegesis to Dogmatics," 165ff., 172ff., 178f.

44. Ibid., 126.

ogy, (6) allegory, and (7) analogy. We will now briefly describe several of these forms, emphasizing those that are of significance for understanding Barth's engagement of Scripture in his treatments of divine unity, constancy, and eternity.

A "concept"[45] is a stable content of meaning that is associated with a particular biblical word or a group of closely related words. Barth often uses a conceptually-oriented exegetical method of "word study," usually relying on the work of others, in order to unfold the meaning of such biblical concepts.[46]

A "theme"[47] refers rather generally to meaning or message that is shared by a number of passages. As such, a theme is a conceptual or logical whole. Barth organizes biblical passages thematically in various ways. He "clusters" passages together that share a common word or concept,[48] speaks of phrases that are characteristic of a book or writer, and variously refers to the themes of a book of the Old or New Testament or of Scripture as a whole.[49]

"A theological statement"[50] is an "unusually doctrinally articulate statement" of doctrine or confession occurring within Scripture itself. Such statements are relatively rare in Scripture. However, according to Baxter, Barth's use of them is "the formative and definitive method" in *CD*.[51] Barth restates or redescribes such statements in his own dogmatic terminology.[52] Partly because of their brevity, Barth employs such biblical theological statements in *CD* as a modified form of "proof texts," frequently in the fine print excursuses and occasionally in the main text.

Besides genres and forms, we can also speak of patterns as aspects of Scripture. A pattern can be defined rather abstractly as an ordered

---

45. Ibid., 127–40.

46. Cf. Bächli, *Alte Testament in der kirchlichen Dogmatic von Karl Barth*, 147–54.

47. Baxter, "Movement from Exegesis to Dogmatics," 141–55.

48. Among those Baxter cites within Barth's doctrine of God are II/1, 385, 459; II/1, 361, and II/1, 392. Cf. Bächli (*Alte Testament in der kirchlichen Dogmatik*, 154–64) on Barth's clusters or catenae of passages.

49. See Bächli comments on Barth's "thematic exegesis" (*Alte Testament in der kirchlichen Dogmatik*, 167–224).

50. Baxter, "Movement from Exegesis to Dogmatics," 155–68.

51. Ibid., 165. According to Baxter (165–68), Ford's prioritizing of narrative results both from his failure to examine all of the explicit uses of Scripture in *CD* (as she does) and his misclassification of those contents of Scripture that he did examine.

52. Ibid., 163ff.

whole that is formed by a construal of various distinct and repeated features of Scripture. These repeated features may be of different kinds (e.g., literary, temporal/historical, conceptual), but for understanding Barth's use of Scripture within his doctrine of God the conceptual features of Scripture are probably the most important.

By saying that a pattern is specifically concerned with the ordered configuration of various distinct features of Scripture, it is important to note that these features are typically not easy to unify in a single theological judgment, but often require the dialectical juxtaposition of two or more apparent contraries. This stands in some contrast to the biblical forms (e.g., themes, concepts or theological statements) that function as the raw materials that patterns include within themselves.

A good example of such a biblical pattern is what we might call the "Trinitarian pattern." Following seminal church theologians like Athanasius, Barth regards this recurring pattern, rather than a series of proof texts, as the primary biblical basis of the doctrine of the Trinity. Thus, Barth contends that the biblical "root" of the doctrine of the Trinity can be summarized in the proposition "God reveals Himself as the Lord."[53] Scripture is paradigmatic for the statement "God reveals Himself as the Lord" even though this statement is not a direct translation of any biblical statement or even a thematic summation of several of them. Rather, this statement sums up the three-fold pattern of God's self-revelation. This pattern involves a conjunction of God's threefold distinctness (as Revealer, Revelation, and "Revealedness") and God's unity as the one Lord.[54]

Concepts Related to Barth's Interpretation of Scripture

Introduction to Barth's Hermeneutics

We now turn to concepts for understanding Barth's interpretation of Scripture. Generally speaking, Barth's distinctive hermeneutical perspective is marked by the predominance of what we could call the "sub-

---

53. I/1, 306 (cf. 304–33). See our comments on Barth's account of the Trinity in chapter 3.

54. The reason why this Trinitarian pattern would not aptly be called a theme, is because it involves a bringing together of two distinct "structural" features that cannot be "thematized" under a unified conceptual rubric. Rather, within the Trinitarian pattern, there is a dialectical interplay between two features or themes: the oneness of the divine being and the distinctness of the divine persons.

ject matter principle." That is, Barth believes that one ought to interpret a text with one's attention fixed primarily on "that which the text says," which he refers to variously as the text's "subject matter" [*Sache*], "content" [*Inhalt*], or "object" [*Gegenstand*].[55] This does not mean that one leaves the text behind in order to contemplate a subject matter independently of the act of interpreting the text. It simply means that one's interpretation of the text should be preoccupied with that which the text itself is preoccupied. This basic conception of textual interpretation, which Barth would also apply to other texts besides Scripture,[56] clearly fulfils the two criteria for dogmatics noted above. That is, one interprets the Bible with a focus on its Christocentric subject matter, but does so in a way that is accountable to the verbal sense of the biblical texts; the subject matter is textually mediated.[57]

THE HERMENEUTICAL PRINCIPLE OF "SUBORDINATION"

In a discussion of the Church's "freedom under the Word" (I/2, § 21.2), Barth discusses the Church's interpretation of the Bible.[58] Here Barth makes it clear that good exegesis is thus not only a matter of technical skill, but of free obedience to God and receptivity to the ongoing divine act of self-revelation.[59]

---

55. General theories of textual hermeneutics often speak of three main factors in interpretation: the author, the text and the reader. Barth joins the few theorists who wish to add a forth factor: the referent or subject matter of the text, and Barth wishes to place the emphasis both here and on the text (see F. Watson, *Text, Church and World* and *Text and Truth* for a similar view of theological hermeneutics somewhat influenced by Barth). See editor Bromiley's comments on the question of how to translate *Gegenstand* (here rendered "object") in Barth's dogmatics (I/1, viii).

56. The subject-matter principle, according to Barth, is true on the level of "general hermeneutics" (I/1, 465ff.). Yet Barth claims that the *source* of this hermeneutical insight is not "general" but scriptural; there is no special biblical hermeneutics, but we get the general hermeneutics from the Bible (466). One reason Barth gives for this claim is that the Bible is marked by an "unusual preponderance of *what is said* in it over the word as such" (468).

57. There is a mutual relation between the text and its subject matter. We need the word to "get to" the object, but we also need the object to "grasp" the words rightly (I/2, 465).

58. I/2, 695–722.

59. Barth also says: "To the question: How does God's Word come to us men in Holy Scripture and how does it exercise sway in the Church of Jesus Christ? We . . . answer, that it happens through free obedience" (I/2, 666).

In this context, Barth's states what he calls the principle of "subordination" as the primary rule of the theological interpretation or exegesis of Scripture. "The necessary and fundamental form of all scriptural exegesis . . . must consist in all circumstances in the freely performed act of subordinating all human concepts, ideas, and convictions to the witness of revelation supplied to us in Scripture."[60] This principle is of great relevance, not only for understanding Barth's way of engaging with Scripture, but also for understanding Barth's theological method as a whole.

Barth says that the theologian must submit to Scripture as a way of submitting to its *unique* subject matter, the God who speaks through it.[61] But how do we do this? We cannot abandon our intellectual framework, Barth says, any more than "we can free ourselves from our own shadow."[62] Rather, we remain ourselves, with our intellectual framework, but we simply subordinate all that we are to the thoughts, ideas, and convictions we find within the Bible.[63] To try to abandon our own ideas for some alleged position of neutrality would be more an act of arrogance than humility. Rather, reverent subordination is letting our ideas, thoughts, and convictions be challenged and confronted. The following passage makes clear what Barth has in mind.

> Subordination implies that the subordinate is there as such and remains there. . . . It cannot mean that we have to allow our ideas, thoughts, and convictions to be supplanted, so to speak, by those of the prophets and apostles, or that we have to speak the language of Canaan instead of our own tongue. In that case we should not have subordinated ourselves to them, but at most adorned ourselves with their feathers. In that case nothing would have been done in the interpretation of their words, for we should merely have repeated them parrot-like. Subordination, if

---

60. I/2, 715.

61. This point implies several other claims. We do not subordinate ourselves to Scripture in the same way as we do to God, but rather we submit to his witnesses in Scripture for the sake of God (717f.). As we submit to the human authors in this way, the Word of God interprets itself to us (718). The object of Scripture, permits no other kind of free human activity in relation to it than that of subordination (715f.). The fog of our intellectual life (and even that of the human authors of Scripture!) needs to become clear in the light of God's Word (716).

62. I/2, 718.

63. This perspective is evident in Barth's early work, such as his 1916 essay "Strange New World Within the Bible" (Barth, *Word of God*, 28–50).

> it is to be sincere, must concern the purpose and meaning indicated in the ideas, thoughts, and convictions of the prophets and apostles, that is, the testimony which ... they wish to bear. To this testimony of their words we must subordinate ourselves—and this is the essential form of scriptural exegesis.[64]

Note that subordination to Scripture does not mean that Theology is a matter of quoting Bible verses. Rather, that would be to repeat Scriptural proof texts parrot-like, without them genuinely transforming us or our ideas. With the attitude and action of subordination, the intellectual and moral framework we bring to the Bible is transformed and affected from the inside out. "The decisive point," Barth says, "is that in scriptural exegesis Scripture itself as a witness to revelation must have *unconditional precedence* over all the evidence of our own being and becoming."[65] As we interpret Scripture, we must allow God to put us humans in our proper place. Of course, this humble attitude rests on assumptions that run directly counter to much of modern theology and surely against the Enlightenment notion of the unconditional autonomy of the rational self (see our concepts for the use of reason later in this chapter). Another quotation helps to illuminate this point.

> The message which Scripture has to give us, even in its apparently most debatable and least assimilable parts, is in all circumstances truer and more important than the best and most necessary things that we ourselves have said and can say.[66]

If we do not recognize this, Barth believes that Scripture and its world and witness remain largely inexplicable. The world of the Bible is only fully accessible, so to speak, "from the bottom up"—by the subordination in which one freely places oneself *under* the Word. Such subordination comes by faith. Barth admits that there is a relative understanding that is possible of the Bible without faith and subordination, namely, the kind of understanding "possible between representatives of different worlds."[67] This understanding can yield many helpful results, as Barth's affirmation and controlled use of higher-critical methods and results would testify. Yet the Bible is best understood, in its proper theologi-

---

64. I/2, 718.
65. Ibid., 719.
66. Ibid.
67. Ibid.

cal depth, by "a human intellectual world the inner security of which has been shaken, and which has become yielding and responsive to the biblical world." In the end, no matter how much readers understand Scripture intellectually—even if they appreciate its "inner consistency" and meaningfulness—they miss the theological *raison d'être* of Scripture if they do not accept what they understand and give way to it.

For Barth, this rule of subordination is the "basic rule" from which all other principles of sound theological interpretation must follow.[68] Such subordination implies that all our theological formulations are provisional and revisable in the face of an ongoing quest for the abiding witness of Scripture. We are never allowed to assume that we have fully subordinated ourselves to Scripture, nor that anyone else has. It is rather a goal towards which the Christian theologian and the Church as a whole must continue to press forward.

Barth's Three Phases of Interpretation

With Barth's principle of subordination in mind, we may now turn to his account of the three phases of interpretation, an account that directly follows his comments on subordination. Barth stresses that all three phases (or aspects) of interpretation are interrelated, mutually inter-dependent, and perichoretically united. They are not to be conceived of in a strictly linear fashion as separate temporal stages, but rather as interrelated aspects of Barth's way of engaging with Scripture theologically.

The first phase of interpretation is what Barth typically calls "observation" [*explicatio*, or *Beobachtung*].[69] Observation involves not only discerning or making intelligible the verbal sense of the text in its historical situation (treating the Bible as a human text), but also involves presenting (re-presenting) the self-presentation of the Word of God (treating the Bible as a witness to the Word). Thus, observation may begin on the plane of "general hermeneutics" with historical criticism as its "presupposition and most important instrument," but later moves beyond this to the object of the text. To be faithful to the object of the

---

68. Ibid., 722.

69. The English Translation of I/2, also sometimes uses the terms "investigation" or "examination" to translate *Beobachtung*, which Barth treats in I/2, 722–27.

A Conceptual Framework for the Exposition of Barth's Theological Method   63

text is not contrary to higher-criticism, but its ultimate fulfillment—letting the text's object have sway over us "without any restrictions."[70]

The second distinguishable phase of biblical exegesis is what Barth calls "reflection" (*meditatio*, or *Nachdenken*; literally, "thinking after").[71] "Reflection" marks the crucial mediating phase between observation (or "explication") of the text and its use or appropriation. As such, it is parallel to the role of the discipline of dogmatic theology in "mediating" the tasks of biblical theology and practical theology.[72] In the act of reflection, the interpreter takes the meaning of the text and relates it to his own thinking, his own philosophy.

Barth's view of reflection assumes that interpreters inevitably possess a philosophy that they bring to the text and that influences their interpretation. There is no neutral exegesis, no exegesis without presuppositions. However, Barth believes that we can determine to a large degree the way in which our philosophies function in our exegesis (see the subsection on "Barth and Philosophy" later in this chapter). Barth's main point is that we should not allow philosophy to function as a systematic pre-understanding (as Heideggerian existentialism did for Bultmann), but rather should allow philosophical categories and convictions to function on an ad hoc basis only as they are helpful in genuinely understanding and responding to the text and its subject matter. In other words, all our reasoning and philosophical inclinations need to be relentlessly subordinated to the text and its object.

The third phase or aspect of interpretation that Barth identifies is "appropriation" (*applicatio*, or *Aneignung*).[73] This is similar to what we are calling the "use" of Scripture in this book, which for Barth means primarily the theological use of Scripture in dogmatics. According to Barth, the word that is declared in Scripture must not only be understood, but must become our own. In order for this to happen, we must move beyond reflecting on that word to in some way *thinking it*

---

70. Ibid., 726.

71. Ibid., 727–36.

72. Ibid., 766ff.; see also our relevant comments on the distinction between biblical and dogmatic theology in "Concepts Related to the Use of Scripture in Dogmatics" below. On how the entire theological enterprise is for Barth a form of *Nachdenken*, see the work of Alan Torrance (e.g., "Trinity," 72f., 89).

73. I/1, 736–40.

ourselves—the ultimate hope of scientific theology.[74] We must think within its categories and with its convictions. To do so is not to respond to Scripture merely as an external norm (heteronomy), but as those have made the scripturally-mediated divine Word their own internal criterion (autonomy). Rather than parrot-like imitation, such reverent autonomy is the proper goal of scriptural interpretation.[75]

Our obedient application of Scripture is rightly a vehicle of this divine act, the act in which the Word of God wills to cross our threshold as the Lord.[76] Ultimately, we can only "use" Scripture rightly, when we let it "use" us.[77] In the next subsection, we turn to a more specific explanation of what is involved in Barth's use of Scripture in dogmatics and how this relates to "exegesis."

Concepts Related to Barth's Use of Scripture in Dogmatics

Exegesis and dogmatics

Barth clearly thought that "exegesis" (*Exegese*), understood broadly as the interpretation and use of the Bible, was crucially important for all branches of theology, including dogmatics.[78] Often Barth uses the terms "exegesis" or "scriptural exegesis" (*Schrifterklärung*; sometimes translated "scriptural exposition") in this comprehensive sense. This is seen in his inclusion of the second and third phases of interpretation ("reflection" and "appropriation"), not merely the first, under the one process of *Schrifterklärung*. However, Barth frequently uses the term *Exegese* in other more narrow senses. This begins to clarify why at times he refers to the work of dogmatics as something distinct from or extending beyond exegesis—even though he consistently speaks of how dogmatics must in some way be based upon exegesis or exegetical theology. This is a point that we will return to below.

---

74. I/2, 736.

75. One implication of this will often be emphasized in this book, namely: reverent subordination to Scripture is often best expressing in a theology that is biblical in an *indirect* rather than a direct manner.

76. Ibid., 738.

77. Ibid.

78. His final parting words to his students in Bonn in 1933 were "Exegesis, exegesis, and again, exegesis.... Then, certainly take care for systematics and dogmatics." (Barth, as cited in Jüngel, *Karl Barth*, 40).

What is clear is that Barth consistently understands exegesis in both its narrow and broad senses as "theological exegesis." According to his own definition given in *Credo*, theological exegesis is exposition of Scripture that occurs "within the pale of the Church" and that asks the question "To what extent is there given to us, here in this text, witness to *God's Word*?"[79] Two important points are made by this definition. First, by speaking of it as exegesis within the pale of the Church, Barth rules out secular exegesis done by the non-believer, with its presumption of neutral scientific objectivity; theological exegesis is self-involving and ecclesial.[80] Second, Barth considers this theological exegesis to be the "norm" (rule, criterion, or basis) for Dogmatics.[81]

To avoid possible confusion arising from Barth's diverse uses of the term "exegesis," we will now provide our own definition of the term. We will use "exegesis" to refer to the direct (and usually detailed) theological exposition of a specific biblical text or group of texts.[82] Although this remains a relatively broad definition, it distinguishes exegesis from other possible ways of interpreting or using Scripture in dogmatics. Specifically, it distinguishes exegesis from the *indirect* uses of Scripture in dogmatics—i.e., uses that appeal to themes or patterns in Scripture without reliance on the citation, interpretation or use of specific texts.

Direct and indirect ways of using Scripture authoritatively

We may clarify this distinction between the direct and indirect ways of interpreting and using Scripture in dogmatics in several ways. First, sometimes Barth uses the term "direct" for what we are here calling "indirect." For example, Barth speaks about a particular view of God's eternity "forcing itself upon us ... directly [*unmittelbar*]" in our reflection on the Bible.[83] However, the complex view he describes in this connec-

---

79. Barth, *Credo*, 177 (Barth's italics).

80. Ibid. Barth goes on to say that the theological exegete works with the dual presupposition that (1) the Church has heard the Word of God in the Bible ("recollection") and that (2) he or she will also hear in the Bible God's Word for his or her time ("expectation").

81. Ibid., 177f.

82. This is similar to the use of "exegesis" in Bächli's work (*Alte Testament in der kirchlichen Dogmatic von Karl Barth*; see our comments on Bächli in chapter 1).

83. II/1, 621. See our comments on this passage in the later part of our discussion of eternity in chapter 6.

tion is certainly not one that can be read directly out of any passage in Scripture. Rather, it is better described as the identification of a complex pattern in Scripture that is then translated freely into dogmatic terms—all of which involves what we would call an *indirect* authorizing relation between Scripture and dogmatics.

Second, at least in the context of Barth's theology, an indirect use of Scripture—no less than a direct use—is a way of using Scripture as a decisive *authority* for dogmatic theology. When Scripture is used to "authorize" a certain theological conclusion, we may call that "scriptural authorization." Indirect scriptural authorization still allows Scripture to determine, often decisively, the content of dogmatics. For example, even though Barth arrives at the doctrine of the Trinity by means of the indirect scriptural authorization provided by biblical patterns (see above), the biblical witness to revelation still has a decisive effect on the shape of his view of the Trinity. Even an indirect use of Scripture can still involve a kind of coercive pressure of the content of Scripture upon the reverent reader.[84]

Third, our use of the term "indirect" needs to be distinguished from the sense in which, according to Barth, *all* dogmatic ideas are "indirectly" related to Scripture. That is, one could say with good reason that Barth teaches that, strictly speaking, the only direct norm and basis for theology is Jesus Christ, the revealed Word of God who is distinguishable from the words of Scripture in themselves. In this respect, the relationship of theology to the text or words of Scripture is *always* indirect, even when specific passages are cited or interpreted. However, we will not typically use the terms "direct" and "indirect" in this sense. When we refer to direct scriptural authorization, we should not forget that, apart from the divine action of revealing, Barth does not believe that even Scripture can provide the final or all-sufficient justification or authorization for any doctrine.

Fourth, the great importance of the *indirect* mode of scriptural authorization in Barth's dogmatic work relates to his consistent stress that dogmatics is *not* a matter of parrot-like repetition of the words of Scripture. Rather, our reverent subordination to Scripture is ultimately subordination to Scripture's personal subject-matter, the Word of God speaking through Scripture. This subordination is a matter of free and

---

84. This paragraph provides further support for the critique of David Kelsey we offered in chapter 1.

A Conceptual Framework for the Exposition of Barth's Theological Method 67

even creative obedience. As we reflect on or "think after" (*Nachdenken*) the biblical witness to God's self-revelation, we are transformed in our thinking. As we are transformed, we are also set free from the specific words of Scripture to state the content, message or Word of Scripture in our own terms and for specific purposes.

Conceptual Terms and Theological Judgments

A helpful distinction made by theologian David Yeago can illuminate the difference between "vain repetition" and faithful adherence to the scriptural message. Yeago distinguishes between theological "judgments" that a passage of Scripture makes and the specific "concepts" or "conceptual terms" in which the passage renders those judgments.[85] Yeago explains:

> We cannot concretely perform an act of judgment without employing some particular, contingent verbal and conceptual resources; judgment-making is an operation performed with words and concepts. At the same time, however, the same judgment can be rendered in a variety of conceptual terms, all of which may be informative about a particular judgment's force and implications.[86]

Thus, the biblical writers and a contemporary theologian like Barth can render essentially the same judgment in quite different conceptual terms. As such, Barth can remain faithful to the message of Scripture (its judgments) without falling into vain repetition of its precise ways of wording and conceiving of things. Of course, Barth recognizes that these precise ways of wording and conceiving of things must be carefully attended to if the judgments of Scripture are to be accurately understood. But once those judgments are understood, one can—indeed one should—"re-describe or re-render those judgments" in one's own conceptual or philosophical terms.[87] For example, Yeago argues that the

---

85. Yeago, "New Testament and Nicene Dogma," 159ff. Childs ("Toward Recovering Theological Exegesis" 16ff.) and Vanhoozer ("Voice and the Actor," 83) offer positive assessments of Yeago's article and his distinction.

86. Yeago, "New Testament and Nicene Dogma," 159. Yeago's distinction is roughly parallel to that of Hunsinger when he speaks (in his definition of Barth's "rationalism") of the difference between "the surface content of scripture" on the one hand, and "scripture's deeper conceptual implications and underlying unity," on the other hand (Hunsinger, *How to Read Karl Barth*, 5).

87. Yeago, "New Testament and Nicene Dogma," 163.

statement that Jesus shares equality with God the Father in Phil 2:6–11 and the statement that "the Son is of one substance with the Father" in the Nicene Creed are two forms of the same judgment. In this book we will consider how many of Barth's theological claims are such redescriptions of judgments that Scripture already affirms.

The Difference between Dogmatics and Biblical Theology

Barth speaks of the "*difference in unity* . . . of the two theological tasks" of biblical (exegetical) theology and dogmatic theology.[88] The differences that Barth saw between these two theological disciplines can be illuminated by our definitions of "exegesis" and the direct and indirect forms of scriptural usage or authorization.

Biblical theology is preoccupied primarily with what we have called exegesis—i.e., with drawing theological conclusions that can be directly authorized by appeal to specific biblical texts. Biblical theology may also appeal secondarily to Scripture in more indirect ways, but even such indirect uses of Scripture are regarded as closely "accountable" to exegesis.

The relation of dogmatics to Scripture is marked by roughly the opposite priorities as biblical theology. Hence, the primary concern with dogmatics is, as Barth notes, with the content or subject matter to which Scripture witnesses. Accordingly, the relation of dogmatics to Scripture is primarily indirect. Only secondarily and occasionally are the main claims of dogmatics supported or justified by exegesis of specific biblical passages. Certainly such exegesis is sometimes significant in Barth's dogmatic work (surely more significant than it is in the work of most modern or contemporary theologians!), but indirect modes of scriptural authorization usually form the grounds of Barth's main conclusions.[89]

This way of defining the difference between biblical and dogmatic theology involves a degree of overlap between the tasks and methods of the two disciplines. Generally speaking, the major method of biblical

---

88. I/2, 821. See also Barth's rhetorical question on I/2, 767: "How can there be dogmatics unless exegesis not only precedes but is included in it?"

89. See Barth's comments on "Dogmatics and Exegesis" in *Credo* (177–79), where he (again) speaks of theological exegesis as the *criterion* of dogmatics. What Barth calls "theological exegesis" here is probably best seen as incorporating both direct and indirect forms of biblical authorization.

theology is the minor method of dogmatics, and vice versa. In each case, engagement with Scripture is crucial, but it tends to take different forms. Speaking more loosely, biblical theology emphasizes the *interpretation* of Scripture in itself, whereas dogmatic theology emphasizes the *use* of Scripture, the specific contemporary appropriation of its teaching.[90]

At the same time, dogmatic theology's concentration on the content of the Church's distinctive God-talk enables it to unpack the internal logic or rationality of the scriptural witness and the revelation to which it points.[91] As such, dogmatic theology does not need to spell out explicitly the direct and detailed exegetical grounding of all of its discourse about God. To do so would be impractical and would even distract it from the overall "implicit logic" (Frei) or the "scope" or "mind" (Athanasius) of Scripture, which is its concern. The fact that Barth continues to appeal to Scripture in his dogmatics, whether directly or indirectly, is an expression of his adherence to the Protestant Scripture principle.

The relationship between direct and indirect authorization, and thus between biblical and dogmatic theology, is one of mutual interdependence. On the one hand, the procedure of indirect authorization (i.e., the typical dogmatic use of Scripture) is dependent on direct authorization (i.e., exegesis of specific texts) to provide it with a detailed exegetical grounding or basis or justification.[92] For example, when Barth employs a Trinitarian pattern of God's self-revelation in Scripture as the biblical basis of his version of the doctrine of the Trinity in *CD* I/1 (a case of indirect authorization), one can ask the further question of how one could ground that biblical Trinitarian pattern itself in the exegesis of various specific biblical texts. Barth (rightly) does not regard it as necessary to spell out fully such an exegetical grounding in his dogmatics (at least not in his explicit treatment of the Trinity in I/1); rather, he is concerned with the *content* of this Trinitarian pattern and its expres-

---

90. See Kelsey, *Proving Doctrine*, 202f.

91. Accordingly, Frei said the following with respect to Barth's dogmatic redescriptions of Scripture: "Barth goes as far, I believe, as one can in articulating the largely implicit logic governing the *sensus literalis*" (*Types of Christian Theology*, 44).

92. "[T]he requirement of a biblical attitude in dogmatics is not interchangeable with the task of reproducing and explaining the text of the Bible. In theology, this is not the task of dogmatics but of exegesis. Biblical exegesis is the *decisive presupposition and source* of dogmatics" (I/2, 821; italics mine).

sion in the creedal statements of the Trinity.[93] However, biblical theology should rightly search out this exegetical basis for this content, and dogmatic theology is indirectly dependent on this.

On the other hand, we can say that the procedure of direct authorization is dependent on the procedure of indirect authorization, and thus biblical theology is dependent on dogmatic theology. In particular, since the exegete is not without presuppositions or philosophy, one could say that the exegete's aim should be to have presuppositions that arise from the subject matter (or object or content) to which Scripture as a whole testifies and that dogmatics elaborates. Since Barth regards even the most "historical" aspects of exegesis to be concerned with the text's subject matter, this "dogmatic" question cannot be bypassed in biblical theology or exegesis. Detailed contextual exegesis depends on some conception of the theological (and, for Barth, Christocentric) content that these passages discuss and how it is related to the whole of Scripture. In relation to the Trinity, Barth would say that one needs *both* the overall pattern evident in Scripture taken as a whole (dogmatics), *and* the proper exegetical grounding of the elements of that pattern in specific passages (biblical theology) to arrive at the full-orbed theological justification of the doctrine.

The Two Criteria of Dogmatics and the Function of Scripture

We earlier identified Barth's "Christocentric" and "biblical" criteria for dogmatics, criteria that distinguish dogmatics from natural theology. We conclude our treatment of the concepts related to the function of Scripture in Barth's dogmatics by commenting on how these two criteria relate to Barth's use of Scripture. While the biblical criterion of dogmatics obviously relates directly to Barth's use of Scripture, the Christocentric criterion is relevant to the specifically Christocentric way that Barth interprets and uses Scripture.

With respect to Scripture, the two criteria function as two hermeneutical rules, which can be stated as follows.[94] (1) The dogmatic theologian should always interpret and use the Bible according to its "Christological sense," its relationship to the Christological center of

---

93. Barth says that dogmatics "will have to keep the text of the Bible continually and constantly in view in its *content*" (ibid., 821).

94. These rules are grounded in our observations of Barth's dogmatic practice.

the Bible, thus avoiding a disjointed and non-theological interpretation of Scripture. (2) The dogmatic theologian should always interpret and use the Bible according to its "verbal sense" (see above), thus avoiding "eisegesis" under the guise of "exegesis."[95]

The first Christocentric rule is an expression of the Christocentric subject-matter or content of dogmatics. It corresponds primarily to the indirect mode of scriptural authorization, since much of Scripture is not directly about Christ (e.g., the verbal sense of much of the Old Testament). Of course, Barth sometimes does authorize his Christocentric proposals quite directly by means of citation or exegesis of specific biblical passages, especially the "theological statements" and the narratives of the New Testament. For the most part, however, Barth's hermeneutical Christocentrism arises from his consideration of the themes and patterns of Scripture that lead him to a synoptic Christocentric construal of Scripture as a whole. As such, Barth is free to draw from Christocentric ecclesial and theological tradition in his dogmatics, without needing to justify such tradition at every point by appeal to the exegesis of Scripture.

The second implicit hermeneutical rule is that Scripture must be interpreted in accordance with its "verbal sense." This is part of what it means for the interpretation of Scripture to be genuinely biblical. This rule expresses the concern that theological interpretations of the Bible, even when they claim to be exegesis, often wind up being forms of "eisegesis"—i.e., occasions in which some idea or meaning or content is read into Scripture that is not really there. Barth himself affirmed the distinction between exegesis and eisegesis in various ways.[96] Even though Barth regarded it as impossible for the theologian to avoid eisegesis entirely, he still regarded exegesis (in broad sense of "reading

---

95. For a similar perspective on theological interpretation of Scripture to that presented in this paragraph, see Watson, *Text and Truth*, see 95–126 (esp. 123f.). Watson derives the metaphor of "the center" from Barth (he cites III/1, 24).

96. Barth himself recognized that the line between "exegesis" (in the sense of "reading out" of the text what is there) and "eisegesis" is often difficult to discern (I/1, 106), a point that is all the more obvious in the face of post-modern hermeneutics. A related point of clarification may be in order. The distinction between exegesis and eisegesis need not be construed in terms of modern preoccupations with "authorial intention." Rather the text itself can be regarded as having relatively stable semantic content, which the interpreter can either attend to or disregard. While Barth sometimes appealed to authorial intention, at other times he appealed to the meaning of the text that transcends the intention of its human authors.

out," not merely in the narrow sense defined above) as an appropriate goal for theological engagement with Scripture.[97] Accordingly, in teaching that the fundamental method of revealed theology (as opposed to invalid natural theology) was "the exposition of Holy Scripture," Barth associates natural theology with eisegesis. Appeals to Scripture cannot be the act of letting one's engagement with Scripture "occasion" the development of ideas that are quite independent of or foreign to the text. To do so would be a tacit refusal to subordinate oneself to Scripture as an authority. Eisegesis runs counter to Barth's adherence to the Protestant Scripture principle. Insofar as the dogmatic theologian interprets specific texts of Scripture, he must, in Barth's words, aim at "a representation" of the text that "will allow even the detailed words of the text to speak exactly as the stand."[98] This does not rule out more indirect ways of handling Scripture, but even those ways need to be distinguished from "reading into" Scripture, from eisegesis and natural theology.

Categories for Tradition and Its Theological Functions

In this section of the chapter we will follow much the same pattern as we did in the previous section on Scripture. Thus, we will move from concepts related variously to the construal of tradition, to the interpretation and use of tradition,[99] and then to the relation of the Christocentric and biblical criteria for dogmatics to the function of tradition. In this book we are concerned with *theological* tradition that Barth cites or tradition by which he is influenced (with or without explicit citation) in his doctrine of God in *CD*. Theological tradition is that subset of Christian church tradition composed of that tradition's various theological writings.

---

97. See Barth's comments on this point on I/1, 106.

98. I/2, 726; cf. Watson, "Bible," 58f. and *Text and Truth*, 123f. Again, although Barth recognized that we could not escape bringing our own presuppositions to the text, he believed that those presuppositions could be revised and overturned by an encounter with the objective reality of the text and the referent that it mediates to us (I/2: 724f.).

99. Unlike our account of Scripture above, we treat "interpretation" and "use" together in this section on tradition and the next one on reason.

Concepts Related to the Construal of Tradition

In a way similar to our way of organizing concepts under the construal of Scripture above, we must distinguish between Barth's construal of tradition as a whole and his way of construing the various parts or aspects of tradition.

THE CONSTRUAL OF TRADITION AS A WHOLE

In contrast to his treatment of Scripture, Barth offers no extended treatment of "tradition" in *CD*.[100] More precisely, he does not do so in a single section under the name "tradition."[101] However, Barth does frequently comment on church or theological tradition, albeit often under other names. Thus, despite the non-systematic character of Barth's construal of tradition, there are certain characteristics he consistently applies to tradition as a whole, i.e., to all instances of tradition.

Barth treats theological tradition primarily under the general category of *church proclamation*, one of the three forms of the Word of God.[102] The writings of theological tradition (including past attempts at dogmatics) are thus an aspect of the past proclamation of the Church. As such, theological tradition can possess an authority for the Church that is real, though secondary to that of Scripture.

The fact that Barth tends to construe "tradition" under the category of "church proclamation" is a manifestation of his Protestant inclinations. Church proclamation is oriented to the exposition or preaching of Scripture. As such, it is accountable to and subordinate to Scripture as a "norm magisterially confronting the Church."[103] Barth thus refers to tradition (especially in the form of church confessions) by means of the metaphor of a "commentary" on Scripture, for to be anything more than a "commentary" is to "try to stand on the same level as Scripture."[104] By this Barth means to ensure that that tradition does not create any "new articles of faith" whose fundamental content is not grounded the

---

100. Cf. Dean, "Relation between Scripture and Tradition," 27.

101. See Barth, *Credo*, 179–83.

102. See I/1, 88–99 and I/2, chapter IV (743–884). For Barth, the paradigmatic case of church proclamation is preaching, but it also includes ecclesial practices such as the administration of the sacraments.

103. Ibid., 106.

104. I/2, 621f. See Leslie, *Trinitarian Hermeneutics*, 134–38, who critiques Barth for construing tradition as commentary (166f.).

content of Scripture. Certainly, traditional formulations can be new in the sense of being spoken in the language and conceptuality of new historical periods, but they are not to create completely new objects of belief. Accordingly, Barth consistently resists that idea of tradition that aims to speak antecedent to or independently of an engagement with God's written word in Scripture, for such church proclamation is essentially "the Church's dialogue with itself," rather than an obedient response to revelation.[105]

Barth uses some of the same key terms he used for Scripture to characterize tradition, or past church proclamation: namely, "witness" and "authority." Yet his conviction that tradition must be hermeneutical and derivative vis-à-vis Scripture now causes him to qualify the sense of these terms. First, Barth uses the concept of tradition as a testimony or witness to biblically-attested revelation. This is evident in Barth's tendency to construe much of the Church's theological tradition along the lines of one of its specific historical forms, namely, "confession."[106] For, much like the self-understanding inscribed in the historic Protestant confessions of the faith, Barth understands normative orthodoxy in terms of adherence to Scripture. Tradition is a kind of secondary witness to revelation, which follows from the primary witness of Scripture.[107]

Accordingly, Barth understands theological tradition as capable of expressing the Church's authority that is subordinate to Scripture, its "authority under the Word."[108] This authority is real, especially over individual Christians. Yet it is at most indirect (mediate), relative and formal authority, rather than the direct, absolute and material authority that Scripture has when it is functioning as the Word of God.[109] Even the

---

105. I/1, 105ff. In the light of the above paragraph, it is not accidental that Barth offers his main comments on the Church's theological tradition (§ 20, "Authority in the Church" and § 21, "Freedom in the Church") in the context of his doctrine of Scripture in CD, chapter III (§§ 19–21). This provides indirect evidence that we are correct to understand the use of Scripture as primary in Barth's method and to understand his use of tradition largely in this context.

106. I/2, 620–60. See Barth's definition of "confession," given in "Construing Scripture according to its diverse forms" below.

107. Thus, tradition is the Church's confession that is limited and established by Scripture's "confession" (ibid., 545ff., 573f.).

108. Ibid., 585–660.

109. Ibid., 516–26; 538.

A Conceptual Framework for the Exposition of Barth's Theological Method 75

authority the Church does have can only operate insofar as it submits to Scripture and applies itself to the reverent interpretation of Scripture.[110]

Construing Tradition according to Its Diverse Forms

Besides offering an explicit or implicit construal of tradition as a whole, Barth also offers a way of construing various parts or subsets of tradition. We can discuss this point by means of several different schemes of organization.

One way in which Barth construes theological tradition is according to the main genres or forms of tradition that existed throughout church history.[111] Besides the Church's recognition of the canon of Scripture,[112] Barth gives two main examples of theological tradition. First, there are the theological works of individual theologians, the "ecclesiastical teachers, i.e., specific expositors and preachers of the Bible."[113] Such works, while they may be influential, do not represent the "confession" of the Church as a whole or even a branch of the Church, though some have approached such a status (e.g., Aquinas' *Summa Theologiae* or Calvin's *Institutes*). As such, they have relatively less authority than corporate statements or confessions of the Church (see below). One way of organizing this vast portion of theological or dogmatic tradition is by the historical period from which the statements or works of an individual theologian comes. We will use the following rough historical categories in this book: the Church Fathers (100–500), the medieval theologians (500–1500), the reformers (1500–1564),[114] the period of Old Protestant Orthodoxy, including both Lutheran and Reformed theologians (1564–1750[115]), and the Modern Period (1750–20th C.). This manner of periodization is a reflection of Barth's priorities, which clearly stress (a) Western theology over the thought of the Christian East (Eastern Orthodoxy), at least from the Medieval Period onwards, and (b) Protestant thought from the Reformation onwards.

110. Ibid., 695–740.
111. Cf. Ibid., 597–660.
112. Ibid., 597–603.
113. Ibid., 603–20.
114. The year 1564 is the date of the death of Calvin.
115. In the context of a treatment of Rousseau, Barth speaks of "the new age in the middle of the eighteenth century" (*Protestant Theology in the Nineteenth Century*, 160).

Second, there is Barth's category of "confessions," which we may define broadly as the corporate statements or works of the Christian church as opposed to the statements or works of the individual theologian. For Barth, "A church confession is a formulation and proclamation of the insight which the Church has been given in a certain direction into the revelation attested by Scripture, reached on the basis of common deliberation and decision."[116] We can divide such "confessions" into "creeds" and "confessions proper." In our usage, *creeds* are the early ecumenical summary statements of faith (like the Apostle's Creed and Nicene Creed) and the statements of certain councils (like the definitions of Chalcedon). These may carry the most authority of all instances of tradition in Barth's work.[117] *Confessions proper* are those specific non-ecumenical statements of doctrine that define the various divisions of belief among those who call themselves Christians (like the Heidelberg or Augsburg Confessions)—which brings us to our next way of categorizing tradition.

Another way of organizing the theological tradition that Barth employs is to speak of various sub-traditions. These sub-traditions are distinguished by their distinctive theological views, rather than their genre or historical period. Thus, sub-traditions are especially important for identifying theological works produced after the Reformation, when distinctions between different streams of Christian Tradition become more important. There are four main sub-traditions that appear in Barth's work: (1) Roman Catholicism, (2) Liberal Protestantism (or Neo-Protestantism, or simply modern Protestantism), (3) Greek (Eastern) Orthodoxy, and (4) his own tradition "Evangelical" Protestantism.[118] The first two are typically Barth's opponents, and thus constitute negative examples of where the Church has strayed from its proper adherence and subordination to the revelation attested in Scripture. The third is largely neglected.[119] The fourth, the "Evangelical" sub-tradition

---

116. I/2, 620.

117. Within his account of the Trinity, see Barth's reflection on fourth century Nicene orthodoxy (I/1, 375ff.) and his use of the Nicene-Constantinopolitan Creed (I/1, 423).

118. CD I/2, 822–30.

119. The few exceptions show that Barth is decidedly Western in his theological preferences (except in relation to the patristic period). E.g., II/1, 331f. has some rather negative comments on certain Eastern theologians and their supposed theological tendencies (cf. Barth's defense of the *filoque* in I/1, 480ff.).

includes the Reformed, Lutheran, and Anglican Churches. The first of these, the Reformed, is the specific tradition with which Barth most readily identifies himself, although his dogmatics are meant to be more broadly "evangelical."[120] Thus, we can generally call Barth's own views as representing a Christocentric version of the "Reformed-Evangelical" theological sub-tradition.[121]

Concepts for the Interpretation and Use of Tradition

INTRODUCTION: POSITIVE AND NEGATIVE FUNCTIONS OF TRADITION

Barth's interpretation and use of tradition differs in several ways from his interpretation and use of Scripture. To begin, the question of *"which tradition?"* is far more significant with respect to tradition than the corresponding question ("which Scripture?") is with respect to Barth's interpretation and use of Scripture. Although Barth believes that Scripture is in some ways varied in its contents, he regards the scriptural canon as fundamentally unified in a way that tradition is not. Specifically, Barth interprets the theological tradition that he cites in either positive or negative ways, while Scripture is treated as uniformly positive and thus authoritative. Some tradition positively witnesses to the prior witness of Scripture to the revelation in Christ, and some tradition stands as a negative example that is unfaithful to Scripture and revelation. Insofar as tradition is interpreted positively, it functions as a *guide* for Barth's dogmatic theology. Insofar as tradition is interpreted negatively, it functions as a *foil* for his theology. In the rest of this subsection, we will explain further this twofold use of tradition, giving examples of tradition functioning as either a guide or as a foil.

---

120. *CD* I/2, 831ff.; cf. I/1, xv–xvi. We note that the "evangelical" character of Barth's dogmatics allows him to be positively engaged not only with Reformed thinkers, but with orthodox Pietists (see our comments on Bengel in "The biblical criterion of dogmatics in relation to tradition" below).

121. That said, Barth states that no single tradition "has all the truth" (as quoted in Godsey, *Karl Barth's Table Talk*, 97).

The Positive Function of Tradition as a Guide

When we speak of the positive "guiding" function of tradition, we must clarify the varying ways in which a given instance of tradition might "guide." Barth could use tradition as a guide in terms of theological content in one case and in terms of theological method in another case. In addition, there are varying degrees to which an instance of tradition might be evaluated positively. One could have a case of tradition in which Barth detects no flaws. Alternatively, there might be a case of tradition that is objectionable in many respects but positive, and thus capable of functioning as a guide, in one or two respects.

An example of tradition functioning positively as a guide for Barth's dogmatic theology is his use of the ancient Trinitarian and Christological creeds of the Church (see the subsection on "Barth's positive use of tradition" in chapter 1). The Apostles' and Nicene Creeds, together with the Chalcedonian Christological formulation, offer theological construals and interpretations of scriptural teaching that stand against various heretical counter-construals and counter-interpretations. In this way, these creeds function both as a hermeneutical guide (a guide for the interpretation of Scripture) and as a guide for theological construction in relation to challenges to the integrity (i.e., unity, purity, catholicity or apostolicity) of Christian doctrine. Thus, Barth recognizes the possible role of church tradition—especially in its ecumenical creeds—in guiding the interpretation and application of Scripture, even though he refuses to regard tradition as a second material source for doctrine alongside Scripture.[122] This "hermeneutical authority" of tradition is not always obvious in Barth's very Protestant theoretical comments on the priority of Scripture over tradition. That said, Barth's practice often converges with his theory in that he frequently makes the effort to show how the "correct interpretations" offered in the creeds are actually grounded in Scripture and its "self-interpretation" as the written form of the Word of God.

Another example of the positive, guiding use of theological tradition is Barth's use of the Protestant reformers, whom Barth refers to as "modern" church fathers. Barth cites Luther more than any other theo-

---

122. It is worth noting that several contemporary Catholic theologians, such as Karl Rahner, appear to share a similar position with Barth in this respect, particularly in their rejection of the older, possibly Tridentine, two-source view of Scripture and tradition (the view that Barth has in his sights in I/2). See Rahner, "Scripture and Tradition."

logian, and is indebted to Luther in many of the important themes of his theology.[123] Calvin is also crucial for Barth as the father of Barth's own Reformed sub-tradition. As with other positive instances of tradition, however, Barth aims to look to the Reformers not as independent authorities but specifically for their ability to interpret and illuminate Scripture.[124] He also freely critiques them when be believes they fail to measure up to Scripture.[125]

The Negative Function of Tradition as a Foil in Dogmatics

In addition to the positive function of tradition in Barth's theology, it can also have a negative function. By this we mean that tradition can show what one should *not* do in theology. The decisive methodological reason why Barth judges certain instances of tradition negatively is that he believes that they fail either to be Christocentric, or biblical, or both.[126] In this book, we will concentrate on the failure of a given instance of tradition to be biblical, i.e., to be a faithful exposition of Scripture.

---

123. See Hunsinger's essay "What Karl Barth Learned from Martin Luther" (*Disruptive Grace*, 279–304).

124. Paul McGlasson draws attention to some possible exceptions to this generalization. In relation to Barth's use of Luther and Calvin, he says: "The point is not just that Barth was guided in his exegesis of the Bible by his reading of classical Christian biblical exegesis, though this too is an interesting and noteworthy fact. But the point is also that Barth did so *in principle*, that is, that he considered the mutual fit of his own biblical exegesis and classical Christian exegesis as a basic requirement" (McGlasson, *Jesus and Judas*, 95f.). While this is slightly overstated, it does speak of the degree to which Barth's practice (like his theory) revered Luther and Calvin as teachers who possess secondary but real authority.

125. For example, in his account of God's holiness, Barth makes the following comments about Luther's tendency to regard the revelation of God's law, holiness and wrath as separate from the revelation of divine grace: "In this respect we do not follow Luther because this scheme cannot honestly be maintained in the face of the ... testimony of Scripture" (II/1, 363). Also, Barth's critique of Calvin on election is well known. That it is based upon Scripture is evident in the words of Barth's preface to volume II/2: "I would have preferred to follow Calvin's doctrine of predestination much more closely, instead of departing from it so radically.... But I could not and cannot do so. As I let the Bible itself speak to me on these matters, as I meditated upon what I seemed to hear, I was driven irresistibly to reconstruction" (II/2, x).

126. As indicated above, that a doctrine is insufficiently Christological is often, to Barth's mind, an indication that it is insufficiently biblical—for the basic orientation or scope of Scripture is Christological.

In referring to Barth's negative use of tradition as a "foil," we mean that Barth critiques examples of theological tradition, not simply for the sake of critique, but specifically to set up his own view on a given theological loci as superior and free of the problems of the view criticized. This happens frequently with his interactions with modern Roman Catholicism and Neo-Protestant Liberalism. It also happens quite often with his treatments of the texts of medieval or later protestant scholasticism, especially when these texts involve what we have called (in chapter 1) classical conceptions of God. These classical conceptions of God, in fact, are the most prominent case of Barth's use of tradition as a foil within Barth's doctrine of God in II/1. We must now turn to a fuller explanation of these classical views, fulfilling the promise we made to do so in chapter 1.

Defining "Classical" Concepts of God

We will generally employ the concepts of "classical theism"[127] or "the classical concept of God"[128] to refer to a relatively consistent conception of God that emerged largely as a result of efforts to synthesize (a) certain classical Greco-Roman philosophical views about what divinity is like and (b) the biblical testimony to God.[129] This definition of "classical

---

127. H. P. Owen (*Concepts of Deity*) presents and defends classical theism (that he often refers to simply as theism) over other views of God such as pantheism or panentheism. He defines theism as "belief in one God, the Creator, who is infinite, self-existent, incorporeal, eternal, immutable, impassible, simple, perfect, omniscient and omnipotent" (1). On the basis of classical theism (as defined in pages 1–48), Owen presents an evaluation (both positive and negative), of Barth (98–107) and other twentieth century theologians.

128. The introduction of Gunton, *Becoming and Being* (1–7), sets forth a way of defining "the classical concept of God" that lays the foundation for his comparative exposition of the doctrines of God of Charles Hartshorne and Barth. He employs Aquinas as the representative example of the classical concept.

129. Cf. Owen, *Concepts of Deity*, 1, where he says "As far as the Western world is concerned, theism has a double origin: the Bible and Greek philosophy. All of the divine properties . . . are implied in the Bible; but the expression and, still more, the amplification of them were due to the influence of Greek philosophy." Owen speaks of the three phases of "attempts to present Scriptural revelation through philosophical concepts": (1) the Jews of the Diaspora before the New Testament, such as Philo, (2) the early Christian apologists, such as Justin Martyr, and (3) the "climax" of synthesis in Augustine and especially Aquinas (1f.).

The average dictionary will contain two definitions of the term "classical" that are relevant to Theology or are commonly used in Theology: (1) That which is of enduring

theism" needs to be qualified and explained. We will do so in the form of five observations.

The first observation is that, historically speaking, it is often more precise to refer to classical *concepts* of God (in the plural), since accounts of the divine nature drawn from a "biblical-classical synthesis" obviously vary according to historical period and individual theological creativity.[130] There are important differences, for example, between the classical doctrines of God of Augustine and Anselm, or Aquinas and Duns Scotus. For this reason, we will, where necessary, refer to classical *concepts* of divine unity, immutability or eternity.

The second observation, in some tension with the first, is this: on the conceptual level, there is a significant and sometimes remarkable similarity that can be observed between the doctrines of God represented by various thinkers like Anselm and Aquinas that makes it appropriate to call them classical theologians. At the least, there is a crucial set of family resemblances, that distinguish classical views from other possible views. In fact, we can legitimately speak (as philosophical theologians often do) of an ideal classical concept of God that consists in a set of logically connected, mutually supporting concepts. This complex concept is rooted in shared metaphysical intuitions or assumptions about God as the first cause or most perfect being. Therefore, we can legitimately speak of "classical theism" or the "classical concept of God" in many contexts, even if no historical figure perfectly exemplifies the ideal classical view.[131]

---

or traditional significance and (2) that which related to the ancient Greek or Roman world. Although some connotations of the first definition may be present in the use of "classical" in this book, the second definition is more specifically relevant. Again, "classical views of God" are a product of a synthesis of the classical Greco-Roman and biblical views of God or divinity.

130. Process theologians sometimes use the term "classical theism" in a historically dubious manner to describe a view that they wish to critique. In a review of a work by Schubert Ogden, Langdon Gilkey has remarked that "what process philosophers of religion call 'classical theism' is a strange hodgepodge that bears little historical scrutiny" (Gilkey, "Theology in Process," 449). He also states that "the argument is very dubious that . . . there has been a *dominant* conception of God in Christendom characterized by Thomist attributes." Our *second* observation in this subsection qualifies the value of Gilkey's comment. See also the comments of William Placher, to the effect that "classical theism" is more a modern (Seventeenth Century) phenomenon than an ancient and medieval one (Placher, *Domestication of Transcendence*, 11 and elsewhere). Our *fifth* observation above clarifies how we depart from Placher on this point.

131. Brian Leftow's comments on classical theism in a recent article ("God,

A third observation about our use of the term "classical" in relation to concepts of God is specific to Barth, namely, that our use of "classical" specifically designates views that involve what Barth called "natural theology." This is based on Barth's patterns of argument rather than his specific use of the term "classical." Barth does not use the adjective *klassisch* (translated as either "classical" or "classic" in English) very frequently, and he does not appear to use it in a consistent way to refer to a particular kind of view of God. However, Barth consistently critiques natural theology, whether in incipient or obvious forms, within what he more often refers to as "traditional" (*traditionell*) views of God.[132] We choose to use the term "classical" to refer to this sub-set of traditional views of God that Barth judges negatively because of their alleged infection with natural theology. In this book, then, the term "classical" will have a primarily negative connotation.[133] Such classical "natural theology" results in a view of God that derived significantly from Greek philosophy, which is not easily compatible with revelation. Specifically, Barth believed it to be the product of idolatrous and arrogant human speculations rather than being derived from the witness of the plain verbal sense of Scripture and its Christocentric subject matter, the "biblical" (methodological) and "Christocentric" (material) criteria of Barth's theology.[134]

A fourth observation is that scholastic concepts of God are typically the fullest and clearest expressions of classical conceptions of divinity. Thus, although Barth sometimes critiques the teachings of church

---

Concepts of") confirm this way of defining classical theism as an "ideal type" that does not depend upon historical thinkers fully instantiating it. Owen attempts to state a contemporary version of such an ideal classical position (*Concepts of Deity*).

132. Meijering (*Von Den Kirchenvatern zu Karl Barth*) claims at several points that one of the main differences between Barth and the Church fathers is that the latter affirmed "natural theology."

133. It is certainly possible that thinkers who synthesize the biblical and Greco-Roman views of God are decisively more biblical than Greco-Roman in content, using the Greek language and conceptuality in the service of the God of revelation. This is evidently what Barth thought of Athanasius' contributions to Nicene creedal orthodoxy. But the thinkers that Barth treats in his doctrine of divine perfections he normally assessed more negatively.

134. For Barth, the biblical portrayal of God resists *any* kind of substantive (rather than merely terminological) synthesis with philosophical or natural views of God. It is all the more problematic for Barth, when he identifies metaphysical views of God that appear to *take precedence over* faithfulness to the biblical witness to God's identity and character.

fathers for tending towards a classical version of natural theology, he more frequently critiques scholastic theologians in his doctrine of God. That said, Barth is by no means consistently critical of scholasticism, as is evident in his often positive assessment of medievals like Anselm and Aquinas, and the Post-Reformation, Protestant scholastics.

Our fifth observation is that we need to clarify the relationship of classical concepts of God to modernity. In this book, we will typically restrict the use of "classical" to pre-modern theologians and their views of God,[135] in keeping with our concentration on the role of pre-modern tradition.[136] Again, we will include post-reformation Scholastics like Polanus under the category of pre-modern theologians.

The Two Criteria of Dogmatics in Relation to Tradition

The Christocentric Criterion of Dogmatics in Relation to Tradition

One of the main factors that determine how Barth relates to tradition is the degree to which that tradition is Christocentric. As a general rule, Barth evaluates and employs tradition in a positive manner if it is Christocentric, and negatively if it is not.[137] In what follows, we provide some examples of the positive use of Christocentric tradition as a guide for Barth's theology.

Although Barth's own style of Christocentrism is distinctive, it also draws on historical precedent, either explicitly or implicitly. The most ancient roots of Barth's Christocentrism lie in the New Testament itself, including its reinterpretation of the Old Testament along Christological lines. This point speaks of the way that the Christocentric and biblical criteria often converge in Barth's theology. But Barth's approach also

---

135. See Placher, *Domestication of Transcendence*, for a different view of the relationship of classical concepts of God to modernity.

136. When we do comment on modern thinkers, our comments will tend to go in one of two directions. (1) Following Barth, we will occasionally comment on the indebtedness of modern theologians to pre-modern metaphysical concepts of God. (2) We will raise the question of the extent to which Barth is helped by or indebted to modern thinking in his critique of classicism. Especially relevant is the new antisubstantialist, dynamic and historical metaphysical thinking of Hegel (and Dorner after him) and the antimetaphysical tendencies of thinkers as varied as Schleiermacher, Kierkegaard, Ritschl, Herrmann, Cremer, and Buber.

137. Exceptions to this rule relate to the degree to which an instance of tradition is biblical. Thus, Barth views non-biblical Christocentrism negatively.

follows certain post-biblical Christocentric traditions of Scripture interpretation and of theology in general. Of special significance are the ancient creeds (Apostles, Nicene, etc.) that defined a certain kind of Christocentrism as basic to Christian orthodoxy. The Chalcedonian formulation continued in this vein by ruling out various heterodox ways of conceiving of Christ.[138] Barth's theology follows such ancient ecumenical Christocentric construals of Christianity in his theology. Even so, these traditional formulations are not adequate to account for the distinctive features of Barth's Christocentrism.

Luther is perhaps the theologian who influenced Barth the most in respect his distinctive Christocentrism. George Hunsinger argues that it was primarily the soteriological Christocentrism of Luther, rather than the later (more formal) Christocentrism of Schleiermacher and Herrmann, that Barth absorbed in his theology.[139] Barth's Christocentrism also goes beyond Luther's in different respects. In some ways, Barth radicalizes Luther's Christocentrism.[140] In other ways, Barth qualifies Luther's Christocentrism by means of a Reformed emphasis on adhering to all parts of the biblical canon (e.g., the book of James), rather than only those parts that "preach Christ" and attest clearly to the gospel of justification by faith.[141]

Before we turn directly to how the second, "biblical" criterion relates to tradition, it may be helpful to offer some transitional comments on the Christocentric traditions of interpreting Scripture. Both Luther

---

138. See Hunsinger on the Chalcedonian character of Barth's Christology (*Disruptive Grace*, 131–47; see also the same essay in Webster, *Cambridge Companion*, 127–42). For a significant argument that qualifies the legitimacy of calling Barth's theology Chalcedonian, see McCormack, "Barths Grundsätzlicher Chalcedonismus"? In this paper, McCormack emphasizes the modern actualist and anti-substantialist tendencies that emerge especially in volume IV of *CD*, tendencies that are not nearly as marked in volume II/1.

139. Hunsinger, *Disruptive Grace*, 283–86. That said, we should not underrate the significance of Herrmann in Barth's *CD*, which frequently alludes to the structure and emphases of Herrmann's writings without actually citing him (I am indebted to Trevor Hart for this point; see also Dorrien, *Barthian Revolt*). We should also note that, according to Hunsinger, Barth's Christocentrism follows Luther more than Calvin, since Barth draws on Luther's "theology of the cross" (*Disruptive Grace*, 287–90).

140. Ibid., 283.

141. Generally speaking, Luther and Lutheranism tended to stress the material principle of the Reformation (soteriological Christocentrism), while Calvin and the Reformed tradition tended to stress the formal Scripture principle of the Reformation (the biblical criterion for theology).

and Calvin regarded Christ as the central unifying subject matter of all of Scripture,[142] and Barth follows them on this point. As such, the Christocentric-soteriological material principle of the Reformation is a form of the traditional Christocentric "ruled readings" of Scripture, hermeneutical applications of the "rule of faith" that shape the Church's understanding of the "plain sense" of Scripture.[143] Barth is guided significantly by such a ruled, Christological construal of Scripture as a whole, especially when he makes global statements about "what Scripture teaches." In such cases, the indirect—but potentially decisive—scriptural authorization of theological proposals is especially important. This way of employing Scripture in dogmatics is drawn to a large extent from Barth's own Neo-Reformational, Christocentric tradition.

The biblical Criterion of Dogmatics in Relation to Tradition

Bart is guided by tradition not only to be Christocentric and "biblical," but also to make being biblical a crucial criterion of his theology. Of course, the primary traditional influences on Barth's thought in this respect are the Reformers and their theological followers. *Sola Scriptura* constituted the "formal principle" of the Reformation, the "Scripture principle." Even if *sola Scriptura* involves the primacy rather than the exclusivity of Scripture over tradition and other potential theological authorities, Barth joins historic Protestantism in emphasizing the need for subordination to Scripture in theology and church. Barth's preoccupation with Scripture over tradition is not a matter of anti-traditionalism, but is itself influenced by a certain (Protestant) ecclesial-theological tradition.[144]

More specifically, the Reformed tradition within Old Protestant Orthodoxy was particularly influential with respect to Barth's view of Scripture and scriptural interpretation. In what follows we will make this point by comparing the treatments of "Holy Scripture" in Heinrich

---

142. Frei, *Eclipse of Biblical Narrative*, 20.

143. Greene-McCreight, *Ad Litteram*, 5ff.; 22.

144. In this connection, it is important to note Barth's consistent rejection of anti-traditionalist forms of Biblicism, which is to be distinguished from the more tradition-friendly Biblicism of the Reformers and of the great Pietist biblical scholar J. A. Bengel (I/2, 607ff.). On Bengel, see our comments below.

Heppe's anthology, *Reformed Dogmatics*,¹⁴⁵ and Barth's *CD*, I/2. We will see that Barth did not follow the Reformed tradition slavishly, which we will indicate partly by noting correspondences between Barth's biblical hermeneutics and those of non-Reformed thinkers like Augustine and the Pietist J. A. Bengel.¹⁴⁶

Barth affirmed several of the "properties" of Scripture defined by Reformed Orthodoxy: authority, perspicuity (clarity of meaning and interpretation), and effectiveness or power.¹⁴⁷ We could also add Barth's affirmation of the unity of Scripture, which Reformed orthodoxy assumed with other pre-moderns. Yet these shared points coexist with other points in which Barth qualified or critiqued Reformed orthodoxy's teachings on Scripture, such as Scripture's inspiration and perfection.¹⁴⁸

Of more immediate relevance are the hermeneutical principles that Barth shared in common with Reformed orthodoxy. To begin with, Barth agreed with Polanus and others that to affirm the perspicuity of Scripture does not exclude the need for exposition.¹⁴⁹ Several other

---

145. Heppe, *Reformed Dogmatics*. Barth used this book as one of his primary sources in preparing his first lectures in dogmatics at Göttingen in the 1920's. His rather positive assessment of the Reformed scholastics is evident in his forward to Heppe, written in 1935 (Heppe, *Reformed Dogmatics*, v–vii).

146. Bengel lived from 1687–1782, and is cited with relative frequency by Barth in *CD* (for some illuminating comments on Bengel, see Frei, *Eclipse of Biblical Narrative*, 175–79). Donald Dayton of Azusa Pacific University informed me in personal conversation (in June 2002) that a copy of Bengel's *Gnommon* on the New Testament is on the shelf of Barth's (well-preserved) personal library in Basel. This circumstantial evidence confirms what careful study of *CD* urges: that Pietism sometimes functions as a positive, formative influence on Barth's theology. Barth's own autobiographical comments about the revision of his "theological foundations" in his early work add additional confirmation of this point, especially in relation to the impact of the two Blumhardts. For example, Barth says that the "very strong influence of Christoph Blumhardt . . . first lead me back simply to more *concrete biblical exegesis*" (italics added; as cited in Bromiley, *Barth-Bultmann Letters*, 157f.; cf. 154).

147. Heppe, *Reformed Dogmatics*, 21–33.

148. In general, there are two main ways in which Barth's perspective on Scripture stood against the mainstream of Reformed orthodoxy. First, Barth distinguished between the Word of God and Scripture (Heppe, *Reformed Dogmatics*, 14ff.). Second, he differed from the view that Scripture was "objectively" inspired by God and therefore infallible and inerrant (Heppe, *Reformed Dogmatics*, 16–21). As a result, Barth does not affirm Scripture's "perfection," although he does affirm its "sufficiency" vis-à-vis tradition (Heppe, *Reformed Dogmatics*, 30).

149. See *CD* I/2, 714; Heppe, *Reformed Dogmatics*, 33. For a similar combination of perspicuity and the need for exposition, see Bengel (*Bengel's New Testament*

principles of interpretation stated by the Reformed scholastics appear to inform Barth's practice. First, the Scripture's perspicuity or clarity only appears as such to the one who "reads it with a believing mind, i.e., according to the *regula fidei et caritatis*."[150] Barth suggests something like this principle both in his general faith-seeking-understanding approach to theology and specifically in his "rule of subordination" (see above). Second, "the obscure passages of Scripture are to be explained by the unambiguously clear ones,"[151] such that "Scripture is its own interpreter." In slightly different terms, obscure passages can be explained by the *analogia fidei* that the Reformed writers regarded as based upon the clear (versus obscure) biblical passages.[152] Third, "the Holy Spirit is the only interpreter of Scripture,"[153] as its divine author. Barth retains the main force of this point, but qualifies it with his more dynamic understanding of inspiration. Fourth, Scripture ought to be interpreted according to the "*constant consent and authority* of the Church," with the qualification that the Church does not have "judicial power by which to control faith and doctrine."[154] This last point shows that the relative authority of catholic or ecumenical tradition was already affirmed before Barth by representatives of the Reformed tradition.

Concepts for Understanding Reason and Its Theological Functions

Following a similar pattern of organization as in the previous two sections of this chapter, this section will explicate concepts relevant to the construal of reason, the use of reason, and the relationship of the two criteria of dogmatics to reason.

Commentary, xii–xiv).

150. Heppe, *Reformed Dogmatics*, 34; cf. Augustine *On Christian Doctrine* III.3.5, III.9.14, and III.10.14. See also Bengel, who regarded uprightness of heart as essential to understanding Scripture's own clear meaning (*Bengel's New Testament Commentary*, xii–xiii).

151. Heppe, *Reformed Dogmatics*, 34; cf. Augustine *On Christian Doctrine* II.10.14.

152. Heppe, *Reformed Dogmatics*, 34.

153. *Conf. Helv.* I.2, as cited in ibid., 34. The connection between the Spirit and the Scriptures was so close in Reformed orthodoxy, that this statement (according to Heppe) was regarded as another way of saying that "Scripture is its own interpreter."

154. *Conf. Helv.* I.2, as cited in Heppe, *Reformed Dogmatics*, 34.

Concepts Related to the Construal of Reason

SOME DEFINITIONS

In this thesis, we will use the term "reason" (and related terms like "rational" or "rationality") in two main senses, "descriptive reason" and "normative reason."[155] In its *descriptive* meaning, reason is simply the human intellectual (or rational) capacity for and activity of forming judgments and making inferences.[156] In this sense, humans use reason all the time, in virtually every aspect of life. In its *normative* meaning, reason refers to the standards or norms for correct reasoning. In this sense, something is "rational" only if it conforms to certain norms for justification, truth or knowledge: e.g., the laws of logic, correspondence to reality, and so on.

We will now apply these two senses of reason to Barth. On the descriptive level, reason includes Barth's construal and use of logic (e.g., deductive and inductive inference),[157] certain uses of his imagination (e.g., Barth's frequent use of "pattern-recognition" in relation to Scripture and tradition)[158] and the intellectual aspects of his experience

---

155. We follow John Frame (*Doctrine of the Knowledge of God*, 329–32) in making this distinction. More indirectly, we follow Barth himself in his book on Anselm, where he offers one of his most extended analyses of the nature of theological rationality (Barth, *Fides Quaerens Intellectum*, 44ff. and passim; cf. Gunton, *Becoming and Being*, 120ff.; 126f. and McCormack, *Karl Barth's Critically Realistic Dialectic Theology*, 428–41, esp. 429–34). Barth here speaks of three senses of reason or rationality: (1) *ratio fidei*, the internal rationality of the creed or Scripture, (2) *ratio veritatis*, the ontic rationality of Jesus Christ, the Word, enacted in ongoing events of self-revelation (and veiling), and (3) *ratio intellectus* (human *intelligere* or *Nachdenken*, thinking-after or reflection, on the *ratio fidei* and ultimately on the *ratio veritatis*). At the risk of oversimplification, our "descriptive reason" corresponds to the *ratio intellectus* and our "normative reason" corresponds to the *ratio veritatis*. To explain further would involve a more detailed exposition of Barth's book on Anselm than is necessary, given the work others have done in this regard. Besides the above sources, see Pugh, *Anselmic Shift*.

156. Barth describes this sense of reason (*ratio*) as "the primary capacity of dealing with experience, of formulating conceptions and judgments" (*Fides Quaerens Intellectum*, 44f.).

157. Barth uses logic, adhering to the law of non-contradiction, especially in his effort to show forth the internal coherence of doctrines with each other (see Barth, *Fides Quaerens Intellectum*, 55; cf. McCormack, *Karl Barth's Critically Realistic Dialectic Theology*, 436f. and Hunsinger, *How to Read Karl Barth*, 281f.). However, Barth's use of standard logic is qualified by the dialectical character of his theology and other factors, as we will see below.

158. John Macquarrie regards Barth as possessing "architectonic reason," "an imaginative reason comparable to that of a great architect" (*Principles of Christian Theology*, 15).

of God's Word.¹⁵⁹ Reason also includes Barth's use of the terms and conceptual resources of philosophy and of other aspects of his intellectual heritage, such as theological tradition. On the normative level, Barth regards theology as rational because it is a "description of what is in fact the case" and in this sense "is concerned to say what is true."¹⁶⁰ That is, theological claims can be true knowledge. The truth of theological statements is determined primarily by "correspondence" to the divine subject matter (i.e., the object or content) of theology and secondarily by its "coherence" with other doctrines (a coherence qualified by the mysterious and dialectical nature of theology).¹⁶¹ Insofar as theology is true, it is a form of knowledge—knowledge that rests on and is imbued with faith.

The above observations indicate that, for Barth, being "rational" is different from being "rationalistic." To be rationalistic would be to develop as system of a priori principles, independent of actual revelation.¹⁶² The rationality evident in Barth's theology is largely a posteriori in character (in relation to the ongoing reality of revelation), which leads him to understand theological proposals as provisional, open-textured or open-ended.¹⁶³

Drawing on the work of Steven G. Smith, we can develop other conceptions of the use of reason that are complementary to the descriptive and normative senses. In our treatment of scholarship on Barth's use of reason in chapter 1, we noted that Smith argued that there were roughly three concepts of reason at work in Barth's theology. Translating Smith's work into our own idiom, we can refer to the following three concepts of reason: (1) instrumental reason (the neutral use), (2) corrupted reason (the negative use), and (3) reconciled reason (positive use).

---

159. Barth includes intellect under the "experience" in which a person's whole self-determining existence (including their thinking) is determined by the Word of God (I/1, 202f.).

160. Gunton, *Becoming and Being*, 126f.

161. Hunsinger, *How to Read Karl Barth*, 281f. The correspondence or "analogy" between theological statements and God's being is ultimately created on an occasional basis by divine actions. As McCormack says, "knowledge of God is an event" (*Karl Barth's Critically Realistic Dialectic Theology*, 432f.).

162. See *CD* I/2, 483, 861f.; cf. Gunton, *Becoming and Being*, 124; and Hunsinger, *How to Read Karl Barth*, 51ff.

163. See A. Torrance, *Persons in Communion*, 31ff.; see also our comments below.

At least in theology, Barth would say that the "neutral" (or strictly formal) use of reason always works in tandem with either (or both) its negative or its positive uses. Such neutral rational capacity may be *involved* in theology, but it is not sufficient to explain how a theologian forms theological judgments. Faith and the theological knowledge derived from it is not neutral, but "self-involving" and "person-specific."[164] Also, observation of Barth's theological practice shows that his social and historical location, and especially the Church and its traditions, shapes his view of what is "rational."[165] The actual use of reason in theology, far from being neutral, is implicated in the dramatic conflict between God's gracious work and human sinfulness.

In its non-neutral theological exercise, then, human reason is not exempt from the inevitable corruption of the whole person that comes with sin; there are noetic effects of sin. This corruption of the mind requires the reconciling work of God to be overcome. As is typical of the "actualistic" elements in Barth's theology, no theologian can ever presume that his reason has reached a state of being finally healed or reconciled. Rather, the Christian theologian must await the unfolding of the ever-repeated miraculous event in which God's self-revelation overcomes the inadequacy of her provisional ways of thinking and speaking.[166]

The positive, reconciled use of reason in Barth's conception of theology can be divided into two primary functions: the "critical" and "constructive."[167] In its critical function, reason can be profitably em-

164. See Hunsinger, *How to Read Karl Barth*, 50f.

165. This is no doubt true of any thinker. As Trevor Hart puts it, "Reason is ... better construed as an intellectual tool working within the horizons provided by particular sets of assumptions about what is possible, credible, meaningful, etc., than as some transcendent set of truths to be applied with equal validity to any time and place" (Hart, "Living with Diversity," 3). Hart appropriately draws on Alasdair MacIntyre in support of this view, and the related concept that rational inquiry is "tradition-constituted" and "tradition-constituting" (see MacIntyre, *Whose Justice? Which Rationality?*, 349).

166. This is an example of the way in which logic and other forms of human theological rationality are conditioned by the actualistic *Realdialectik* of God's ontic veiling and unveiling (see McCormack, *Karl Barth's Critically Realistic Dialectic Theology*, 432f., 436f.).

167. In making this distinction we are again drawing on Smith ("Karl Barth and Fideism"), but are using different terms for what he referred to as the constraining and freeing functions of reason (see chapter 1). See also Hunsinger (*How to Read Karl Barth*, 5) on Barth's rationalism.

Macquarrie (*Principles of Christian Theology*, 14f.) describes the main theological uses of reason as "speculative reason" (both a priori and a posteriori), and "critical

ployed in the critique of various theological arguments or positions, such as those represented by classical conceptions of God's attributes. In this critical role, a reconciled use of reason, based on and trained by God's self-revelation attested in Scripture, can properly judge theological proposals. For Barth, a theological proposal can be judged inadequate because it fails to attend to the distinctive rational norms of theology found in God's self-revelation in Christ as attested in Scripture.[168] Instead it falls into errors such as speculation about God and rationalistic systematization. This is what happens in natural theology, which is for Barth the paradigmatic expression of "corrupted reason." The critical role of reason, far from involving an autonomous or independent use of reason, is rather a critique of any such claims to autonomy.

In its constructive function, by contrast, reconciled reason constructs theological proposals and arguments by various procedures that move from faith to understanding. As Hunsinger states, for Barth there is "no faith without knowledge," for faith possesses intrinsic and distinctive cognitive content.[169] Barth's constructive use of reason is constructive in only a weak sense, since it is based upon the subordination to and reception of the revelation attested in Scripture. It is not (or at least it does not aim to be) constructive in the strong sense of producing speculative or metaphysical truths entirely out of the resources of one's own autonomous intellect. However, rather than merely passively receiving and repeating revelation in a parrot-like manner, Barth does use his mind actively and creatively to explicate the content of revelation and, specifically, to interpret and apply Scripture rightly.[170]

Barth clearly uses mainly "internal" rather than "external" norms of reason or rationality in his dogmatics. In other words, the norms of theology are usually drawn from within the sphere of the Church and

---

reason" (both "elucidatory" and "corrective"). He associates the quasi-speculative category of "architectonic reason" specifically with Barth (15). The "elucidatory" aspect of Macquarrie's "critical reason" might aptly describe much of Barth's use of reason, but the "corrective" aspect (autonomous reason capable of critiquing revelation-claims) would not (15f; cf. 90ff.).

168. Such faulty theological proposals often attempt to impose improper (nontheological) norms upon theological judgments and inferences, such as the "general norms" of science (see I/1, 8ff.).

169. Hunsinger, *How to Read Karl Barth*, 54f.

170. See our treatment of the principle of subordination above in the section entitled "Concepts Related to Barth's Interpretation of Scripture."

its God-talk rather than being derived from without or being shared with all spheres of human rational activity. This is because the thinking and speaking of theology are derived from Christocentric revelation, which is known by faith. There is a limited sense in which Barth recognizes that certain rational norms are shared by theology and other disciplines or forms of life outside of the practice of theology: e.g., the rules of grammar and, to a large extent, the rules of logic.[171] This is what enables theology to be largely intelligible to non-Christians and non-theologians. However, Barth's particularistic impulse causes him to be ever-ready to overturn the rational norms appropriate for other subject matters in order to conform his theological reasoning to the unique subject matter of God and his revelation.[172]

A Construal of the Rational Intelligibility of the Gospel

Aspects of Barth's construal of reason are evident in a passage in *CD* IV/3 on the Christian community's explanation of the gospel. Although this passage comes late in *CD*, it appears to shed light on the way Barth understood reason in the earlier volumes, such as II/1. In context, Barth is unfolding of the claim that, in the ministry of witness that it does in the power of the Holy Spirit, the Church is called not only to *declare* the gospel, but to *explain* it.[173] To explain the gospel, is to show forth its inherent perceptibility and intelligibility. The human work of explaining is not autonomous, but rests on and follows the prior divine work in which the Word of the gospel explains itself. Yet there is still a human work of explaining to be done, and this is a *rational* work. Barth emphatically avers that the Church's human witnesses must discard "the illusion that [theological] knowledge is possible only in the form of a

---

171. In his discussion of "secular parables to the truth" and the "lesser lights" Barth does argues for relative analogies between theological truths and the truths of wider human experience and reasoning (see IV/3, 38–165 and Hunsinger's fine exposition in *How to Read Karl Barth*, 234–80). Theology has a secondary task of relating its claims to non-theological realities and truths (see Dalferth's chapter in Sykes, *Karl Barth*).

172. In this respect, T. F. Torrance correctly understands Barth's basic rule of rationality as "conformity to the object of knowledge" whether it is divine or created (see *Karl Barth: An Introduction*: 182f.; *Karl Barth: Biblical and Evangelical Theologian*, 52–60; cf. Barth, *Fides Quaerens Intellectum*, 53f. and I/1, 190). Since the nature of the object (or subject matter) varies considerably the appropriate rational norms can vary considerably. Rationality as conformity to the object is related to Barth's "objectivism" (Hunsinger, *How to Read Karl Barth*, 35–39).

173. IV/3, 846–50.

sacrificium intellectus."[174] Rather, the gospel message is rational; human reasoning is part of what is required to show this, as the following quotation shows.

> For it is surely possible for even the most obstinate of unbelievers, whether or not they can come to a knowledge of the truth, at least to appreciate the inner consistency and to that extent the meaning of the evangelical message. If they do not, the community is well advised to ask itself whether this is not because of a deficiency in its own attention to the inner clarity, rationality and perspicuity of the Gospel on the one side and neglect of the human means at its disposal on the other. It is thus advised to seek the fault in itself rather than on the wicked world, and therefore with new zest and seriousness to make now and more energetic efforts in this direction. But it is generally intelligible and explicable. For its content is rational and not irrational. (Ibid.)

In this passage, Barth distinguishes between "knowledge of the truth" of the gospel that is open only to believers and an appreciation of the "inner consistency" and meaning of the gospel that are open to believers and unbelievers alike.[175] If unbelievers do not appreciate the intelligibility of the gospel (its inner consistency, rationality and perspicuity), Barth implies that this is the fault, not of the gospel nor of the unbelievers, but of the Church.

Barth's speaking of the "inner consistency" of the gospel is illuminating, and can be unfolded dialectically. First, it is "*inner* consistency." In that sense, it may not be consistent with human knowledge at large; it is internal rationality. It is concerned rather with interpreting the mysterious world of revelation, the "strange new world within the Bible."[176] The truth of the gospel is often at odds with the conclusions of history, philosophy and natural theology.[177] Yet, second, the intel-

---

174. Ibid., 848.

175. One could argue that a non-believer's appreciation of the inner consistency of the gospel requires an imaginative recognition of the meaningful pattern within it. This makes communication between believers and non-believers possible.

176. Barth, *Word of God*, 30ff.

177. As such, Barth differs from Wolfhart Pannenberg and other theologians who lay great emphasis on demonstrating the compatibility between the truth-claims of theology and the truth-claims of other non-theological disciplines (history, philosophy and science). But Barth is not simply a fideist. The reason is that he does claim the rationality and general intelligibility of the gospel and of dogmatics. Barth simply

lectual world of the gospel possesses "inner *consistency.*" It remains intelligible. Possessing this inner consistency, theology is meaningful. In this respect, Barth's theology is marked by what George Hunsinger calls a "weak" form of "Anselmian coherentism." By this Hunsinger means that, for Barth as for Anselm, "no cognitive assertions can be justified independently of other theological assertions and beliefs"[178] It is *weak* coherentism, since it is not purely the internal coherence or consistency of these proposals that grants them meaningfulness or justification. Rather, doctrinal beliefs are "thought to be justified also *and primarily* because they are suitably grounded in revelation as normatively attested in Scripture."[179] Hence, the "consistency" he is concerned to affirm is qualified by correspondence to the dialectical nature of revelation and of our limited human understanding of it.[180]

Concepts for the Use of Reason

In this subsection, we will describe various critical and constructive functions of reason. In his use of various rational tools, Barth consistently aims to subordinate himself to Scripture and its subject matter.

---

recognizes that the rational grounds that enable a person to come to knowledge of theological truth are rooted in revelation, as it is received in faith.

178. Hunsinger, *How to Read Karl Barth*, 55; cf. 281f. On Anselm in this respect, see Barth, *Fides Quaerens Intellectum*, 55f.

179. Hunsinger, *How to Read Karl Barth*, 281. This is Barth's incorporation of elements of the correspondence theory of truth and is related to his concern for "hermeneutical adequacy" (Hunsinger, *Disruptive Grace*, 191f.). Moving beyond what Hunsinger has shown, we can offer a couple of further provisional observations. First, the implicit approach to or theory of *meaning* evident in Barth's theology seems to be largely "coherentist." This is what allows a non-believer who is not personally acquainted with the divine referent of theological language to grasp its internal meaningfulness and intelligibility—even in regard to its first-order discourse. Second, Barth's implicit theory of *truth* seems to be largely a correspondence theory of truth. Revelation supplies the reality to which theological statements must correspond to be true. Barth's implicit theory of *justification* (Hunsinger's concern) involves elements of both coherence and correspondence theories.

180. See McCormack, *Karl Barth's Critically Realistic Dialectic Theology*, 432f. A related point is that Barth appears to believe that no human theory or system, in any discipline, can be totally without internal contradictions (II/1, 105; 580; cf. Hunsinger, *How to Read Karl Barth*, 282).

Hans Frei on the Three Levels of Discourse and "Conceptual Redescription"

In his posthumously published work entitled *Types of Theology*, Hans Frei employs several helpful categories for the analysis and comparison of various theologians and theologies. One set of categories is his reference to first-order, second-order and third-order discourse. Barth's theology has a certain way of relating these three levels of discourse in his theology, which sets it apart from other types of theology.

We may define the three levels of discourse briefly as follows. First-order discourse is both "first-person direct address *to* God, speaking and acting in his presence"[181] and the basic testimony to God's self-revelation found in biblical narratives, especially those about Jesus. Such self-involving statements are at the heart of the Church's native language of prayer and worship, its distinctive language-game. Second-order discourse is reflective "talk *about* God" that typically takes the form of conceptual analysis or redescription of the self-involving first-order statements about God. This is the heart of the language and task of theology. Third-order discourse is formal and technical philosophical language, which Barth employs in a qualified manner within his theology.[182]

Frei observes that, in Barth's theology, the relationships between these three levels of discourse are ad hoc rather than systematic. This has several specific implications. For one thing the first two orders of discourse "are not nearly so sharply distinguishable as they are for some other theologians."[183] This means that theological language, even if it is predominantly second-order "conceptual redescription," is also self-involving. As the Church's self-criticism, it is still the language of the Church and of faith.[184] The second-order speech of theology is essentially Christian "self-description," a sort of description and analysis of the rules that govern the theological discourse of the Christian community. In addition, Barth employs philosophical conceptuality freely on an ad hoc basis, but in a way that retains the primacy of the distinctive

---

181. Frei, *Types of Christian Theology*, 39. See A. Torrance (*Persons in Communion*) on the significance of the doxological (first-order) aspect of God-talk and how Barth ought to have emphasized it more.

182. See Frei, *Types of Christian Theology*, 41.

183. Ibid., 39.

184. Again, see Hunsinger, *How to Read Karl Barth*, 50f.

theological subject matter and discourse (see below).[185] In sum, Frei regards Barth's *CD* as primarily second-order redescription or conceptual analysis of first-order language of the biblical text, with the use of third-order discourse that aids this analysis.[186]

Although Frei's interpretation of Barth is basically accurate and insightful, it does need to be qualified in one respect. This qualification concerns how Frei refers to the second-order discourse of theology as "self-description." The trouble with this language is that Barth believes that this Christian God-talk is, at its best, not merely the self-expression of a particular religious community but is genuinely grounded in and expressive of God's self-revelation.[187] Barth's theocentric realism leads him to consistently speak of the objective theological referentiality of theological language, rather than any anthropocentric reduction of it to the self-enclosed world of a cultural-linguistic system.[188] Barth repeatedly declares that, because of the ongoing gift of revelation, theologians can be set free to talk not only about themselves but *about God*. At times Frei seems aware of this point, but sometimes, (like George Lindbeck) he does not give sufficient attention to Barth's theological realism—i.e., to his unswerving commitment to the adequate connection between theological language and the extratextual, transcommunal reality of God.[189]

---

185. Indeed, Frei claims that, for Barth, "One not only can but must make use of technical philosophical schemes of a metaphysical sort in the process of using Christian language in its descriptive or assertive mode" (*Types of Christian Theology*, 41).

186. Frei, *Types of Christian Theology*, 44; cf. 81, 125. See the work of Paul McGlasson (*Jesus and Judas*), who, probably being influenced by Frei (Frei taught at Yale, where McGlasson did his PhD), calls "conceptual analysis" the primary exegetical method that Barth uses, at least in the first two volumes of *CD* (see our comments on McGlasson in chapter 1).

187. In a relevant comment, Frei says that if Barth "sounds like a traditional metaphysician . . . the impression is misleading. . . . He is indeed talking about knowledge appropriate to reality, but there is no theory of reality and no theory of [the] classes of assertions involved" (*Types of Christian Theology*, 45). Jenson (*God after God*) is one interpreter of Barth who is more quick to speak of Barth as offering a metaphysic or theory of reality, and in this his view differs somewhat from Frei's. But even Jenson is well aware that if Barth is doing metaphysics, it is surely a distinctive *theological* kind.

188. Webster appropriately associates this with "ecclesial subjectivism" (*Barth's Ethics*, 27).

189. This point is made with exceptional force by Webster (*Barth's Ethics*, 26–33), who critiques Lindbeck (*Nature of Doctrine*), and to a lesser extent Frei, in the light of an exposition of Barth's unique revelational realism. See also Hunsinger's helpful com-

A Conceptual Framework for the Exposition of Barth's Theological Method 97

Thus, there is a polemical point implicit in the title of this book: "Redescribing God." Barth's theological method surely involves redescription of first-order Christian language, but in faith this is properly seen as in some sense "redescribing *God*," albeit dialectically and provisionally—and not merely another effort at communal self-description. Understood correctly, "redescribing God" in obedient response to *God's own self-description*, i.e., his self-revelation in Jesus Christ attested in Scripture, is the primary goal of Barth's theological method.[190] This is the *telos* of Barth's distinctive and disciplined way of integrating the roles of Scripture, tradition and reason within his theology.[191] We will observe this "realist principle" at work in the remainder of the book.[192]

Barth's Use of Logic and Argument in CD

We will now examine some of the various ways of using logic and argument that Barth employs in CD. To begin, we will consider why we think it is appropriate to use the term "argument" as a way of characterizing what Barth is doing in CD.

Some interpreters have regarded "argument" as inappropriate to Barth's theological method. For example, Frei says that "Barth's theology proceeds by narrative and conceptually descriptive statement

---

ments on the motif of realism in Barth (*How to Read Karl Barth*, 43–49, and *Disruptive Grace*, 210–25).

190. The term "redescribing God" admittedly stands in danger of overstate the "realism" of Barth's approach and understating its "eschatological reserve." We could perhaps make the same point by speaking of "reinterpreting God's self-interpretation" or "re-articulating God's self-revelation."

191. This is especially important in relation to Scripture, and again, Webster's comments get to the heart of the issue. In some contrast to the work of Lindbeck and Frei, he says: "For Barth, it is not Scripture as *text*, and certainly not Scripture in its *use* by a determinate religious community, which is of overarching significance, but Scripture as normative *testimony* to the absolute act of God's self-manifestation in free grace. Barth's understanding of Scripture as the 'basic text' is inseparable from his emphasis on the divine action by which it becomes God's Word" (Webster, *Barth's Ethics*, 31; the reference to Scripture as "basic text" [*Urtext*] alludes to Barth's comment on I/1, xii).

192. This realism in human theological language (see Hunsinger, *How to Read Karl Barth*, 43–49) is rooted in the ontic "realism of revelation." This ontic realism, as Gunton says, "provides the ontological grounding for Barth's understanding of revelation and therefore for his doctrine of God" (*Becoming and Being*, 129). Hunsinger discuses this ontic realism largely under the category of "objectivism" (*How to Read Karl Barth*, 35–39).

rather than by arguments or by way of explanatory theory."[193] But Frei's statement does not hold if we define the term "argument" broadly, as something like "making a case for a particular view," such as a lawyer might do on the basis of varied pieces of forensic evidence. This is the kind of informal "argument" that the linguistic philosopher Stephen Toulmin had in mind in his book *The Uses of Argument*, the concepts of which David Kelsey helpfully applies to the uses of Scripture in theology.[194] There are a great variety of ways that one can make a case for various conclusions, and hence a great variety of kinds of argument. When we forego a monolithic conception of what arguments are, then perhaps "conceptual description" can itself be a form of argument—an argument that follows and traces out the internal logic and conceptual implications of the revelation attested in Scripture.[195]

According to Toulmin, and Kelsey after him, the variety of informal arguments nonetheless tends to involve a fairly stable set of elements, each of which plays of particular role in making a case for a particular conclusion.[196] Kelsey shows how Scripture tends to play certain roles rather than others, and we can say the same for tradition. Reason is at work in different ways in all aspects of an argument, forming judgments and making inferences under the constraint of certain rational norms.

The key insight afforded by Kelsey's analysis of Barth's arguments[197] is that there are *multiple* sources and resources that a theologian like Barth might employ to authorize a *single* theological conclusion. Indeed, it is unlikely that a single strand of the "threefold cord"—even Scripture—authorizes Barth's theological conclusions all by itself. Scripture does not play all the authorizing roles of the argument.

---

193. Frei, *Types of Christian Theology*, 161. The context of this statement is Frei's legitimate claim that the divine-human relationship can be narrated and redescribed, but cannot be proven by argument or by a general explanatory theory of possibility. Frei's point is directed against arguments resting on general a priori assumptions about reality, and may not apply directly to informal arguments rooted in a posteriori assumptions (like those rooted in specific narratives).

194. Toulmin, *Uses of Argument*; Kelsey, *Proving Doctrine*, 122–47. Toulmin regards formal arguments (strict syllogistic logical arguments) as of limited value in the analysis of how people argue in ordinary speech or in many disciplines other than Logic.

195. David Ford's use of the term "argument" in relation to Barth confirms this (*Barth and God's Story*, 12).

196. See Kelsey, *Proving Doctrine*, 125–34. The elements identified are data, warrant, backing (for the warrant), qualifiers, rebuttal and conclusion.

197. See especially Kelsey, *Proving Doctrine*, 133f.

Rather, Barth's typical informal argument involves Scripture, tradition and reason with each playing a distinctive but essential role. As we will see below, it is nonetheless true that Scripture usually retains a certain primacy in authorizing Barth's theological proposals.

Barth's Use of Philosophy in Theology

Barth's theoretical comments, observations of his actual practice, and the interpretation offered by others, are all relevant to the process of developing concepts about how philosophy functions in his theology.

We begin with his theoretical comments on the role of philosophy in theology, drawn from his discussion of the phase of "reflection" in the theological interpretation of Scripture.[198] The following is our summary of Barth's five points about the role of philosophy in biblical interpretation,[199] which can also illuminate the circumscribed role that Barth saw for philosophy in his biblically-oriented dogmatic theology.

1. Given that everyone has a philosophy (or philosophies), a theologian needs to be aware of her philosophy and how it affects her scriptural interpretation.

2. A philosophy should be no more than a revisable hypothesis.

3. Philosophy should not become an end in itself, an independent interest. Otherwise, it becomes dangerous, and transforms interpretation into the support of an ideology.

4. There is no essential reason for preferring one philosophy or scheme of thought to another; all of them are fallible and provisional.

5. Using a philosophy is fruitful only when "it is determined and controlled by the text and the object mirrored in the text."[200] Only then is it rightly self-critical.

These comments are fairly self-explanatory. The restrictions that Barth imposed on the use of philosophy are clearly in keeping with the non-systematic and revelation-based character of his theology.

---

198. See also Barth's helpful comments on "dogmatics and philosophy" in *Credo* (183–86).
199. I/2, 730–75.
200. Ibid., 734.

With these theoretical directives of Barth in mind, we may now consider some examples of his actual use of philosophy. We will concentrate on his use of Kant and (neo-) Kantian philosophy. There are several ways that Barth is indebted to Kant and Kantian philosophy. First, Barth uses Kantian terms and conceptual forms. We noted in chapter 1 that Barth makes use of Kantian distinctions such as: analytic and synthetic and a priori and a posteriori. Barth does not always use these terms in the same way that Kant used them, but rather adapts them for use in theology, often using them more loosely and casually. In fact, Barth sometimes uses the conceptuality of Kant without using Kant's terminology, thus concealing his indebtedness to Kant to some degree.[201] Second, interpreters of Barth have regarded Barth's overall epistemology and view of rationality as a distinctive theological form of "critical realism." The adjective "critical" highlights the influence of Kant and his followers (such as the Marburg Neo-Kantians) upon Barth.[202] Third, and most significantly for our purposes, Barth employs certain quasi-Kantian transcendental arguments in his theology, not least within his account of divine perfections.[203]

It is worth examining this last "Kantian" feature in more detail. In his *Critique of Pure Reason*, Kant famously used the transcendental method of argument to move from the factual claim that humans made "synthetic a priori judgments" to the conditions of possibility of this fact. The key distinguishing characteristic of such an argument is that one starts with a statement of fact, describing what is the case and then

---

201. George Hendry believes this point applies generally to Barth's use of philosophy, not only to Kant and Hegel: "It became Barth's practice to conceal his philosophical obligations by translating them into general and less technical terms" ("Transcendental Method," 213; cf. 219).

202. However, Barth's "critical realism" is distinctively theological and does not result from an a priori adherence to a *general* view of epistemology or rationality (see McCormack, *Karl Barth's Critically Realistic Dialectic Theology*). Also, we might note that, considered broadly, the critical aspects of Barth's theological epistemology include categories such as "imagination" (understood as the capacity to recognize or construct meaningful patterns), which would be more closely connected with Kant's Third Critique, *Critique of Judgment*. We are here using the term "critical" in the sense developed by the Kantian tradition, which is somewhat different than the way we defined the "critical" function of reason above.

203. See Hendry "The Transcendental Method"; see also our comments on such arguments in chapter 3. W. S. Johnson offers a loose statement of a transcendental argument in Barth (*Mystery of God*, 45, 200). More generally, see Roderick Chisholm's philosophical analysis of the transcendental procedure (*Foundations of Knowing*, 96f.).

infers the conditions that make it *possible*.²⁰⁴ For, Kant to move from the actual to the possible rather than the other way around signaled a "move toward 'concreteness' that offered an epistemology less dependent on speculation about what is abstractly possible."²⁰⁵ In this respect, the transcendental method is congenial to Barth's theology, which consistently tends to move from particular actualities to general possibilities, rather than vice versa.²⁰⁶ The main difference between Kant and Barth is that Barth draws his initial factual claims, not from general human experience, but from God's self-revelation known by faith.²⁰⁷ By transcendental reasoning, Barth then aims to show forth the inherent intelligibility and rationality of such a claim of faith. The result is that, instead of Kant's "religion within the bounds of reason alone" Barth aims at a use of reason that is within the bounds of revelation alone.

A closing comment about Barth's use of philosophy is this: the fact that Barth uses philosophy at all—whether its terms, ideas, or forms of argument—is another indication of how his dogmatic claims are often authorized by biblically-attested revelation in an *indirect* rather than direct manner.

The Two Criteria in Relation to Reason

We now turn to the concepts pertinent to understanding the relationship of reason to the biblical and Christological criteria of Barth's dogmatics that we identified above. In keeping with our relative concentration on

---

204. Hunsinger describes this same kind of argument or inference as the rational procedure of "grounding," which is a part of Barth's "rationalism" (*How to Read Karl Barth*, 57f.). He points out that this kind of procedure is typical in Barth's doctrine of the knowledge of God (II/1, 63–178). For here the actual fact of human knowledge is grounded in the divine freedom, as known by revelation, which provides the necessary and sufficient conditions of the fact of knowledge.

205. Frame, *Doctrine of the Knowledge of God*, 175. Also, if Schwöbel is correct, an actuality-possibility order is typically pre-modern, which would (surprisingly) make Kant an atypical modern thinker in this respect—together with Barth ("Theology," 29f.).

206. See Hunsinger on Barth's "particularism" (*How to Read Karl Barth*, 32–35) and A. Torrance on Barth as a "methodological actualist" (*Persons in Communion*, 47).

207. Hendry "Transcendental Method," 221. Kant did not believe God could be an object of rational knowledge at all. Barth did, but only because God *makes himself* an object of our knowledge. Also, Barth denied immediate knowledge of God, affirming that we know God only through the signs he has appointed to reveal (and conceal) him (see II/1, 16f., 49).

Barth's method over his content, we will give more space below to the consideration of the more methodologically-oriented biblical criterion of dogmatics.

The Primacy of Scripture in Theological Arguments

We may now clarify in what sense Scripture has an overall primacy among the threefold cord in authorizing Barth's dogmatic proposals. Some steps in Barth's informal arguments for his proposals will not be directly based upon Scripture, but even these steps are often at least *indirectly* based upon Scripture. This is part of what allows Scripture to retain primacy, without exclusivity, in the grounding of Barth's claims. This point may be clarified by making some observations related to a distinction that Kelsey makes between "macro-arguments" and "micro-arguments."[208]

Macro-arguments provide a "gross anatomical structure" of argument that incorporates several more specific micro-arguments.[209] The micro-arguments justify, support and ground aspects of the macro-argument. As such, the micro-arguments can stand on their own (although their significance may be restricted to a very narrow scope), but the macro-arguments depends on these micro-arguments.

This bottom-up (rather than top down) structure of epistemic justification sheds light on the way Scripture functions in Barth's theology. Most of the claims supporting Barth's wide-ranging macro-arguments often do not take the form of direct quotations or exegeses of specific passages of Scripture. In other words, Barth's macro-arguments usually operate mostly or entirely by means of indirect scriptural authorization. However, this indirect scriptural authorization in principle could be supported, and sometimes is supported, by the *direct* scriptural authorization of many micro-arguments.[210] This is in keeping with Barth's claim that biblical (exegetical) theology is principally concerned with the basis of the Church's God-talk (see the first subsection of this chapter).

---

208. Kelsey, *Proving Doctrine*, 130f.

209. Ibid.

210. We use the concept of "direct authorization" in a slightly less restrictive way than Kelsey does (ibid., 139ff.). For example, it seems appropriate to allow direct authorization to include exegetical summaries or paraphrases of specific texts rather than only direct quotations of them. See our definitions in 2.3 above.

However, because Barth is doing dogmatics, rather than biblical theology, he does not provide this kind of full exegetical basis for all his doctrinal claims. (If he did, *CD* would be even more massive and prolix than it is!) Yet Barth does offer a large number of exegetical micro-arguments in *CD*, often by means of excursuses that provide evidence for part of a macro-argument. At times, he provides such a micro-argument inadvertently in another context and volume of *CD*. Yet Barth often uses indirect biblical authorization even for micro-arguments. This confirms that, even in Barth's *CD*, it is very difficult to find a theological argument that is truly an example of direct scriptural authorization from beginning to end.[211]

Barth's Use of the Historical-Critical Approach to Biblical Interpretation

Our consideration of the concepts relevant to the intersection between Scripture and reason in Barth's work includes Barth's appropriation of aspects of the modern historical critical approach to interpretation. A good place to start is Christina Baxter's excellent discussion of the issue of Barth's relationship to the historical critical approach to interpretation.[212] In short, Baxter argues that Barth's usage of historical critical methods is ad hoc. As with Barth's use of philosophy, Barth uses higher critical methods when they are consistent with and helpful for accomplishing his theological purposes. This is the basic position that will be both assumed and corroborated in this book. This view stands in contrast to other interpretations of Barth, either those that affirm that Barth's practice shows a basic rejection of the higher critical approach (despite the superficial acceptance of it in his theoretical comments) or those that hold that there is an incoherent dualism in Barth's thought on the matter.[213] It is clear that no matter how much Barth used higher critical methods or conclusions, he did not follow them slavishly, but always subjected them to a searching theological critique.[214]

    211. Ibid., 139ff.

    212. Baxter, "Movement from Exegesis to Dogmatics," chapter 1. See Barth's comments in "Exegesis and the Science of History" in *Credo*, which offer a qualified critique of historical criticism (186–91). See also McCormack, "Historical Criticism and Dogmatic Interest."

    213. Baxter, "The Movement from Exegesis to Dogmatics," 72ff.

    214. Ibid., 62; cf. *CD* I/2, 715f.; I/2, 466; I/1, 283–86.

There are two main ways in which Barth tends to depart from the typical methods and conclusions of historical criticism. First, Barth has a strong orientation to and reverence for the canonical form of the text as a theological witness, and does not wish to probe behind the text to discern its historical pre-history. Accordingly, Barth's is concerned to interpret the verbal sense of this final form of the text, not some critically reconstructed form.[215] Second, Barth believes that historical-critics are often guilty of neglecting the central Christological object or subject matter of Scripture.[216] Clearly, Barth believes that the theological interpretation of Scripture is "Christocentric," as with all of theology, and he does not believe that higher-criticism has the authority to override this.[217] So long as Scripture is interpreted with reverence for the text and in light of its subject matter, then higher criticism can be profitably used as a rational tool for uncovering the meaning of the text.

The Relation between Barth's Christocentrism and His Use of Reason

We now turn to the primary material criterion of Barth's dogmatics, that it be Christocentric. The role of reason in Barth's dogmatic theology is constrained by this criterion just as it is by the biblical (methodological) criterion.

In our comments on the construal of reason above, we noted that Barth uses reason in both critical and constructive ways. We can apply this distinction to Barth's concern that dogmatics be Christocentric. An example of the Christocentric-critical function of reason is found in Barth's emphatic rejection of the *analogia entis* of much scholastic theology and of Roman Catholic theology. This rejection has largely to do with Barth's actualistic, non-substantialist perspective in which it is only in the act of the incarnation that God "shares being" with the cre-

---

215. This is one among several respects in which Brevard Childs is similar to Barth (see Scalise, "Canonical Hermeneutics: Childs and Barth").

216. I/2, 466ff.

217. In this respect Barth is very similar to his colleague Wilhelm Vischer, who wrote approvingly of Barth in his *Witness of the Old Testament to Christ*, 28ff. Likewise, Barth cites Vischer approvingly on many occasions and often follows his exegesis (e.g., I/2, 80; cf. 47, 68, 87; II/1, 118, 412).

ated order.[218] Although this is basically a material claim, it is not without methodological import (as in Barth's rejection of natural theology).

An example the Christocentric-constructive function of reason is found in Barth's broad tendency to develop what we might call "Christocentric metaphysics." In the words of Robert Jenson,

> In Barth's interpretation of reality, the life-history of one human person has taken the place held in the West's traditional metaphysics by . . . the Ground of Being. The *Church Dogmatics* is the first grand system of Western metaphysics since the collapse of Hegelianism, but a thoroughly revisionary one. It casts a vision of reality founded in a particular temporal entity [i.e., Jesus Christ] . . . an encompassing, flexible, and drastically coherent Christological interpretation of reality.[219]

Whether or not we agree with the details of Jenson's comments (Is Barth's really the *first* grand metaphysic since Hegelianism? Is it best to call it a "system"?), he makes a worthwhile point about the extraordinary creative and constructive capacities of Barth's Christocentric use of reason. We wish to add that Barth's metaphysics are biblical as well (the other criterion of dogmatics), for Barth would not be interested in a Christological metaphysic that was not well grounded in Scripture.[220]

As a final comment on Barth's Christocentric use of reason, we wish to reemphasis the close connection of Barth's Christocentrism to his use of tradition. That is, we wish to stress that Barth's Christocentric way of reasoning is not simply the product of his own mind, or even his own reading of Scripture. Rather, it is in large measure shaped by his appropriation of Christocentric theological traditions and their Christocentric ways of using reason. Thus, even though Barth's appropriation is in some ways novel and creative (and thus is tradition-constituting), it also draws from a tradition-constituted theological understanding of rationality that aims to place Christological revelation as the center of reality.

---

218. See McCormack, "Barths Grundsätzlicher Chalcedonismus"?

219. Jenson, "Karl Barth," 31; cf. 28–32.

220. It is along these lines that David Ford speaks of Barth's doctrine of God in II/1 as "metaphysics in support of story" (*Karl Barth and God's Story*; see our comments in chapter 3).

Conclusion: Moving from Categories towards a Conceptual Framework

In this final section of the chapter, we will attempt to draw out some important ways in which the various concepts we have described in this chapter can be interrelated within Barth's theological method. Our key claim is that Barth's theological method is marked by *five key features*. It is: (1) reverent, (2) Christocentric, (3) textually-based, (4) ecclesial, and (5) creative.[221] As we expound these five features we will give some indication how they are prioritized and interrelated. The first feature of reverence towards revelation is a kind of "master feature" and it is expressed in the other features according to two sets of two features each.

The Basic Stance of the Theologian: Reverence towards Revelation

According to Barth, the fundamental attitude or disposition of the theologian should be one of reverence and subordination towards God's revelation. Since the time of his early break with liberal theology, Barth proclaimed the fundamental axiom: "God is God." The reverence implicit in this statement is the first and most basic feature of Barth's theological method. The other four features, which are forms of subordination to God and God's revelation, result in some sense from this feature.

Among the five features, this feature touches most directly on what we could call the "spirituality" of Barth as a theologian. In accordance with his Reformed ecclesial background, Barth stressed the spiritual discipline or ascesis of Bible reading.[222] In Barth's distinctive view, proper theological reading of the Bible means reading it with an expectation that one will hear God himself speaking though Scripture.[223] In *CD*, Barth also frequently speaks of the importance of prayer for the theologian.[224] In this way, Barth may be drawing in a qualified way on

---

221. For an explanation of these five features in relation to Barth's theological use of Scripture in particular, see Pokrifka-Joe, "Appropriating Karl Barth's Use of Scripture."

222. See Ford, *Barth and God's Story*, 165ff.

223. See T. F. Torrance, *Karl Barth: Biblical and Evangelical Theologian*, 83ff.

224. Barth also emphasizes the link between prayer and theology in his book on Anselm (*Fides Quaerens Intellectum*, 31ff., esp. 39).

the Pietist tradition. In any case, both Scripture reading and prayer are expressions of Barth's basic reverence to God and God's self-revelation.

Another specific expression of this reverence before God and God's self-revelation is Barth's a posteriori rather than a priori approach to theological questions and concerns.[225] Barth consistently refused to attempt to settle questions about what God could or must be like before or apart from observing what God has actually revealed in Jesus Christ. God is God, so we must defer to that which God, in his freedom, has determined to reveal of himself rather than projecting anthropomorphic conceptions of possibility and necessity upon God. This is an ongoing requirement, because, in keeping with Barth's actualism, our knowledge of God is an event that depends on the event of God's self-revelation.[226] Such actualism, grounded in God's freedom, leads to methodological particularism.[227]

Finally, Barth's hermeneutical principle of subordination to Scripture and to its subject matter is another clear manifestation of basic reverence. Without such subordination, the reader of Scripture conforms Scripture to his own thought forms rather than vice versa. Whether or not he is successful, Barth always strives to let the text and its object continually revise his worldview.

The Principal Expressions of the Theologian's Reverence: A Theology That Is Christocentric and Textually-Based

Barth's reverence for God and his revelation expresses itself clearly in two features of his method that we have already encountered: namely, theology should strive to be Christocentric and be based in the text of Scripture, for God has chosen to reveal himself in Jesus Christ and this revelation is definitively attested in Scripture. Put precisely, the "textually-based" character of Barth's method is an aspect of the biblical criterion of his theology, and is most clearly seen in instances of "direct scriptural authorization" in which a close exegetical analysis of specific texts is brought to bear upon his theology.[228] Here we need only to draw

---

225. See Gunton, *Becoming and Being*, 124ff.; 130, and passim.
226. See McCormack, *Karl Barth's Critically Realistic Dialectic Theology*, 432ff.
227. See chapter 3 for fuller support of the last two paragraphs.
228. The other four features of his theology, including his Christocentrism can also be seen as expressions of the biblical criterion of Barth's method, as forms of *indirect* scriptural authorization.

together a few relevant strands of our discussion in anticipation of what is to come in the later chapters.

In chapters three to six, we will see that within his account of God's perfections—and specifically his treatment of God's unity, constancy and eternity—Barth's dogmatic theology can be both biblical and Christocentric in either direct or indirect ways. This leaves us with the following four options within Barth's theological practice at a given moment (the examples given point forward to future chapters).

1. *Directly biblical and directly Christocentric*: e.g., Barth's exegesis of Phil 2:6–11 in his account of constancy (chapter 5).

2. *Directly biblical and indirectly Christocentric*: e.g., Barth's treatment of Old Testament texts on God's repentance in his account of constancy (chapter 5).

3. *Indirectly biblical and directly Christocentric*: e.g., Barth's assertion that "God's being is in act" (chapter 4).

4. *Indirectly biblical and indirectly Christocentric*: e.g., Barth's proposed connection between God's simplicity and faithfulness (chapter 4) or Barth's thematic treatment of "salvation history" in his account of constancy (chapter 5).

This analysis is arranged in the relative order of occurrence, from the least frequent to the most frequent. This highlights a significant point about Barth's theological method in *CD* II/1, namely, that it involves (in the words of our thesis statement) "a predominantly indirect way of relating Scripture and theological proposals" (see the conclusion of chapter 1).

Two Further Derivative Features of the Theologian's Reverence: The Ecclesial and Creative Character of Dogmatics

Our strong emphasis on the first three features of Barth's method in this chapter does not mean that there are no more significant features of Barth's method besides these three. Instead, we also need to attend to the ecclesial and creative features of Barth's theology to have an adequately comprehensive and accurate account of his work.

The ecclesial characteristic of Barth's method refers to how it is rooted in and oriented to the Church as his basic community.

Accordingly, this feature partly corresponds to Barth's use of theological tradition (respect and engagement with the Church of the past), but it also goes farther by emphasizing Barth's respect for and ongoing involvement with the Church of his day.[229] The Church, and not the academy, was the primary community by which he was shaped and for which he wrote; hence, the title of his great work: **Church** Dogmatics.

The creative feature of Barth's work describes the imaginative and innovative nature of Barth's theological reasoning. As such, it is closely related, though not restricted, to his distinctive use of reason in his theology, his way of making intellectual judgments and drawing inferences. Although it is perhaps not immediately obvious, the creative character of Barth's approach to theology is also an expression of his basic reverence to God and God's revelation. The reason for this is two-fold, with a divine side and a human side.[230] On the divine side, God's revelation continues to take place in new divine actions, and thus, reverence for God requires that we creatively adapt to the newness of God's free acts of revelation in new situations and contexts. On the human side, our response to God is an ongoing response of active and free obedience. Therefore, theology is a matter of freely reflecting on the spirit of God's Word rather than a legalistic repetition of the letter of God's Word. Along with the other four features, the creativity of Barth's theological method will become clearer in the remaining chapters of this book.[231]

---

229. See Barth's comments on the "confessional" and "churchly" attitudes required of the theologian (see our explanation of dogmatic method in the first section of this chapter).

230. For further, more general, reflections on the divine and human sides of revelation and theological response, see chapter 7.

231. For more on the role of imagination in the human reception of and participation in divine revelation, see Clark, *Divine Revelation and Human Practice*.

3

Scripture, Tradition, and Reason within Barth's Doctrine of God

This chapter provides an overview of Barth's doctrine of God, with particular reference to the function of the "threefold cord" within this doctrine. This will provide a background for the more detailed exposition of divine unity, constancy, and eternity that will follow in chapters 4–6.

The chapter has four main sections. In the first, we will comment on Barth's doctrine of the Trinity, which forms the background of his doctrine of God proper. In the next three sections, we will survey aspects of Barth's doctrine of God proper, as found in chapter VI ("The Doctrine of the Reality of God"). Our primary concerns throughout this chapter are expressed in the following two questions: (1) "what are the main distinctive features of Barth's doctrine of God?" and (2) "how do these features relate to Barth's theological method?"

Background: Barth's Theological Method and His Doctrine of the Trinity

Introduction: Method, Trinity, and Revelation

Several scholars have noted, for good reason, that Barth's account of the doctrine of the Trinity is crucial for understanding his dogmatics as a whole.[1] Barth himself said that "a Church dogmatics derives from a doctrine of the Trinity."[2] Regardless of the extent to which these claims are true, it is definitely true that Barth's doctrine of the Trinity forms the crucial background for Barth's "Doctrine of the Reality of God"

---

1. Jüngel, *Doctrine of the Trinity*; Leslie, *Trinitarian Hermeneutics*; and A. Torrance, *Persons in Communion* and "Trinity."

2. II/1, 261.

and specifically his account of divine perfections. Others have made this point, either in general terms[3] or with respect to particular divine perfections.[4]

We will pay particular attention to the theological method that Barth employs within his doctrine of the Trinity. If Barth's doctrine of God is thoroughly Trinitarian, then it would make sense for the theological method that he employs here to shed light on the theological method he employs in his doctrine of God as a whole. We will pay special attention to the role of Scripture in his work, but will also comment on the roles of tradition and reason. As we do so, we will also note various features of the material content of Barth's doctrine of the Trinity, which are interwoven with these methodological features. In this way we will provide the necessary methodological and material background for understanding his doctrine of God in II/1.

Barth's doctrine of "the Triune God" is found in *CD* I/1, §§8–12. It is the first part of chapter II, a long chapter on "The Revelation of God," which Barth continues in I/2. Further, his account of the Revelation of God occurs within his first volume of *CD*, on the "Doctrine of the Word of God." It is significant that Barth unfolds his doctrine of the Trinity in the context of his accounts of the Word and Revelation of God.

The Trinity-revelation connection is obvious in §8 (on "God in his Revelation"), with which Barth opens his account of the Trinity.[5] The opening boldface "thesis statement" that summarizes Barth's argument in this paragraph reads as follows:

> God's Word is God Himself in His revelation. For God reveals Himself as the Lord and according to Scripture this signifies for the concept of revelation that God Himself in unimpaired unity yet also in unimpaired distinction is Revealer, Revelation, and Revealedness.[6]

We ought to notice several things about what Barth is saying in this dense formulation. First, the doctrines of the Word of God and of God's revelation are doctrines about God himself and, in that sense, are aspects of the doctrine of God. This is related to the point that, for Barth,

---

3. Gunton, *Being and Becoming*, 127–85.

4. Hunsinger, *Disruptive Grace*, 186–209, which is a chapter on divine eternity (see chapter 6 below).

5. I/1, 295–347.

6. I/1, 295.

God's revelation is self-revelation.[7] Second, and more specifically, "God's reveals himself as the Lord." Barth later explicates this statement as "the root of the doctrine of the Trinity."[8] Third, "according to Scripture," this statement that "God reveals himself as the Lord" implies or "signifies that God Himself... is Revealer, Revelation, and Revealedness," a three-fold characterization[9] that corresponds to the Father, Son, and the Holy Spirit. Put differently, "God reveals Himself. He reveals Himself through Himself. He reveals Himself."[10]

Barth says that the reality of revelation requires us to ask three interrelated questions: who is the self-revealing God, how does it come about that God reveals himself and what is the result of this revelation in humanity?[11] All three of these questions converge in a single point, namely, that Barth grounds his doctrine of the Trinity in his doctrine of Revelation and only in the doctrine of revelation. In Barth's words, "It is only—but very truly—by observing the unity and the differentiation of God in His biblically-attested revelation that we are set before the doctrine of the Trinity."[12]

But how does Barth ground his distinctive doctrine of the Trinity in revelation? What theological method does Barth use to authorize his doctrine of the Trinity? What is the role of Scripture, tradition, and reason in this authorization? This is a set of questions that has received a wide variety of answers by Barth's interpreters and critics. We will only be able to answer these questions by carefully attending to what Barth actually says and does in I/1. What we will find is that Barth understands his Trinitarian doctrine to be an attempt to be faithful to what Scripture teaches about God and God's self-revelation. Accordingly, Barth's practice gives primacy to Scripture, with "supporting roles" provided by tradition and reason.

---

7. Indeed, Barth appears to assume that God's revelation is not only *primarily* self-revelation (the view that many Christian thinkers have held since the early church) but *exclusively* self-revelation (a modern idea probably initiated in definitive form by Hegel). See Pannenberg, *Revelation as History*, 3ff.

8. I/1, 304–33.

9. Eberhard Jüngel paraphrases this as "revealer, becoming revealed, and being revealed" (*Doctrine of the Trinity*, 127).

10. I/1, 296.

11. Ibid., 295ff.

12. Ibid., 299.

The Role of Scripture within Barth's Doctrine of the Trinity

For Barth, the doctrine of the Trinity is an expression of what could be called exposition of Scripture—whether Barth's own exposition or that of past theologians of the Church.[13] This "exposition," taken in a broad sense, does not mean that Trinitarian doctrine is simply the exegesis of individual biblical texts, although this is part of what Barth does here. In the main, it means that Barth indirectly authorizes his Trinitarian doctrine on the basis of Scripture. We now wish to summarize several relevant aspects of Barth's account of the Trinity in I/1.

From the beginning of his doctrine of the Trinity, Barth states his intention to link revelation and Trinity in terms of the interpretation and use of Scripture. On virtually every page we find phrases that attest this. For example, in the first subsection of his treatment of the Trinity, we find the phrases: "measured by Holy Scripture,"[14] "by subordination to Scripture,"[15] "the biblical answer to the question,"[16] "according to the direction of the whole Bible,"[17] and "guided by the Bible."[18] Put simply, Barth does not wish to pursue his own idea of revelation or even the Church's idea of revelation, but to enquire into "what Holy Scripture attests as revelation"[19] or "the concept of revelation taken from the Bible"[20] or simply what he calls on several occasions "biblical revelation."[21]

---

13. More specifically, Barth's doctrine of the Trinity is a combination of the acceptance of the theological exposition of Scripture performed by others such as Athanasius (as such it is an acceptance of an aspect of theological tradition) and his own creative theological exposition in the context of the contemporary church. Barth's prior settling of fundamental exegetical-theological matters (i.e., the "double-homoousion," the unity and distinction of the immanent and economic Trinities) with respect to the Trinity in I/1 allows him to assume these Trinitarian conclusions in the context of the divine perfections in II/1, chapter 6.

14. Ibid., 295.
15. Ibid., 1, 296.
16. Ibid., 297.
17. Ibid., 298.
18. Ibid., 300.
19. Ibid., 304.
20. Ibid., 332.
21. That this is Barth's intention does not guarantee, or course, that Barth is successful in carrying out this intention. But here, as elsewhere in this book, we are not concerned with evaluating Barth's success, but with describing the nature of his methodological practice. Also, we will continue to expect that his theory is consistent with his practice, unless it is obvious that it is not.

How in more specific terms does Barth say that Scripture should function as an authority in the doctrine of the Trinity? Barth believes that the Bible presents a certain concept or doctrine of revelation and that this doctrine of revelation is "the root of the doctrine of the trinity" [*Die Wurzel der Trinitätslehre*].[22] As we noted above, Barth summarizes this "root" in the statement: "God reveals Himself as the Lord."[23] And as we indicated in chapter 2, this statement is best seen as a summary of a certain pattern in Scripture — the pattern having to do with the character of revelation. As such, it is not a direct quotation or literal translation of any one passage of Scripture.

Rather, Barth states that the relationship between the biblical root or ground to the Trinitarian doctrine is one of "indirect identity." Being indirectly identical with the biblical root, there is no identity or repetition on the textual level between Scripture and the Church dogma of the Trinity.[24] As such, the Trinity is only an "interpretation" of Scripture and of the revelation to which Scripture witnesses; Scripture does not contain the doctrine of the Trinity explicitly. Yet as indirectly identical with each other, Barth can say that the biblical doctrine of revelation and the doctrine of the Trinity say "the same thing" in different words or that the latter draws out some of the implications of the former.[25] Barth

---

22. Ibid., 304–33. While Barth uses "root" [*Wurzel*] much more frequently, he appears to uses it more or less interchangeably with "ground" [*Grund*], as in the phrase "the *root or ground* of the doctrine of the trinity" (332).

23. Ibid., 306. In using the term "concept of revelation" [*Offenbarungsbegriff*] in this context, Barth refers to a complex pattern of judgments (i.e., a doctrine), rather than a unitary linguistic concept or conceptual term (see the subsection in chapter 2 on "Concepts Related to the Construal of Scripture"). This is what R. Kendall Soulen has in mind when he says that the statement "God reveals himself as the Lord" occurs on the "conceptual" level of Barth's dogmatic analysis, as distinct from both the "exegetical" level (e.g., the compound divine name *Yahweh-Kyrios*) or the level of the Church doctrine of the Trinity (e.g., the Nicene Creed) (Soulen, "*YHWH* the Triune God," 36f.). In relation to the Trinity, then, Barth and Soulen use the terms "concept" and "conceptual" in a way quite different from David Yeago ("New Testament and Nicene Dogma"), who uses "concepts" or "conceptual terms" to refer primarily to the specific linguistic forms in which a judgment may be stated in either Scripture or theology (see our comments in chapter 2). Yet the three authors are making similar substantial points.

24. I/1, 308; cf. 313f. In the terminology of Yeago ("New Testament and Nicene Dogma"), there is no strict identity or continuity on the level of terminology or "conceptual terms" (see the subsection in chapter 2 called "conceptual terms and theological judgments").

25. Again, in Yeago's terminology, there *is* an identity or continuity on the level of theological judgments ("New Testament and Nicene Dogma").

regards the Trinitarian dogma "as a necessary and relevant analysis of revelation, and we thus think that revelation itself is correctly interpreted by the dogma."[26] As such, the Trinity is rooted in biblical revelation; there is "an authentic and well-established connection between the two."[27] Yet again, this "well-established connection" does not rest primarily on explicit references to the Trinity in the Bible (e.g., Matt 28:29, 2 Cor 13:13, etc.), even though these passages "prefigure" the problems that the later Trinitarian doctrine addressed. Indeed, Barth regards this indirect relationship between the Bible and church dogma (or doctrine) to be typical of the relationship between the Bible and other dogmas.[28] We will return to the Church's Trinitarian dogmas themselves below, as an instance of the role tradition in his work.

We can see that Barth wishes to use Scripture indirectly, but decisively, to authorize the doctrine of the Trinity by the "mediation" of the biblical doctrine of revelation, "the root of the Trinity." But what are the concrete contours of this mode of authorization? For one thing, we must ask the "historical question" of how "biblical revelation and the [church] doctrine of the Trinity are interconnected," of "how the second could and did proceed out of the first."[29] The background of this question is Barth's assumption that in both biblical revelation and the doctrine of the Trinity, there is roughly equal emphasis on both the oneness of God and the "threeness" of God. Thus, "The God who has revealed himself according to the witness of Scripture is the same in unimpaired unity and yet also the same thrice in unimpaired distinction."[30] An initial indication of this point is found in Barth's belief in the equal material importance of God the revealer (subject), God the revelation (the predicate), and God being revealed (the object)—a schema that corresponds roughly to the Father, the Son, and the Holy Spirit in their equality. But Barth says that historically (i.e., in the historical development of the doctrine in the early centuries of church history) these three aspects of the reality of revelation "do not have the same importance"[31] and indicates that this has relevance for understanding

26. Ibid., 310.
27. Ibid., 311.
28. Ibid., 310.
29. Ibid., 314.
30. Ibid., 307.
31. Ibid., 314.

how Scripture grounds the doctrine of the Trinity. "The true theme of the biblical witness is the second of these concepts, God's action in revelation." In other words, the Bible is primarily about the verbal predicate "reveals" in the statement "God reveals himself as the Lord." For Barth, this is another way of saying that the biblical doctrine of revelation and the development of the doctrine of the Trinity are both marked by a decisive Christocentrism, which we must now explain in more detail.

According to Barth, the questions of identity of the Revealer and the nature of "revealedness" to humanity should only be pursued in the course of answering the primary question of how God revealed himself in Christ, the embodiment of "God's action in revelation."[32] The common Christological starting point and focus of the doctrines of revelation and Trinity imply a shared order or structure: Christ (Son) first, then God (Father), and then the Holy Spirit.[33] This is the typical order of revelation, the order in which the Trinity is known.[34] The Father and the Spirit are known through Jesus Christ, the Son. In our words, Barth presents the following in this order: God's self-unveiling (the Son; the resurrection), God's unveiling as the one who remains veiled (the Father; Good Friday), and God's impartation to humanity of this self-unveiling (the Spirit; Pentecost).[35] This is the kind of pattern that Barth has in mind when he says that "the threefold yet single Lordship of God as Father, Son, and Spirit, is the root of the doctrine of the Trinity. In other words, the biblical concept of revelation is itself the root of the doctrine of the Trinity."[36] Once again, Barth's method here is best conceived of as bringing Scripture authoritatively but indirectly to bear upon the formulation of doctrine.[37]

---

32. Ibid., 315.

33. Ibid., 315. Cf. 2 Cor 13:13.

34. This "order of knowing" (essentially Barth's "economic Trinity") is distinct from the "order of being" (Father, Son, and Holy Spirit).

35. Ibid., 315–32. In parentheses, we have included the mode of being (i.e., person) and event that Barth associated with each aspect of revelation.

36. Ibid., 334.

37. See Barth's own statement of the indirect rather than direct nature of the relationship between Scripture and Trinitarian doctrine in his summary of the biblically revealed root of the doctrine of the Trinity (ibid., 332f.).

The Roles of Tradition and Reason within the Doctrine of the Trinity

The role of tradition within Barth's doctrine of the Trinity is perhaps more obvious to readers of *CD* than the role of Scripture. Although the ultimate, authoritative basis of the doctrine is found in the revelation attested in Scripture, the doctrine of the Trinity is clearly a doctrine that was formulated by the Church and stands at the heart of orthodox Christian tradition. Barth receives the doctrine from the Church and, with some qualifications, preserves it in the form in which he has received it—including most of the traditional philosophical conceptual language used in the creeds.[38]

However, Barth does sometimes depart from what might be regarded as the "majority view" of Christian tradition, as is so when he prefers the term "ways" or "modes" of being [*Seinsweise*] over "persons" to refer to the Father, Son, and Holy Spirit.[39] This shows that his adherence to theological tradition, while generally present in his work, is not slavish or automatic. Rather, Barth generally follows the traditional ecumenical consensus on the Trinity because he believes it follows the revelation attested in Scripture. For example, we have alluded to how Barth believes that the Christocentrism of the traditional Trinitarian developments and formulations matches the Christocentrism of God's self-revelation attested in Scripture. Yet it is also clear that Barth is definitely willing to depart from the theological tradition insofar as it fails to uphold biblically-attested revelation.[40] The authority of Trinitarian creeds is derivative, and thus subject to scripturally-based critique.

---

38. In particular, Barth retains the Western form (with the *filoque* clause) of the Niceno-Contantinopolitan Creed (see ibid., 423ff.). Leslie (*Trinitarian Hermeneutics*, chapter 4) believes that Barth is overly and inconsistently concerned to retain the specific traditional wording of the Trinitarian creeds, but Leslie's argument is somewhat overstated (see below and also chapter 1).

39. We should emphasize here that Barth opts for *Seinsweise* partly because he believes it is actually more faithful to the meaning and intention of the early Trinitarian formulations (e.g., the use of *hypostasis*), and that modern language about "persons" obfuscates this meaning. See Bromiley's comments on the translation of *Seinsweise* in his editorial preface to *CD*, I/1 (viii).

40. Trevor Hart shows that Barth's preference for *Seinsweise* over "persons" is not merely a matter of surface-level terminology, but involves a fairly significant departure from the "logic" of the Trinitarian creeds, which Hart thinks is to the detriment of Barth's doctrine (*Regarding Karl Barth*, 102–9). Barth no doubt intends for his doctrine to be more relentlessly attentive to revelation than preceding doctrines, whether or not he succeeds in carrying out that intention.

In sum, we could say that tradition is the direct or proximate basis for Barth's doctrine of the Trinity, while Scripture is its indirect basis. While the direct and relative authorization by tradition is easier to grasp, the more decisive and normative authorization for his doctrine is indirect and is provided by Scripture.

Barth's distinctive use of reason is also evident in his Trinitarian doctrine. Barth clearly does not appeal to reason as an independent authority. But Barth's entire doctrine of the Trinity, as with all of dogmatics, is the product of a rigorous process of reasoning. Barth's Trinitarian doctrine can be described as an attempt to unfold the internal logic or rationality of God's self-revelation, as attested in Scripture.

Wolfhart Pannenberg, Jürgen Moltmann, and others draw on the orderly logical character of Barth's Trinitarian doctrine in order to critique Barth. Specifically, they say that his doctrine is rooted in a logical development of the "idealist" concept of divine self-revelation rather than in careful attention to the actual revelation of God in history.[41] Whether or not this is the case, it surely was not Barth's intention. Barth's intention is well described in the words of Alan Torrance, who is particularly critical of Moltmann's evaluation of Barth: "Barth's argument is not that any self-revelation will possess a triadic structure and thus affirm divine triunity. Rather, he is suggesting that the specific dynamic of revelation to which Scripture attests requires, as a matter of fact, to be interpreted in terms of a Trinitarian logic."[42] Whether Barth's way of reasoning is more akin to an a priori deduction (Pannenberg and Moltmann), an a posteriori analysis (A. Torrance), or some mixture of the two, it is clear that Barth is employing a distinctive pattern of reasoning in his doctrine of the Trinity.

Pannenberg and Moltmann are at least correct on one point: that implicit in Barth's doctrine of the Trinity is the influence of the modern understanding of God as a free, self-identical personal Subject, which Barth develops in terms of the idea of God's threefold self-repetition [Wiederholung]. Even though the Church fathers may have employed

---

41. Pannenberg, "Subjecktivität Gottes und der Trinitätslehre," 96–111, and *Systematic Theology*, 1:295f., 304; Moltmann, *Trinity and the Kingdom*, 39–144. See also the related critique of Rowan Williams in Sykes, *Karl Barth*. For a comparison of Barth and Pannenberg (and of both to Hegel) on the Trinity, see Bradshaw, *Trinity and Ontology*. For a critical analysis of Moltmann, see Colwell, *Actuality and Provisionality*, 208–14, and A. Torrance, *Persons in Communion* and "Trinity" (see below).

42. Torrance, "The Trinity," 77.

a subject-predicate logic or grammar in their Trinitarian doctrines, Barth's modern way of conceiving of God still distinguishes his doctrine from theirs.[43] All of this raises an evaluative question about Barth's method and specifically about the use of "reason" within it. Is Barth's use of such a modern "philosophical" perspective better characterized as: (a) a helpful ad hoc commandeering of conceptual forms in the service of a lucid interpretation of revelation or (b) as the entrapment of revelation within a materially-foreign set of metaphysical judgments?[44] In his discussion of the vestigia trinitatis, Barth thoroughly spells out his theoretical resistance to and ideas about God's triunity that are not exclusively governed by the revelation of God in Christ as attested in Scripture.[45] The debate will no doubt continue about whether Barth's practice in his doctrine of the Trinity contravenes this theoretical commitment.

Some Influences of Barth's View of the Trinity on his Larger View of God

The Trinity provides a foundational perspective for understanding Barth's doctrine of God as a whole. It identifies the God about whom Barth wishes to speak in his Theology. Against the classical tradition, Barth says that our conceptions of the essence of God "ought never to have been an abstraction from the Trinity, and that means from the act of divine revelation."[46] In placing the Trinity before the rest of the doctrine of God (i.e., the doctrine of God) Barth follows only two major theologians (Peter Lombard and Bonaventura)[47] and sets his dogmatics on a different course from the classical tradition represented by Aquinas (the first to reverse Lombard's order).[48] In what follows we

43. See Hart, *Regarding Karl Barth*, 104–7 and Frei, *Types of Christian Theology*, 124f; cf. A. Torrance, *Persons in Communion*, 103f.

44. See Colwell, *Actuality and Provisionality*, 211ff. See also his comments on the distinction between a priori and a posteriori necessity, which bear on what kind of "logic" is at work in Barth's Trinitarian account (221f.).

45. I/1, 333–47. Many would argue that Barth's Trinitarianism (or perhaps any consistent Trinitarianism) involves a critique of classical metaphysics in response to revelation (e.g., Gunton, *Becoming and Being*; T. F. Torrance, *Karl Barth: Biblical and Evangelical Theologian*).

46. II/1, 261.

47. I/1, 300.

48. See Jüngel, *Doctrine of the Trinity*, 4f., where he interprets Barth's dogmatic order

will highlight some of the more important ways that Barth's distinctive treatment of the doctrine of the Trinity influenced the rest of Barth's doctrine of God.

First of all, Barth's doctrine of the Trinity manifests a certain way of relating the being and act of God—or, in the language more typical of Trinitarian theology—a certain way of relating the "immanent Trinity" and the "economic Trinity." Put simply, these two "sides" of the Christian doctrine of God stand in a dialectical relationship to each other. On the one hand, Barth believes that God himself is present in his self-revealing action in the economy of creation and salvation (in his works *ad extra*) and that, therefore, there is no ontic or noetic gulf between the economic Trinity and the immanent Trinity. Further, the only way for humans to know the immanent Trinity is through the economic Trinity, and so the order of knowing must proceed from divine act to divine being or essence. But on the other hand, God's internal being is by no means "swallowed up" or "exhausted" in his external actions.[49] Rather, the "ontic basis" of the work of God in the earthly economy is God's eternally *free* being, an inexhaustible freedom that resides in God's immanent Trinity. Again, the reason why we need to affirm God's immanent Trinity, is not because we wish to speak of a God essentially other than the God revealed in his revelatory action, but simply to remind ourselves that God's actions have a basis in the free decisions of God. In the words of Colin Gunton's summary of Barth: "God's reality is not exhausted by his acts. If he is to be a gracious God, this giving of himself must be a free, unnecessitated act."[50] We will see in the course of our considerations of Barth's doctrine of God, that Barth places great emphasis on the divine freedom, yet in a way that does not detract from the unity between God's being and acts that is necessary for divine reconciling love.

Many of the same points made above are clarified further by the "Christological concentration" of Barth's doctrine of the Trinity. The su-

---

as implying that the Trinity is the hermeneutical foundation for dogmatics (5; cf. Leslie, *Trinitarian Hermeneutics*). For more comments on the issue of order, see chapter 4).

49. See II/1, 260 and our comments later in this chapter.

50. Gunton, *Becoming and Being*, 147. Barth says that God's works "are bound to Him but He is not bound to them" (II/1, 260; cf. I/1, 371). Paul Molnar ("The Function of the Immanent Trinity," "Toward a Contemporary Doctrine of the Immanent Trinity," and *Divine Freedom and the Immanent Trinity*) underscores at length the significance of the immanent Trinity in Barth's work in relation to God's freedom.

preme free act of God in relation to the world is his act of revelation and reconciliation accomplished in Jesus Christ. This act is the unifying centre of all the other *ad extra* divine acts. Indeed, Barth believes that God cannot be known other than through Christ—and this includes God the Father and God the Holy Spirit. Barth implies that Scripture provides no independent, non-Christological testimony to God, even in the Old Testament; there is no other way to find out who God is *ad intra*.

We may further clarify the Christocentrism of Barth's understanding of the dialectical relationship between the economic Trinity and the immanent Trinity by commenting on Barth's Christological doctrine of *election*. For the supreme unifying self-revelatory act of God in Jesus Christ proceeds from the "eternal" act in which God decides to elect humanity in Christ. In fact, in the distinctive view Barth unfolds in his "doctrine of election" in II/2, the God-man Jesus Christ (and not merely the Son as *logos asarkos*) is himself the *Subject* of election, not only its object.[51] By this daring move, Barth wishes to ensure that there is no speculation about another different God behind the God known in Jesus Christ.[52] In this respect, Barth's Christocentric doctrine of election is significant for understanding his doctrine of divine perfections in II/1, even if he does not consistently draw out the implications of his view there.[53] It is at least clear that Barth understands God's perfec-

51. McCormack, "Grace and Being," 93–95.

52. Barth was influenced to make this "daring move" by a lecture of Pierre Maury in 1936 (although Maury himself did not make this move) and thus moved into the final Christocentric phase of his theological development (McCormack, *Karl Barth's Critically Realistic Dialectic Theology*, 453–63).

53. Although Barth wrote his detailed account of election in II/2 after he wrote his account of the perfections, there is evidence (both internal and external) that the "germ idea" of Christocentric election had already taken hold before he wrote the "doctrine of the reality of God in II/1, VI" (see McCormack, *Karl Barth's Critically Realistic Dialectic Theology*, 461). McCormack believes that Barth was never fully consistent with his Christocentric view of election in this and other parts of his work ("Grace and Being," 101–4; cf. McCormack, "Barth's grundsätzlicher Chalcedonismus?").

A couple of points are in order in regard to McCormack's overall argument concerning Barth's election (especially in his 2000 essay, "Grace and Being"). McCormack shows clearly that, on both ontic and noetic levels, Barth's view of election argues that there can be no *logos asarkos* that is in any sense separate from or independent of the *logos sarkos* (a parallel point could be made about the relationship between the immanent Trinity and the economic Trinity). But McCormack does not offer a compelling argument as to why this would require that Barth believes that the decision of God to be incarnate *constitutes* the eternal being of God (what we might call the "actualist" constitution-thesis) rather than being constituted by God's eternal being (the "essen-

tions as manifestations or expressions of the God who is known to have elected humanity in Jesus Christ, which Barth regards as a summary of the gospel. This is fitting for Barth, who included the doctrine of election within the doctrine of God.[54]

A Summary of "The Reality of God": God as "One Who Loves in Freedom"

We now turn to Barth's doctrine of God proper. This Barth calls the doctrine of the Reality (*Wirklichkeit*) of God, because this term *Wirklichkeit* "holds together being and act."[55] Barth unfolds the two-fold reality of God—a reality conjoining being and act—in the course of chapter VI. In Gunton's words, in this chapter Barth states "the things that we have to say that God *really is* if we are to be true to what happens in revelation."[56] In general, Barth's presentation of the doctrine of God in chapter VI starts with fairly abstract statements about God (e.g., his description of "The Being of God in Act" in §28.1) and moves to progressively concrete statements (such as his accounts of twelve specific divine perfections in §§30 and 31).[57] He begins, in §28, with a summary of this doctrine of God under the rubric of "The One Who Loves in Freedom," which will be our concern in this section of the chapter.

Barth notes that the statement that "God is" is the basis and content of the rest of dogmatics (257).[58] Despite its wide-ranging significance, a particular development of "God is," i.e., a doctrine of God, is both pos-

---

tialist" expression-thesis). McCormack thinks it is inadequate to say that the being of the *logos asarkos* (or the immanent Trinity) is *perfectly expressed in and present in* God's acts in the *logos ensarkos* (or the economic Trinity)? This view appears to be Barth's dominant view in II/1: God is one whose being "*is in* act," not necessarily one whose being "*is* act" or whose being is constituted by act (see below).

54. See Gunton, "Karl Barth's Doctrine of Election."

55. II/1, 262.

56. Gunton, *Being and Becoming*, 186.

57. This observation about Barth's abstract-to-concrete order of presentation should not be construed as a contradiction of his methodological "Particularism" (see Hunsinger, *How to Read Karl Barth*), in which he moves from the particular to the general. This is so for two reasons. First, Hunsinger rightly notes that it is possible for an abstract claim to be a "particular" (*How to Read Karl Barth*, 284f. n. 2). Second, the order in which Barth *presents* his conclusions is not necessarily the same as the order in which he *arrived* at those conclusions (i.e., what we are calling his "method").

58. The numbers in parentheses from this point forward in this chapter refer to *CD* II/1.

sible and necessary. We cannot adequately describe God's actions and working (say, in the doctrines of Creation and Reconciliation), without understanding the God who is their incomparable Subject (258f.).

The Being of God in Act

INTRODUCTORY REFLECTIONS

The first section of §28 on God as the "The One Who Loves in Freedom" is entitled "The being of God in Act" (§28.1). Barth's comments in a brief excursus near the beginning of this section may help to orient us to Barth's understanding of the proper method and role of the doctrine of God in dogmatics. The excursus concerns two errors of Melanchthon, "the first dogmatician of the Evangelical Church" (259). Melanchthon's first error, in his *Loci* of 1521, was to "suppress the special doctrine of God in order to turn at once to the statement of the *beneficia Christi* [benefits of Christ]." Against this, Barth wishes to develop a special doctrine of God—largely in order to understand the Subject whose acts result in Christ's benefits. Otherwise, one risks reducing theology to the anthropocentric exploration of the subjective benefits of God's acts.[59] Melanchthon's second and more serious mistake, committed in a later version of the *Loci*, was to develop a special doctrine of God, but to "create it from another source than from the revelation of God, namely, from an independently formed and general idea of God." As such, Melanchthon developed an a priori doctrine of God that was detached from the proper basis for knowing God in his revelation and his benefits.[60] Barth wishes to avoid assiduously any such independently formed, general conception of God and to base all that he says about God on what God has actually revealed of himself, i.e., one needs to speak of God's being only on the basis of God's works (260).[61]

---

59. Barth states that we should not revolt against speaking of God's "being," since "God is not swallowed up in the relation and attitude of himself to the world . . ." (260). Yet it is *God* and not "being" that is our subject, or else "being" only as it is defined by God (260f.), by God in his *act* of revelation. It is in this vein that Barth will later show a preference for God's more concretely defined "eternity" and temporality over God's "being" in his account of God's eternity (609f.; see chapter 6).

60. In this way, Barth says, Melanchthon followed "late medieval scholasticism" and thus afforded "a disastrous example to the whole of Protestant orthodoxy" (260).

61. This is a point that Barth has already made clearly earlier in *CD*, especially in

The transcendental condition or presupposition that makes Barth's distinctive approach to the doctrine of God possible is this: that God's *being is in act*.[62] If God's being were detached from and not wholly present in his actions, then God's actions would not provide a reliable basis for knowing his being.[63] But God's being is "in act"—i.e., God's being is fully present in God's actions in the world. (Indeed, as we will see, God's eternal being apart from the world is inherently active in some sense; it is not "in act" simply as a consequence of having created a world to act in.) This is a clear example of how Barth's method of rooting all dogmatic statements in revelation is closely linked to and grounded in the material content of his doctrine of God.

Before we turn to a fuller explication of Barth's concept of God's "being in act," we may glean insight from another illuminating excursus in which he critiques theological tradition. Barth regards the fundamental error of the "older theology" and "Protestant orthodoxy" (forms of what we have called "classical" doctrines of God) to be that they began elsewhere than "God's act in His revelation" (261). Rather than starting and remaining with the God's revelation attested in Scripture, natural a priori axioms are "interwoven ... with ... biblical reminiscences." Barth regards the need to base one's doctrine of God in revelation as inseparable from the need to have a *Trinitarian* doctrine of God (see our comments earlier in this chapter). Barth believes we must remain "vigorously aloof" from this classical tradition and its speculations.

The foregoing points lead Barth to a series of statements that, he claims, are progressively concrete explications of the statement that "God is," statements that we will now explicate in turn.

The Reality of God in the Act of Revelation (Actualism)

The first proposition Barth presents is that "*God is who He is in the act of His revelation*" (262). Again, Barth is concerned to articulate the concept [*Begriff*] of "the Reality of God" [*Die Wirklichkeit Gottes*], which holds together being and act [*Sein und Tat*] unlike the concept of "essence"

II/1, chapter 5, "Doctrine of the Knowledge of God." Here he argues that God is known only by God, through his "secondary objectivity."

62. See our comments on Barth's transcendental arguments and method in our consideration of concepts for "reason" in chapter 2.

63. See the similar point made by Johnson (*Mystery of God*, 44ff.).

[*Wesen*]. In his act of revelation, God declares his reality, not only for us [*pro nobis*] but also God's reality in himself [*a se*].

What does Barth mean by saying that, in revelation "we have to do with God's *act* (262)? This act is an event [*Ereignis*], but a unique event that is "in no sense to be transcended." This event of self-revelation is not only past (i.e., completed), but also present (contemporaneous) and future. As such, it is in time, but it transcends the usual limitations of time. Although Barth does not use the term here, we could say that God's act of self-revelation is an "eternal" act, in Barth's distinctive sense of "eternal" (see chapter 6). Barth appeals to Heb 13:8 ("Jesus Christ is the same yesterday, today, and forever") to ground this view, an indication of his attempt to be both biblical and Christocentric (262). Barth repeats the point that the act of God in his revelation is also Trinitarian: God in his threefold self-repetition is its subject (the revealer), predicate (the act of revelation), and object (the revealed) (263).

Barth's description of God as one whose being or reality is "in act" leads to the question of whether it is appropriate to say that Barth is a theological "actualist" or whether he is marked by "actualism." The answer to this question depends on one's definition of "actualism." If one means generally that God's reality must be described in the language of act or event, then it seems clear that Barth is an "actualist."[64] Barth goes as far as to say that "With regard to the being of God, the word 'event' or 'act' is final" and that "God's Godhead . . . is an event" (263). However, if by actualism one means that God's being or reality is reduced to God's works, his acts *ad extra*, then Barth is not an actualist.[65] This is plain in the following comment of Barth:

> God is who He is in His works. He is the same even in Himself, even before and after and over His work, and without them. They are bound to Him, but He is not bound to them. He is not, therefore, who He is only in His works. Yet in Himself He is not another than He is in His works. (260)

---

64. See Hunsinger's account of Barth's "actualism" (*How to Read Karl Barth*, 30ff.).

65. This appears to be the reason behind A. Torrance's rejection of the claim that Barth is a theological actualist ("The Trinity," 90 n. 28; cf. Gunton, *Being and Becoming*, 147f. and McCormack, "Grace and Being"). Elsewhere however, Torrance does refer Barth's "methodological actualism" and relates this to the sense of actualism used by some analytic philosophers (*Persons in Communion*, 47).

Barth here expresses the view that God has an antecedent reality that is expressed in (rather than constituted by) his works. Yet, at the same time, God's antecedent, eternal reality itself has an "event-character"; it is best described in terms of the categories of decision and act.

For Barth, the category of act is closely related to the category of God's "life."[66] Unlike Barth's indirect conceptual redescription of God under the category of act, this claim is rooted *directly* in the Bible's witness to "the living God" (263). From the point of view of a method of theology rooted in Scripture, then, Barth says: "The definition we must use as a *starting-point* is that God's being is life" (263; italics added). For Barth, the biblical affirmation that God is "the living God" is no metaphor or parable [*Gleichnis*], but a description or designation [*Bezeichnung*] of God, even of God as he is in himself (263).[67] Barth develops this point in a later comment, where he says, "As we remember from the doctrine of the knowledge of God,[68] not only some but *all human standpoints and concepts, even those used by scripture, are 'anthropomorphisms'*" (265; emphasis added). Even anthropomorphisms in the narrower and more typical sense are "specially adapted to describe the special life and being of God, although quite useless to describe the highest ideal in Plato's teaching" (265).

God's Act and Life as Free and Unique (Particularism)

So far Barth has argued that God reveals himself "as event, as act and as life" (264). But Barth believes it is necessary to be more precise, so as to avoid confusing God with "a sum or content of event, act or life generally." God's act in revelation is a *particular* action. God is thus not only *actus purus*, but is *actus purus et singularis*. As such, God's acts

---

66. Jüngel regards the claim that "God's being is in becoming" (his paraphrase of Barth) is "an attempt to think out theologically how far God *is the living God*" (*Doctrine of the Trinity*, vii).

67. Barth unfolds this point in two brief excursuses. In the first, Barth cites and comments on many biblical citations as well as positive references to traditional theologians who made statements in keeping with the biblical affirmation of God's life (263). In the second, Barth broadens his consideration of the issue of "anthropomorphism" beyond the phrase the "living God." He says that many of the biblical expressions designated anthropomorphic such as "remembrance and forgetting" are not mere simile or metaphor; they are not *attributa metaphorica*. In our treatment of Barth's use of Scripture in chapter 5 we will consider Barth's related comments on Old Testament passages referring to divine repentance.

68. Barth is referring to his comments in II/1, 222f.; cf. 286 and 369f.

"contradict" all other acts or events. Neither is God's transcendence a "dialectical transcendence" that "*must be* understood with equal strictness as immanence" (264; emphasis added). Divine Freedom is the "undialectical transcendence," a "saving contradiction of God found in His revelation" that "cannot be removed dialectically" (265).[69] Put simply, God is subject to no external necessity whatsoever. Therefore, "God is in Himself free event, free act, and free life" (264).

Barth wishes to be yet more specific about the nature of God's "specific freedom" and how it distinguishes God's act and life from all other non-divine expressions of act or life. To do so, Barth first states how the difference between the divine and non-divine is *not* to be conceived. It is not to be construed along the lines of a various dualistic ontologies. In Barth's words, "The differentiation of the divine happening from the non-divine does not coincide in Holy Scripture with the distinction between nature and grace, soul and body, inner and outer, visible and invisible" (265). Against the "idealistic" assumptions that God's act is to be consistently and exclusively associated with the "spiritual," Barth insists that the event of revelation has a natural, outer, historical element. God is not to be confused with the spiritual world or even with absolute spirit, for spiritual reality (in the general sense) is also created reality (265f.).[70] Accordingly, "The divine being must be allowed to transcend both spirit and nature, yet also to overlap and comprehend both" (266). Here Barth states his belief that "pure spirit" cannot really act in this world. According to this more holistic ontology, "Acts only happen in the unity of spirit and nature." The concept of Spirit acting alone is best considered to be an idolatrous "hypostatisation of our own created spirit" (267). Such statements appear to be attempts to state, in ontological terms, the implications of the fact of the incarnation for understanding God's reality.

---

69. See Cross, "Use of Dialectic in Karl Barth's Doctrine of God," 177f.

70. Barth notes that Scripture speaks unashamedly of God's bodily parts—his nose, back, and so on. Instead of glibly following Amandus Polanus and others who understood such passages "non-theologically" or "figuratively" (*uneigentlich*), Barth wishes to take them as depicting something true about God. Like all theological language, it is *both* anthropomorphic *and* descriptive. Otherwise, Barth says, we will have to raise questions as to the appropriateness of other more basic terms such as: Father, Son, and Holy Spirit! Barth believes that Protestant orthodoxy (e.g., Polanus) has here been determined by the classical philosophy of pagan antiquity, and, as such, paves the way for the Enlightenment (266).

God's Being as "Personal" (Personalism)

Yet Barth does regard the freedom of God as "the freedom of the spirit" in some sense (267). God's own special spiritual freedom "is not . . . accident or necessity," and "it does not have the orderliness or fatality of a natural event, although nature is not excluded." Rather, "it is the freedom of a knowing and willing I," i.e., the freedom of a *personal Subject*. "The particularity of the divine event, act and life is the particularity of the being of a *person*" (267).

Before we unpack what Barth means by God's personal being, we would do well to review the flow of Barth's thought in his treatment of "the Being of God in Act." Using the "motifs" that George Hunsinger identifies in Barth's work, we can say that Barth has moved from actualism (the being of God is in act or life) to particularism (the being of God is specific and free act or life) and now to personalism (the being of God is personal being—personal act and life).[71]

What does Barth mean by saying that God's being is "being in person"? In clarifying his meaning, Barth states that the nature of the event of revelation leads us to reject both a "false spiritualizing on the one hand and a false realism on the other" (268). False spiritualizing, as we have noted above, denies the presence of "nature" in God's act. False realism, by contrast, makes nature and spirit equal and symmetrically-related. The following passage clarifies the nature of Barth's opposition to false realism.

> [T]he peak of all happening in revelation, according to Holy Scripture, consists in the fact that God speaks as an I, and is heard by the thou who is addressed . . . In this happening the world of nature and sense is undoubtedly subordinate. It is the servant. It is the component which is not important and necessary for its own sake, but only in its relationship and function. (267)

We could say that, in order to reveal himself, God commandeers the natural order. In this act, the natural order is necessary (how else could God's self revelation be mediated to humans who exist as a part

---

71. See Hunsinger, *How to Read Karl Barth*, 4f., 30–35, 40ff. The motif of objectivism, and other motifs, are also implicit in Barth's account of God's dynamic being in §28.1.

of this order?), but God is free in using it as he pleases.⁷² This implies a certain Christocentric theological-ontological claim.⁷³

A similar emphasis on God's freedom is found in Barth's definition of a person as one who is "self-moved" and "self-motivated" (268ff.).⁷⁴ God is entirely self-moved and entirely unmoved by anything or anyone outside himself. Therefore, Barth thinks that only God is, properly speaking, a person (271). The Triune God's being is self-disposing and self-sufficient, and in this is the meaning of the biblical claim that "God is spirit" (John 4:24) (268). In being "self-moved," the transcendent God is different from either nature or spirit, which, are ultimately either "unmoved" or "moved," but never "self-moved" (269).⁷⁵ In God's revelation we recognize that, despite our relative capacity to move and motivate ourselves or other beings, we are not absolutely self-moved and self-motivated, as only God is.⁷⁶ Furthermore, God's works are in no sense reducible to human "movements" (270f.).⁷⁷ "No other being exists abso-

72. Cf. II/1, 267f.

73. To elaborate more fully, Barth appears to have an ontological perspective in which God's acts (at least acts *ad extra*) require both spirit and nature, but in which nature is clearly subordinate to spirit. This way of relating spirit to nature is not a *general* ontology (i.e., applicable to all reality), but ought to be interpreted as a way of speaking of God in particular. It is derived from the particular divine act of the incarnation in which the human nature of Christ is necessary, but is subordinate to the divine person-in-act. We may thus speak of the hypostatic Christological "inclusion" of the "natural" order within the divine being in the act of revelation or reconciliation. We will see that Barth's treatments of divine unity, constancy, and eternity demonstrate a similar ontological pattern. Aspects of this "Christological ontology" are illuminated by what Ingolf Dalferth refers to as Barth's "eschatological realism" ("Karl Barth's Eschatological Realism").

74. That this applies also to human persons is evident in Barth's account of "experience" in I/1, 198ff.

75. In a brief excursus, Barth launches a polemic against "naturalistic or spiritualistic Deism" and "mystical Pantheism" in which God is an unmoved being identified with an abstract view of either nature or spirit as the measure of all things (269). On this point, Barth sounds similar to I. A. Dorner (*Divine Immutability*, 110f.), as at other points (see our comments in chapter 4 and especially chapter 5).

76. Donna Bowman's article ("Barth and Whitehead on Divine Self-Determination") notes that despite their drastically differing methods, Barth and Whitehead converge in their affirmation of divine self-determination. Yet even this convergence in content must be qualified by Barth's distinctive understanding of God's personal sovereignty. God is only voluntarily (and never necessarily) "passible" or affected by what happens in the world (see Fiddes, *Creative Suffering of God*).

77. In a page-long excursus, Barth shows the flaw of any view of God that is equivalent to shouting "man" loudly (269f.). Barth treats Kant, Hegel, Schleiermacher, and Ritschl in this light (270).

lutely in its act... in its own conscious, willed, executed decision" (271).[78] Therefore, "the real person is not man but God ... God lives from and by Himself" (272).

In affirming God's unique self-determining personhood, Barth makes explicit an implicit transcendental argument that has been running through this whole subsection (§28.1).[79] That is, God's being totally self-moved is what *makes it possible* for God's being to be "in act." Otherwise, God's actions would (like ours) be moved partly by external influences; as such, God's being would not be fully present in his action. But since God is totally self-moved, God and God alone can be totally faithful to his character or being in all his actions.[80]

Barth's Theological Method in §28.1

With his affirmation of God's unique personhood, Barth concludes this introductory section of his doctrine of the reality of God (§28.1). We may conclude our treatment of this section of *CD* by asking how Barth's theological method has been evident within it. Once again, we will do so by asking how Scripture, tradition, and reason function in this section.

If we ask which strand of the threefold cord is primarily at work in §28.1, the most natural answer is probably: "reason." This is because Barth is principally concerned to do a kind of "conceptual analysis" of the ideas most appropriate to describing God's being as known in revelation. In fact, this section is about as close as Barth comes to doing theological metaphysics or ontology, an activity which would be an instance of the constructive use of reason.[81] While Barth does engage Scripture and tradition quite often in this section, it is mainly in his

---

78. Such a quotation does not imply that Barth believes God's freedom is arbitrary. We will see that God's freedom is in some sense constrained internally by his determinate loving character (see II/1, 284ff. and our comments below).

79. See Johnson, *Mystery of God*, 44f., 200. To use the language of Paul Ricoeur, it is possible (as it is not for us humans) for God's "idem-identity" and "ipse-identity" to fully converge (see the excursus on Barth and Ricoeur in chapter 5).

80. Barth's development of God's unique capacity to "act out" his decisions qualifies David Kelsey's claim that Barth develops a "rudimentary ontology of personal agency" here in II/1 (*Proving Doctrine*, 134). While Barth does develop a definition of a "person" that applies to humans in a derivative way, the specific claims that Kelsey associates with this "ontology" fully apply only to God and not to personal agents in general.

81. Jüngel indicates that Barth makes ontological statements but is not doing ontology (*Doctrine of the Trinity*, 62), at least not in the typical systematic or comprehensive sense.

excursuses and affects the large print discussion only in a highly indirect manner. That said, when Barth does appeal to Scripture, he takes it as an authority that shows him the true nature of God and God's self-revelation. As such, reason remains clearly subordinate to Scripture. Tradition does as well, functioning primarily in a negative way in this section. Tradition is here subject to a critique that aims to be based on revelation as attested in Scripture.

But again, it is the role of reason that is most prominent in this section of *CD*. Reason is present both in its critical and constructive capacities in this section, although the constructive function is probably primary. Barth incorporates insights of idealism and realism on an ad hoc basis.[82] Barth strives to ensure that he uses reason in such a way that it is conformed to the unique demands of its subject matter, rather than subjecting God to the illegitimate strictures of a priori general concepts. For example, he concludes with a reminder that when we speak of God as the living God, "our quality of life can never be confused with His, or compared or contrasted with it as commensurate" (272). Such confusions will be avoided, Barth says, if we are clear about the rule that all further statements about God "are found alone in his act . . . because only in His act He is who He is." We will not go wrong if our thoughts are in this way "grasped by God's action" instead of being about ourselves.

The Being of God as One Who Loves (CD §28.2)

Now that Barth has sketched the divine essence in relatively abstract and formal terms as his being-in-act, he now pursues further the specific content of this being-in-act: "We must now further enquire what is this act of His" (273). God's revelation is self-revelation and, as such, tells us more than simply that "God is God." It is rather the revelation of his *name*, a personal name that we cannot "go behind." Barth is here referring to the Triune name of God, his identity as Father, Son, and Holy Spirit (274). The question is "what this name has to say about the particular being of God in His act" (273). Using our own terminology, we could say that Barth is asking about how one can relate the question of identity—the question of who God is, which is answered by the Triune

---

82. In this process of incorporating philosophical ideas, Barth employs the rational procedure of "assimilation" in which the ideas are transformed so that they may be appropriate to the distinctive subject matter of theology (Hunsinger, *How to Read Karl Barth*, 61ff.).

"name"—to the question of character—the question of what God is like. Barth's answer is: "This name definitely has this primary decisive thing to say to us in all its constituents: that *God is He who, without having to do so, seeks and creates fellowship between Himself and us* (273). In other words, God is One who *loves*.

"God is He who, *without having to do so*, seeks and creates fellowship between Himself and us." In other words, God loves *in freedom*—as Barth will say later. More specifically, Barth says that God's internal fellowship within the eternal Trinity overflows, as it were, towards us and includes us. This overflow is neither the product of internal nor external necessity, but is entirely self-moved.

But Barth's primary concern in this section (§28.2) is not with God's freedom, which he unfolds in §28.3, but with a positive statement of God's love, his seeking and creation of fellowship (273f.). Put differently, Barth is here concerned with the content of the verb that best sums up God's action for us (i.e., that God *loves*) rather than the adverbial modifier of that verb (i.e., that God loves *in freedom*).

Barth begins by showing how all the great works of God *ad extra* are works of love for us. The act of creation is already an expression of this love, this free seeking and creation of fellowship. Yet this work of love is "is heightened in the work of revelation itself" and "finds its crown and final confirmation in the future destiny of mankind as redeemed in Jesus Christ" (274).[83] In addition, Barth notes that "what God does in all this He is"; God's being and his act, his character and his work, are inseparable.

To say that God loves means that God "wills to be ours, and He wills that we should be His" (274). God desires a relationship of fellowship, of *koinonia*, of mutual belonging. In this loving, God remains Creator and we remain creatures. God remains the judge who hates sin. God remains the Lord over us and all creation. Yet in all his works, God is always the one who wills *this one thing*—to have fellowship with us (274f.). In fact, this seeking and creation of fellowship—this one thing— is the divine, the divinity or essence of God [*Wesen Gottes*] found in

---

83. Here Barth refers to how God's love is God's motivating factor in the three great works of creation, reconciliation (revelation), and redemption. Also, although this passage contains one of few explicit references to Jesus Christ in §28, Barth's whole conception of God's being revealed in his act of revelation is implicitly Christocentric (and Trinitarian) throughout.

the revelation of his Triune name (275). In his eternal being, God has fellowship in himself. In giving us fellowship with him, God gives us himself. God is one who loves.

In a brief excursus, Barth makes some exegetical comments on the biblical statement that "God is love" (1 John 4:8 and 16) that illuminate the nature of his theological use of Scripture. Specifically, Barth points out that taking the phrase "God is love" out of its context is "forced exegesis" (275). Against the comment of historical-critic Martin Dibelius that "God is love" provides "an equation of God," Barth shows how the context of this statement defines God's love specifically by reference to the acts of God in Jesus Christ (see 1 John 4:9 and 15). Barth identifies a similar pattern at work in John 3:16. Thus, Barth appeals to a contextual[84] interpretation of Scripture in order to show that, as far as our knowledge of God is concerned, God's concrete acts of "loving" (the verb) are prior to any abstract claims that we might make about God's love (the noun). Accordingly, Barth's effort to interpret Scripture carefully and contextually goes hand in hand with his more general principle that we know God's unique being only through God's works. Barth speaks of this principle as making a "decisive turn" to revelation as the only proper basis of the doctrine of God. This methodological turn implies that we must not now take our general concept of love and impose it on God (275f.). Therefore, we cannot reverse 1 John 4's statement and say that "love is God." This principle of the "non-reversibility" of the Subject-predicate order runs throughout Barth's doctrine of God.[85] Since Scripture is the only adequate and reliable witness to God's self-revelation, Barth's appeal to the specific features of this scriptural witness is his concrete methodological alternative to speculative attempts to define God's being on the basis of speculative, general concepts of predicates such as love.

Barth further elucidates this love of God found in revelation in four theses (276–83), which we will now examine in turn. In the first thesis, Barth speaks of the inherent *goodness* of God's love: "God's loving is concerned with a seeking and creation of fellowship for its own sake"

---

84. Barth here demonstrates his capacity to critique and transcend the older "prooftexting" method of Scripture usage through attention to its immediate literary context and its larger canonical context.

85. For some helpful reflection on the issues raised in this paragraph, see Hart, *Regarding Karl Barth*, 188ff.

(280). Barth explains, "God is not . . . the *Good* first, and then the One who loves," but is good in the very act of divine loving. "The "positively good content" [Thomasius] of God's personal life does not exist behind or apart from His communication, but consists in the fact that it is the self-communicating life as such" (277). By giving the loved the gift of love, God gives us himself. The Gift *is* the Giver.

Barth's second thesis about God's love states that "God's loving is concerned with a seeking and creation of fellowship without any reference to an existing aptitude or worthiness on the part of the loved" (278). Here Barth speaks about the *basis* of God's love—a basis found entirely in the Lover, not in the loved. "God's love always throws a bridge over a crevasse." In an excursus, Barth supports this second thesis by appealing to several scriptural passages. He begins by citing texts in the gospels that speak of Jesus Christ as one who came to seek sinners— the sick and the lost among humanity (Matt 15:24; Luke 5:31, 19:10). He also notes Pauline texts such as Rom 4:5 (the justification of the ungodly) and Rom 5:8 (God's love for his enemies). In this same excursus, Barth critiques Protestant scholastics Polanus and Quenstedt for suggesting that God's love is motivated by some "preceding pleasure in the loved" (278). Such a conception, Barth thinks, is based not on the cross of Christ or other aspects of the biblical view of God's love, but on a problematic general concept of love (278f.). According to the revelation attested in Scripture, God's love is grounded in God himself, in "the event in the triune God himself in all eternity" (279).

The third thesis speaks of the *purpose* of God's love: "God's loving is an end in itself" not a means to an end (279). God's love is not subordinate to other goals as self-glorification or the achievement of human salvation (279). Indeed, God loves in eternity within the Trinity, where such *ad extra* purposes are not inherently necessary. Barth supports such claims, once again, by appealing to scriptural passages in an excursus. Barth cites several passages that show that God's saving acts are based upon God's prior love, not *vice versa* (Deut 7:8, Jer 31:3, Isa 63:9). Again, Barth moves directly from the quotation of such passages to a (scriptural) critique of theological tradition that he thinks has departed from the point of these passages. In this case, Barth criticizes Ritschl's view of God's love as grounded in God's purposes for humanity. According to Barth, Ritschl forsakes God's transcendent freedom by riveting God inflexibly to his specific purposes in the economy of salvation (279f.). What God does in free love is dissolved into "inflexibility of purpose" (280).[86]

Barth's fourth and final thesis about God's love is that "God's loving is necessary, for it is the being, the essence and the nature of God" (280). In speaking thus about the *necessity* of God's love, Barth makes clear that no external necessities are imposed on God; rather, he speaks of an internal necessity. The point of speaking of this internal necessity is to ensure that the concept of God's freedom does not lead to the view that God's free decisions and actions are libertine or arbitrary,[87] nor that God's being is finally indeterminate. Rather, Barth here shows that God has a stable, determinate character; God is necessarily loving in his being and his acts. Yet God is entirely free in the sense of being entirely self-determining. "We are tied to God, but not God to us" (281). God freely chooses, however, to take us up into his eternal love, his eternal fellowship and blessedness. Put differently, God freely chooses to allow his eternal love within the Trinity to overflow into our temporal humanity. God necessarily loves (this is his eternal nature or character), but he does not necessarily love *us* (for even our existence is an expression of his freedom).

These four theses show in various ways that God "loves as only He can love" (283). When God's love is understood in all its richness and concreteness, then we understand that all talk about God must be a development of this basic definition that God loves (284).

Barth concludes his consideration of God's being as "one who loves" in §28.2 with a fuller explanation of his claim, made first in §28.1, that "God is a person" (284f.). God is *the* person and we only become persons in virtue of God's love for us (i.e., we are dependent, derivative persons). God alone is the "I" who is fully able to love in himself. Furthermore, Jesus Christ is *the* human person who shows us what it means to be a human in all its fullness (286). Such an understanding allows us to take the Bible at face value when it speaks of God in per-

---

86. This is relevant to Barth's view that God's "constancy" is flexible and informed by free decisions, unlike classical immutability (see chapter 5).

87. Commenting on the diversity of conceptions of divine freedom at work in Barth, Hendry says that caprice or arbitrariness is "the only conception of freedom that [Barth] expressly eliminates" ("The Freedom of God," 236; cf. II/1, 318 and II/2, 26). While this may be true, we believe (contra Hendry) that the varying nuances of Barth's view of divine freedom can be coherently related under the rubric of "self-determination."

sonal terms (286). For God really is a person to the core of his being, the perfect person. Again, who God has revealed himself to be to us is who God truly is in his eternal being (287). There is no tension between God's "personality" and his "absoluteness" within his being. God is one and in this unity of his being, he is the one who loves.[88] And "the one God is revealed to us absolutely in Jesus Christ" (297).

The Being of God in Freedom (CD §28.3)

In this subsection we turn from love to freedom, from one side of the dialectic of Barth's doctrine of God to the other. As noted earlier, Barth tends to speak of God's freedom in adverbial terms, as that which modifies God's fundamental activity of loving. God loves *in freedom*. In a more obvious way than in the last two subsections, we will focus in this subsection on Barth's method and specifically on the methodological implications of his conception of divine freedom. To do so, much of following analysis will employ the rubric of the "five features" that we introduced at the end of chapter 2.

Despite our methodological concentration in this subsection, we do not wish to neglect the essential contours of Barth's understanding of God's freedom. Therefore, we will begin with a summary of some of the main concepts that Barth uses to unfold his understanding of God's freedom.

Important Distinctives of Barth's View of Divine Freedom

Barth employs several terms to speak of God's freedom. Some of the most frequent are lordship (301), aseity or self-existence (302), sovereignty, and absoluteness (see below). Perhaps Barth's most significant way of defining divine freedom is his affirmation (encountered above) that God is self-moved or self-determining. Barth further clarifies the

---

[88]. Barth concludes §28.2 with a lengthy excursus on the modern discussion of the personality of God (287–97; see Gordon Clark's exposition in *Karl Barth's Theological Method*, 33–38; cf. I/1, 403 on Barth's own objection to "persons"). Barth starts with the ancient pagan historical origins of this problem in the Middle Ages in which the Trinity was placed after the nature and attributes, and in which people began to speak of God apart from revelation and Scripture (i.e., apart from his being as one who loves). This led first to the error of understanding God as three human personalities and then to a reduction of theology to anthropology. We do not need to affirm that God has or is a "personality" (although we may do so), but only that he loves. Barth clearly regards God as one person (and perhaps one personality), not three.

meaning of this concept by making a distinction between God's primary and secondary freedom. God's *primary freedom* is his positive freedom to be "grounded in [his] own being, to be determined and moved by [himself]" (301). As such, God is free in himself even apart from relationship to the world. God's *secondary freedom* is God's "negative" freedom from all external constraints and limitations—in all the works and acts he carries out in relation to the world. The primary positive, internal side of God's freedom is the basis of the secondary, negative, external freedom (see 302f., 305, 307f.).[89]

Besides his distinction between God's primary and secondary freedom, Barth also clarifies the relationship between divine freedom and the concept of *causation*. Barth thinks that it is inappropriate to speak of God as self-caused or self-realized. Rather God should be seen only as the cause of the particular existence of all things other than himself. God does not cause himself because God "is in no need of origination" (306).[90] God already is all that he is, for he is eternally actual in his Triune being. We need to keep this in mind when Barth uses terms like "self-determination" or "self-positing" in relation to God. Although Barth has a dynamic, actualistic conception of God, he does not believe in God's "self-realization" in a sense that implies fundamental growth or change in God's identity.[91]

Barth also uses the concept of God's *absoluteness* to clarify the nature of divine freedom (309ff.). Barth uses this concept specifically to illuminate God's secondary freedom, the freedom or lordship God has in his relationship to the world. Barth distinguishes between God's noetic and ontic absoluteness (310ff.). God's *noetic absoluteness* resists placing God under any general concept (being, personhood, love, freedom etc.) in which God is grouped together in a genus along with non-divine objects of knowledge. This noetic absoluteness, Barth says, is grounded in God's *ontic absoluteness*, his self-sufficiency and independence in relation to all that is not God.[92] Here Barth wishes to maintain what

---

89. This is an aspect of the more general point we have noted above about the ontic priority of the immanent Trinity over the economic Trinity in Barth's doctrine of God.

90. Cf. Hunsinger, *How to Read Karl Barth*, 193.

91. This matter will be clarified in chapter 5 on God's "constancy."

92. Robert Brown ("On God's Ontic and Noetic Absoluteness") argues, against Barth, that noetic absoluteness does not follow from ontic absoluteness. However, Brown's critique is largely misplaced (see Colwell, *Actuality and Provisionality*, 187).

Kierkegaard called the "infinite qualitative distinction" between God and the created order, while at the same time showing that God is free to be immanent in the world. Barth explicates the dynamic and flexible character of God's freedom in an effort to show the inadequacy of all static and mutually-oppositional views of God's otherness or transcendence (314f.).

Methodological Reverence and Particularism

We will now turn to the more distinctly methodological aspects or implications of Barth's view of divine freedom. To begin, we wish to underline how Barth opens his consideration of God's freedom: namely, by saying that God's being, act, and love are "His own" (297). In other words, they are unique to God and flow from God's own self-determination. Barth moves from this point to the methodological implication that the theologian must always retain a proper respect for God as a unique object—or, more precisely, as the unique Subject who freely makes himself an object for our thought and speech in his own way. "This object permits and indeed commands us to speak of a life and a love, of a living and loving I ... But ... He also requires us to understand and name Him beyond all our insights and ideas as the I who lives and loves *in His unique way*" (298; emphasis added). A respectful recognition of God's freedom leads to a kind of methodological "particularism," a tendency to form judgments about God only on the basis of his particular acts of self-revelation. We may ask: "*what* is God" "only if we are aware that with the greatest *childlikeness* which in this connection is also the greatest, the only possible, profundity, we are again asking: *Who* is He?" (298; emphasis added).[93] When this is remembered, theological inquiry does not proceed according to "universal criteria and standards" but according to "the reality revealed to us by God himself."

In another passage, Barth draws out the link between a reverent approach to theology and a particular spirituality marked by disciplines such as hearing the Word and prayer. With respect to the question of God's "necessity" or "necessary existence," Barth distinguishes two methods. The first marks the "classical" and modern Catholic doctrines of God and the second is Barth's preferred approach. In his words, "The

---

93. To refer to the proper theological attitude as "childlikeness" speaks of humility that is willing to let the reality of God's self-revelation overturn one's own pre-conceived notions of God.

former proceeds automatically from the development of an idea, but the latter can be won only from the hearing of the divine Word in prayer and supplication, from the experience of the struggle between the flesh and the spirit, from the real overcoming of real temptation" (307). One such "real temptation" is "wishing to cling to something [i.e., some idea of God] supposedly higher and better than the God who in freedom lives as He who He is." The theologian must always resist this temptation, deferring always to what we know on the basis of God's sovereign self-revelation.

Christocentrism and Textual-Basis

Barth's methodological reverence—his continual deference to God's self-revelation—expresses itself decisively and primarily in two concrete features of his theological method: its Christocentrism and its textually-based character (see chapter 2). We will now consider how these two features appear in Barth's discussion of God's freedom.

For Barth, the content of God's sovereign self-revelation is always to be understood primarily in terms of what God has done in Christ and God's Christocentric self-revelation that manifests God's freedom. Barth unfolds these truths in an illuminating passage (304f.). God chooses to love creatures distinct from him and thus chooses to let those creatures know him and have fellowship with him. Since this *has* taken place, we know that it is *possible* for it to take place—i.e., we know that what has happened "lies within the scope of God's freedom" (304).[94] God "shows and proves in His revelation His freedom to begin with Himself." That is, in the "event" of Christ, God acts wholly by himself and out of his own self-determination: "this is the freedom of His incarnation in Jesus Christ foreshadowed in his election and rule of Israel." Indeed, in Jesus Christ, God "proves his own existence."[95]

The textually-based character of Barth's theology, as we have said, is the "exegetical" part of the larger phenomenon of the role of Scripture within Barth's method. While indirect scriptural authorization pervades much of this section on divine freedom, these directly

---

94. We note again the transcendental method that Barth employs here.

95. In this context Barth refers to Anselm's so called "ontological proof" of God's existence as an attempt to testify to God's prior "self-demonstration" in his revelation (305). This, of course, expresses the interpretation of Anselm Barth made famous in his 1931 book on Anselm.

exegetical engagements with Scripture are relatively rare, perhaps due do the relatively abstract character of much of this section.[96] That said, such references sometimes appear at important points. For example, when Barth begins to unfold the meaning of divine freedom as self-determining Lordship, he turns to an excursus that explains its textual basis. The excursus opens like this:

> There is no plainer description of the divinity of God than the phrase which occurs so frequently in the Pentateuch and again in the Book of Ezekiel "I am the Lord." It is followed hard by that other, analytical phrase "I am the Lord your (or thy) God," and it has its exact New Testament parallel in the "I am" of the Johannine Jesus. It is, of course, obvious that in this biblical "I am" the Subject posits itself and in that way posits itself as the living and loving Lord, in doing so, this Subject is God. He who does this is the God of the Bible. (301f.)

In this quotation, the direct and indirect modes of scriptural authorization are interwoven, so we need to discuss both in relation to each other. While specific passages are quoted, they are set in the context of a biblical pattern that might not be obvious to all readers; at the least it requires a Nicene-Chalcedonian interpretative grid (see below). Barth sees a coherent theological pattern at work in the biblical repetition of a set of related phrases in which God, as Subject, posits himself.[97] Barth goes on to say that because God posits himself as nothing else does, "everything outside of him depends on His good-pleasure or its opposite" (302). Barth follows this with a series of "proof-texts" that speak of what we could refer to as God's uniqueness, sovereignty and "aseity"—all terms that Barth will use later in his exposition of divine freedom. In this excursus, then, we see two different ways (identification of patterns and citations of specific texts) in which Barth grounds his view of divine freedom in Scripture.

---

96. That said, Barth does use terms like "the biblical idea of God" fairly frequently in this section. This is a kind of shorthand for the view of God that he derives from Scripture, either directly or indirectly.

97. While Barth's use of the language of philosophical idealism to speak of God here ("the Subject posits itself"), he redefines these terms somewhat in light of the unique God of the biblical witness.

Ecclesial and Creative

The remaining two of the five main features of Barth's method are that it is ecclesial and creative. We begin with the ecclesial character of Barth's treatment of divine freedom.

For example, Barth appeals frequently to the Church's theological traditions in his account of divine freedom. While Barth's treatment of church tradition is largely negative in this section (due to the "classical" tendency to define God's freedom according to general a priori ideas), positive uses of church tradition are also evident. For example, Barth's interpretation, mentioned above, of the "I am" sayings of Jesus seems to be guided by the early church's Nicene creed and Chalcedonian formulation. His positive reception of the Trinitarian and Christological heritage of the early church enables Barth to regard the "I am" statements of Jesus as standing in an "exact parallel" to the "I am" statements of God in the Old Testament (302; see our comments above). Also, we have already noted Barth's positive assessment of Anselm and his "proof" (305).[98] Barth's negative assessments of theological tradition are evident in his critique of the scholastic tendency to interpret God's "aseity" almost exclusively in terms of God's independence (302) or its related tendency to define God's transcendence strictly in terms of opposition to the world (303f.).[99]

The creative character of Barth's theological method is evident mainly in his creative use of reason to construct and expound his own position.[100] This is evident in his flexible use of "idealistic" concepts such as the "self-positing" of the Absolute in relation to God. To use the example again that we employed above, Barth's creatively redescribes the "I am" statements in John as evidence that Jesus is the divine

---

98. See Gunton, *Becoming and Being*, 117ff.

99. In relation to the ecclesial character of Barth's work, we could recall that, as we noted in our account of Barth's reverence above, Barth's approach to the doctrine of God implies a spirituality of prayer and hearing the Word of God. This suggests that the theologian ought to be actively involved in the practices of church life.

100. We ought not to forget the critical role of Barth's use of reason in his doctrine of divine freedom that is manifest in his criticism of theological tradition that we have already mentioned. Barth continually exposes the tendency of various thinkers to "deify" their own human concepts rather than subordinating their ideas to God's actual self-revelation. For example, Barth critiques the neo-Platonic concept of God as "a hypostatised summary of His nonbeing in relation to all other kind of being, a God who is certainly conceivable as an idealisation of man . . ." (305).

Subject positing himself (302). Such rational reconstruction presupposes the constant deconstruction or critique of inappropriate ways of conceiving of God, but also moves beyond deconstruction to develop an understanding of God on the basis of revelation. More generally, Barth explicates God's internal relations by using the conceptuality of the modern idealist subject: self-realization, self-affirmation, and self-confirmation (306). As such, Barth uses imaginative resourcefulness in critically-appropriating philosophical terminology in the service of the interpretation and application of revelation.

The Perfections of God

Introduction to Barth's Account of Divine Perfections

In this section of the chapter, we turn to Barth's account of the perfections (or attributes) of God (*CD* §§29–31). Barth offers a general treatment of God's perfections in §29 and then turns to his accounts of specific perfections in §30 and §31.

Scripture, tradition, and reason each have important functions in Barth's account of divine perfections. Barth's relatively abstract and general description of God's perfections in §29 (like his understanding of God's "being in act" in §28.1) could be seen as an example of "scriptural reasoning," a highly indirect form of the scriptural authorization of doctrine formed in critical dialogue with theological tradition. Specifically, Barth's theological language of "perfections" follows indirectly from the scriptural testimony to God as (1) uniquely perfect, (2) both "one" and "many," and (3) describable in an ordered dialectical pattern of love and freedom. We will consider the first two of these three elements in the remainder of this subsection and the third in much greater length in the subsections that follow this one.

The opening synopsis of Barth's paragraph on the "Perfections of God" (§29) reads as follows:

> God lives His perfect life in the abundance of many individual and distinct perfections. Each of these is perfect in itself and in combination with all the others. For whether it is a form of love in which God is free, or a form of freedom in which God loves, it is nothing else but God Himself, His one, simple, distinctive being. (322)

From this synopsis and the statements that follow, we see that Barth regards God as "the perfect being," as the only being who lives a "perfect life" (322). Barth reinforced this foundational assumption by stressing the language of divine "perfections" rather than the more typical language of divine "attributes" or "properties." That God alone is perfect implies that God alone has perfections. In Barth's words, "How can He be anything except in perfection, and what can be perfect except in Him?" (323). Clearly, Barth uses the term "perfections" in order to emphasize God's uniqueness. "Attributes" or "properties," while they can be used to describe God, can also be used to describe non-divine beings. But only God's being can be described as a "multitude of perfections" (322).

Another issue that arises from the above quotation is how God can be a plurality of "individual and distinct perfections" and it also be true that each perfection "is nothing else but God Himself, His one, simple, distinctive being." How can God be both one and many? The short answer is that Barth does not tell us how this is possible. Rather, he simply declares that, according to revelation, it is *actually the case*: God is "who he is and what he is in both unity and multiplicity" (323). The longer answer is that this combination of oneness and multiplicity is bound up with a Trinitarian understanding of God—a God who is both one and three (323). We will pursue these matters further in chapter 4, where we consider Barth's conception of divine unity. There we will see that Barth has a concept of divine "simplicity" (God's undivided and inseparable oneness) that is capable of including a diversity of perfections within it. The key point we need to be aware of here is that Barth wishes to carefully avoid the classical tendency to undermine the full reality of diverse divine perfections, an error that he refers to a "nominalism" and "semi-nominalism." The diverse perfections of God are not merely names or metaphors that we humans improperly impose upon a God who is really an undifferentiated unity. Rather, they are aspects of God himself that are made plain in the revelation of God attested in Scripture.[101]

---

101. See Barth's extensive consideration of the issue of how God is both one and many in II/1, 322–55, to which we will return in parts of chapter 5.

The Perfections of Love and Freedom

Introductory Questions About the Divine Perfections

After addressing the question of the sense in which God is marked by a multiplicity of individual and distinct perfections, Barth turns to the question of how we are to conceive of these perfections and how they are related to one another. In the traditional language, Barth raises the question of the "derivation and distribution of the divine attributes" (335). In other words, what are the "contours of God's being?" (336).

For our purposes, there are two key questions that Barth raises in this connection. First, Barth asks on what basis and in what sense we are to affirm these perfections as real in God? In sum, Barth's answer is that God's revelation leads us to affirm with confidence that God is "almighty, eternal, just, wise, merciful," and so on, "*not merely for us but in Himself*" (336). Yet this objective knowledge of God is provisional, not a once-for-all reality in our control. Barth wishes to ensure that the theologian is ever reliant on ongoing divine acts of revelation—acts that freshly authorize our language about God's perfections. As Barth says, when we are "authorized by his revelation to name Him with these words of ours" then we can be confident that "we are moving in the sphere of truth and not falsehood *so long as we are always willing to allow Him to be Himself the interpreter of these human words which He has placed upon our lips*" (336; emphasis added). Thus, we can speak of God's real perfections (that are true of God *a se* rather than simply *pro nobis*) only by means of a trustful subordination to ongoing divine action in which God places words upon our lips and then interprets those words for us. We can see Barth's actualism and his dialectical understanding of revelation and religious language at work in his method here.[102]

For Barth, the dialectical or eschatological reserve with which we must speak of God does not vitiate confidence in the real objectivity and rationality of our God-talk. Barth says, "The objectivity of God in His revelation has to be taken seriously, so that in regard to God we cannot be content merely with a devout silence or a rapturous whisper" (336).[103] The use of human reasoning and speech to understand God's

---

102. See McCormack, *Karl Barth's Critically Realistic Dialectic Theology*, 428–41 for a helpful commentary on these themes in relation to Barth's account of Anselm's theological method.

103. See Hunsinger on Barth's "objectivism" (*How to Read Karl Barth*, 35–39).

revelation is fully appropriate, so long as it remains obedient to that revelation and does not speculate beyond it.[104] Therefore, although God remains mysterious and hidden even in his self-revelation, the question of the nature and organization of God's perfections is not meaningless (335ff.), and this leads us to the next question.

Second, Barth raises the question of whether our account of God's perfections ought to be organized in any particular way, and if so, what is the basis for this organization of them. Barth's answers to these questions can be summarized in the following way. Revelation leads us to organize God's perfections in a two-fold series, which is most adequately done under the rubric of the perfections of divine loving and the perfections of divine freedom (337–44). Because Barth believes in the *perichoresis* of the divine perfections, no divine perfection is exclusively a manifestation of either love or freedom. Yet certain perfections are more fittingly associated (*per appropriationem*, as it were) with the divine loving (even though they also partake of divine freedom), and other perfections are more fittingly associated with the divine freedom (even though they also partake of divine loving). Further, despite the perichoretic interpenetration of the perfections, love, and freedom, the order in which the perfections are presented is important rather than wholly arbitrary. The knowledge of God that revelation grants to us itself urges us to begin with the perfections of love and to conclude with the perfections of freedom.

Love, Freedom, and the "Threefold Cord"

In this subsection, we will explain Barth's proposal about the love-freedom arrangement of the divine perfections in more detail. In doing so, we will pay special attention to the role of Scripture, tradition, and reason in his theological method.[105] The key question is this: In what

---

104. A few pages later, Barth will emphasize both "the obedience of knowledge and the humility of ignorance" (342). In other words, a reverent response to revelation requires a forthright acknowledgment of both what revelation gives us to know *and* what it does not give us to know.

105. The dissertations of Thomas Currie ("Being in Act") and Terry Cross ("Use of Dialectic in Karl Barth's Doctrine of God") are among the most helpful in doing an exposition of this aspect of Barth's work, not to mention other aspects of Barth's doctrine of God. Currie explicates clearly the nature of the integration of and interplay between freedom and love in the account of perfections. Currie also speaks helpfully of other matters such as the relation of the perfections to the Trinity and to their Christocentric

concrete ways does revelation suggest a twofold rational account of the perfections of God in which the perfections of love are treated first and then the perfections of freedom?

In answering this question, Barth gives extended consideration the Church's theological tradition, evaluating it both negatively and positively. The negative side of Barth's assessment of tradition is evident in his rejection of any approach insofar as it aims to "define and order the perfections of God as though they were the various perfections of a kind of general being presupposed as known already" (337). Against this, Barth wishes to recognize fully that each one of God's perfections is "the characteristic being of God Himself as He discloses Himself in His revelation." Barth continues his critical dialogue with tradition in an extensive excursus that outlines three problematic modern ways of organizing the doctrine of divine perfections into "psychological," "religio-genetic" or "historical-intuitive" categories (337–41). In each case there is a problematic anthropocentrism that diminishes the proper theocentric objectivity of God's perfections as they are disclosed in revelation.

The positive side of Barth's evaluation is evident in his reference to "a classical, and to some extent ecumenical, line of theological reflection" (337) in which God's perfections are organized within some kind of two-fold series.[106] Barth's version of this "better way" (340) is the love-freedom series. But this finds precedent in other versions of the two-fold series. In Protestant orthodoxy, the perfections were classed as negative or positive, absolute or relative, or incommunicable or communicable. Yet even beyond Protestant orthodoxy, Barth believes there was an ecumenical theological consensus that God needs to be described in a two-fold manner. On the one hand, we need speak of "God's aseity, absoluteness, and freedom" in distinction from all of creation (341). On the other hand, we need to speak of "the love of God, of the activity of His personal being."

Following his evaluation of theological tradition, Barth moves into the more directly constructive phase of his account of perfections. In this aspect of his work, Barth employs a constructive use of reason in

---

centre. Cross (esp. 176–201 and 209ff.) offers an illuminating discussion of the role of a specific form of "dialectical method" within Barth's account of divine perfections.

106. Barth's use of "classical" here is quite different from our typically negative use of it in this book (see chapter 2, within the section on "the role of tradition").

the service of an argument in which Scripture indirectly authorizes his theological proposals.

How does Barth rework the tradition of organizing the perfections in a two-fold series in the light of scriptural revelation? One of the most important ways is that Barth relates the categories of God's love and freedom to the dialectic of God's self-disclosure and God's hiddenness in revelation (341ff.). In this way, Barth uses dialectic as a rational tool by which to speak appropriately of God.[107] God is known first as one who acts in love and yet as one who, in his freedom, remains hidden—even in his act of revelation. Barth thus closely relates the dialectic of unveiling and veiling in revelation to the dialectic of God's love and freedom. In both dialectics, "opposing" ideas exist in "complete reciprocity" to each other. In Barth's words,

> Each of the opposing ideas not only augments but absolutely fulfils the other, yet it does not render it superfluous or supplant it. On the contrary, it is only in conjunction with the other—and together with it affirming the same thing—that each can describe the Subject, God. (343)

This perichoretic kind of dialectic is crucial for understanding not only the relationship of love and freedom in Barth's doctrine of God, but also for understanding the relationship of each perfection to each other and to God's being as a whole.[108]

Further Observations

In the latter part of §29, Barth makes three observations that help to clarify the distinctive character of his proposed love-freedom model. Firstly, he points out that freedom and love are not to be strictly identified with transcendence and immanent self-giving respectively. Due to the *perichoresis* between freedom and love in God's being, God's love describes God's transcendent being *a se*, and God's freedom is expressed in God's self-giving immanence. In the end, the distinction between "God in himself" and "God for us" can have only "heuristic rather than

---

107. On the secondary literature on "dialectic" (as a distinctive use of reason), see our comments in chapter 1.

108. See Cross, "Use of Dialectic in Karl Barth's Doctrine of God," 186f.; Hunsinger ably expounds upon the same dialectic in other terms: as a "Trinitarian pattern" of "dialectical inclusion" (*How to Read Karl Barth*, 58, 86, etc.).

essential significance" (345).[109] There is no absolute rift or separation within God's being. The God known in Christ is emphatically the same as the God who exists *a se*.

Secondly, Barth observes that we need to avoid "attempted epistemological deductions" that move from the created realm to conceptions of God's perfections. Specifically, Barth considers the traditional doctrine of the "threefold way" or *via triplex*: (1) the "way of negation" (*via negationis* or *via negativa*), (2) the "way of eminence" (*via eminentiae*), and (3) the "way of causation" (*via causalitatis*) (346f.). Regarding the third way (causation), not as a third method, but as a "common presupposition and crown" of the first two methods, Barth concentrates on the first and second ways. For Barth, the perfections of the divine freedom should not be regarded as the straightforward result of the way of negation, i.e., the simple denial of created concepts (the finite becomes infinite, temporality becomes timeless eternity, etc.). The trouble with this is that, when we pay attention to revelation, "God's freedom is not in any way identical with God's being over against the world" (347).[110] Likewise, Barth sees the possible temptation of thinking that the perfections of divine loving can be derived from the application of the way of eminence, i.e., by choosing certain concepts from the created order (i.e., human love, patience, and so on) and fitting them to God (taking them to a superlative degree and removing any objectionable qualities in them). But again, when we consider the God known in revelation, we realize that God's unique ways of loving are not simply quantitatively different than ours. Furthermore, God's love, because it is an eternal feature of his being, "is in no way coincident with His being for us" (347). Barth concedes that, in the appropriate context of the reception of revelation, the theologian may well employ something like the methods of negation or eminence,[111] but he is emphatic in his denial that these methods (and those humans using them) have any inherent

---

109. Barth considers problematic the traditional pairs for the two categories of divine perfections (absolute and relative, incommunicable and communicable, and so on) because they imply that this distinction is essential, rather than merely heuristic.

110. In the chapters to follow, we will see that this point is a repeated feature of Barth's critique of classical concepts of God.

111. We will see in chapter 6 that Barth refers to God as "supremely temporal" (*CD* III/2, 437), which sounds like the *via eminentiae*. That said, such language is not typical of Barth, who more commonly wishes to emphasize the uniqueness of God's perfections in contrast to creation (see his denial of *analogia entis*, at least in a static form).

capacity to speak adequately about God (347f.). Again, our correct use of theological concepts is ultimately an event of correspondence with God constituted by God's ongoing revelatory action.

Last but not least, Barth observes that "the order in which these two series of divine attributes are formulated is not a matter of indifference." Indeed, it is significant enough that Barth wishes to reverse the order typical of the traditional or "classical" two-fold arrangements. Barth wishes to treat the perfections of love (associated loosely with the traditional "relative" or "communicable" attributes) *before* the perfections of freedom (associated loosely with the "absolute" or "incommunicable" attributes), rather than after them, as had been typical. For Barth, "[t]he fundamental error of the whole earlier doctrine of God is reflected in this [traditional] arrangement" (348). The reason is that, the practice of considering the perfections of God's freedom or aseity *first* tends to lead to abstract speculations about what God must be like in himself, apart from God's revelation. Instead, we must start with the God who loves us, the personal Triune God. Only from that point may we move to considerations of God's sovereign self-existence.[112] In the following passage, Barth makes this point as well as others that serve to summarize this subsection.

> [W]e must first say that it is as the personal triune God that He is self-existent; as the One who loves that His is the One who is free. If there is full reciprocity [between love and freedom], as we have seen, this order obtains even in the full reciprocity, not signifying a difference of value between the two aspects of divinity, but the movement of life in which God is God, corresponding exactly to His revelation of Himself as God. And in

---

112. Thus, it is the need to begin with God's concrete loving acts of self-revelation that leads Barth to start with God's love rather than freedom. This is a more adequate explanation than David Ford's suggestion that "the relationship between the two moments" of love and freedom "is to be understood through the crucifixion and the resurrection" (Ford, *Barth and God's Story*, 139). Ford continues, "It is the resurrection which demonstrates the freedom of God in the loving act of the crucifixion; and the irreversible order of the two events in their rendering of one identity shows how such attributes as God's judgment ... and grace are to be held together." There may be a kind of analogy between the crucifixion and resurrection and God's love and freedom (that, by the way, is not strictly parallel to the relationship of grace and judgment), but there is no evidence that Barth regarded this as the basis of the order of the doctrine of the perfections. Ford's speculative claim here is indicative of his attempt to overstress the significance of biblical *narrative* in Barth's theological method.

our apprehension and exposition of the perfections of God, we must adhere to this sequence. (348)

In this passage we see that Barth wishes to affirm two complementary dynamics in his doctrine of divine perfections: (1) the perichoretic *reciprocity* of love and freedom (and also of each perfection to the other) and (2) the revealed *order* of God's being and life, an order of love first and then freedom.[113] We will see these two dynamics at work throughout our further exposition of individual divine perfections.

"The Perfections of Divine Loving" (§30)

We now turn to a survey of Barth's six perfections of divine loving. Since our primary concern in this book is with three of the perfections of divine freedom, we need only to indicate some structural and methodological features of his account of God's love. The following general pattern is evident in §30. The six perfections of divine loving are organized into three pairs: grace and holiness, mercy and righteousness, and patience and wisdom. The first members of each pair (grace, mercy, and patience) are perfections that abundantly emphasize God's love or "relationality" in his act of self-revelation, while the second members of each pair (holiness, righteousness, and wisdom) are perfections that speak of the freedom or "integrity" of God that is apparent when God acts in love (see 352f.).[114]

Any adequate consideration of Barth's account of divine perfections must address the questions of selection and arrangement. Why does he select *these* perfections, and why does he place them in *this* arrangement? We have already considered some reasons for Barth's selection and arrangement on the macro-level. We saw that Barth's interpretation of God's self-revelation causes him to select love and freedom as two macro-categories or meta-perfections by which to organize his account of perfections. We also saw how, against the grain of the classical tradition, he believed that revelation urged that they stand in the order of love-freedom, rather than freedom-love. On the macro-level, the relationship between

---

113. Again, see Cross, "Use of Dialectic in Karl Barth's Doctrine of God," 185ff.

114. The terms "relationality" and "integrity" are taken from W. S. Johnson, *Mystery of God*, 52ff. While these terms are helpful in drawing out certain aspects of Barth's love and freedom respectively, they are liable to neglect other aspects of Barth's terms. Therefore, we will employ Johnson's terms only occasionally in this book, where they seem appropriate and illuminating.

the revelation attested in Scripture and Barth's proposals of selection and arrangement was indirect. There were no direct appeals to specific biblical passages. Rather, Barth appealed to overall patterns evident in God's revelation and drew implications from these.

With a few qualifications, the same pattern of indirect scriptural-revelational authorization is present on the micro-level: i.e., on the level of Barth's selection of specific perfections and his arrangement of these. Again, there is a careful balance between the theologian's freedom and constraint under revelation (see the subsection on dogmatic method near the beginning of chapter 2). Barth clarifies this point in a brief excursus (352f.) within his introductory comments on "the perfections of divine loving" (§30).[115] Barth states: "Every doctrine of God's perfections has to come down, in detail, to a certain choice and grouping of concepts—a choice and summary which as such *will not be able to appeal to any direct intimation of Holy Scripture nor to the voice of any sort of relative authority*" (352). In this way, Barth affirms his freedom as a dogmatic theologian to work in a way that does not follow the *direct* precedent of either Scripture or church tradition (the prime example of a "relative authority"). The Church's theological traditions show great variety on these matters, and Scripture "does not anywhere give authoritative directions." According to Barth, this is a "specific form of the problem that has already arisen regarding the order of dogmatics as a whole." In the following passage, he highlights the significance of this comparison.

> *Methodus arbitraria* was our conclusion then, and we repeat it now.[116] The kind of choice and grouping which we must now attempt can always have the basic character only of a trial and proposal. But it must not on that account be arbitrary [*Wilkürlich*] i.e., unreasonable [*sinnlos*] or perverse [*eigensinnig*]. (352)[117]

Clearly then, despite Barth's apparently positive use of the traditional phrase *methodus arbitraria*, Barth does not actually believe that either his account of the order of dogmatics or of the specific order

---

115. As we will note later, a very similar excursus is found at the beginning of his consideration of the six perfections of divine freedom (441f.).

116. See *CD* I/2, 860f.; cf. 869, where Barth refers to the "fundamental lack of principle in the dogmatic method."

117. A more accurate translation of the last phrase would be "arbitrary, i.e., senseless and obstinate" (*KD* II/1, 396).

of the perfections is "arbitrary" or "indiscriminate" in any strong sense. True, the relevant order or selection is in neither case directly prescribed by any theological authority, and therefore can only be provisional. Yet Barth *does* wish to be guided in some indirect sense by such authorities—especially Scripture—in making responsible, rather than capricious, dogmatic decisions.

What kind of indirect function does scriptural revelation have in shaping Barth's decisions about the selection and arrangement of the perfections of divine freedom? Barth suggests an answer to this question when he explains (on 352) the two questions that he kept in mind in his attempt to make this selection and arrangement.

1. "[B]y what specific determinations [*Bestimmungen*] does the love of God—not love according to a general conception, but the love of God in Jesus Christ, as attested in Holy Scripture—become for us an event and reality so that we may and must infer in consequence that these are the determinations of the divine being?"

2. "[I]n what determinations does the freedom of God stand—again not a universal idea of freedom but the freedom of God in Jesus Christ—when his love is actualised for us?"

Barth's answers to these two questions take the form of two series of three perfections each. The first question is answered by grace, mercy, and patience, the first members of the three pairs of attributes Barth considers in §30. These three attributes could be called the leading attributes of divine mercy. The second question is answered by holiness, righteousness, and wisdom, the second members of these three pairs. These three attributes emphasize what we might call the freedom-side of God's love. Thus, Barth's presentation interweaves discussion of both (a) the concrete forms or determinations of divine loving itself and (b) the concrete forms or determinations of divine freedom in the context of God's love in act. Barth has given careful thought to ensure that a counterbalancing dialectic of love and freedom is maintained in the very selection and order of the perfections of divine loving. As such, Barth aims to be faithful to the main themes and contours of Christological revelation to which Scripture witnesses. Barth reinforces this point by saying: "Whether these two answers are correct, satisfying, or compelling, and whether our proposal is serviceable, can be seen only from our exposition itself *or from [its] relationship to the biblical witness to revela-*

tion" (352; emphasis added). Clearly, he wishes to stand in an accountable relationship to Scripture on these matters of dogmatic selection and organization, even though it is a basically *indirect* relationship.[118]

This does not mean that there are no direct supports for Barth's selection and arrangement of certain perfections—despite what he says in his comments at the beginning of §30 (352f.). Barth later mentions a series of biblical passages that could be construed as a "direct" basis pattern of selection and arrangement, and thus may constitute an exception to the typically "indirect" character of this relationship. At the beginning of his account of divine patience, Barth says: "In view of certain *specific scriptural passages*, there is a *clear necessity* that after speaking of God's grace and mercy, we should consider the perfection of divine patience as a special perfection of the love and therefore the being of God" (407). In a brief excursus here, Barth cites a series of Old Testament texts (e.g., Exodus 34:6, Joel 2:13, Jonah 4:2, etc.) that lift up these three perfections as a special and almost formulaic set of "distinctive marks of the God revealed and active in Israel."[119]

"The Perfections of Divine Freedom" (§31)

We now turn to a survey of Barth's consideration of the perfections of divine freedom. This is crucial for this book, since it provides the immediate context of the three perfections on which we have chosen to concentrate our attention in the next three chapters: unity, constancy, and eternity. Although we will provide a detailed exposition of those three perfections in these upcoming chapters, we now wish to include brief characterizations of them along with the other three perfections with which they are paired. Here is a summary of the six perfections of divine freedom in the order in which Barth treats them.

- **Unity**: "The word oneness has two meanings, uniqueness, and simplicity. As a statement about God it must in fact mean both" (442). God's uniqueness means that "God alone is God" (442).

---

118. Ultimately, the dogmatician is responsible not to Scripture itself, but to God—the divine "object" to which Scripture witnesses (353). The dogmatic theologian's reverent and rational form of obedience to God, then, requires a "certain degree of systematisation" yet one that is "controlled as far as possible by this object in its self-manifestation." We will see Barth maintains the same methodological commitment in his treatment of the perfections of divine freedom.

119. II/1, 407; cf. I/2, 68.

For God to be simple "signifies that in all He is and He does, He is wholly and undividedly Himself" and "in Himself there is no separation, distance, contradiction, or opposition" (445). "His uniqueness ... is based upon his simplicity."

- **Omnipresence**: This is "the sovereignty in which, as the One He is, existing and acting in the way that corresponds to His essence, He is present to everything else, to everything that is not Himself but is distinct from himself. It is the sovereignty on the basis of which everything that exists cannot exist without Him, but only with Him, possessing its own presence only on the presupposition of His presence" (461). Omnipresence includes both "remoteness" and "proximity." "God's omnipresence, to speak in general terms, is the perfection in which He is present, and in which He, the One, who is distinct from and pre-eminent over everything else, possesses a place, His own place, which is distinct from all other places and also pre-eminent over them all" (468).

- **Constancy**: This perfection means that "the one, omnipotent God remains the One He is" (491). In God "there neither is nor can be ... any deviation, diminution, or addition, nor any degeneration or rejuvenation, any alteration or non-identity, nor discontinuity" (491).

- **Omnipotence**: This is "the perfection in which He is able to do what He wills" (522). Omnipotence includes both God's *de facto* and his *de jure* ability to do what he wills (526). Included in the discussion of omnipotence is God's omniscience, his "omnipotent knowledge," which is "complete in its range" and is "the one unique and all-embracing knowledge" (552).

- **Eternity**: "The being is eternal in whose duration, beginning, succession, and end are not three but one, not separate as a first, second, and third occasion, but one simultaneous occasion as beginning, middle, and end. Eternity is the simultaneity of beginning, middle, and end, and to that extent, it is pure duration. Eternity is God in the sense in which in Himself and in all things God is simultaneous, i.e., beginning and middle as well as end, without separation, distance, or contradiction... Eternity has and is the duration that is lacking to time. It has and is simultaneity" (608).

- **Glory**: This is God's "dignity and right not only to maintain, but to prove and declare, to denote and as it were to make Himself conspicuous and everywhere apparent as the One He is. He does this negatively by distinguishing himself from what He is not, and positively by naming Himself, pointing to Himself, manifesting Himself in various ways. It is further his right to create recognition for himself. . . . To sum up, God's glory is God Himself in the truth and capacity and act in which He makes Himself known as God" (641).

With respect to these perfections of divine freedom, we need to ask the question of selection and order, much as we did in relation to the perfections of loving. The explicit answer that Barth provides to this question is almost identical to what he said with respect to the perfections of divine loving: that "method is arbitrary" in this context. Yet the selection and arrangement of the perfections of freedom are again in some sense indirectly authorized by Scripture and the revelation to which it witnesses.[120] Hence, Barth says that in regard to these questions "we certainly cannot rely on, or appeal to, any direct (or verbal) precept of Holy Scripture or even to the precedent of any other dogmatics" (441). Therefore, the selection and arrangement can only "have the character of an attempt or a suggestion." Here again, one would expect that the selection and arrangement of the divine perfections would remain at most *indirectly* authorized by Scripture or tradition. In fact, this "indirectness" is more obvious here in §31 than it was in §30, where Barth's actual selection and arrangement of the divine perfections showed some direct precedent in Scripture, against his explicit programmatic comments (352f.; see above).

But even now there are important, indirect precedents to Barth's decisions, though this time they are found in tradition rather than in Scripture. This is evident in Barth's choice of unity, constancy, and eternity as the "leading" perfections of divine freedom, for one finds in medieval and Protestant scholasticism a strong emphasis on God's unity (simplicity), constancy (immutability), and eternity (timelessness). In fact, one even finds evidence in such classical treatments for an order-

---

120. Compare the very similar wording and emphasis of Barth's excursus on the selection and arrangement of the perfections of freedom (441f.) with the parallel excursus on the perfection of loving that we discuss above (352f.).

ing of these attributes similar to Barth's; at least, it was common to begin with a treatment of God's unity or simplicity and to treat other attributes (including immutability and eternity) later.[121] That said, the manner in which he expounds upon each of these three perfections, as the next three chapters show, represents a rigorous scripturally-based critique of and alternative to some influential classical traditions. Similarly, there are no direct precedents for Barth's precise selection and creative dialectical arrangement of six perfections of divine freedom.

The Threefold Cord in §30 and §31

We may conclude this subsection with some generalizations about the role of the threefold cord within *CD*, §30 and §31, with an emphasis on comparing Barth's method in the two paragraphs.

We begin with the role of Scripture. Scripture plays an important role in both paragraphs, but in somewhat different ways. In §30, Scripture *directly* authorizes Barth's claims to a much greater degree than he does in other parts of his doctrine of the reality of God. The reason for this is that it is far easier for Barth to appeal to specific scriptural passages to authorize claims about those characteristics of God that are directly expressed in the divine acts of love, for it is with this that Scripture is primarily concerned.

In Barth's account of the perfections of divine freedom in §31, by contrast, his dogmatic claims are only rarely directly authorized by Scripture. The reasons for this have to do with how the claims Barth makes in this context have a more abstract or even "metaphysical" character than his statements about the perfections of divine loving. The discourse found in §31 (largely a mixture of second or third-order discourse) is rather different than the discourse of Scripture (largely

---

121. In his doctrine of the nature of God in the *Summa Theologiae* (vol. 2), Aquinas treats simplicity first (Pt. 1, Q. 3). Then, after dealing with several other questions, he turns to God's unchangeableness (Q. 9) and eternity (Q. 10). Finally, he closes his comments on the nature of God with a treatment of God's oneness, another way of treating God's unity and underlying its importance (Q. 11) See Wolterstorff, "Divine Simplicity," on the theoretical fecundity of simplicity, especially as illustrated in Aquinas. See also Heppe's collection of the comments of various Reformed dogmaticians on the "incommunicable" attributes, which begin with God's simplicity (*Reformed Dogmatics*, 62–68). On the role of these attributes of God in "classical theism" more generally, see Leftow, "God, Concepts of," 98ff.

first-order discourse). Some comments of David Ford about §31 are illuminating in this regard:

> It is under the heading of God's freedom, as understood by Barth, that traditional "general" ideas about God such as transcendence, independence, and infinity arise, and Barth's interpretation of them is perhaps the most severe test of his story-centred method. His solution is what might be called a descriptive metaphysics in support of the overarching story.[122]

If we alter "story-centered method" to "Scripture-centered method" (in order to account for the variety of genres in Scripture that are important to Barth), then this statement is an accurate and insightful estimation of the challenge Barth faces in §31 as well as his solution to it. Ford rightly sees that see that, in contrast to the perfections of freedom, "the perfections of the divine loving lend themselves fairly straightforwardly to being given their content by the story of Jesus Christ" (139).[123] Barth's solution to the challenge of how to relate the revelation attested in Scripture to the perfections of freedom is appropriately described as a kind of "descriptive metaphysics," to which we will return below in our comments on the role of reason.

Tradition also plays somewhat different roles in §30 (love) and §31 (freedom). In §30, Barth interacts with theological tradition somewhat less frequently than in §31. In particular, Barth spends significantly less time critiquing various classical conceptions of God in his treatment of the perfections of divine loving. The main reason is that Barth usually regards the classical tradition's treatment of these attributes of love to be more or less faithful to Scripture, and thus in little need of correction. This stands in contrast to Barth's extensive criticism of certain classical accounts of the perfections of divine freedom, as we will see in chapters 4–6. But these are only differences of emphasis; tradition functions in the same basic ways throughout §§30 and 31 and the rest of Barth's doctrine of God. For example, the ancient Trinitarian and Christological formulations consistently guide and shape Barth's doctrine, while Barth consistently remains allergic to any hint of natural theology.

---

122. Ford, *Barth and God's Story*, 139.

123. Again, however, we would add that Barth is concerned not only to authorize these perfections by means of the Christological "story," but also by the wider witness of Scripture.

The role of reason remains relatively consistent in Barth's doctrine of God, always showing a concern to develop a distinctive theological rationality that is constrained by the particulars of revelation. However, there are some differences of emphasis in §30 and §31. For example, Barth more frequently employs an "exegetical" use of reason in §30 (i.e., the use of reasoning in the context of exegetical excursuses) and a more frequent "constructive" (though not strongly speculative) use in §31. Barth's theological work in §31 can be seen as "descriptive metaphysics" in the following qualified way. It is "*descriptive* metaphysics" because it is an attempt to conceptually redescribe what is found in scripturally-attested revelation, rather than being a *speculative* metaphysics rooted in autonomous rational reflection.[124] Neither is it a rigorously systematic metaphysics. It is "descriptive *metaphysics*," not because it imposes an established philosophical metaphysical system upon Scripture and revelation, but because it offers a view of reality that freely uses and adapts metaphysical concepts and categories (drawn from third-order discourse like that of philosophy) in an effort to describe the revealed reality of God encountered in Scripture.

Despite these slight shifts in the function of Scripture, tradition, and reason between §30 and §31, Barth's overall theological method remains consistent and stable. Scripture retains primacy as the "norming norm" over tradition and reason, tradition retains a two-fold (positive or negative) character, and reason remains consistently hermeneutical and subordinate to Scripture and revelation (whether in its critical or constructive modes). We will need to test these claims in the course of our "close reading" of Barth in the next three chapters.

---

124. The term "descriptive metaphysics" was defined influentially by British philosopher P. F. Strauson (see his 1959 work *Individuals*) as "the actual structure of our thought about the world," and hence an a posteriori endeavor that stands in contrast to "revisionist metaphysics." For further comments pertinent to Barth's "metaphysics" or (moral) "ontology," see Jenson ("Karl Barth, 31ff.), Frei (*Types of Christian Theology*, 45), and Webster (*Barth's Ethics*, 4 and passim).

4

Barth's Doctrine of Divine Unity

In this chapter, we begin the expository analysis that forms the core of this book. In this and the next two chapters, we will examine Barth's treatments of three specific perfections of the divine freedom: unity, constancy, and eternity.

This chapter will unfold in three main parts. First, we will describe Barth's own presentation and critique of classical notions of God's unity, focusing on the concept of divine "simplicity." Second, we will describe Barth's alternative account of divine simplicity. Third, we will examine the particular role that the theological interpretation and use of Scripture plays in Barth's work, both in his critique of classical traditions and in his own constructive alternative to them. The next two chapters on constancy and eternity will follow a similar pattern.[1]

For Barth, God's unity (or "oneness," *Einheit*) has two main senses: uniqueness (*Einzigkeit; singularitas*) and simplicity (*Einfachheit; simplicitas*).[2] In Barth's thinking, these two senses of God's unity mutually interpret each other, each depending on the other for its full meaning. Thus, it is impossible completely to separate his treatment of one from that of the other. However, uniqueness and simplicity are still relatively distinct concepts. We will focus primarily on his presenta-

---

1. In the exposition of Barth in this chapter and in chapters 5 and 6, we will refer to Barth's work by the following abbreviated method: the first page number in parentheses (in the main text or in the footnotes) refers to the English translation in *CD* II/1 and the second to the German original in *KD* II/1.

2. God's unity is the first of what Barth calls the "perfections of the divine Freedom." Barth's division of the term into simplicity and uniqueness has a long history that appears to date as far back as Tertullian (Stead, *Divine Substance*, 182 [citing R. Braun]) and that was likely mediated to Barth through the medieval and Protestant scholastics (see Barth's early use of the distinction in his *Göttingen Dogmatics*, 428–32).

tion of simplicity, because it is more illuminating for understanding his theological method.

Barth's Presentation and Critique of Classical Notions of God's Simplicity

Introduction

Barth's presentation of classical notions of divine unity is inseparable from his critique of them. Thus, Barth's presentation—including his selective citation and description of the classical view—is not a "neutral" account. As such, it may be challenged by alternative construals and interpretations of doctrinal history and of classical theological texts. Yet in keeping with the purpose of this book, we will take Barth's representation of the past at face value without questioning its soundness as an historical account. Rather, we will ask how he evaluates and critiques the theological past and how this relates to his overall theological method.

Before we turn to his treatment of divine unity as simplicity, we should say a few words about Barth treatment of divine unity as uniqueness.[3] Barth regards the main classical theologians (he makes reference, among others, to Origen, Tertullian, Irenaeus, Anselm, Aquinas, and Calvin) as having admirably testified to the uniqueness of God, even when they employed Hellenistic philosophical categories to do so. Thus, although Barth's treatment of divine uniqueness includes negative evaluations of non-Christian religious traditions like Islam and even Judaism,[4] he has virtually nothing negative to say about the Christian

---

3. Despite our focus on simplicity in this chapter, uniqueness is probably even more prominent in Barth's discussion of unity in II/1. David Ford comments, "In the unity of God Barth sees two aspects, uniqueness and simplicity, but as the latter was dealt with in his doctrine of the Trinity he concentrates on the uniqueness" (*Barth and God's Story*, 180). The uniqueness-aspect of God's unity is central to Barth's whole account of God's freedom, as when he speaks of God's freedom under the affirmation that "God is uniquely who He is" (297; 335). God's being unique means that "God alone is God" (442; 498). See also Webster, *Barth's Ethics*, 41ff. on God's uniqueness.

4. In an excursus, Barth offers a pointed critique of Islamic monotheism, as "a good example of the absolutising of 'uniqueness'" (*CD* 448; *KD* 504). Monotheism is an idea that can be "constructed without God," and apart from revelation, as the pagan "religious glorification of the number 'one'" (448f.; 504f.). According to Barth, nothing separates Islam and Christianity "so radically as the different ways in that they appear to say the same thing—that there is only one God" (449; 505). In another excursus, Barth calls the monotheism of Islam the "later caricature" of the "Jewish monotheism" that existed at the time of Jesus (453; 510).

theological tradition at this point. Rather, he employs the statements of traditional Christian writers in his own constructive development of God's unique unity, seeing them as helpful ways of drawing out the scriptural truth that God is unique.

But as we will see, Barth does not believe that such theologians always remained true to their affirmation of divine uniqueness in their accounts of divine simplicity. Barth tends to subsume various traditional treatments of divine simplicity under a certain type in an effort to draw out the main tendencies of the view he wishes to critique. We will call this view the "classical view of simplicity," the "classical approach to simplicity," or just "classical simplicity," recognizing that it may not correspond in every respect to the historical view of any one thinker. Sometimes we will refer to "classical views of simplicity" to indicate something of the plurality of historical views lying behind Barth's critique.[5]

Barth on Classical Simplicity: Departures from a Good Beginning

For Barth, that "God is simple" signifies that "in all He is and does, He is wholly and undividedly Himself" (445; 501). The classical position associates simplicity with God's undividedness, but tends to regard the primary meaning of "simple" as "non-composite."[6] Also, such classical writers are different from Barth in the way in which they construe the relation of the doctrine of simplicity to other parts of the doctrine of God.

To understand Barth's critique of the classical approach to simplicity, we must begin where he begins. The proper starting point for any understanding of God's unity, according to Barth, is the view of unity that emerges from the Trinitarian and Christological doctrines of the ancient church. Barth believes that the early Christian church correctly worked out its understanding of divine simplicity in the context of these doctrines. In his words, "the early battle for a recognition of the simplicity of God was the same as [the battle] for the recognition of the Trinity and of the relation between the divine and human natures in Jesus Christ" (446; 502). Whether or not Barth's comment is accurate as

---

5. See our comments on the "classical" concept of God and "classical theism" in chapter 2.

6. Wolterstorff, "Divine Simplicity," 134.

an historical assessment,[7] clearly he wants to highlight the theological point that the only concept of simplicity he regards as appropriate is one that is closely connected with the Trinitarian and Christological doctrines of the early church. As we saw clearly in chapter 3, Barth regards the Trinitarian God of the creeds as the same as the God who revealed himself in Jesus Christ. Thus, the reason Barth believes the early church "began well" is because it began with the unique God known in revelation.

Yet, in Barth's view, it did not take long for the Church's doctrine of God to go awry. In his words, "the later theology of the Church appears to be *of a purely logical and metaphysical kind*" (446; 502; emphasis added). Here, as is often true of Barth, he speaks in somewhat exaggerated terms to intensify the rhetorical force of the point he is trying to make. The crucial point for Barth is that the Church's doctrine had departed from proper theological method (rooted exclusively in revelation), in exchange for a method that was dominated by philosophical conceptions of God that were not derived from revelation.

Barth's citations of passages from Augustine and Anselm are helpful in identifying what he regards as problematic about their classical approach. A passage from Augustine (that he cites without significant comment) provides Barth's first example of this negative development within the doctrine of God's simplicity. This passage draws out one of the axioms of classical simplicity, namely, that whatever we predicate of God we predicate of God *as a whole*, not as a part of God, because God is simple and is not divided into parts.[8]

> For to [God] it is not one thing to be, and another to live, as though he could be, not living; nor is it to Him one thing to live and another thing to understand, as though He could live, not understanding; nor is it to Him one thing to understand, another thing to be blessed, as though He could understand

---

7. Stead's comments on the Trinitarian context of the early Christian discussions of divine unity seems to confirm Barth's interpretation of history (*Divine Substance*, 180ff.).

8. Wolterstorff describes this claim as the "theistic identity claim," stating that "God has no properties distinct from God's essence" ("Divine Simplicity," 145; cf. 145ff.). For discussion of an early form of this claim in Irenaeus, see Stead, *Divine Substance*, 187ff.

without being blessed. But to Him to live, to understand, to be blessed are *to be*.⁹

Barth then quotes disapprovingly several passages from Anselm on divine simplicity (the same Anselm whom he earlier cited approvingly with respect to God's "uniqueness"). Barth cites the following passage from the *Proslogion*, where, after listing a series of God's attributes, Anselm says:

> How, then, O Lord, are You all these things? Are they your parts, or, instead, is each one of them wholly what You are? . . . Now whatever is composed of parts is not absolutely one but is in a way many and is different from itself and can be divided either actually or conceivably (*intellectu*). But these consequences are foreign to You, than whom nothing better can be thought. Therefore, there are no parts in You, Lord. Instead of being composite You are something so one and so identical with yourself that in no respect are You dissimilar to Yourself. Indeed, You are Unity itself, divisible in no [conceivable] respect (*nullo intellectu*).¹⁰

Following these quotations from Augustine and Anselm, Barth concludes his survey of "classical" understanding of simplicity by commenting on the treatment given it by the Protestant scholastics. He asserts that "the older Protestant orthodoxy, too, usually adopted much the same arguments and explanation when it placed and expounded the simplicity of God first among the divine attributes" (446–47; 502).¹¹ It is important to notice that Barth draws attention to the order in which these Protestant theologians presented the doctrine of God. Simplicity was presented at the head of the doctrine of God before all the other attributes, just as in medieval scholasticism.¹² In light of the Trinitarian

---

9. Augustine *City of God* 8.6 (Schaff translation, 148; emphasis added). Earlier (in II/1, 263), Barth cites more approvingly a similar passage from Augustine's *Confessions* 1.6.10.

10. *Proslogion* 18 (Anselm, *Anselm of Canterbury*, 105f.). For further discussion of this and related passages in Anselm, see Padgett, *Eternity and the Nature of Time*, 46ff.

11. He cites the definition of simplicity given by Lutheran scholastic J. Wolleb as typical: "Simplicity is that by which God is understood as a being that is truly one and free from all composition" (II/1, 447). This English translation is provided by Harry M. Hine of the School of Greek, Latin and Ancient History at the University of St Andrews, Scotland.

12. Protestant orthodoxy appeared to follow Aquinas' account of simplicity (*Summa Theologiae*, 1a.3). Although Barth begins with divine unity in his treatment of perfec-

and Christological doctrines, then, Barth presents the following critique of this classical version of simplicity represented by Augustine, Anselm, and the Protestant scholastics.

> There could be no objection to the logic, metaphysics, and mathematics of these lines of thought if they had been used only to perform the service of explanation—a service which it is quite possible and even up to a point necessary to render in this way. But we cannot read these things in the older writers with unmixed joy. The trouble is that they are put at the head, and not, as we are trying to do here, in their proper turn. They thus give the impression that what is argued and considered is the general idea of an *ens vere unum* and not the God of the doctrine of the Trinity and of Christology—although this is in flat contradiction to the way in which this recognition originally forced itself on the Church. (447; 503)

This passage indicates several things about the nature of Barth's criticism of the classical version of simplicity. First, he is not concerned about the theological use of logic or metaphysics *per se*, but rather that logic and metaphysics had failed to be simply tools "used only to perform the service of explanation." He implies that the logical and metaphysical reflections of theologians like Augustine and Anselm on divine simplicity had become ends in themselves, rather than expounding the revealed nature of the Triune God. The proper hermeneutical *function* or role of the doctrine and its use of reason had been lost. Second, Barth makes a related point about the *placement* of the doctrine. Theologians placed simplicity at the head of the doctrine of God, rather than at some later point. This is problematic because of the false "impression" (*Eindruck*) this order gives, namely, that for much of the doctrine of God one is talking about a general idea of God (i.e., "god") as *ens vere unum* ("a being truly one"), instead of the distinctly Christian God, the Triune God revealed in Christ. When it was placed before rather than after the doctrines of the Trinity and Christology, the doctrine of simplicity failed to function properly as an "explanation" of the only true God. This is an example of how Barth sometimes regards the order and structure of dogmatics as important and accountable to revelation.

---

tions of divine freedom, it follows his treatment of the six perfections of divine freedom (see chapter 3).

This "misplacement" of the doctrine, both in dogmatic order and dogmatic role leads to larger and more serious distortions in the whole doctrine of God's perfections or attributes. Starting with a general or abstract concept of God and God's simplicity "leads to a nominalism or semi-nominalism in the doctrine of the attributes" (447; 503). Barth makes this point at greater length in his general account of divine perfections (II/1, §29). Barth cites Eunomius (the Arian), William Ockham, Gabriel Biel, and (with some hesitation) Schleiermacher as representatives of the "strict nominalist thesis" and John of Damascus, Aquinas, and Calvin as representatives of a partial form of nominalism (327ff.; 368ff.). Barth recognizes the good intentions of the semi-nominalists,[13] but believes that they water down the full reality of the diverse divine perfections that are attested to in Scripture. In virtually all of these cases, an abstract logical view of divine simplicity was responsible for nominalistic tendencies that undercut God's "many and distinct divine perfections" (322; 362).

The multiplicity and unity of the perfections should be understood, not primarily in terms of general rational schemes of logic or metaphysics, but in distinctively Trinitarian terms. Barth does not wish to deny the strong affirmation of God's oneness or simplicity that is present in the passages cited above. He simply wants to resist the kind of philosophical logic that tends to deny that the one God can *also* have many real perfections.

Despite all of the dangers Barth uncovers within the classical doctrine of simplicity, his criticism of the classical tradition concerning simplicity remains relatively moderate in comparison to his criticism of other parts of his doctrine of God.[14] This is because he regards the traditional affirmation of God's simplicity—at least if we define it as God's undividedness—as a necessary and important recognition. The Church rightly has always faithfully resisted tri-theism or any other view that would separate God into parts.[15] Rather than a wholesale

---

13. For example, Barth says: "there is no desire simply to abandon and deny the attributes of God" (328; 369) and "the themes suggested by the Bible were not simply abandoned" (329; 370f.).

14. As compared, for example, with his radical criticism of classical versions of immutability (chapter 5).

15. As we will see in our exposition of Barth's own view of simplicity, Barth's main concern is to ensure that God "remains himself" rather than being a divided and potentially self-contradictory self. There is no "God against God" in Barth (Berkouwer, *Triumph of Grace*, 307f.).

rejection of the doctrine of simplicity, then, Barth aims "to give it a more distinctly biblical and therefore Christian basis than it had in the Early Church, the Middle Ages, and Protestant orthodoxy" (447; 503). In this new methodological orientation, Barth will make much the same affirmations about God's simplicity as the classical treatments of it did, but does so in a manner that restores their proper Trinitarian and Christological context (see the relevant parts of the final section of this chapter, "Reflections on the Role of Scripture in Barth's Account of Simplicity").

Barth's Methodological Critique of the Classical View of Divine Simplicity

Barth's critique of classical simplicity, as we have explained it thus far, involves and presupposes a methodological critique, that we must now examine more closely. In this way, we will gain a deeper appreciation for the reasons that Barth feels an alternative approach is necessary in the doctrine of God's unity and the other divine perfections.

We have seen that Barth retains the language of simplicity but aims to give it "a more distinctly biblical and therefore Christian basis." This intended reconceptualization stands in contrast to all attempts to define God, the Subject, by means of an independently defined predicate of simplicity. The theological methods of many classical theologians from the early church to the post-Reformation scholastics have failed to be true to their understanding of God as absolutely unique. Barth declares, "[T]he assertion of the simplicity of God is not reversible in the sense that it could equally well be said that the simple is God" (449; 505). The irreversibility of the defining relation between God the Subject and God's perfections as predicates is a kind of methodological axiom for Barth: "The relation between subject and predicate is an irreversible one when it is a matter of God's perfections" (448; 504). Barth recites this axiom with respect to virtually every perfection of God[16] in order to ensure that every predicate ascribed to God is uniquely defined by God as its Subject. This axiom is an instance of Barth methodological "particularism," his insistence that theology starts with the particular act

---

16. See Camfield, *Reformation Old and New*, 70. For a helpful discussion of Barth's view of divine love in this respect (in comparison to other theologians), see Hart, *Regarding Karl Barth*, 173–94.

or acts of God's self-revelation rather than with general philosophical ideas of what a divine being must or must not be like.

In the course of his critique of the use of general human ideas of simplicity, Barth makes another point that is important to his polemic against classical concepts of God throughout the doctrine of divine perfections. "It is not true," he says, "that the simple as such ... can be unequivocally ... contrasted as that which is divine with what is not simple but complex" (449; 506). That is, a methodology that simply *contrasts* God with an aspect of creation as its opposite, is just as much a symptom of "natural theology" as to identify God with an aspect of creation.[17] In either case, a preconceived human idea of the nature of "divinity" controls our picture of God, rather than God's own self-revelation.

Two further quotations clarify the methodological aspects of Barth's critique of classical versions of divine simplicity and direct us to an alternative method grounded in God's self-revelation. Classical orthodoxy, Barth says,

> seemed to imagine that the simplicity of God can be attested and presented—more simply than by reference to God himself—by all kinds of speculation on the idea of the uncomposed and indivisible as such and in general. It did not see that the scientific accuracy necessary to present the object requires us absolutely to accept God Himself in His revelation attested in Scripture as the absolutely simple One, the One who is in fact uncomposed and indivisible, and to allow Him to assert Himself as such. (457f.; 515)

This passage manifests several of the basic assumptions and motifs of Barth's theology.[18] Perhaps most importantly, we see the force of Barth's methodological particularism in his reference to "the scientific accuracy necessary to present the object," namely the unique God of Scripture. As we "redescribe God," we "allow Him to assert Himself." In a closely related passage, Barth says,

---

17. On this point, see Gunton (*Becoming and Being*, 1ff.), where he identifies this logic of contrast between God and creation as integral to "classical theism." Similarly, William Placher (drawing from Kathryn Tanner) speaks of a "contrastive" conception of divine transcendence, but does not regard such a view as typical of classical premodern thinkers (*Domestication of Transcendence*, 111ff.).

18. To use George Hunsinger's categories, we see in this passage Barth's particularism, objectivism, and rationalism (*How to Read Karl Barth*).

> If we examine its treatment of the *simplicitas Dei*, we can only be amazed at the way in which orthodox dogmatics entered on and lost itself in logical and mathematical reflections. For the results reached it naturally could not produce *a single scriptural proof*, and yet this was to form the fundamental presupposition of its whole doctrine of God and therefore finally of its whole Christian doctrine. (457; 515)

This passage summarizes many of the key themes of Barth's critique of classical simplicity as we have presented it. It highlights how classical orthodoxy lost itself in reflections on general ideas rather than reflections on the object (or subject matter) of revelation. As such, orthodoxy was occupied with logical and mathematical reflections that were not in the service of genuinely theological explanation. These reflections yielded results for which "it naturally could not produce a single scriptural proof" (*Schriftgrund*).[19] Since the interpretation and use of Scripture is the primary way in which dogmatics comes to understand God as its proper subject matter, Barth wants to restore and develop the scriptural grounds of all traditional doctrines. Furthermore, the lack of scriptural underpinnings in the classical doctrine had particularly disastrous potential in the case of simplicity, since the doctrine was placed at the foundational starting point of the doctrine of God and thus in a position where it could distort the entirety of Christian doctrine. We hasten to add here that Barth did not think that classical simplicity, for the most part, actually exercised such a pernicious influence. "Fortunately," Barth says, the "subsequent progress" of orthodox dogmatics "was generally better than its customary beginning" in the simplicity of God (457; 515). "Later it said everything about God which has to be said if scripture is guide."[20] Barth hopes to develop a view in

---

19. "Scriptural ground" or "basis" would be a better translation, avoiding the "geometric" connotations of "proof" in English.

20. Thus, Barth can follow Protestant scholastics like Polanus (Reformed) and Quenstedt (Lutheran) as his guides in *most* of his doctrine of God (see 426; 479). He continues, "It is a pity that this happy inconsistency did not survive in the teaching of a later period" (457; 515)—and here he presumably refers primarily to the modern Neo-Protestantism of Schleiermacher and his followers. Yet despite the benefits of an older orthodoxy whose "happy inconsistency" resisted reduction to a uniformly non-biblical approach to the doctrine of God, Barth does lay the blame on this orthodoxy for starting the Church off on the wrong foot. For this bad start afforded "a later period the possibility of deducing from this unhappy starting point far more unhappy consequences." Again, we see the link Barth makes between earlier classical errors and modern ones.

which Scripture is the guide also of the doctrine of divine simplicity itself.

Barth's Alternative Doctrine of Divine Simplicity

The "Classical" Aspects of Barth's Doctrine of Divine Simplicity

Despite Barth's critique of the classical view on simplicity (as he understands it), Barth's opening definition of simplicity at first appears to place him very close to the classical treatments of the doctrine. That God is simple, Barth says,

> signifies that in all that He is and does, He is wholly and undividedly Himself. At no time or place is He composed out of what is distinct from Himself. At no time or place, then, is He divided or divisible. (445; 501)

Another passage is even more forceful: "God is simple without the least possibility of either internal or external composition ... He is absolutely simple" (447; 504). These descriptions of God's absolute simplicity manifest a strong continuity with the language and conceptuality used for simplicity by the classical writers. Classical thinkers like Anselm (see the quotation above) and Aquinas defined the concept of simplicity primarily as the absence of all "composition" or parts, whether "internal" or "external" (i.e., "composed out of what is distinct from himself"). Barth clearly picks up and employs this terminology. Yet the primary concept that Barth uses for God's simplicity is not "non-composition" but the concept of God being "undivided" and "indivisible" (445; 501 and throughout). This concept is also closely allied to the classical notions of simplicity, although it appears to offer slightly more logical and semantic flexibility. Barth exploits this flexibility and invests the old classical terminology with new connotations and emphases.

For Barth, God's simplicity includes at least three distinct but related conceptions; in God there is (1) an absence of division, (2) an absence of separation, and (3) an absence of contradiction. This rich concept of simplicity is a concept that is basic to the shape of Barth's overall doctrine of God.[21]

---

21. Terry Cross believes that "there seems to be in Barth's God a primacy of his unity" by which he means primarily God's complete freedom from ontological self-

If God's simplicity is defined in such apparently classical terms, then in what sense does Barth develop the concept of simplicity in a more "biblical and thus Christian" manner than classical orthodoxy does? The main ways in which Barth's view is distinctive lie not so much in his terminology or in his affirmations themselves, but rather in what Barth regards as the proper *conceptual relationships* between simplicity and the other aspects of the doctrine of God. Such conceptual relationships are what give Barth's doctrine its distinctive "non-classical" meaning.

The Relationship Between Simplicity and Other Aspects of the Doctrine of God

The differences between Barth and the classical thinkers on the relationship of simplicity to other doctrines begin with the different judgments about where to place simplicity in dogmatic order. Instead of placing simplicity at the beginning of the doctrine of God, Barth places it *after* the doctrine of the Trinity (I/1) and his initial Christological reflections (I/2). Furthermore, he treats the unity of God *after* his doctrine of the knowledge of God (II/1, §§ 25–27), his general account of God's being and perfections (§§ 28–29), and his account of the perfections of divine loving (§ 31). He also purposefully treats it as the first of the perfections of divine freedom.[22] The placement of the doctrine of simplicity is not arbitrary or insignificant for Barth. Rather the placement of divine simplicity (and unity as a whole) in a particular dogmatic location yields at least the following four important implications.

1. Most obviously, Barth's account of simplicity *presupposes* both that God is Triune and that God has multiple perfections, in virtue of his treating of simplicity (and unity in general) after his accounts of these two doctrines.

2. This results in the distinct hermeneutical or "redescriptive" function of the doctrine of simplicity. Since this function is to *explain*

---

contradiction, despite any apparent contradictions (Cross, "Use of Dialectic in Karl Barth's Doctrine of God," 199; cf. 197).

22. In treating unity (uniqueness and simplicity) first among the perfection of freedom, Barth does follow the classical order to some degree (see chapter 3). This speaks of the foundational role that his revised doctrine of unity, and specifically simplicity, has within his doctrine of divine freedom.

the revealed God,²³ the doctrine of simplicity (as indivisibility or inseparability) must presupposes rather than deny what revelation asserts about God, including God's real internal multiplicity (whether in divine persons, perfections, or actions).

3. Barth's treatment of a given doctrine (e.g., divine simplicity or divine unity as a whole) is shaped significantly by its relation to his treatment of other doctrines.²⁴ In this sense, Barth's dogmatic theology is "systematic."²⁵

4. Despite point 3, complete logical consistency or coherence is neither possible nor proper for theology. Thus the aim to have consistency in the sense of freedom from contradiction must be subordinated to the aim to have theology that is descriptively and hermeneutically adequate in correspondence to the unique God who is its revealed object.²⁶ This results in Barth's dialectical approach in which incomplete, and sometimes apparently contradictory, perspectives of God are juxtaposed. As such, God remains mysterious.

The most significant result of these four points is probably that, according to Barth, simplicity does not and cannot require any weakening of the affirmation that God has a real multiplicity within himself. We must dialectically assert both God's unity on one side and God's diversity on the other. The kinds of diversity in God that have been typically thought to threaten God's absolute simplicity are (1) "the distinctions of the divine persons"²⁷ and (2) "the real wealth of [God's] distinguishable perfections." We will now treat these two kinds of diversity in turn,

---

23. Barth speaks of simplicity as the "*explanation (Erklärung)* of the diversity and unity of His perfections" (447; 503).

24. More tentatively, we could say that a given doctrine (e.g., divine unity) is shaped primarily and uniquely by doctrines treated in the text *before* it (e.g., the Trinity and the general treatment of divine perfections) and secondarily (and in a different way) by those doctrines treated *after* it (e.g., the doctrine of reconciliation).

25. See Gunton, "Salvation," 143. See our discussion of the sense in which Barth's dogmatic method is "systematic" in chapter 2.

26. Hunsinger, *Disruptive Grace*, 191f.

27. It is interesting to note that Barth uses the term "persons" (*Personen*) here (445; 501) instead of his typical preference for the term "modes of being" (*Seinsweisen*).

which will enable us to see how the four points stated tersely above are fleshed out concretely in Barth's own account of simplicity.[28]

The Mysterious Unity of Trinity

By mentioning the "divine persons" early in his exposition of divine unity, Barth makes clear that his doctrine of unity is from the start a doctrine of the Triune God known in Christ. We recall that this recognition, according to Barth, constituted the "good beginning" of the early church in regards to God's simplicity. Barth ensured that this beginning was structurally incorporated into his *CD* by treating the Trinity in Volume I, before his formal doctrine of God and divine perfections in Volume II.[29] This has several implications.

As noted above, one crucial effect of this arrangement is that Barth's concept of simplicity retains a quality of mystery. This is clarified by what Barth said in his consideration of the Trinity in I/1: "The unity of God's oneness-in-threeness and threeness-in oneness" is a unity for which "we have no formula, but which we can know only as the incomprehensible truth of the object itself."[30] The Trinitarian background and character of Barth's concept of simplicity stands in contrast to what we find, for example, in Aquinas, who is representative of classical scholasticism. In the *Summa Theologiae*, Aquinas does not refer to the Trinity in his discussion of God's simplicity and does not treat the doctrine of the Trinity until much later.[31] In contrast, Barth construes God's simplicity itself in Trinitarian terms. Barth takes the approach that Aquinas and other scholastics had for doctrines like the Trinity (i.e., treating it as a revealed mystery) and *applies it to the whole doctrine of God and ultimately all of dogmatics*. For Barth, all doctrines are *equally* revealed doctrines, i.e., given by grace and transcending the corrupted rational

---

28. See the Appendix to this book for further comments about how divine unity is related to diversity, and how this relates to broader structures within Barth's doctrine of God that find parallels in his accounts of divine constancy and eternity.

29. Barth also began to discuss God's simplicity within his treatment of the Trinity in I/1 (Ford, *Barth and God's Story*, 180).

30. I/1, 368. Rather, we can and must state that God is both one and three "only in interpretation of the revelation attested in the Bible and with reference to this object" (I/1, 367).

31. Aquinas treats simplicity in *Summa Theologica* 1a, 3, and the Trinity in *ST* 1a, 27–32.

capacities of natural humanity.³² The revealed Triune God always remains mysterious or "hidden," even in self-revelation. Theology must be dialectical, for no human concept (of unity, love, etc.) can express at once the fullness and richness of what needs to be said of God in correspondence to revelation.³³

The Unity of Diverse Divine Perfections

According to Barth, our understanding of God's many perfections and their unity stands in "an exact parallel" to the Trinity (326; 367). George Hunsinger summarizes well how Barth's carrying the Trinitarian pattern over into the doctrine of perfections distinguishes him from the classical tradition: "Barth separates himself from the venerable theological tradition that regards simplicity as more basic in God than multiplicity." Hunsinger continues, "Traditionally, it has typically been held that because God's simplicity is proper to his being, multiplicity can only be ascribed to his being improperly."³⁴ In contrast to this, Barth wants to say that God is properly both simple and multiple, just as God is properly both one and three in the Trinity.

As noted above, Barth's account of perfections involves a constant effort to resist the "nominalism" and "semi-nominalism" that, he thinks, marked the classical treatments of the divine attributes.³⁵ While clearly affirming God's simplicity, Barth also desires to develop the truth of "the multiplicity, individuality, and diversity of God's perfections."³⁶ Indeed,

---

32. Recent accounts of Aquinas have shown that Aquinas is closer to Barth in this respect (and others) than has traditionally been held either by Thomists or their critics (see especially Rogers, *Thomas Aquinas and Karl Barth*). However, this should not be taken to deny that Aquinas' work displays a much greater tendency than Barth's to treat many doctrines in philosophical terms (as in the "negative theology" dominating his discussion of simplicity), rather than in significant dependence on revelation or Scripture.

33. See I/1, 369; cf. Hunsinger, *Disruptive Grace*, 189–97.

34. Hunsinger, *Disruptive Grace*, 194f. Barth treats these matters in a fascinating excursus (327–30; 368–72). Again, see our general discussion of *CD* §29 in chapter 3.

35. At their best, classical theologians resisted nominalism by asserting that the distinctions between perfections were real or *distinctionae formales* and not merely "mental conveniences or *distinctionae rationis ratiocinatae*" (Hunsinger, *Disruptive Grace*, 196 n. 11). Barth either does not fully recognise this resistance to nominalism within orthodoxy or else he judges their strategies to be unsuccessful.

36. II/1, 330. He does this by means of three propositions, which are stated and developed on 331–35.

he says that one of the proper functions of the doctrine of simplicity is to be the "*explanation* (*Erklärung*) of the diversity and unity of His perfections" (447; 503). Simplicity, then, should explain not only the unity of the perfections, but their *diversity* as well. More generally, Barth does not want to develop a system that excludes or attenuates any part of what one needs to say about God on the basis of revelation. Accordingly, Hunsinger notes that Barth subordinates systematic coherence or consistency to "descriptive adequacy."[37] Thus, it is more important to affirm *that* the God of Scripture (a) has both multiple perfections and (b) is one than it is to affirm *how* (a) and (b) are logically consistent with each other. Barth does not, for example, say that these two propositions are true on different logical levels, nor does he deny that this is the case. Rather, Barth employs a "strategy of dialectical interconnection and juxtaposition,"[38] which moves back and forth between God's unity and the distinctness of the perfections and shows their "perichoretic" interconnection (a relation of "mutual indwelling") with each other. "Both the unity and the distinction describe God's being as a whole, not two separate parts that constitute the whole."[39] The interconnection between both sides of this dialectic, or generally between various doctrines, does go some way to showing their coherence and consistency with each other. But it is not the consistency of a system of logic in which all paradox is eliminated. Rather it is a consistency of method (the disavowal of any ideas of God except those derived from Christological and scriptural revelation) and subject matter (the God revealed in Christ and Scripture) that allows for mystery. Thus, the oneness of God—the oneness that exists between the divine perfections and the three persons of the Trinity—is a mysterious and paradoxical oneness. On the one hand, the diverse perfections or persons are not parts of a whole, but in some sense the whole itself. On the other hand, these multiple forms of the whole somehow do not add up to more than one whole.[40] But as difficult as such things are to grasp, Barth believes

---

37. Hunsinger, *Disruptive Grace*, 191ff. See also Hunsinger, *How to Read Karl Barth*, 281f.

38. Hunsinger, *Disruptive Grace*, 193.

39. Ibid.

40. See Hunsinger (*How to Read Karl Barth*, 58, 107ff.) for his related description of Barth's "Trinitarian pattern" of "dialectical inclusion." In this pattern, "the part is included in the whole and the whole in the part" (58). In our present discussion, simplicity/unity is included within the whole of God's diverse perfections and the whole of God's

they are warranted by revelation, a revelation in which "multiplicity, individuality, and diversity do not stand in any contradiction to unity" (332).

The "Inclusive" and "Personal" Logic of Barth's Approach to Divine Simplicity

We have seen how Barth is more comfortable than the classical writers he cites with affirming that there are real "distinctions" in God's being and actions. Yet he is clear that the internal *distinctions* in God do not involve any real *divisions* in God; there is no true "separation" or "opposition" in God. This can be understood better by reflecting on what we may call the "logic" that Barth employs in his account of simplicity, an aspect of his distinctive use of reason.[41]

Barth's theology is marked by what we could call an "inclusive" rather than "exclusive" logic. The following quotation summarizes well the inclusive dialectical logic that marks Barth's doctrine of divine unity and his doctrine of divine perfections as a whole.

> God's being transcends the contrast of *simplicitas* and *multiplicitas* including and reconciling both. . . . [W]e cannot emphasise either his *simplicitas* or his *multiplicitas* as though the one or the other *in abstracto* were the very being of God, as though the one inevitably excluded the other. We can only accept and interpret God's *simplicitas* and *multiplicitas* in such a way as to imply that they are not mutually exclusive but inclusive, or rather that they are both included in God himself. (II/1, 333)

---

diverse perfections are included within God's simplicity/unity. The term "part" cannot be taken strictly here because it actually refers to the whole and is a "reiteration" or "form" or "mode" of the whole (the persons of the Trinity and the perfections ought not to be called "parts" of God). Hunsinger also points out that in this pattern of dialectical inclusion, each form is not superfluous, but makes a distinctive and irreplaceable contribution to the whole (107).

41. By "logical" and "logic" in this subsection, we refer to the highly informal and implicit patterns of and evaluative criteria that characterise the conceptual relationships in Barth's theology. When we speak of such "logic," we are striving to discern and articulate what conceptual relations and inferences Barth thinks are appropriate and inappropriate and, if possible, why he thinks so. This is related to Barth's (implicit) view of language in general, a view of language that is, among other things, "strongly revisionist" (Hunsinger, *How to Read Karl Barth*, 33), because of the need to revise the ordinary meanings of terms in light of the particularities of revelation.

This passage points to the idea that true correspondence to the reality of God (in which both simplicity and multiplicity are included) requires a revision of the way concepts for God are understood and related to each other. These concepts need to be understood according to a Trinitarian logic of "mutual indwelling." Otherwise, they would inevitably come into conflict with each other and ultimately with the God whom they are meant to describe. When Barth articulates various divine perfections, each perfection has a range of meaning marked by a clear centre that makes it distinct from other perfections, but with "fuzzy" or permeable boundaries between it and the concepts of other divine perfections.[42] For example, mercy (*Barmherzigkeit*) and righteousness (*Gerechtigkeit*) are concepts distinct from each other at their respective "centers" (where they make distinct contributions to our understanding of what God is like), but they tend to converge with each other around their "edges" as aspects of God's love (368–406; 413–57). Accordingly, there is something of mercy in the concept of God's righteousness and something of righteousness in the concept of God's mercy. These perfections exhibit a conceptual inter-penetration made possible by a legitimate kind of conceptual vagueness.

Precise and sharply differentiated concepts have the advantage of clarity, but they also lack the flexibility and conceptual inter-connectedness (a kind of coherence) that are made possible by more vague or ambiguous terms. Barth's theology constitutes an implicit argument for the value of such imprecise language in the description of theological mystery. Barth's resistance to conceiving of dogmatics as a deductive, quasi-geometric system implies this, since one can only have a deductive system if every term in one's system is precisely defined and clearly related to the others.[43] Indeed, Barth believed that when theology

---

42. To say that words or concepts often have "fuzzy boundaries" is virtually commonplace in contemporary semantics and philosophy of (ordinary) language (see Poythress, *Symphonic Theology*, 64–68, 81f.). Barth's approach adds particular theological force and significance to this observation.

43. Such as system would seem to require that one follow Descartes in two respects: (1) one should define theological concepts or judgments as "clear and distinct" ideas and (2) one should apply the laws of logic (e.g., the law of non-contradiction and the law of the excluded middle) to the relations between theological concepts or judgments without exceptions. Barth resists both of these strictures for theology, as is evident in his rejection of H. Scholtz's general requirements for theology to be a "science" (I/1, 4ff.). Gordon Clark (*Karl Barth's Theological Method*) critiques Barth for failing to adhere to such a (Cartesian) geometric-deductive conception of theological rationality.

"deals with revelation as a systematic principle that can be worked out logically and consistently," then such as theology inevitably (and ironically) becomes "inconsistent at some point and necessarily [involves] contradiction."[44]

We could add (and perhaps this is part of what Barth has in mind in some of his anti-systematic statements) that the procedure of precisely defining theological terms can actually *create* unnecessary contradictions between theological concepts. For example, if one defines God's oneness or simplicity precisely in a way that excludes multiplicity then one has a contradiction when one affirms the Trinity or the divine perfections, whereas one could define these terms in more loose and inclusive ways that would not "generate" such a contradiction (even if it does not remove all mystery). Such "contradictions," once generated, can too easily be resolved in favor of a consistent system that clings to only some, but not all, of the truths of revelation—e.g., that God is one but is not really multiple (Trinitarian modalism or semi-nominalism in regard to the perfections).

Barth's dialectical theological method, by contrast, shows attentiveness to the particularities of God's revelation in Scripture and resists facile harmonization of apparent tensions between them. Yet Barth also believes that the diverse aspects of the revealed God are all ontologically interrelated and unified in God. Barth's inclusive logic helps to make that partially epistemologically and linguistically understandable. But an element of paradox and mystery, and thus an appropriate degree of conceptual vagueness, will always be present in the human endeavor of theology. Although humans cannot fully comprehend God's unity and especially *how* it relates to the multiplicity in God, Barth believes the scriptural testimony to God yields the conclusion *that* God is simple, and that scriptural testimony is adequate warrant for him to assert that God is simple.

The nature of Barth's inclusive logic is further illuminated when we stress that it is a "personal" logic.[45] The various aspects of who God is and the nature of God's relation to humanity are best understood when we regard God as a "person," so long as we see that the meaning of "person" here must be decisively determined by God as the unique Subject,

---

44. II/1, 106, cf. 105ff. See also Hunsinger, *How to Read Karl Barth*, 282.

45. See Cole ("Towards a New Metaphysic of the Exodus") for an account of the kind of "personal logic" that seems to underlie much of Barth's work.

rather than ordinary ideas of person-hood or personality.[46] Therefore, the nature of Barth's account of God's simplicity is illuminated by an appropriately-qualified conception of "narrative personal identity" as explored by Paul Ricoeur and others (see our excursus one Barth and Ricoeur in chapter 5). The following quotes from Barth appear to speak of God's simplicity in primarily personal rather than impersonal terms (another difference from the classical views). Barth avers that "in the specific things [God] is and does, He never exists in such a way as to be *apart from* other things that He also is and does" (445; 501). Barth also asserts here that "every distinction of being and working is simply a repetition and corroboration of the one being."[47] These assertions would probably not be sufficient to keep God from being "composite" according to the impersonal and substantialist terms used by Anselm, Aquinas, and other scholastics for God's simplicity. The reason is that the "repetition" (*Wiederholung*) that Barth speaks of is not primarily about strict sameness (Ricoeur's *idem*-identity) but implies a *self*-continuity of the more dynamic kind, like that present in rendering a subject in a narrative (Ricoeur's *ipse*-identity). Such personal self-identity is inclusive of variation and distinction within God's being. For example, Barth emphasizes often in his dogmatics that when God became incarnate, he became human as he was not before, yet he did not become any less God. In light of the mystery of the inclusion of humanity in his simple identity, the "perichoretic" unity of the perfections is easier to comprehend.

These reflections on Barth's logic enable us to expand further on how his theological method differs from classical method. We noted above that the irreversibility of the statement that "God is simple" is, among other things, a clear manifestation of Barth's persistent methodological "particularism"—his constant tendency to ensure that theological claims are rooted in the particular, concrete, and mysterious revelation of God attested in Scripture instead of general ideas not

---

46. For Barth, we recall, if a person is "being in act," then "by the concept of the being of a person, in the strict and proper sense, we can understand *only* the being of God" (271). We also recall Barth's preference for *Seinsweise* ("mode of being" or "way of being") over *Person* to refer to the *hypostases* of the Trinity. See the first section in chapter 3.

47. We recall from the first part of chapter 3 the significance of the concept of such "repetition" (*Wiederholung*) for Barth understanding of the Trinity and also for the divine perfections.

derived from revelation.[48] We may add here that this particularism gains special grounding within Barth's discussion of God's unity. The reason is this: the ultimate basis for Barth's method of particularism is his substantive affirmation that God is absolutely unique. Because God is unique, our methods of knowing and speaking of God must correspond to that uniqueness. Theology therefore must have a distinctive method, for we cannot expect to know a unique God with the methods we apply to other objects of knowledge. This method is one of obedience to God's self-revelation as attested in Scripture.[49] God's uniqueness (one aspect of divine unity) must govern our understanding of God's simplicity (the other aspect of God's unity).[50] The God revealed in Jesus Christ is simple in a way that no created thing is, or could be, simple.

Conclusion: The Significance of Simplicity in Barth's Doctrine of God

We close this section with one final question: what is the significance of God's simplicity for Barth's view of God and ultimately his whole theology? For Barth, simplicity (and unity in general) is what holds together our understanding of God. Without the concept that God is undivided and that no aspect of God is separable from another, he thinks that we might have a God of self-conflict. Simplicity understood in this way is a fundamental feature of Barth's doctrine of God.[51]

---

48. See Hunsinger, *How to Read Karl Barth*, 32–35, for his helpful account of Barth's "particularism." Barth strives to move from the particular to the general rather than from the general to the particular, and to do so in such a way that he never leaves the particular behind when he gets to the general (see II/1, 602). Hunsinger points out that "a specific statement might well be abstract and a general statement might well be concrete" (*How to Read Karl Barth*, 284).

49. God only becomes an object of our knowledge because God chooses to be so in a prior act of self-revelation; that is, God is an object only as a Subject, as the unique Subject of all that is. God's uniqueness is also why Barth prefers the term "perfections" (of God, the only one who is Perfect) to "attributes" (322f.).

50. As we stated at the beginning of the chapter, the two main senses of God's unity are interdependent. As such, simplicity can also be seen at the basis of divine uniqueness, as Barth explicitly states: "His uniqueness too is based on his simplicity" (445; 501). Indeed, Barth stresses that the irreversibility of subject and predicate applies to uniqueness as well. We cannot say "the unique is God," as Barth believes Islam does (448f.; 504f.), for then we would only be absolutising a human conception or ideal.

51. Again, see Cross ("The Use of Dialectic in Karl Barth's Doctrine of God," 199; cf. 197): "there seems to be in Barth's God a primacy of his unity."

From one perspective, Barth speaks of simplicity as the foundation of God's uniqueness, for a God who is divided would no longer be unique, but would be allowing a second or third "god" to arise as a genuine rival (445ff., 500ff.). Thus, Barth can speak of simplicity as "the basis of His uniqueness" (447; 501). In the same context, Barth shows the significance of simplicity for Barth's doctrine of God as a whole. Simplicity is "the explanation of the diversity and unity of His perfections, and finally the criterion for understanding his relation to the creature." The last phrase presumably refers to how God's incomparable simplicity sets God apart from everything in the created order, which strictly speaking cannot be "simple." As we will see in our treatment of the role of Scripture in Barth's account of unity (the third and last section of this chapter), this incommunicable simplicity of God is revealed in God's unparalleled faithfulness and trustworthiness shown in Christ.

Now that we have a good understanding of Barth's view of divine unity and specifically of simplicity, we must ask to what extent his view is biblical. If his view is not fundamentally grounded in the Bible, it would be virtually impossible for him to say that it is nonetheless grounded in the particulars of revelation; for Barth's understanding of revelation is "textually-mediated." Is Barth's distinctive non-classical understanding of simplicity truly a "more biblical" development of the doctrine, in accordance with his stated aim? And if so, in what *way* is it biblical?

Reflections on the Role of Scripture in Barth's Account of Simplicity

We have surveyed the overall landscape of Barth's critique and constructive alternative to classical simplicity. We now focus our attention on a particular feature of that landscape, namely the function the Scripture has in all of it. In all of Barth's treatment of divine unity,[52] he does not undertake an extensive exegesis of a passage of Scripture. However, Scripture comes into play in other important ways.

Barth employs a mixture of direct and indirect ways of grounding doctrine in Scripture in his treatment of divine unity (see our use of the distinction between direct and indirect in chapters 1 and 2). First, Barth

---

52. This treatment is found primarily in CD II/1, 442–61 (our focus above) and secondarily and more diffusely in his general account of divine perfections in 322–50 or in his account of the unity of the Trinity in I/1.

supports his theological claims directly by citing and briefly commenting on collections of biblical texts. Second, he supports his theological claims indirectly by offering descriptions of biblical themes or patterns and without the citation of specific texts. The direct (text) approach and the indirect (theme) approach are inter-related. The two approaches are often interwoven in a way that is difficult to separate. However, sometimes themes are more prominent and at other times the citation of specific texts comes to the fore.

We will reflect on these approaches and their interrelationship in our treatment below. We will treat Barth's construal of two scriptural themes or patterns, divine faithfulness and the Christological construal of the divine identity. In each case, we will begin with Barth's general descriptions of the given theme or pattern and then turn to his handling of specific biblical texts related to the given theme. Once again, we will concentrate on Barth's use of Scripture with respect to the simplicity-aspect of the divine unity rather than on divine uniqueness.

Divine Simplicity as Divine Faithfulness or Trustworthiness

THE BIBLICAL MOTIF OF GOD'S FAITHFULNESS OR TRUSTWORTHINESS

In Barth's theory and practice, the Bible is the normative and authoritative testimony to God's self-revelation as "one" or as "simple."[53] But it is only in the concluding excursus of his treatment of God's unity (457–61) that he explicitly turns to the biblical roots of his understanding of simplicity.[54] That said, Barth regards these biblical roots as undergirding his doctrine of simplicity from the beginning. For it is primarily by means of a "biblical" method that Barth arrives at his conclusions about simplicity.

How, then, does Barth understand the biblical witness regarding simplicity? Barth begins to answer this question with what we could call

---

53. Turning to Scripture is the concrete way that Barth as theologian is able to attend to God's own self-revelation as the basis of his view of simplicity: "*In scripture* the utterly simple is 'simply' God Himself in the actuality [and] the factuality in which He is present as God and deals as God with the creature, with man" (457; 514; emphasis added).

54. However, he had made reference to many biblical texts and themes earlier in regard to God's uniqueness.

a narrative account of God's personal identity.[55] The God of the Bible "is simply the One of whom all prophets and apostles explained that they had heard his voice and had to obey him" (458). God is the Lord, "the Subject of creation, reconciliation, and redemption" (458).[56] Barth then makes the point that this God, though witnessed to in different forms and at different times, is always *the same God*. This same God is characterized by the prophets and apostles as gracious and holy, patient and wise, omnipotent and eternal. Barth says that "He is all this indivisibly, indissolubly, and inflexibly."

Barth employs the biblical motif of God's trustworthiness or faithfulness as the key concept by which he wishes to establish the link between "the testimony of the Bible" and the theological concept of simplicity.[57] Barth assumes that trustworthiness and simplicity are conceptual terms that are at some level commensurable with one another (this is an assumption that we will analyze in a subsection later in this chapter). At this stage, we turn our attention to the nature of the conceptual relationships between trustworthiness and simplicity as Barth describes them.

Barth speaks of at least three distinct conceptual relationships between trustworthiness and simplicity in the course of his discussion in this excursus. First, Barth *equates* simplicity with trustworthiness, or vice versa. For example, he declares that "[God] is trustworthy in his essence ... and this is His simplicity" (459; 516).[58] Second, trustworthiness is *dependent upon* simplicity, or, in other words, simplicity is the *basis of* trustworthiness. "If [God] were divisible, dissoluble, or flexible, He would not be trustworthy" (458; 516).[59] Third, and the apparent "op-

55. Again, see the account of *ipse* identity described by Paul Ricoeur (for more detail, see the excursus on Barth and Ricoeur in chapter 5).

56. See our comments in section one of chapter 3 on Barth's "root of the Trinity" in I/1: "God reveals himself as the Lord."

57. Following Barth's usage, we will use either "trustworthiness" or "faithfulness" below to refer to one rich concept that includes notions of God's "fidelity" or "truthfulness."

58. As is evident in the first part of this quotation, Barth regards God's trustworthiness as a non-negotiable datum of the revelation attested in Scripture. Nearby in the context he writes, "The God of the prophets and apostles is trustworthy" (458; 516).

59. Although Barth does not spell out what he means here, we presume he is reasoning something like this: that without simplicity there could be a division in God, for example, between a part of God that made a promise and another part that was not committed to keeping that promise.

posite" of the last point, simplicity is *dependent upon* trustworthiness; trustworthiness is the *basis of* simplicity. "The faithfulness and truthfulness of God are to be regarded and understood as the real meaning and *basis of* his simplicity" (460; 518; emphasis added).

Barth does not explain how these three conceptual or logical relationships between God's trustworthiness and God's simplicity coherently co-exist with one another. However, our discussion above of Barth's inclusive logic earlier in this chapter should give us pause before we easily assume that these logical relationships are contradictory to one another. Rather, a more proper hermeneutical goal would be to try to interpret them as complementary ways of speaking and to call them contradictory only if this proves impossible. As such, we could say that biblical trustworthiness and doctrinal simplicity are *mutually-dependent*, each being the basis of the other in differing ways. Further, they are united (if not literally equivalent as Barth's language would indicate) in highlighting similar aspects of the same reality, the God of self-revelation. (We will return to these conceptual relations further in the subsection entitled "Reading between the lines" below.)

Regardless of whether this interpretation of the conceptual links between faithfulness and unity correctly portrays Barth's view, it is clear that Barth develops the close tie between simplicity and God's self-identity in ways that touch on the unity of the whole biblical message. He states, "God's simplicity reveals itself and consists in His continual self-confirmation and self-attestation in his speech and action" (460; 518).[60] "This involves" he says, "the repetition and fulfillment of His promise" and "the unity of His promise and His command, of the Gospel and the Law." He goes on to state how God's continual "self-confession" involves "the unity of the election and calling" of Israel and the Church, "the unity of grace and holiness," and the unity of all his perfections. (Barth concludes by pointing out how this divine unity is known especially in Christ, but we will leave that point until the next subsection.) For Barth,

---

60. Note again the fittingness of Ricoeur's concept of self-identity or *ipse*-identity to describe Barth's language, which is, in turn, an attempt to "conceptually describe" (Frei's terms) the biblical language. Barth (and indirectly Ricoeur) is similar to Isaak A. Dorner in that he refers to God as "self-positing" and "self-establishing," language that Dorner wants to distinguish from mere self-sameness (*Einerleiheit*) in God. In this way, Dorner anticipated Barth's critique of a conception of divine simplicity in which God is a "rigid dead substance" that is "motionless in itself" (Dorner, *Divine Immutability*, 136f.). See more on Dorner below and in the concluding section of chapter 5.

then, a major theme of the Bible is that God is faithful and completely simple, rather than self-divided and unreliable. Barth relates this to the unity of the message or witness and overall narrative of the two-testament biblical canon, because Barth regards the undivided God as the one in whom the Bible finds its unity.

Biblical Passages on God's Faithfulness or Trustworthiness

Barth cites a number of biblical passages under the theme or pattern of God's simplicity as trustworthiness and faithfulness (459f.; 517f.). He begins with two passages from Deuteronomy, where God is called the "faithful God" ("*der getreue Gott*"; Deut 7:9) or "God of truth" ("*ein Gott der Treue*"; 32:4; translated "a faithful God" in the NRSV). In Kantian language, Barth states that the affirmation that God is faithful in these passages "may be called an analytical judgement" (459; 517). By this Barth means "a biblical statement [e.g., that God is faithful] in which a biblical concept [e.g., the "general" biblical concept of God] is clarified but not expanded informatively by the addition of further concepts."[61] In both the Old and New Testaments, Barth points out how God is known as faithful by his self-demonstration in word and action within the context of covenant relationship. Accordingly, Barth draws attention to the fuller statement of God's faithfulness given in Deut 7:9: The Lord is one who "keeps covenant and mercy with them that love him and keep his commandments to a thousand generations." Likewise, it is because God has redeemed the psalmist that God is called the "God of faithfulness [*Treue*]" (Ps 32:5). In the New Testament, Paul affirms that "God is faithful" in the context of God being the one who calls the believers into the fellowship of Christ (1 Cor 1:9) and the one who will guard them from evil (1 Thess 3:3). 1 John 1:9 affirms God is faithful to forgive and cleanse the believer from all unrighteousness. By reference

---

61. McGlasson, *Jesus and Judas*, 90 (comments in brackets added). McGlasson describes this as what "Barth usually means by an analytic judgment" (90). Barth's usage of analytic and synthetic, he says, "roughly corresponds to the famous definition ... in the preface to Kant's *Critique of Pure Reason*, but Barth was no doubt aware of the history of the distinction in Protestant orthodoxy." Barth uses the terms more loosely than Kant, as is typical of his use of philosophical terms (see Hendry, "The Transcendental Method"; see also our subsection on "Barth's use of Philosophy in Theology" in chapter 2 above).

to these passages, Barth wishes to offer some direct scriptural grounds for the basic theological judgment that God is faithful.

Barth also draws attention to an illuminating pattern, namely how often Scripture states God's faithfulness in "contrast to men's unfaithfulness" (459; 517). Citing a number of passages that demonstrate this pattern (including Rom 3:3 and 2 Tim 2:13), he notes that the "analytical judgement" that God is faithful and humans unfaithful involves the recognition of the unworthiness of those to whom God has shown his faithfulness. By God's grace, humans can show a measure of faithfulness (Ps 33:4), but they must always remember the truth of Rom 3:4: "God is true, but every man a liar." These passages show that the biblical concept of God's faithfulness or truth is fundamentally a moral category that involves a contrast with human moral corruption.[62]

In Barth's description God's faithfulness and in the passages that he discusses in relation to this theme, we have seen something of the biblical grounding (*Schriftgrund*) that Barth aimed to give to simplicity. Later in this chapter, we will return to this linkage between faithfulness and simplicity. But first we turn to his treatment of another biblical theme or pattern, namely, the Christological and Trinitarian nature of God's unity or simplicity.

A Christological Interpretation of Divine Unity

The Biblical Motif of the Christological Unity of God

We begin with a reminder about the relation of Christology to the Trinity for Barth. Despite frequent references by Barth's critics to his "Christomonism," Barth's Christocentrism—his "Christological concentration"—is a way of being thoroughly Trinitarian. To speak of

---

62. Dorner develops the concepts of God's ethical immutability (parallel to Barth's "constancy") and ethical self-sameness (parallel to Barth's simplicity). He does so with reference to scriptural references to God's "unity" and especially "God's truth and steadfastness" (*Divine Immutability*, 88f.). The similarities between Dorner and Barth are difficult to explain as accidental. The correspondence between the two thinkers is confirmed by their reference to many of the same scriptural passages (Sherman, "Isaak August Dorner on Divine Immutability," has pointed this out with respect to divine immutability or constancy, but not with respect to divine simplicity or unity). Shared references to God's steadfastness, trustworthiness, or faithfulness include virtually all the New Testament passages cited above, namely: Rom 3:3, 1 Cor 3:9, 2 Tim 2:13, and 1 John 3:9 (Dorner, *Divine Immutability*, 89). Again, see the concluding subsection of chapter 5, an excursus on Barth and Dorner.

Christ and his incarnation as the centre of the biblical witness presupposes a Trinitarian understanding of God. Christ reveals not simply himself (his own "way of being"), but the whole Trinity. Thus, for Barth to speak of how the biblical witness to Christ supremely manifests God's unity is a way of saying that Christ manifests the unity of the Trinity—a point that Barth's conception of simplicity is specifically designed to accommodate. We will see the integral relation of Barth's Christocentrism and the doctrine of the Trinity when we observe how he interprets the passages cited below.[63]

We may begin unpacking Barth's Christocentric use of the Bible by considering the last part of the exegetical excursus with which Barth closes his section on God's unity (457–61; 515–18). Barth makes a subtle reference to a Christocentric conception of God's faithfulness and thus simplicity in the following statement. "It is precisely God's faithfulness and truthfulness and therefore His simplicity which in a special way characterize God Himself *as the One who gives Himself* to man to be His God" (459f.; 517; emphasis added). This is reference to God as he reveals himself in Christ. Accordingly, the whole group of passages that follows this statement is Christological passages from the New Testament (see 460; 517f.). We will consider some of these passages below. But before we do that, we must fill out Barth's general description of the biblical motif of the "Christological concentration" of God's revealed unity.

We saw above that Barth speaks of God's faithfulness and simplicity as his "continual self-confirmation" in word and deed, as attested in Scripture. Barth concludes this discussion by saying: "But the name in which this witness to His unity is made is the name of Jesus Christ ... All the lines we mentioned, promise and fulfillment, Gospel and Law, Israel and Church, the love and freedom of God, are not separate, but meet and unite in Christ" (460; 518). Barth is sketching the rudiments of a Christocentric biblical theology, an account of the economy of salvation in which a series of scriptural themes (that have sometimes been deemed "contradictory") are harmoniously inter-related and united in Christ. Barth does not merely wish to argue that the works of God in

---

63. Subtle indications of the relationship between Barth's Christocentrism and his Trinitarian commitment appear throughout his treatment of God's unity, in places besides his treatment of biblical texts. For example, he indicates in one place that God's work in the incarnation presupposes the unity of the Trinity and thus is a work of the whole Godhead, not simply of the Son (460; 518).

the economy of salvation (*ad extra*) are united and that this can be seen in the centre in Jesus Christ. Rather, Barth wants to say that in Christ's works and person there is a perfect manifestation of the eternal unity and simplicity of God *in himself* (*ad intra*). Again, God's acts reveal God's being (see chapter 3).

This "revealed" simplicity of God is known through faith in Jesus Christ.[64] In the very last sentence of his treatment of the perfection of divine unity in II/1, Barth makes the following strong claim. The true and simple faith of the Christian "does not deviate a hair's breath from its committal to the name of Jesus Christ"[65] and this commitment is "the *conditio sine qua non* of a knowledge of the simple God" (461; 518). In this case, where Barth *ends* his dogmatic presentation is actually where, according to his Christocentric particularism, he has *begun* his dogmatic reflections: namely, with the particular biblical testimony to God's action in Jesus Christ, the centre and pinnacle of God's self-revelation. In Barth's theological method, there is a clear distinction between formulations or reflections and the subsequent presentations of such formulations.

Biblical Passages on the Christological Unity of God

When Barth states that the biblical witness to God's unity is "made in the name of Jesus Christ," he adds, "as all the New Testament passages cited above show" (460; 518). Specific biblical passages and the patterns implicit in them are the intended basis of Barth's Christocentric understanding of God's unity. We will highlight Barth's treatment of the passages that best illuminate his Christocentric claim that the faithfulness of Jesus is the faithfulness of God, which Barth here continues to relate closely to God's unity or simplicity. As is often the case in his use

---

64. Barth ends this concluding excursus (and thus his whole treatment of divine unity) with a discussion of faith as the Christian's "simplicity" that corresponds to God's unique simplicity (460f.; 518). Saying that God's simplicity is known by faith is another way in which Barth resists the idea that such simplicity is subject to general rational criteria.

65. By referring to the "*name* of Jesus Christ," Barth is employing a kind of idiomatic expression that has roots in Scripture and that appears frequently in Barth's writings. The sense of the phrase is to place the emphasis on Christ, on the one hand, *as one who is revealed and known* (one whose name we know) and yet, on the other hand, to stress that this name is to be *identified with* the (eternal) person of Christ himself. In CD II/1, see Barth's references to the name of God (59, 273, and 647) and the name of Jesus Christ (153, 249, 373f., 517, and 615).

of Scripture, Barth does not discuss any of these passages in detail, but organizes them into certain arrangement and then quotes them or cites their references, making occasional comments or paraphrases. Barth apparently regards the interpretation of these passages as relatively self-explanatory.

Barth quotes a collection of related passages in the book of Revelation, where Jesus Christ is called "true" (Rev 3:7), "faithful and true" (Rev 19:11), and the "true witness" (Rev 1:5 and 3:14). Picking up on the understanding of Christ as "true witness," Barth offers the following paraphrase of John 3:33: "those who receive the testimony [of Christ] confirm that *God is true*" (460; 517; emphasis added).[66] This brings out Barth's key point that Christ's words and actions reveal the truth or trustworthiness of God. He quotes 1 John 5:20, in which the identification of the faithfulness or truth of Jesus and God is yet more plain: "He has come and hath given us an understanding that we may know him that is true, and we are in him that is true, even his Son Jesus Christ" (460; 517). Jesus Christ "is true" in the sense that he is included in the unique identity of the God who is true. We know that "God is true," Barth says, "because Jesus Christ is "in truth arisen" according to Luke 24:34." If we read between the lines, Barth's reference to this passage in Luke indicates that, for him, the resurrection, as perhaps the supreme revelatory act of God, speaks of the undivided unity that exists between God's promises and his carrying out of those promises, and this unity in turn manifests the unity of God's own personal being. A similar train of thought is evident in Barth's reference to 2 Cor 1:18–20. This is a passage that for him speaks decisively of the Christological unity of the biblical witness, including its apparent tension between law and gospel.[67] Barth says that it is because of Jesus Christ that Paul was able to speak a message that was not "a Yes and No, but a word of truth and therefore a simple word" (460; 517). Barth then quotes the passage, which concludes with Paul's statement: "For all the promises of God in him [Christ] are yea and in him, amen" (2 Cor 1:20). In Christ, there is no division between the God of Israel and the God of the Christian church. Nor is there in Christ any other potential division that might

---

66. See Barth's extensive treatment of Christ as "true Witness" in *CD* IV/3.

67. Here as elsewhere Barth regards the unity of the biblical witness to God's revelation, the unity of God's narrated "history," as a reliable indicator of the unity of God's personal identity.

sever various parts of God's life-giving message. There is one Lord whose gracious promises are all "yes" in Christ.[68]

We conclude our treatment of Barth's Christological use of specific biblical passages by noting Barth's use of a passage that shows the link between Barth's Christocentrism and a Trinitarian reading of Scripture. It occurs in the context of an excursus in which Barth articulates a Christian conception of God's unique oneness in contrast to that of Jewish monotheism.[69]

Barth's treatment of two passages in particular highlights the Christological and Trinitarian aspects of the scriptural testimony to God's unity: 1 Cor 8:6 and 1 Tim 2:5.[70]

> For us there is one God, the Father, from whom are all things and for whom we exist, and one Lord, Jesus Christ, through whom are all things and through whom we exist. (1 Cor 8:6)

> For there is one God; there is also one mediator between God and humankind, Christ Jesus, himself human, who gave himself a ransom for all. (1 Tim 2:5f.)

For Barth, these passages make plain that the knowledge of God's singleness and uniqueness, properly conceived, stands or falls on "Jesus the Messiah, rejected by monotheistic Judaism" (455; 512). Barth highlights the two-fold structure that the two passages share: (1) a confession of the one God, which is followed by (2) a confession of the one Lord or mediator, Jesus Christ. We should not understand either passage, he says, "as if a second unique being is being named alongside the first." In other words, these passages do not postulate a kind of "bi-theism." Rather, the second Christological affirmation, according to "a common usage" found in both passages, merely "emphasizes and interprets what

---

68. See also Barth's allusions to 2 Cor 1:18ff. in the context of his argument denying that the Bible offers contradictory perspectives on the question of natural theology (II/1, 105f.).

69. In a programmatic statement, Barth claims that what primarily distinguishes "these two possibilities" of monotheism "is the resurrection and ascension of Jesus Christ, the outpouring of the Spirit and faith" (454). We also note that for Barth "Jewish monotheism" is not to be equated with the monotheism of the Old Testament, which can be interpreted in "Christian" terms as well, as the witness of the Jewish-Christian writers of New Testament would indicate.

70. Both passages are cited here in the NRSV translation. Barth cites the relevant parts of both verses in Greek (455; 512). These two passages may allude to Deuteronomy 6:4: "Hear O Israel: The Lord our God, the Lord is one."

stands in front of it." "Thus," Barth states, "mention of the One Lord and Mediator simply expresses the fact and extent that God the Father is the unique being," a point not inconsistent with Christ *also* being identified with or included within the identity of "the one unique being."[71] While this identification of God and Christ may be problematic to natural reason, Barth believes it is fundamental to the knowledge of God that comes by faith.

Clearly, Barth here employs a conception of theological exegesis and reasoning that is guided by the ancient Trinitarian church creeds, especially the Nicene Creed.[72] In any case, Barth here assumes a high degree of commensurability between traditional Trinitarian discourse and biblical discourse. As Paul McGlasson says, Barth's exegesis and theology are marked by the "seemingly unquestioned assumption of the mutual fit of biblical language and traditional Christian theological language ... The mutual fit, the mutual addressability ... is the condition for the possibility of the kind of biblical exegesis that Barth does."[73] This is a sub-set of the larger issue of the commensurability of extra-biblical theological discourse and biblical discourse, to which we now turn.

The "Commensurability" of Scriptural and Dogmatic Discourse

An orientation to the problem of commensurability

We conclude this chapter with a consideration of the question of the manner and degree of comparability or commensurability between scriptural and dogmatic discourse in Barth's theology. As we will see, this question touches on the nature of the relationship between Scripture, tradition, and reason in Barth's work.

We begin by defining our terms. Simply put, different things (entities, theories, concepts, or viewpoints) are commensurable if they are capable of being compared with one another and incommensurable if they are not. Since the early 1960's, this terminology has been widely ap-

---

71. For an independent confirmation of this conclusion of theological exegesis, see Bauckham, *God Crucified*, 25–42.

72. That said, Barth does not repeat the tradition slavishly, for he uses his own terms and conceptuality to interpret and apply the tradition.

73. McGlasson, *Jesus and Judas*, 94.

plied to scientific theories and traditions[74] and, more recently, has been applied to philosophical, moral, and theological traditions.[75] How does Barth assess the degree of "semantic distance," the differences in meaning, between (1) biblical discourse (terms, sentences, and texts) and (2) theological discourse (terms, sentences, and texts)?[76]

We have noted above how Barth moves rather easily back and forth between the biblical language of God's faithfulness[77] and the theological language of God's simplicity. Barth sometimes treats faithfulness and simplicity as if they were virtually equivalent and always regards them as easily comparable and "relatable." This feature of Barth's work is objectionable to some readers, who regard Barth as blurring the lines of two incommensurable discourses or conceptualities. In fact Barth's own theoretical comments about the relationship between Scripture and theology might be interpreted so as to bring his practice into question here. Specifically, Barth could be seen as engaging in a form of "eisegesis" (or even "natural theology") in which he reads theological concepts into biblical concepts, e.g., reading simplicity into the biblical affirmation of divine faithfulness.[78] Although we will not definitively

---

74. In the field of Philosophy of Science, Thomas Kuhn and Paul Feyerabend both put forth versions of what is often called the "incommensurability thesis."

75. See especially the works of Alasdair MacIntyre (*Whose Justice? Which Rationality?* and *Three Rival Versions*).

76. Consideration of this question involves a sub-question about the relationship between the terms and concepts of theological tradition and Barth's own theological terms and concepts. If Barth is going "back to the Bible" for his understanding of God, one might ask what hangs on keeping classical theological language of "simplicity." Does Barth place independent value of maintaining traditional language? We can offer a tentative affirmative answer to this question, since Barth tends to treat the tradition as "innocent until proven guilty" and thus worthy of maintaining unless it fails to witness to the revelation of God attested in Scripture.

77. Although Barth treats the biblical motif of God's trustworthiness or faithfulness most extensively in his treatment of divine unity (with specific reference to simplicity), he also speaks of it as an important biblical foundation for the doctrine of God's constancy (see chapter 5) and, perhaps to a lesser extent, God's Eternity (see chapter 6). All three attributes appear to presuppose or imply God's faithful self-identity.

78. Barth might also be seen as reading biblical concepts into theological ones (e.g., reading faithfulness into simplicity or radically redefining simplicity in terms of faithfulness), with the ultimate result that the theological concepts become superfluous repetitions of semantically-equivalent biblical concepts. Consider the following set of critical questions raised by Nicholas Wolterstorff in regards to Barth's account of simplicity.

refute this charge, we will show in the next subsection that Barth can be interpreted as avoiding "eisegesis."

Reading between the lines: an interpretation of Barth on commensurability

In the effort to understand Barth better, we turn again to Paul McGlasson's reflections on the question to the relationship of biblical and theological language in his study of Barth's biblical exegesis.[79] McGlasson observes rather uncontroversially that biblical exegesis stands in "conceptual interdependency" with doctrinal presentation in the *Church Dogmatics*.[80] Accordingly, he correctly points out that the kind of exegesis that Barth does is most commonly an "explication of the text"[81] in the form of "conceptual analysis."[82] In referring to "conceptual analysis" McGlasson draws on Hans Frei, who uses this phrase as a synonym for "conceptual (re-) description."[83] Accordingly, Barth assumes that there are "theological judgments" and concepts in the biblical text that are commensurable with the theological concepts and judgments of dogmatic theology of the past or present.[84]

But what exactly does this "mutual fit" or commensurability involve in Barth's work? In order to escape the abstractions that might result from trying to answer this question in general terms (as Barth

---

If simplicity is grounded in God's trustworthy character, then Barth has to show how simplicity follows from that, or give it up. What hangs on keeping simplicity, and is it really still simplicity? He is probably working with very different intuitions than the Medievals, and his use of traditional terminology conceals that.

These are unpublished comments (handwritten on the author's unpublished paper on the topic of divine simplicity in Aquinas and Barth) made in 1998 by Wolterstorff in private communication with the author. Although he referred to the last sentence as an "uninformed hunch," the questions he raises are instructive.

79. McGlasson, *Jesus and Judas*.

80. Ibid., 80.

81. See ibid., chapter 5 on "The Explication of the Text."

82. Ibid., 81–97 and passim.

83. See Frei, *Types of Christian Theology*; see our related comments on Frei in chapter 2.

84. See McGrath (*Genesis of Doctrine*, 58ff.) on the relationship between the biblical text (especially narrative) and doctrine.

says, *Latet periculum in generalibus!*[85]), we will begin our inquiry by asking a more specific question: "What is the nature of the alleged conceptual commensurability that exists between the biblical concept of divine faithfulness and Barth's doctrinal concept of divine simplicity?" Above we interpreted the conceptual relationship between biblical faithfulness and doctrinal simplicity to involve both *mutual-dependence* and *equivalence of referent and judgment*. Such a relationship implies a real and significant commensurability between biblical discourse and Barth's dogmatic discourse. We must now explain this further.

First, Barth's statements about simplicity and biblical statements about divine faithfulness are *mutually-dependent* on each other. This means that when Barth says that "God is simple" and the Bible says "God is faithful," each of these statements provide the ground or basis for the other in different ways. We may apply George Hunsinger's description to two of the rational procedures that Barth's employs to make sense of this. First, it seems accurate to say that Barth implicitly employs the "procedure of grounding"[86] to ground the biblical statement of fact that "God is faithful" in the transcendental condition of its possibility, namely, that "God is simple." The dogmatic statement "God is simple" provides the necessary and sufficient (ontological) condition for the biblical statement that "God is faithful." More generally, this is an example of the move from faith to understanding, from the first-order biblical faith claim of God's faithfulness to understanding something of its doctrinal ontological grounds. In this way, we could say that Barth regards God's faithfulness as ontologically dependent on God's simplicity (the order of essence or being; *ordo essendi*). Second, Barth also appears to employ the "procedure of deriving"[87] to derive the statement "God is simple" at least partly from the statement "God is faithful." As such, Barth's doctrine of simplicity is hermeneutically-based in the biblical text, not only directly in assertions such as "God is faithful" but also indirectly in its "essential underlying conceptual patterns."[88] We could say that the knowledge of God's simplicity is epistemologically dependent on the prior knowledge of God's faithfulness (the order of knowing or *ordo cognoscendi*).

85. Barth, *CD* II/2, 48f., 51.
86. Hunsinger, *How to Read Karl Barth*, 57f.
87. Ibid., 55ff.
88. Ibid., 56.

With the help of Hunsinger's categories, then, we are able to see at least one coherent way in which it would be possible for doctrinal simplicity and biblical faithfulness to be mutually-dependent on each other in different respects. This, in turn, shows an aspect of the complex view of commensurability or mutual fit of biblical and theological language implied within Barth's doctrine of simplicity.

The second thing that our analysis above showed is that the relationship between biblical faithfulness and doctrinal simplicity in Barth's work involved an *equivalency of referent and judgment*. By this we mean that, when the Bible says that "God is faithful" and Barth says that "God is simple," (a) faithfulness and simplicity are predicates that describe the same God as their subject or referent and (b) the Bible and Barth are making essentially the same judgment about this God, but are using differing conceptual terms.[89] Claim (a) implies that Barth is not speaking about the "God of the philosophers" but the God of the Bible, even when he using philosophical language (perhaps including the concept of simplicity itself) to do so. In Barth's method, this implies that the third-order philosophical language must be transformed so that it can be fittingly applied to the unique God of revelation; i.e., so that the subject has sway over the predicate. Claim (b), if it is true, would imply a very strong sense of commensurability bordering on "identity." This strong commensurability is implied when Barth says that God "is trustworthy . . . and this is His simplicity" (459; 516). It is probably best to interpret Barth as not asserting a direct identity but an "indirect identity" between the two concepts. In this relationship of indirect identity, Barth aims to revise the general concept of simplicity according to the particular biblical concept of faithfulness. If this interpretation is correct, then Barth's view of simplicity means something like this: God remains the same, single person (or subject) in all his diverse ways of being and acting.[90]

In Barth's view, then, theological concepts from one "language-game" can be used to support those in another. For example, the first-order biblical language-game of covenant faithfulness within the economy of salvation can ground the second-order theological reflec-

---

89. See Yeago, "New Testament and Nicene Dogma" and our discussion of his distinction in chapter 2.

90. As we will see in chapter 5, this is very much like the way Barth describes God's constancy.

tion about God's essential simplicity. Both "language-games" refer to the same reality, the God known in Jesus Christ, and thus we could also say that biblical language and doctrinal language are parts (*sub*-language-games) within the same overall language-game of Christian speech, the speech of the Church.[91]

All of these observations go some way towards showing that, while Barth's does present such biblical and doctrinal concepts as commensurable, he does not do so in a naïve or simplistic way.[92] Yet this interpretation does not resolve the question of whether Barth overestimates the commensurability (or consistency) of biblical and doctrinal language or whether this would involve "eisegesis." Is simplicity really presupposed or implied by faithfulness, and is this an appropriate "exegesis" (in the broad sense of "reading out") of the theological judgments of the biblical text? Or does Barth read simplicity into the text, such that the *real* basis of the doctrine is found in extra-biblical "philosophical" judgments about what God must be like in order to be "faithful"? This is a difficult question to resolve, as it involves a whole series of assumptions about what constitutes good and faithful theological interpretation of the Bible. Our tentative response is that Barth's usage of simplicity is sufficiently "transformed" or "revised" by the biblical concept of faithfulness so as to make it legitimate. Barth's version of simplicity does seem to be something that is either presupposed or implied by the Bible when it refers to God's faithfulness. For example, Scripture seems to assume that the God who promises is the same person as the God who keeps the promise; these are not two "parts" of God that are or even could be in conflict with each other. But it is not our concern in this book to evaluate Barth's success, not even his success in following his own stated

---

91. This implies that the line between first-order and second-order discourse is somewhat blurred in Barth's work, or at least that the rules for the transposition from first-order statements and second-order ones are ad hoc, or situation-specific (see Frei, *Types of Christian Theology*, 39f. and our discussion in chapter 2 in the subsection called "Hans Frei on the three levels of discourse and conceptual redescription"). First-order and second-order discourse offer *mutual* justification and warrant to each other; the justification is not simply one-way. This is related to the "weak coherentism" (rather than foundationalism) implicit in the modes of justification in Barth's theological practice (Hunsinger, *How to Read Karl Barth*, 281f.).

92. McGlasson is probably correct to say that "The Bible *can*, in Barth's hands, be more or less immediately used to discriminate against certain traditional theological options" (*Jesus and Judas*, 95; my emphasis). But in the case of simplicity Barth's scriptural mode of critique is better described as mediate or indirect.

methodological principles. Rather, we aim to offer a fair and accurate description and analysis of Barth's Scripture-oriented methodological practice.

5

Barth's Doctrine of Divine Constancy

In this chapter, we take up an expository analysis of Barth's account of divine "constancy" in *CD* II/1. We will defend the view that Barth's rejection of a representative classical view of immutability proceeds primarily from a conviction that it is incompatible with Scripture. Accordingly, Barth's alternative is to develop what he regards as a more biblical account of God's unchangeableness, which he calls divine "constancy."[1]

This chapter, like chapters 4 and 6, is composed of three main parts. In the first part, we will describe Barth's description and critique of the classical view of divine immutability. In the second part, we will explain, in fairly general terms, Barth's response and Barth's alternative to the classical view. In the third part, we will undertake a specific examination of what in our view is the major factor driving Barth's critical response to the classical view, namely, his theological use of Scripture.

Barth's Description and Critique of Classical Versions of Immutability

Barth's Presentation and Critique of Polanus

In an excursus near the beginning of his exposition of the doctrine of constancy (492f; 553f.), Barth cites passages from Polanus and Augustine as representatives of the classical or traditional doctrine of divine immutability. For our purposes, Barth's treatment of Polanus is more instructive.

---

1. Barth treatment of God's constancy is found in *CD* II/1, 491–522 (*KD* II/1, 552–87). As in chapters 4 and 6, we will cite these sources by means of page numbers in in-text parentheses, referring to the English translation first (before the semicolon) and the German second (after the semicolon).

Barth is decidedly critical of Polanus. Barth begins by quoting a number of biblical passages that Polanus and other traditional theologians considered crucial to formulating the doctrine of immutability (Exod 3:14, Num 23:19, Mal 3:6, Ps 102:25f., Jas 1:17, and Heb 6:13ff.). Barth states: "In both substance and terminology we are transported to quite a different world [than that of these biblical passages] when we read Polanus" exposition and demonstration of God's 'immutability'" (492; 553).[2] Here is a translation of the full passage Barth quotes from Polanus.

> God can be moved or changed by no substance existing outside Himself; for in that case He would not be the prime mover and efficient cause of all the good things in nature. He cannot be moved or changed by some internal principle either. In anything that is moved or changed by some internal first cause, it is necessary that there be in that thing something which causes movement and something which is the subject of movement, and accordingly it is composed of different things. In the case of God, however, His absolute simplicity, his immeasurability, and ultimate perfection do not permit us to postulate the combination of different substances. The question therefore does not arise. Consequently, He is entirely immutable.[3]

Despite being a Reformed theologian, Polanus here offers us a typical scholastic, and largely Aristotelian, argument similar to what we might expect from Aquinas. Polanus considers two possible ways in which God might be moved to change, from the outside or from the inside. God cannot be changed from the outside because this would conflict with God being the prime mover of all things in nature. Further, God cannot be changed from the inside because that would imply a

---

2. When Barth speaks of Polanus' world as different in "substance and terminology," the German reads *"nicht nur sprachlich, sondern sachlich"* (*KD*, 553); hence, a more accurate translation might be: "not just linguistically, in its terminology, but in its content." When Barth says this, he refers to a contradiction or perhaps an incommensurability between the biblical world and Polanus' world. To use David Yeago's terms, the difference between the two worlds is not only in "concepts" or "conceptual terms" ("terminology") but in actual "judgments" ("substance") ("The New Testament and Nicene Dogma").

3. Amandus Polanus a Polansdorf, *Syntagma Theologiae Christianae*, 1609, col. 967, as quoted by Barth in *CD* II/1, 492; 553f.). With the exception of slight modifications, this English translation was provided by Prof. Adrian C. Gratwick of the School of Greek, Latin & Ancient History, University of St. Andrews, Scotland.

form of composition in God in which one part is being changed and another is doing the changing. This is ruled out by God's perfect simplicity or absolute, non-composite oneness (see chapter 4). Therefore, God is entirely immutable.

Barth does not engage in a detailed, systematic critique of Polanus' argument. It is enough for Barth, here and later, to concentrate on three related points. Barth shows how Polanus' view departs from what Barth thinks is the biblical view in three ways: (1) origin, (2) method, and (3) content.

1. First, Barth believes the source (*Quelle*)—and here Barth means the ultimate, normative source—of Polanus' view is not Scripture, nor even faithful church tradition. Rather, it is classical Greek philosophy, especially the philosophy of Aristotle—with its assumptions about God as the Unmoved Mover and so forth.[4] With such a starting point, it is not surprising that Polanus ends up with a view of immutability that is not satisfactory. This leads to our next point.[5]

2. Second, Barth discerns in Polanus a dangerous tendency towards what may be called "methodological anti-particularism." Polanus is controlled by general philosophical axioms about what a supreme divinity *must* be like, rather than following what God's concrete actual self-revelation *shows* God to be like. Barth notes that Polanus and other Protestant scholastics use scriptural passages as "proof texts" for their views. But Polanus' proof for divine immutability stands in "a different world" from that of these texts and "does not correspond in the least with the biblical

---

4. Immediately following his quotation of Polanus, Barth asks, "Does this derive from the biblical passage quoted? Is it therefore true of the God who attests Himself in His revelation? (492; 554). Barth goes on to give his answer: "The source [*Quelle*] ... from which Polanus draws is different [from the passages Polanus quoted] and is expressly mentioned. It is his development of the idea of the *ipsum ens,* the *actus simplex et perfectissimus,* the *immensitas,* the *primum principium et primum movens*. By definition this is necessarily *immutabile,* and *immutabile* in this sense, which does not correspond in the least to the biblical passages" (492f., 554).

5. Before his quote from Polanus, Barth offers us a list of biblical quotations from passages that Polanus and other traditional theologians considered crucial to formulating the doctrine of immutability. Barth follows this list with the statement "we are transported to quite a different world" from that of these biblical passages when we turn to Polanus, a world different both in "substance and terminology" (492).

passages" (493; 554). Barth implies, therefore, that the classical model of "proof texting" (arguing from so called *dicta probantia* in Scripture), at least as employed by Polanus, is not sufficient to ensure that Scripture is functioning appropriately as a determinative theological authority.[6]

3. Third, the problems of origin and method in the classical approach of Polanus result in problems with its *content*—problematic claims about who God is and what God is like. Polanus' view of immutability is not adequately scriptural nor Christological, and thus it is "in irreparable conflict with God's freedom, love, and life" (493; 554), which are three features basic to Barth's own biblically-governed, "personal" understanding of God (see chapter 3). If the widespread classical view represented by Polanus is true, than "God is the pure *immobile*" (494; 555). The classical versions of immutability as immobility replace the living God of the Bible with a God who is essentially dead, or, more precisely, with a view in which "death is God" (494; 554). This obviously renders problematic all theological assertions about God rooted in the revelation of the living God.

Further Development of Barth's Critique of Classical Immutability

After the initial critical treatment of the classical view of immutability of Polanus summarized above, Barth continues to delineate what he regards as the problematic tendencies of the classical view of God's immutability. Barth's critique involves both methodological and substantive aspects.

Barth develops his *methodological* critique of classical immutability (as represented by Polanus) as follows. Barth first points out that the divine perfection of God's immutability, like all divine perfections is a predicate that must be determined by God as its subject, rather than

---

6. The reason for this may be that the proof-texting method, which can allow one to take a statement of Scripture out of the context of its message as a whole, does not ensure that one take seriously the Scriptural testimony to God's Christocentric self-revelation. In any case, Barth implies that Polanus is doing "natural theology." The fundamental *method* of his theology is other than "exposition of Holy Scripture," and the fundamental *content* of his theology is other than the self-revelation of God in Christ (Barth and Brunner, *Natural Theology*, 74f.).

vice versa. Barth consistently moves from the particular to the general, from the concrete, Scripturally-attested realities of God's self-revelation in time and space to the more general statements about the character of the Triune God who loves in freedom. One of the most troubling aspects of the classical doctrine of divine immutability is its tendency to move in the opposite direction, from abstract philosophical ideas of what perfect divine immutability must be, to the particular determinations and applications of that immutability. In the end, God and the scriptural language that witnesses to him are interpreted systematically in light of a priori philosophical conceptions rather than vice versa. Barth's method, by contrast, is a posteriori and proceeds from the "bottom up," moving from the concrete particulars known in revelation to general truths about God. Barth does not believe that we can entirely rid ourselves of philosophical presuppositions in our interpretation of Scripture and efforts at doctrinal construction. But he does believe that we can and should consciously subordinate our assumptions to the revelation given in Scripture so that they may be revised accordingly.[7] For Barth, a methodological "generalism" marks much traditional theology, but it is perhaps nowhere more problematic than in the doctrine of immutability, where the material manifestations of a flawed methodology are so devastating.

We turn, then, to Barth's further development of his *substantive* critique of classical immutability. In his striking words, "if the 'immutable' as such is in fact to be God, this is undoubtedly *the most dangerous assumption conceivable* not only for the doctrine of God in particular but for every statement about God" (493; 555; emphasis added). He then indicates some of the reasons why this is so. If the widespread classical view represented by Polanus' is true, than "God is the pure *immobile*" (494; 555).[8] And if that is so, Barth says, "it is quite impossible that there

---

7. See our comments Barth's rule of "subordination" in biblical interpretation in chapter 2.

8. Barth seems to regard *immobile* roughly as the English "immobile" or "inactive." Richard Muller is probably correct in pointing out that this term meant something more like "unmoved" [by an external force or entity] for the classical theologians ("Incarnation, Immutability, and the Case for Classical Theism," 27). Although Barth may have misrepresented the classical thinkers somewhat on this terminological point re *immobile*, this does not undermine his overall critique of them. Barth recognizes that classical views of immutability speak of God as "acting" or "moving" in some sense, but critiques the way in which they construe this.

should be any relationship between Himself and a reality distinct from Himself—or at any rate a relationship . . . that includes God's concern for this other reality." This problem in the classical view Barth is critiquing is one that he refers to under the rubric of a "dualistic" understanding of the relationship between God and creation (see below). The classical version of immutability renders problematic God's real, personal[9] relationship with creation. If immutability does allow for any relationship between God and creation at all, it would be at the most an impersonal relation of "pure mutual negativity," of mutual opposition.[10] Barth continues, "This being the case, it is only *in the most highly figurative way* . . . that we can speak of God as the Creator and Lord of the world, or the work of reconciliation and revelation as His real work." Classical versions of immutability as immobility replace the living God of the Bible with a God who is essentially dead. Indeed, classical immutability, by a grave reversal of subject and predicate, in effect says that "death is God."

Thus, such traditional or classical understandings of God as immutable come into conflict with basic affirmations about God that we must make on the basis of the Christocentric revelation that is found and attested in Scripture. For Barth, the God witnessed to in Scripture is, by definition, the only legitimate God of the Christian church and of Christian theology.[11]

Barth thinks that other theologians sometimes did relatively better than Polanus in their treatments of the nature of God's immutabil-

---

9. Although Barth does not use the adjective "personal" here, it expresses the concrete content of what Barth appears to have in mind in speaking of the relationship between God and the world.

10. This is exactly what one would expect if God is defined purely in contrast and opposition to creation, as is the case in the standard classical views of God (see Gunton, *Becoming and Being*, 2, 190, and elsewhere). We note that Barth does not say that classical immutability rules out relationship with God entirely, but only that it wrongly delimits and characterizes the nature of that relationship. This runs *contra* what Muller's selective quotation and exposition of Barth on this point would suggest ("Incarnation, Immutability, and the Case for Classical Theism," 26).

11. Barth supplements this primary argument from the incompatibility of classical immutability with Scripture with historical arguments about the deleterious effects of classical immutability. In the end, Schleiermacher's anthropocentrism and even modern atheism are laid at the door of classical immutability (494; 555f.). Despite its occasional attempts to make contact with Scripture, the classical doctrine of divine immutability represents a historical trajectory of unbelief running from pagan Greece to modern atheism.

ity, as is evident in Barth's more positive treatment of a passage from Augustine that Barth regards as "much nearer to the facts" (493; 555). But on the whole, Barth finds little in the theologians who have gone before him that is worthy of following on the matter of divine immutability. With the exception of the German nineteenth century thinker Isaac August Dorner (see our comments in the excursus at the end of this chapter), Barth must chart his own way forward on this matter. As we look Barth's proposed view, we will encounter further dimensions of Barth's Scripture-based critique of the classical view of immutability.

Barth's Development of an Alternative to the Classical View

Barth's Basic View of Constancy Summarized

Barth develops an alternative to immutability (*Unveränderlichkeit*), and this is what he calls God's "constancy" (*Beständigkeit*).[12] Barth believes that the term "constancy" describes reality of God found in Scripture far better than the "suspiciously negative" term "immutability" (495; 557).[13] How does Barth understand God's constancy? Several short descriptions serve as an initial answer to this question. Constancy is the divine perfection by which "God remains the one He is" (491) and "does not cease to be himself" (491; 553).[14] Constancy also means that God lives

---

12. F. W. Camfield translates *Beständigkeit* as "permanence" in his fine summary of Barth's treatment of this divine perfection (*Reformation Old and New*, 61ff.). "Permanence" is a possible translation, but it more naturally translates the term *Beharrlichkeit*. We will use "constancy" as the translation of *Beständigkeit*, following the translators of *CD* II/1. We note that in 1924/5, Barth was happy to use the term *Unveränderlichkeit* consistently in *Unterricht in der christlichen Religion* (78, 165; in the English Translation published under the title *The Göttingen Dogmatics* [*GD*], the relevant pages are 375 and 439). Evidently, Barth's further reflections over the next twelve years or so led him to see the value of adopting the new term *Beständigkeit* for God in *CD* (although he continues to use *Unveränderlichkeit* in a revised sense throughout his treatment of "constancy").

13. Barth avoids using "negative terms" for God's perfections in all twelve of the perfections of God that he treats in II/1, VI. We may speculate that this is one reason why Barth did not use "immutability" as his primary designation for the perfection of constancy. In any case, while Barth maintains the traditional terms "simplicity" and "eternity," he changes their meaning significantly—arguably as radically as the change in meaning involved in the shift from "immutability" to "constancy."

14. We note the similarity of this formulation to the definition of immutability given by the Reformed Scholastic Heidanus: immutability as that "by which God is

"in eternal self-repetition and self-affirmation [*in ewiger Wiederholung and Bestätigung seiner selbst*]" (492; 553). Or, in a revision of the meaning of "immutability," Barth declares: "This living God in His self-affirmation [*Selbstbehauptung*] is the immutable" (495; 556). Barth's entire exposition of God's constancy unfolds the meaning of these definitions or descriptions.

Barth's claim that "God remains the one that he is" stands in a felicitous relationship with the other important affirmations that we must make on the basis of Scripture about God's life, love, or freedom. It expresses the "immutable vitality" in which God loves in freedom. As one who constantly loves, God's basic character remains stable both in himself and in relation to the world. Yet, as a God who loves *in freedom*—as one who is constantly and uniquely free—God is free to express his constant love in a variety of changing and often-surprising ways. Accordingly, the constancy of the living God who loves in freedom is a constancy that is "elastic" enough to allow God to be marked by a kind of "holy mutability" [*heilege Veränderlichkeit*] (496; 557).[15] In keeping with his affirmation of divine simplicity (see chapter 4) Barth does not affirm that God is self-contradictory—i.e., that God is immutable and mutable *in the same respect*. Rather, God is self-constant in his personal being (his fundamental character and purpose) yet also mutable with respect to "attitudes and actions" (498; 560)—a distinction to which we will return in what follows.

God is thus "immutable" in the sense that He "remains himself" and that "at no place or time can He or will He turn against Himself or contradict Himself" (494f.; 556). This immutability is "the constancy of His knowing, willing, and acting and therefore of His person" (495; 557; see chapter 3 on Barth's view of God as a person). This immutability is a positive feature of God's being, rather than implying "the death of his life." As we will see, the divine constancy that Barth wishes to speak of can be fittingly described under the rubric of God's personal self-

---

necessarily that which He is and as He is" (Heppe, *Reformed Dogmatics*, 68). Barth cites this definition in his brief account of immutability in his *GD* (*Göttingen Dogmatics*, 165).

15. For comments on how the relationship between divine constancy and (divine) mutability fit into a larger structural pattern in Barth's doctrine of God, see the Appendix to this book.

identity.[16] This is the kind of constancy that he believes is present in Scripture's testimony to God.

In keeping with his methodological particularism, Barth does not let a general concept of personhood rule improperly over the particular, concrete realities of God's self-revelation. This point is clarified further by a closer look at how Barth regards the relationship between God and creation, a relationship in which God is both free and loving.

God's Constancy and the God-World Relation

Barth is concerned to forge a biblically-grounded answer to the question of God's relation to the world that avoids either of two errors. These are the speculative metaphysical alternatives Barth calls "monism" and "dualism" (see the excursus on 500–502; 562–65).

On the one hand, Barth wants to avoid all kinds of monism (*monistiche Spekulation*), either (1) in the form of one God who swallows up the world or (2) in the form of one world that swallows up God. In this view God takes up the world's mutability and change and suffering into his very essence (500; 562).[17] An abstract conception of God's metaphysical mutability and passibility is asserted in a manner that threatens any genuine sense of divine transcendence.[18] Monism thus undermines the truth that God loves *in freedom* over the world.

On the other hand, Barth wants to avoid all forms of dualism (*dualistiche Spekulation*)—a view in which an abstract concept of immutability is straightforwardly ascribed to the Creator and all mutability, in

---

16. See the excursus on "Barth and Ricoeur" later in this chapter as well as Hunsinger, *How to Read Karl Barth*, on Barth's use of the motif of "personalism" and Cole, "Toward a New Metaphysic of the Exodus," for an account of "personal" metaphysics and reasoning that is comparable to what is implicit in Barth. In a limited sense, Barth's view includes "personal" or "ethical immutability," to use the terminology of Dorner (see the excursus on Barth and Dorner at the end of this chapter).

17. Barth's understanding of monism, we note, would likely include contemporary advocates of "panentheism," such as most process theologians. In his earlier work, *Göttingen Dogmatics*, Barth identified "panentheism" as an indulgent term for "a spiritualistic pantheism" (430).

18. Unlike modern philosophers like Hegel and process theologians like Charles Hartshorne, Barth definitely does not adopt an abstract divine *mutability* as the comprehensive alternative to classical immutability. To affirm this simple opposite of immutability, would be one more example of letting a general metaphysical concept rule improperly over the particular, concrete realities of God's self-revelation.

stark contrast, is ascribed to the creature (501f.; 563f.).[19] Classical views of immutability—such as those of Polanus and, to a lesser extent, of Augustine—tend to fall into such dualism. A key problem with dualism for Barth, as we have seen above, is that it denies the full reality of the concrete (i.e., Christologically-grounded and determined) personal relationship of God and the creature. Dualism undermines the truth that God *loves* in freedom.

For Barth, monism and dualism alike "arise from a failure to see that the world is *freely posited by the divine love*" (502; 564; emphasis added). Against monism, God is free in that God is under no obligation to create the world, nor does God change fundamentally in virtue of the act of creating the world. Accordingly, there is a unity and consistency in all of God's acts in the world that is driven by God's own will rather than being captive to the alterations of the created order (see 502ff.; 565ff.). Yet, against dualism, God also stands in a "real history in and with the world created by Him" (502; 565).[20] God stands in a real loving relation to creation in this history—a history in which he is free to alter his actions and attitudes in ways that conform and correspond to, and even respond to, the free acts of his creatures (cf. 496; 557 and 499; 561). Yet as the One who is constantly a free Subject, "He himself does not alter in the alteration of His attitudes and actions" (498; 560).[21]

Now that we have seen how Barth avoids the dangers of monism and dualism, we may unfold more fully Barth's own positive view of the God-world relation. Barth consistently claims that in whatever way God might be said to change in relation to the changing world, this does not change "God himself" or the "being of God." The function of phrases like "God himself," "He himself," or "the one He is" or "the Being of God" are clarified when we recall that, for Barth, "the being of God is in Act" (see our discussion of *CD* §28 in chapter 3). God is the ultimate

---

19. This is an example of the "contrastive" or "oppositional" logic that infects the classical view (Gunton, *Becoming and Being*, 2ff., etc.). To define God in terms of a simple contrast with creation still fails to define God on *his own* terms.

20. For an exposition Barth's view of God's "life" and "history," see T. F. Torrance, *Christian Doctrine of God*, 240ff. (cf. Jüngel, *Doctrine of the Trinity*).

21. This point occurs in the context of an excursus in which Barth does theological exegesis, much of it on biblical language about divine "repentance." In fact, Barth places a parenthetical reference to Psalm 102:26f. at the end of the statement that we have cited above. For further discussion, see the section below on Barth's use of Scripture in his doctrine of constancy.

Subject or Person, in whom there is no separation between his being and his act.

God's central self-determining act is *the act* of God in Jesus Christ, and this act demonstrates *the* attitude or basic "disposition" of God towards the created world. Therefore, it is in light of this *constant* attitude and this *constant* act that we are to understand God's alterations in individual "attitudes and actions" [*Gesinnungen und Taten*]. When seen in this light, in fact, we will see that the alternations may be a *necessary* expression of God's constancy. As Eberhard Jüngel says, "God's being remains a being-in-act only in the constantly new acts of God's self-affirmation."[22] God remains who he is even in the realm of historical becoming. God does so only *by ever new acts by which he corresponds to himself*—i.e., corresponds to his stable character or to one who he has determined himself to be in Jesus Christ. Therefore, the central act of God in Jesus Christ and its relationship to God's derivative acts governs and gives content to Barth's claim that God "has a real history in and with the world created by him" (502; 565)—a point that Barth goes on to explicate (513ff.; 576ff.). We will turn to the nature of the "Christological concentration" evident in his doctrine of constancy in the next subsection below.

Before we do so, we need to mention an important feature of Barth's constructive view of the God-world relation. This feature is God's gracious response to sin through the special history of salvation. Given the reality of the fall, we cannot conceive of God's relationship to the world simply in terms of a general understanding of God as Creator and the world as created. Therefore, Barth does not rest content with his own statements that "God has a real history in and with the world created by Him" and that "God is the real subject of this history" (502; 565). He must be more concrete and particular. God's creation is not merely "creaturely," but is infected with sin and evil. God's relates to the world not merely as its Creator, but as one who responds to its fallen condition. God is not only the world's Creator (*CD* III) but also the Savior of the world, that is, its Reconciler (*CD* IV) and Redeemer (what would have been *CD* V, had Barth finished it). In Barth's view, God is constantly *both* (a) Creator and (b) Reconciler or Redeemer, and there is no conflict between the two (see 515; 579). Indeed, as Barth says several times in his treatment of constancy (and in the later volumes

---

22. Jüngel, *Doctrine of the Trinity*, 88; cf. 95 and passim.

of *CD*), we only understand God's work as Creator adequately when we understand it *through* and *in relation to* God's work as Reconciler.[23] This is an expression of Barth's "Christological particularism"—his voluntary submission to the rule that one should always move from the particular reconciling acts of God (especially the act of God in Christ) to the general (in this case, the "general work" of God in creating and preserving the world).[24] This is very clear in Barth's treatment of takes place in God's special work in "salvation history," a work that has Jesus Christ as its presupposition, center, and fulfillment (see below).

Divine Constancy and Christology

All that we have said so far about Barth's understanding of God's constancy can be definitively summarized and clarified by turning concretely to Jesus Christ. In accordance with Barth's usual pattern in his accounts of the perfections of God, Barth closes his discussion of divine constancy by turning to the special significance of Jesus Christ, in whom we find God's supreme self-revelation (512–22; 576–87).[25] "In the investigation of the constant will and being of God we cannot go behind Jesus Christ" (513; 577). Barth opposes any theology (like that of Polanus) insofar as it fails to speak of God's constancy or immutability in a way that is decisively determined by the scripturally-attested revelation of God in Christ. Barth intends his view of constancy to be thoroughly Christocentric.

---

23. As we have noted before, the full justification (including the scriptural grounding) of the points that Barth makes here in II/1—especially about matters such a creation and reconciliation—will be found in the later volumes of *CD*.

24. Speaking of the particular Christological event in which the biblical language about God's will gains its unity, Barth says: "We must deduce from its particularity what is always involved in the general relation between God and the world as determined and ordered by the divine will" (521; 586). Barth can indicate this methodological rule in a simple phrase: "because in particular, in general too" (513); "weil im Besonderen, darum auch im Allgemeinen" (577). See the helpful account of Tanner ("Creation and Providence") on the complex relationship between the general truths of creation and providence to the particular truths of reconciliation.

25. "Here too, then, we must speak finally and supremely about Him—not only as the Last, but as both the First and the Last—if we are to speak correctly about the confirmation and manifestation of God's immutable vitality" (512; 576). Although this Christological discussion typically comes last in Barth's order of presentation, there is a sense in which it is "the First" in the sense of being methodologically prior to the rest of his discussion.

What, then, does Jesus Christ reveal to us about God's constancy? The short answer is that Jesus Christ shows that God is one who constantly *loves in freedom*. How does God perform this ongoing act? In Jesus Christ, God "has become a creature," a human being, and this is the basis of God's constant purpose of obtaining reconciling fellowship with the creature (514; 578). In Christ, we see the inter-personal content of God's relationship with creation: "God has befriended and continually befriends fallen creation" (515; 579). God's gracious election of and faithful covenant love for a world that rejects him is the concrete content of God's constancy.[26]

Barth is sensitive to the fact that the striking language of God becoming a creature could be taken to imply that God has changed. At least according to "classical" assumptions, this would raise a serious problem for God's constancy (515f.; 579f.). If God has changed, then perhaps God has become less than divine. But, in agreement with the "older theology," Barth denies that God, or God's being, changes in the incarnation.

Such a denial begs for further explanation in the light of Barth's strong critique of classical views of immutability. Barth offers two main reasons for the claim that God himself (in his divine being) does not change. The first is drawn significantly from traditional Christology and the second from his own constructive theological interpretation of Scripture.

First, Barth follows a line of thought present in traditional Chalcedonian Christology.[27] In this line of thought, God, in the second person of the Trinity, did not *change into* a human creature, but "assumed"—took upon himself—a human nature. Barth cites a passage from Polanus in support of the Word's assumption of a human nature, which, like the divine nature of the Word, was "not abrogated

---

26. Bruce McCormack stresses the significance of Barth's Christological doctrine of gracious election (cf. II/2) for Barth's doctrine of God in II/1 (McCormack "Grace and Being" and *Karl Barth's Critically Realistic Dialectic Theology*, 458–63; cf. Jüngel, *Doctrine of the Trinity*, 68–83).

27. With McCormack, we observe that Barth is marked by "a highly actualistic, a posterioi Chalcedonianism" (*Karl Barth's Critically Realistic Dialectic Theology*, 454). This means that Barth places traditional Chalcedonian terminology and forms of thought into a non-traditional interpretative framework. McCormack has since questioned whether it is appropriate to call Barth's non-substantialist Christology "Chalcedonian" at all ("Barths Grundsätzlicher Chalcedonismus"?).

or destroyed" by this assumption into unity with the divine Word (515; 580). In other words, God freely unites himself to created humanity by assuming it, and, as such, the divine nature does not change. Thus, Barth qualifies the statement "God Himself has become a creature" with the following paraphrase: "that is to say, He became *one with* the creature, with man" (514). In this respect, Barth is following traditional Chalcedonian Christology.

However, from other aspects of Barth's argument, we realize that Barth is not concerned to deny *entirely* that the incarnation expresses change in God. Rather, Barth denies "any alteration in the divine being" in the *specific sense* of denying "any declension of God from Himself" (515).[28] God does not become any less divine.[29]

Second, Barth goes a step beyond such classical Christology through his own creative Christological reading of Scripture. Barth asserts not only that God's being does not fundamentally change in the incarnation, but also that God's being is revealed in the incarnation in all its fullness and perfection (515; 580). This is the case even—or rather especially—in the humiliation, suffering, and death of Christ. On the

---

28. In other ways, Barth affirms God's "alteration," at least in what he calls God's "attitudes and actions." Barth even goes as far as to say that in being "the King of the ages" (1 Tim 1:17), God "partakes in [the] alteration" of the ages he rules over "so that there is something corresponding to that alteration *in His own essence*" (496; 557). Accordingly, in a more directly Christological passage later in the dogmatics, Barth distinguishes between (a) the legitimate ascription to God of a "determination of divine essence" that comes from the hypostatic union and (b) an illegitimate ascription of "alteration" of the divine nature through this union (IV/2, 84). The determination of the essence is real, such that Barth can speak of the "profoundly unchristian conception of a God whose Godhead is supposed not to be affected at all by its union with humanity" (85). But Barth's denies that this constitutes any alteration of the divine nature of the Son, presumably because God, at some level, is has determined himself to become incarnate from eternity (see McCormack "Grace and Being" and "Barths Grundsätzlicher Chalcedonismus"?). Instead, he says, what is needed is to "think of the Godhead of God in biblical rather than pagan terms," that is, in "a kind of immutability that does not prevent Him from humbling Himself and therefore doing what He willed to do and actually did do in Jesus Christ" (85). Given his extensive use of the Chalcedonian definition and other ecumenical formulations—formulations that include the use of extra-biblical terms like "being," "nature," and "essence"—Barth is clearly thinking primarily of biblical versus pagan "judgments" rather than "concepts" or "conceptual terms" (see Yeago, "New Testament and Nicene Dogma").

29. Barth avoids "kenotic" understandings of the incarnation such as those of the 19th century German theologians Thomasius or Gess. Dorner also took a strongly anti-kenotic line in his Christology (*Divine Immutability*, 5–9 and 49–81; see the concluding subsection of this chapter on Barth and Dorner).

basis of his interpretation of Philippians 2 (see below), Barth believes that God's self-humiliation in the death of Jesus on the cross literally shows us what the constant God is like. As Eberhard Jüngel puts it, "God's being is in becoming." That is, God freely chooses for his eternal constant being to be "ontologically localised" in the changing, historical world of becoming—specifically, in the person and work of Jesus Christ.[30] Because God's being is constantly and eternally free and self-determining, God is free to become what he is not (a human creature) without ceasing to be who he is.

Traditional or classical Christology, especially the basis of its presuppositions of divine immutability and impassibility, tended to see the humiliation and passion of Jesus Christ as demonstrating or revealing the *humanity* of Christ (in the stage or mode of *humiliation*), but as saying little about the nature or determinations of his divinity. Barth however, wants to speak plainly of the real humiliation and self-offering *of God*, albeit in a form of self-concealment (again, see his treatment of Phil 2:5ff. below). This is closely related to God's eternal decision to be the God who elects Jesus Christ and all humanity in him. This Christological election and divine self-determination are clearly not arbitrary decisions unrelated to God's eternal being. Rather, God's constancy is about God's being faithful to his self-determining election and act of self-revelation in Jesus Christ; and this act is God's eternal being and will in action. So God does not change when he humbles himself in Christ's suffering; rather, God is *eternally* the one who determines himself to do this.[31] Christ thus reveals clearly what it means to say God is constant, that he has remained and will always remain Himself.[32]

---

30. Jüngel, *Doctrine of the Trinity*, especially viif.

31. This paragraph raises a number of questions about the precise relation of the eternal Christological determination of God in election and the nature of God's constancy. Among the most important is whether the election and incarnation ought to be regarded as an "expressing" or as "constituting" God's eternal being, or perhaps both. See Jüngel, *Doctrine of the Trinity*, for an interpretation of Barth's doctrine of God that appears to see both elements as more-or-less equal importance; cf. McCormack ("Grace and Being") for an interpretation that stresses the "constituting" option. While we will not resolve this question, we will return to issues related to it occasionally below.

32. For an excellent statement of Barth's thinking regarding the relationship between God's constancy and the incarnation see F. W. Camfield, *Reformation Old and New*, 62f.

Excursus: Barth and Ricoeur

The nature of Barth's dogmatic theology resists a final resolution of certain kinds of questions, such as the metaphysical or ontological questions that arise in the effort to clarify the nature of God's constancy.[33] That said, in this section we will address some of those philosophical issues. We will do so by turning in this excursus to the work of the contemporary French philosopher Paul Ricoeur in an effort to shed light on Barth's view of divine constancy.

Although Ricoeur is known best for his work in hermeneutical theory, he has written a significant book on the question of personal identity entitled *Soi-même comme une autre*, which in English is published as *Oneself as Another* (1992).[34] In this work, Ricoeur develops his constructive account of human personal identity under the rubric of "narrative identity."[35] Although Ricoeur's conceptions are concerned with human identity, we will inquire as to how they may be applied to divine identity, so long as the appropriate qualifications are made.[36] Our use of Ricoeur will be in keeping with Barth's view that philosophy (an expression of reason) can be employed positively to illuminate revelation, so long as it is not applied systematically but with due subordination to the divine Subject, who is known in Scripturally-attested revelation (see chapter 2).

---

33. Barth does not spell out his ontological assumptions, nor does his language have the precision and clarity that would lend itself to rigorous philosophical analysis. However, it is possible to draw together the strands of an implicit ontology of an appropriate kind by means of disciplined imaginative reflection on Barth's work.

34. The book *Oneself as Another* is based upon Ricoeur's 1986 Gifford Lectures in Edinburgh.

35. For Ricoeur's account of narrative personal identity, see *Oneself as Another*, 113–68.

36. The author asked Ricoeur about the application of his "model" of personal narrative identity to God in a seminar at the University of St. Andrews on June 1, 2000. He expressed caution and a strong degree of agnosticism about what we can say about God. That said, we will attempt to show in what follows that there is much that Barth thinks we can say about God's identity on the basis of revelation, and that much of it is very similar to what Ricoeur says about human identity.

A Summary of Ricoeur's Understanding of Narrative Personal Identity

The crucial backdrop to Ricoeur's concept of personal narrative identity is what he calls the dialectic of "sameness" and "selfhood."[37] This dialectic of Western thought results in "two major uses of the concept of identity": (1) *idem*-identity (*idem* is Latin for "same") and (2) *ipse*-identity (*ipse* is Latin for "self").[38] Since "selfhood... is not sameness," these two types of identity are irreducibly different from each other.

Each type of identity provides a distinctive answer to the question of the self's "permanence in time." Idem-identity speaks of this permanence in static and "essentialist" or "substantialist" categories; the identity of something is viewed as a "substance." It is thus variously expressed under the sameness-criteria of "numerical identity," "qualitative identity" ("extreme resemblance" or similitude), and "uninterrupted continuity" within the same individual.[39] The last criterion opens up the possibility of genuine change within sameness, such as the organic development of the same oak tree from an acorn to a mature tree. Yet even here, the *identity* of the developing tree is described under the rubric of sameness, such as the invariable structural feature of the oak tree's genetic code.[40] Thus, idem-identity regards "*change as happening to something that does not change*" rather than regarding change as a series of events that actually constitute the identity of that something.[41] Under the rubric of sameness, then, this "something that does not change"— this unchanging essence, substance, substratum, or "character"—is an individual thing's identity, its permanence in and through time. Hence, idem-identity answers the question of *what* something or someone is.

But one can also conceive of identity or "permanence in time" as "selfhood." Such ipse-identity takes the question "Who am I?" as its leading question. Thus, its model of temporal permanence is not reducible to the question of *what* I am or *what* someone is. Under this model, personal identity consists not so much in constant character, but in "faithfulness to oneself," especially as "keeping one's word."[42] Indeed,

37. Ibid., 115.
38. Ibid., 116.
39. Ibid., 116f.
40. Ibid., 117.
41. Ibid., 118; emphasis added.
42. Ibid.

such "self-constancy" or "self-maintenance" allows for a kind of ethical persistence through time—a holding to one's words, promises, or commitments—which may coexist with radical changes in one's dispositions, desires, or character.[43]

Ricoeur's initially defines "character" as "the set of distinctive marks which permit the reidentification of a human being as being the same."[44] But Ricoeur develops this definition of character by reinterpreting the "distinctive marks" of character "in terms of *acquired disposition*."[45] As such, character "*adds self-identity to the identity of the same*."[46] Thus, Ricoeur questions the "immutable status of character" (pure *idem*-identity without *ipse*-identity) and expresses the "*temporal* dimension of character."[47] Accordingly, Ricoeur offers a second definition of character that slightly revises the first: "the set of lasting *dispositions* by which a person is recognized."[48]

Ricoeur continues, "In this way character is able to constitute the limit point where the problematic of *ipse* becomes indiscernible from that of *idem*, and where one is inclined not to distinguish them from each other."[49] In this way, character points to an overlapping of *ipse*-identity and *idem*-identity, an overlapping that theoretically could be complete. We can see this overlapping to some degree in the notion that consistently keeping promises is a kind of disposition of character. Yet in Ricoeur's view, to speak of actual human persons as those whose selfhood is *just* their sameness of character is a "confusion of *idem* and *ipse*" in which the self is in danger of being reduced to sameness.[50]

It is at this point that Ricoeur brings his *narrative* account of personal identity into play. Narrative identity mediates sameness and selfhood and brings together these two poles of the dialectic of identity in a way that allows their differences to be maintained. By means of a quasi-Hegelian pattern of argument, Ricoeur takes the thesis of *idem*-identity (i.e., character) and the antithesis of *ipse*-identity (i.e.,

---

43. Ibid., 123f.
44. Ibid., 119.
45. Ibid., 120; emphasis added.
46. Ibid., 119; emphasis added.
47. Ibid., 120.
48. Ibid., 121; emphasis added.
49. Ibid.
50. Ibid.

self-maintenance as keeping one's word) and variously affirms them, cancels them, and then reconstitutes them within a narrative "synthesis" (*Aufhebung*).[51] Narrative identity thus oscillates between:

> [i] a lower limit, where permanence in time expresses the confusion of *idem* and *ipse*; and [ii] an upper limit, where the *ipse* poses the question of its identity without the aid and support of the *idem*.[52]

Avoiding both of these limits, narrative personal identity avoids the disappearance of the question of "who?" into the question of "what?" and vice versa. By examining the narration of a self in time, one can arrive at a view of the identity that includes *both* (a) a properly revised notion of character as "the 'what' of the 'who'"[53] and (b) a revised view of the self as "the 'who' of the 'what.'"[54]

Narrative identity is related to a revised view of character. For Ricoeur, "it is the identity of the story that makes identity the identity of the character."[55] One important implication of this point proceeds from Ricoeur's observation that the integrity of a narrative's plot contains, and to some extent is threatened by, the discordant, "unforeseeable events that punctuate it," although such events are in some sense incorporated into the plot.[56] An implication is drawn from plot to character: "the contingency of the event contributes to the [retroactive] necessity . . . of the history of a life" and hence contributes to "the identity of the character."

Constancy as Divine Personal Identity of Character and Selfhood

Ricoeur's work on personal narrative identity aids us in a deeper analysis of the nature of Barth's understanding of God's constancy. Most importantly, we will examine the role of the dialectic of sameness and

---

51. See ibid., 124 and passim. Aside from the use of the "term" dialectic, the Ricoeur does not explicitly employ the Hegelian conceptuality that we are using here to describe him.

52. Ibid., 124.

53. Ibid., 122.

54. This phrase is our own, but finds indirect support in several passages in Ricoeur, ibid., such as 166f.

55. Ibid., 148.

56. Ibid., 147.

selfhood, of *idem*-identity and *ipse*-identity, within Barth's view. In our view, *Barth's conception of God's constancy includes strong emphasis on both forms of personal identity, while giving relative emphasis or priority to ipse-identity.* (As we unfold this basic interpretation below, we will strive to "speak in Barth's voice" even when not citing Barth or mentioning his name.)

We may begin supporting this interpretation by recalling some of the basic ways that Barth defines God's constancy (see above). God's constancy is the divine perfection by which "God remains the one He is" (491; 553). Such a definition allows for both sameness and selfhood, but puts the emphasis on the latter. That is, it stresses the "who" question and answers that God is "the one who he is" or even "the one who he determines himself to be."[57] We also recall Barth's references to constancy as God's life "in eternal self-repetition and self-affirmation [*in ewiger Wiederholung and Bestätigung seiner selbst*]" (492; 553). Again, by stressing that God's constancy is a kind of self-constancy, the faithfulness of God to himself, Barth is able to affirm "holy mutability" in God. When Barth says that God himself does not alter in the alternation of his attitudes and actions, he seems to be referring to something like the stable identity of God's unique self. While God's self-identity includes an element of sameness—e.g., a consistently loving character—it is neither a predictable sameness, nor a sameness that is incapable of moving and being moved.[58]

Ricoeur's categories also illuminate Barth's critique of "classical immutability"[59] and thereby clarify the nature of Barth's constructive alternative to it. Such immutability (*Unveränderlichkeit*) represents the *reduction of the category of personal selfhood to the category of impersonal sameness.* The following quotation from Ricoeur highlights the difference between such a reductionistic view and a view (like Barth's) that gives "personal selfhood" its due.

---

57. This is confirmed by Barth's comments on Exod 3:15 ("I am that I am"), one of the key proof texts for the classical view of God and specifically of God's immutability. See *CD* II/1, 495f. (cf. 302), where Barth claims that the text speaks of a "*self-affirmation of God*" that is consistent with God's "holy mutability."

58. See the similar comments of Gunton, *Becoming and Being*, 147f.

59. Again, by this term we refer especially to the view represented by Barth's account of Polanus (see the first section of this chapter).

> Keeping one's word expresses a self-constancy which cannot be inscribed, as character was, within the dimension of *something in general but solely within the dimension of "who?"*[60]

Ricoeur's comment is in keeping with Barth's methodological particularism and his related assertion that God, as the unique Subject, must govern all our predications of God. This implies that instead of relying on general a priori God-concepts, one must give due attention to God's particular self-determinations in particular acts of self-revelation. Such particular acts may express a consistent pattern of character, but in themselves, they are irreducibly particular acts (e.g., particular promises to particular people). As such, all of God's acts are "miracles" that are "completely new."[61] Again, for Barth the "who?" question is prior to the "what?" question.[62]

We can take our Ricoeurian redescription of Barth's view of constancy further, albeit now more provisionally. We do so by noting some possible parallels that exist between the dialectic of sameness and selfhood on the one hand and Barth's dialectic of God's love and freedom on the other (on the latter, see chapter 3). God's love, we could say, corresponds to God's idem-identity: his stable, determinate character as one who loves. God's freedom corresponds to God's ipse-identity: his constant self-determination and his faithfulness to himself.

If we follow these correspondences, we can, with some caution, transpose basic theological claims of Barth's doctrine of God into statements made in Ricoeurian idiom. Thus, Barth's claim that "God is the One who loves in freedom" becomes: "God is the One whose loving character exists in the context of free self-determination." Or, Barth's claim that "the divine predicate must be determined by the divine Subject" becomes: "The meaning of God's character-identity (e.g., that "God *is loving*") must be determined by God's ipse-identity or unique selfhood (e.g., that "*God* is loving" and "loves *in freedom*"). Indeed, perhaps the main emphasis of Barth's account of God's freedom is to stress God's uniqueness and thus the inappropriateness of all general conceptions of "divinity" or of the various divine perfections.

---

60. Ricoeur, *Oneself as Another*, 123; emphasis added.
61. CD II/1, 509.
62. A similar dynamic is expressed by D. Bonhoeffer's references to the priority of the "who" question over the "how" question in Christology (see A. Torrance, *Persons in Communion*, 71ff.).

Constancy, which Barth classifies as a perfection of divine freedom, naturally places more emphasis on God's freedom than God's love. Yet, Barth does not develop God's free self-constancy in a way that contradicts the affirmation that God has a determinate loving character and reveals himself as such. Indeed, we could say that we only know God's self-affirming freedom by means of the acts of love that God has shown—acts that form a definite pattern, which forms a coherent plot that witnesses to God's consistent character. But as such, God's character is still "the constancy of *His* knowing, willing and acting and therefore of His *person*" (495; 557)—a person or self who is inherently *free*.[63]

In what remains of this analysis or redescription of Barth's view of constancy (under the dialectic of sameness and selfhood), we turn to an aspect of the question of what makes God's personal identity *different from* human personal identity. Following some remarks in an unpublished paper by Trevor Hart, we make the tentative suggestion that in God's case "idem- and ipse-identity coincide entirely, rather than being held in tension" or threatening to fly apart.[64] The primary reason that Hart gives for this suggestion is the biblical witness to God's faithfulness. Such faithfulness is appropriately, and perhaps necessarily, described as *both* "faithfulness to his promises and purposes" (*ipse*-identity) and faithfulness "to his own character" (*idem*-identity). Indeed, in the biblical story, such faithfulness can itself be seen as an expression of divine character, "as a virtue or disposition of character."[65]

We can clarify and reinforce Hart's suggestion that God's character and self-constancy are one and the same by appealing to Barth's view

---

63. Evidence supporting several of the assertions in this paragraph is found in Barth's account of the "Being of God in Freedom" (§28.3) in II/1, 297–321 (see our comments on this section of *CD* in chapter 3). Here the similarity between Barth's understanding of freedom and his understanding of constancy is obvious, and the congruency of both with Ricouer's ipse-identity seems strong. For example, in the opening page of the section, Barth says "In His being and act God is who He is" and "He is uniquely who He is" (*CD* II/1, 297).

64. Hart, "Spirit of the Age or Spirit of Truth?" 5.

65. Ibid., 5. We note that Barth himself seems to treat God's faithfulness as a constant disposition in his treatment of it as the primary biblical "correlate" for the theological concept of divine simplicity (see our comments on Barth's use of Scripture within his account of divine simplicity in chapter 4). Barth would likely join Ricouer in saying that all *human* expressions of faithfulness are too inconstant to allow for a complete overlapping of faithfulness as self-maintenance and faithfulness as character (Ricouer, *Oneself as Another*, 124; see above).

that God alone is strictly and properly a "person." Barth's reason for this view, we recall, is that only God is "a being in act" in an unqualified sense.[66] As the only completely self-motivated and self-determined person, God's being is completely consistent with God's actions and vice versa. This means that, in some sense, God *is* his own decision, his own act. What all of this implies is that there can be no fundamental tension between any one act of God (say, his promise to redeem Israel) and God's character (his love, justice, or freedom). Rather, all God's acts (promises, judgments, and so on) are consistent with God's character (either as expressions of it or as that which forms and constitutes it). While the disruptions caused by "contingent events" (such as the "fall" of Gen 3) affect God's life or narrative identity, they do not cause God to act in any way that is inconsistent with who he is or inconsistent with his revealed character.[67]

We close this section by responding to Ricoeur's negative assessment of the possibility of a complete overlapping of *idem*-identity and *ipse*-identity in a person's character. We have given reasons to think that this overlapping exists in God, but what are we to make of Ricoeur's charge that such an overlapping (at least on the human level) represents the overtaking of selfhood by sameness? Simply put, while this charge may well apply on the human level, it is not at all clear that it would apply to God, the supremely self-determined one. We cannot assume that God faces a "problem" of self-identity similar to the one that we face.[68]

For Barth, God's character is itself simultaneously marked by permanence of character and the flexibility of self-constancy, the flexibility by which God can freely modify his actions and attitudes (i.e., dispositions)—yet again, in ways that are in keeping with the broad patterns of what God is like. This capacity for "self-change" is most striking in God's relationship to his creation. For in this relationship, Barth says, God freely alters his attitudes and actions in ways that *correspond to* the contingent alterations of the created order (e.g., human actions). In this sense, God's "contingent" (i.e., free) actions constitute God's character. Yet God's character is not captive to "contingencies" outside of himself.[69]

---

66. *CD* II/1, 271 (see our relevant comments in chapter 3).
67. See *CD* II/1, 503f., 507 (see above at several points).
68. Hart, "Spirit of the Age or Spirit of Truth?" 4f.
69. See *CD* II/1, 496, 499, and 506 and our discussion above.

Thus, there is a unique, ordered dynamic of "innovation and sedimentation" in the divine life.[70]

Constancy as Divine Narrative Identity Rendered in Scripture

God's constant personal identity is not only helpfully understood in terms of an integration of idem- and ipse-identity, but can also be specifically understood as a *narrative* identity. In Barth's approach, we could say that God has a narrative identity in two main senses: the ontic sense and the noetic sense. That is, there is the narrative identity that God has, and the narrative identity that we understand God to have. On the *ontic* level, God's life is (or at least includes) a "history," and, as such, is a story that has a "direction" that proceeds from a "beginning" and to an "end."[71] God has determined himself to be *for us* (*pro nobis*), and this involves a determinate pattern of actions in history. This self-determination may imply not only the self-determination of God *ad extra*, but also in some sense the determination of God *ad intra*.[72] On the *noetic* level, we come to know who God is and what God is like by means of the story we find in Scripture—and this is a faithful rendering of God's ontic idenity. We come to know God's identity through Scripture, not so much in a series of propositions (although there are these), but in a story that is *told*. In this story we learn of God as an unsubstitutable subject or agent. Through God's Scripturally-attested acts in the "economy of salvation" (God *ad extra*, the economic trinity) we come to know God in himself (God *ad intra*, the immanent trinity). In several different respects, these observations are harmonious with Barth's use of Scripture and mode of

---

70. Accordingly, the divine constancy of character to which Barth's exposition appears to refer may not be obvious to human eyes; God sometimes *appears* to act "out of character." Even to the eyes of faith, there is a level of unpredictability to God's actions. The question of *how* "surprising" acts of God are in fact consistent with God's constant set of dispositions can often only be answered with hindsight, at a further stage in the story when faith becomes sight (e.g., the crucifixion in the light of the resurrection). This, indeed, is the hope of the Christian: that in the final *eschaton*, she will be able to see how all the alterations of God's attitudes and actions were a part of a coherent "plot." This is the positive emphasis of Barth's largely noetic account of eschatological redemption (see below).

71. See T. F. Torrance, *Christian Doctrine of God*, 240ff. God's story does not have an end in the sense of a termination, but perhaps in terms of a *telos*. See also chapter 6 for a clarification of the concepts of time and eternity in Barth.

72. See our comments earlier in this chapter about eternal Christological election.

doctrinal construction in his account of God's constancy and indeed with his wider approach to theology.[73] This will be confirmed especially by our exposition of Barth's treatment of constancy of God in "salvation history" (see below).[74]

The Role of Scripture in Barth's Account of Divine Constancy

Introduction to the Role of Scripture in Barth's Treatment of Constancy

At this point, we have a grasp of the main contours of Barth's understanding of divine constancy and how it differs from the classical doctrine of divine immutability represented by Polanus and others. We will now develop a fuller answer to the question of *why* Barth's way of doing theology causes him to depart from this classical view in the way that he does. We have already gone some way towards an answer by making reference to his particularism, and specifically in saying that it is Christocentric particularism. Barth's view of constancy, unlike that of classical immutability, arises out of "Christological concentration" in which God's act in Christ is the epistemological basis and hermeneutical centre for what we say about God. But, if we apply the method of particularism rigorously to our understanding of Barth's particularism itself, then we must be still more specific or concrete about what methodological Christocentrism involves for him. Thus, we must reflect on the particular theological practices that Barth engages in order to, as it

---

73. The following citations from secondary literature on Barth add credence to this claim. Ford asserts that "constancy is a concept that develops *the interpretation of the Bible as rendering one subject*" (*Barth and God's Story*, 161; emphasis added). Hunsinger notes that "the ground on which [Barth's] Christology takes shape here is much closer to "narratology," or the study of narrative structures and strategies, than it is to metaphysics" (*Disruptive Grace*, 137). Both Kelsey and Frei speak of Barth as employing scriptural narrative to form identity descriptions of Jesus Christ (and/or God) by rendering him an agent (Kelsey, *Proving Doctrine*, 39–40; and Frei, *Types of Christian Theology*, 90).

74. New Testament scholar Richard Bauckham, in his book *God Crucified* (1999), presents a view of Christology under the rubric of divine personal identity that draws indirectly on Ricoeur. Bauckham's way of interpreting Scripture is similar to Barth's in various ways and indicates in some respects what Barth's account of constancy might have looked like if he had more openly employed the conceptuality of "identity" (which came into its own only after his death).

were, "put him in contact" with the Christological particulars of God's self-revelation. The most important of all such practices is the reverent theological interpretation and use of Scripture in theology.

Accordingly, we will now develop the distinctly *scriptural* (and, as such, exegetical or hermeneutical) aspect of Barth's particularism in his account of God's constancy—an aspect of Barth's work that has been implicit in many of our comments above. Barth's Christocentrism is basically a Christocentrism that arises out of Scripture, albeit a distinctive, Christological version of a theological reading of Scripture.[75] More generally, we will see that Barth's critique of classical immutability and his alternative to it are to great extent driven by his engagement with Scripture.

Barth's small-print excursuses in *CD* often provide exegetical substantiation for the dogmatic claims Barth makes in large-print.[76] At least in his treatment of constancy, Barth's theological engagement with Scripture in these excursuses takes *three different forms* according to the level at which Barth engages with the biblical text. These three forms of the function of Scripture in Barth's dogmatics correspond to the next three subsections of this chapter, where examples of each of the three forms will be treated. First and most commonly, Barth cites a group of specific passages that he has collected in a catena or group to make a particular point. In such cases, Barth often quotes important passages in full, but rarely engages in any detailed exegetical comments on any one of them. Second, and more rarely (only once in his treatment of constancy), Barth undertakes a rather extensive theological exegesis of a single passage (Phil 2:6ff.) and draws doctrinal conclusions from it. In the third, Barth engages in a form of theological exegesis in which primary reference is made not to particular biblical texts, but rather to larger biblical themes or patterns.

---

75. The role of Scripture stands out as an independent feature of his theological method in some ways more important than his Christocentrism. Indeed, from one point of view, his Christocentrism is a sub-category of the priority that he gives to testimony of Scripture, for Scripture is the primary source and basis for Barth's portrait of who Christ is. Perhaps it is more accurate to say that that this primary source is his Christocentric *reading* of Scripture.

76. Indeed, in his preface to *CD*, Barth calls the Scripture passages in the excursuses a pointer to the "real ground text" of all that he wants to say (I/1, Thompson tr., 1936, ix; Bromiley's translation in the 1975 edition refers to Scripture here as "the basic text," xii). We note that although Barth also engages Scripture in his main print discussion of constancy, we will focus on his engagement with Scripture in his fine-print excursuses.

A Topical Grouping of Texts: The Question of Divine "Repentance"

We now turn to an example of the first and most common form of Barth's engagement with Scripture in his section on constancy—a grouping of texts related to a single theological issue.[77] Our example is Barth's treatment of biblical texts, primarily from the Old Testament, that variously affirm or deny divine "repentance" or that God "changes his mind." Barth's engagement with these texts related to God's repentance occur in the context of a four-page excursus in which Barth presents scriptural evidence *against* God's nature being "motionless" or absolutely immutable and *for* God's "holy mutability" (495–99; 557–61). Apart from rather schematic comments, Barth does not discuss most of the passages that he cites or quotes on the matter of divine repentance, apparently regarding it sufficient to let the biblical texts "speak for themselves." This is probably related to Barth's view that, in theological exegesis, the interpreter's primary calling is to listen for a "witness to God's Word" that is conjoined to God's own capacity for self-witness.[78]

Barth's use of his selected texts on divine repentance falls into two groups. First, there are those passages that Barth believes to have been misread by proponents of the classical understanding of immutability—misunderstandings that Barth goes on to correct. Second, there are passages that Barth uses to develop his own constructive understanding of God's constancy. These passages were often not considered relevant by the classical writers on immutability. We will consider these two kinds of passages in turn.

First then, Barth critiques and corrects classical misreadings of biblical passages. He deals with two kinds of misreadings: (1) those misreadings in which a passage is wrongly taken to support a classical version of absolute immutability[79] and (2) those misreadings that ob-

---

77. Other examples of this form of a "catena" pertaining to a specific topic are: God not growing weary in redemption (504f.), God's response to prayer (510ff.), or the passages traditionally taken to support a doctrine of the divine "decree" or "decrees" (520f.).

78. See Barth, *Credo*, 177. Barth speaks of God's capacity for self-witness in the section on constancy when he speaks of Polanus' failure to give ear to "the God who attests Himself in His revelation" (492; 554).

79. The first such passage he actually considers here is Exod 3:14, a passage that became a sort of *locus classicus* for classical understanding of God. Barth claims that we cannot distil a motionless *ipsum ens*, or Being Itself, from this passage. To do so,

fuscate the meaning of a text that could prove contrary to the classical view.[80] In both cases, Barth charges that classical interpreters misread Scripture on the basis of a priori philosophical assumptions about what God must be like.

One of several passages that Barth regards as having been misconstrued as evidence for absolute immutability is Malachi 3:6. In this text, the God of Israel declares, "I the Lord change not." Barth points out that when this passage is read in its context, we see that the Lord is being contrasted with the Israelites. But the contrast between God and Israel in this passage is primarily a *moral* contrast between God's consistently good and holy character and Israel's "wicked inconstancy" or "unholy mutability" (496; 558). Therefore, Mal 3:6 cannot rightly be used to support the classical view's metaphysical assumption of a "mathematical sameness" in God's being.[81] By this phrase, Barth refers to the tendency of classical views of immutability to regard all distinctions in God's being and action as mere accidents of our perception (see the problem of "nominalism" and "semi-nominalism" discussed in chapters 3 and 4). To do so, Barth says, is to uphold the God of Platonism, the God who is basically without life, word, or act. This is emphatically not the personal God of the Bible. God's faithfulness to his moral nature and his covenant promises is not the same as the abstract Platonic immutability and Mal 3:6 cannot be used as a proof-text for the latter.

Falling under the second category of "obfuscated texts" are several Old Testament passages that directly state that God "repented" or "changed his mind" (such as Gen 6:6f., Gen 18:20ff., Exod 32:9ff.). These texts, which could have served as counter-evidence to an extreme understanding of God's immutability, were instead interpreted *figuratively* as instances of anthropomorphism. In a vigorous response, Barth

---

is to wrongly separate God's self-declaration here from its context, in which God "approaches Moses and Israel and deals with both in a very definite manner" in time and space (495f.).

80. The first text he considers of this kind is the divine title "King of the ages" from 1 Tim 1:17. Barth says that although God is *above* all ages as their Lord, as such he must "partake of their alteration, so that there is something corresponding to that alteration in His own essence" (496). In this context, Barth says that there is such a thing as the "holy mutability of God." As King of the ages, God is constant, but he is constant *in* every change.

81. Barth is using "mathematical" here and elsewhere in a loose sense for its rhetorical associations. But he is also implicitly resisting the Cartesian geometric model of knowledge and asserting that it is inappropriate for theology.

declares, "Biblical thinking about God would rather submit to confusion with the grossest anthropomorphism [*Anthropopathismus*] than to confusion with a God who is absolutely immutable and thus immobile" (496; 558). Barth concludes his discussion by saying:

> It would be most unwise, then, to try to understand what the Bible says about God's repentance as if it were *merely* figurative [*als nur bildlich*]. For what *truth* is denoted by the "figure" [*Bild*] if we are not to deny that there is an underlying truth? (498; 560; emphasis added)

Barth wishes to press into the "underlying truth" pregnant within these texts. When Scripture says that God changed or repented, we cannot explain it away in terms of changes in humanity. Even if we concede that the Bible presents us with "figures" or "pictures" *of God*, these figures or pictures surely stand for something *about God* that *changes*. Barth tends to read passages "literally"—even "anthropomorphically"—rather than "figuratively," at least when "figurative" reading obfuscates the plain sense of the Bible.

With this hermeneutical rule in place, Barth considers the apparent contradiction between biblical passages that variously deny and affirm that God repents or changes his mind. Barth considers Numbers 23:19 in which God says "I am not a son of man that he should repent" (or, in an alternate translation, "should change his mind") and relates it to the passages in which God is said to repent (such as Gen 6:6f., Gen 18:20ff. and Exod 32:9ff.). Barth affirms with the classical view that these passages are indeed consistent with one another. However, in contrast to the classical view, he states that this consistency cannot be gained by giving definite priority to the passages that deny God's repentance, writing off the force of the others as anthropomorphism. Instead, Barth wants to take both kinds of passages equally seriously, and, in this case, as equally literal or proper speech—as *eigentlich* rather than *uneigentliche Rede* (see 496; 558).[82]

The theological result of Barth's interpretation is that, according to Scripture, there is some sense in which God really does repent and another sense in which God really does not repent. God remains self-constant ("He remains himself") even in the alteration of his attitude and actions. Yet God is not "self-limited to an inflexible immobility"

---

82. *CD* uses the term "figurative" (on 496 and 498) for both *uneigentliche* (*KD*, 558) and *bildlich* (*KD*, 560) respectively.

that "deprives God of the capacity to alter His attitudes and actions" (498; 560). To say that would be to deny that God is constantly free, and freedom is one of God's unchanging perfections! Rather, God's self-constancy is flexible, allowing for "holy mutability"—for "something corresponding" to the "alteration" of the world "in his own essence" (496; 557f.).

How God can be said to be both mutable and immutable is clarified by Barth's employment of two biblical passages as positive ground for his view. We select these two passages (Ps 18:25ff. and Jer 18:1-10) because, if we read between the lines, they serve to unlock the apparent deadlock that faces us initially in trying to reconcile the various passages pertinent to divine repentance. They do so by showing how the biblical view of God's constancy is not only consistent with a kind of divine mutability but actually *requires* it.[83] Barth chooses to quote these two passages in full and juxtapose them with the other biblical passages he quotes. In this way Barth brings these passages (that classical interpreters apparently neglected) into fruitful "conversation" with the other passages he considers, albeit with only a minimum of commentary.

The first passage is Psalm 18:25ff., which reads as follows (NRSV):

> With the loyal you show yourself loyal; with the blameless you show yourself blameless; with the pure your show yourself pure; with the crooked you show yourself perverse [or "shrewd," NIV]. For you deliver a humble people, but the haughty eyes you bring down.

Barth wishes to ensure that we do not explain away the force of this passage through improper "figurative" readings of it: "It is not . . . a figurative [*uneigentliche*] but a strictly literal [*eigentlich*] statement, and one which does not contradict but bears testimony to the constancy of God." (496; 558). Again: "This is really the way that the immutable and as such the living God acted." Barth does not spell out what is it about the content of this passage that is so important. But we may safely assume that it is that God consistently acts in ways that *appropriately correspond* to human actions, whether bad or good. This means that

---

83. Barth does not explicitly say this, nor does he refer to these passages as "hermeneutical keys" this is clearly our own interpretation of these passages. This is our attempt to dig below the surface level of Barth's prose for the "deep literal sense" of what he says, including why he quotes certain biblical passages and why he arranges those quotations in a certain order.

God's constancy is marked by an "elasticity [*Elastizität*]" (496; 558) that allows God to act in different ways at different times. Indeed, if God is to be constantly righteous in response to human inconstancy, he must be "elastic" in this way.

Barth appears to draw a similar message from another biblical passage, Jeremiah 18:1-10 (quoted on 497; 559; cf. Amos 7:1-6, which Barth also quotes here). This is a passage in which God describes himself as the potter and Israel as the clay in his hands. Verses 7 and 8 are especially pertinent, for in these verses the Lord refers to his ability to change his mind:

> At one moment I may declare concerning a nation or a kingdom, that I will pluck up and break down and destroy it, but if that nation, concerning which I have spoken, turns from evil, I will change my mind about the disaster that I intended to bring upon it. (Jer 18:7f.; NRSV)

The passage goes on to describe how God will also repent in the case of the reverse scenario, in which God originally intended good for a nation, but finds it doing evil. In this case, God will "repent" and bring judgment upon them.[84] Again, God's personal and moral constancy is such that it actually *requires* changes, and the changes are *orderly and consistent*.

We have seen how Psalm 18 and Jeremiah 18 can be understood as "hermeneutical keys" for Barth's understanding of the biblical witness to God's constancy, even though Barth does not spell out explicitly the logical connections between these texts and his dogmatic conclusions. But with disciplined hermeneutical imagination, these texts speak of one way in which Barth might consistently and appropriately link change with constancy in the being of God. For according to Psalm 18 and Jeremiah 18, God can and does change his attitudes and actions with respect to specific nations or persons. God does not change arbitrarily, but in conformity with constant patterns of relating to human action. According to God's unchanging moral nature, God consistently responds to human obedience with blessing and to human sinfulness with opposition and judgment.

Barth's biblical view of God's constancy allows for divine repentance and mutability. But more must be said about God's concrete and

---

84. Cf. Joel 2:13 and Jonah 4:2, where God is called one who "repents of evil."

consistent patterns of relating to humanity and how these are related to Scripture as a whole, as it is united in Jesus Christ. This is the very task Barth takes up in the latter part of his excursus (497ff.; 559ff.).

Barth says, "It should be noted that in both Amos and Jeremiah the two possibilities of divine repentance are put in a definite order" (497; 559). In saying this, Barth refers to the possibilities of God repenting from intended evil and repenting from intended good. He points out how the former "gracious" possibility is consistently listed first and is given the overall emphasis in both Jer 18 and Amos 7 and draws attention to a similar pattern in a host of other passages.[85] In the Bible, "the repentance in which God repents of evil" always has "a position of advantage or preponderance over that other repentance," and "this preponderance may be observed even in Ps 18:25ff." (498; 560). Barth appropriately employs this comprehensive biblical pattern to establish the following dogmatic point. In God's actions towards us, there is a constant priority given to God's gracious "Yes" over the "No" of his judgment or "chiding" (497ff.; 559ff.). As such, one side of Barth's theological application of these passages is to emphasize God as the one who is constantly loving and gracious, the one who "*loves* in freedom."[86]

We conclude this subsection with some comments on how what Barth has said about divine repentance relates to his Christocentrism. While Barth does not explicitly refer to Jesus Christ in this discussion, Christ is no doubt on his mind. We could say that Barth's drawing out of

---

85. Barth cites Jer 26:2-3, 13, 19; 36:3; 42:10; Joel 2:13; Jonah 4:2. In the New Testament, he cites and comments on Rom 9:21ff., which picks up the potter and clay imagery from Jer 18 and Rom 11:29 (498; 559f.).

86. As such, Barth is quite content to speak of what we might call "internally-motivated" changes in God, in a way that Polanus would not. More specifically, God freely changes his attitudes and actions without changing himself. Polanus, we recall, had ruled out any such change on the basis of it violating a strict classical understanding of God's absolute unity or simplicity. Barth has already critiqued such an understanding of God in his treatment of the perfection of divine "unity" (see chapter 4).

Indeed, Barth's views of divine unity and constancy are closely related (as are his views of eternity). David Ford rightly notes that "constancy is a concept which expands on God's unity and so develops the interpretation of the Bible as rendering one subject" (Ford, *Barth and God's Story*, 161). This means avoiding any sense of dualism internal to God's being in which an unchanging aspect of God stands opposed to a changing aspect (as if there were two subjects in conflict in God). However difficult it is to grasp, Barth would want to say that any internal distinctions in God are harmoniously united with each other, in a way similar to the unity and plurality implied in God being Triune.

the pattern of the priority of God's gracious repentance over his judging repentance is in some sense a Christological reading of the Bible. But the priority of God's grace no doubt finds support in the individual texts he cites in their contexts—including those of the Old Testament. Indeed, we could say that in Barth's engagement with Scripture, there is a tacit Christological construal of various texts. Such a construal is by no means imposed on those texts (as a "hard reading"); it is carefully drawn out of them in terms of their own "resources." Later on Barth simply makes explicit what was hitherto tacit. He says that all divine reconciliation and revelation are the execution and fulfillment of "one fixed" decision (505; 567; cf. 521f.; 586f.). He also identifies that "one fixed divine decision" with God's gracious election in Jesus Christ, as attested in Scripture. Such a reading seems to make the most sense of Barth's earlier discussion of the concrete order and preponderance of grace in divine repentance. Accordingly, it is in Christ that we find the supreme basis for the key claim that God is constant as the one whose being is in Act and as the one who loves in freedom. This Christological ground forms a basic perspective or framework for Barth's engagement with particular biblical texts. When God changes in his attitude or actions, he changes in faithfulness to his own constant attitude of holy, reconciling love that is rooted in his election of Jesus Christ and all humanity in him.

In this sense it is appropriate to describe Barth's theological exegesis, even of the Old Testament, as "Christocentric" exegesis. This is so, even though we have been able to summarize much of Barth's discussion of Old Testament texts on divine repentance without mentioning Christ. This fact shows that Barth's exegesis is "Christocentric," not in a sense that requires *explicit* reference to Christ, but in the sense that his effort to discern the theological import of the verbal sense of the text is affected by an *implicit* relation to Christ as the centre of Scripture. For Barth, the God known in Christ is the central subject matter to which all biblical texts refer at some level, including texts about God's repentance and non-repentance.

Exegesis of a Single Passage: Barth on Philippians 2:5–11

In this subsection, we turn to Barth's treatment, in an important excursus, of Phil 2:5–11.[87] This excursus occurs within a larger discussion of the significance of Christ for understanding God's constancy. To foreshadow something of the doctrinal import that Barth wishes to draw out of his engagement with Philippians two, we begin by quoting the passage that immediately precedes it.

> The incarnation not only does not mean any curtailment of compromising of the immutable divine nature, but ... it means the revelation of it in its perfection, a perfection which *we recognize* in God the Creator, Reconciler, and Redeemer *only because* he is the God revealed, present, and active in the God-manhood of Jesus Christ. (516f.; 580; emphasis added)

In keeping with this basic Christological thesis, Barth's exposition of Phil 2:5ff. aims to show the nature of Christ's voluntary self-humiliation ("he emptied himself," v. 7). He says the incarnation is an act in which Jesus Christ is and reveals himself to be truly divine while at the same time concealing his true divinity before sinful human eyes. Barth's exegesis of Phil 2 provides part of the basis for Barth's claim that Christ's self-humiliation reveals the character of God's constant and immutable purpose and being.

Barth begins by recounting the narrative pattern of Phil 2:7–9. "Jesus Christ emptied himself, taking the form of a servant, going about in the likeness of man ... and that as such He humbled Himself, becoming obedient to death, even the death of the cross" (516; 580). Here and elsewhere in his exposition, Barth considers the claims Paul makes to be commensurable with the claims of post-biblical theologians (see our treatment of commensurability in chapter 4). Accordingly, he claims that "like the older theology" Paul "did not believe that ... Jesus Christ surrendered, lost, or even curtailed his deity." Barth appeals to v. 6 as his reason: "For [Jesus] did it all *ev morphē theou huparchōn*, being in the form of God." Barth goes on to make the following exegetical observation about Christ's self-emptying against the view of the so called "kenoticists." Christ's self-emptying is a voluntary "veiling" of his deity

---

87. We note that when Barth wrote this passage in II/1, he had already written (in 1928) a commentary on the book of Philippians (Barth, *Epistle to the Philippians*).

to humans (a noetic veiling) without any diminution of his deity (his ontic constancy).

> The self-emptying does not refer to his divine being. It refers in a *negative* sense to the fact of that he did not consider or treat his equality with God as His one exclusive possibility ... *Positively* His self-emptying refers to the fact that, without detracting from His being in the form of God, He was able and willing to assume the form of a servant and go about in the likeness of man, so that the creature would know him only as a creature, and he alone could know himself as God. In other words, He was ready to accept a position in which He could not be known in the world as God, but His divine glory was concealed from the world. (516; 580; emphasis added)

In this passage, we see that Christ shows forth the freedom of God—a freedom that, through Christ, God exercised in love through his act of self-emptying. In this way, Christ "did what man does not do because he is a sinner," namely, "He was obedient unto death." Not only so, "He took upon Himself ... the curse and punishment over the rebellion which He had not Himself committed." But none of this has anything to do with "a surrender or loss of His deity." Rather, Christ in his self-humiliation is a true and perfect enactment of the constant "free love" of God, which "is the one true God himself" (517; 582).

But most human observers of a man being crucified on Golgotha know none of this; God's self-concealment of his deity in the humiliation of Jesus Christ veils it from their eyes. Since God has done this, God is free to do this; God's freedom is the transcendental condition of the former fact. God is free to become a creature who is known to others only as a creature and to do this without becoming any less divine.

With this point established, Barth turns to an exposition of vv. 9–11, which begins with the decisive phrase, "*Therefore* God also highly exalted him" (NRSV). In Barth's words,

> [T]he exaltation of Jesus Christ by the power of God, and therefore the revelation of the divine form hidden under the form of a servant, is not introduced with a Nevertheless or an And but with a Therefore. The name *Kyrios* does not belong to him *in spite of* the fact that the self-offering and concealment of God took place in Jesus Christ, but *just because* it took place. *Because* he emptied and humbled himself this name is His as His resurrection reveals. (517; 581; emphasis added)

In his usual "fugal" style, Barth repeats this passage's motif in several variations and as such brings it into relationship both with another New Testament text related to the humiliation of Jesus Christ (Matt 11:28f.) and with the inadequate Christological doctrine of the "older theology" of the Protestant scholastics (517; 581f.). Barth perceives in the text here is expressed well in what he elsewhere calls a "teleologically ordered dialectic" (236; 266) in which "veiling occurs for the purpose of unveiling."[88] Barth is not alluding to a purely non-temporal, symmetrical dialectic here, but to an ontic dialectic in which God's self-concealment exists as the necessary prelude to God's self-revelation and in which the latter is the purpose of the former. The humility of Christ's life and death exists for (and makes possible) the exaltation of his resurrection, ascension, and heavenly session. In this we see that Barth's dialectical thinking is significantly constrained by the ordered temporal pattern of the gospel story—the narrative of Jesus' life, death, and resurrection, of his humiliation and exaltation. Thus, the same acts by which God hides himself in Jesus Christ also bring about God's full and perfect self-revelation in Jesus Christ.

> The truth is that it is by the incarnation that God has revealed his truly immutable being as free love in the perfection in which, on the basis of the incarnation, we recognize it *again* and find it confirmed in His acts as Creator, Reconciler, and Redeemer. God is "immutably" the one whose reality is seen in His condescension in Jesus Christ . . . He is not a God who is what he is in a majesty *behind* this condescension, behind the cross on Golgotha. On the contrary, the cross of Golgotha *is itself the divine majesty*, and all the "exaltation" necessary on account of his deity (i.e., the revelation of what He is) can reveal only . . . that God on high is the One who was able and willing and in fact did condescend so completely to us in His Son. This *free love* is the one true God Himself. (517; 581f.; emphasis added)

In this passage we see that Barth enjoins upon dogmatics the task of rigorously revising all its theological conceptions of divinity, exaltation, and constancy in the light of the definitive self-revelation of God in Jesus Christ attested in Scripture. Abandoning all a priori concepts of God, the theologian can only add his humble and obedient "acknowl-

---

88. The later phrase comes from McCormack, *Karl Barth's Critically Realistic Dialectic Theology*, 460. See our general comments about dialectic in chapter 1.

edgement and confirmation" to what God has already done in Christ (517; 581). Barth concludes,[89]

> All statements about God and His exaltation which omit or deviate from this [i.e., God's humility in Christ] deny and violate His *constancy* . . . We must not forget that the *only reason* why the name of Jesus is "the name above every other name" [v. 9], the name of God's glory itself, is that it is the name of him who humbled and emptied himself. (517; 582; emphasis added)

We close this subsection on Phil 2:5–11 with a consideration of two questions. First, how does this instance of Barth's theological interpretation of Scripture fit into his larger dogmatic argument regarding constancy? Second, in what sense can Barth's theological interpretation of Phil 2:5–11 be regarded as exegesis of the verbal sense of this passage?

In answer to the first question, we have seen how Barth's exposition of Philippians 2 functions not only to underscore but also to ground the major motifs and claims of the main text. As such, the placement of this engagement with Scripture within an excursus cannot mean that its contribution is peripheral or unimportant. Rather, without such a concrete exegetical excursus, several of Barth's claims could appear rather more like the general a priori conceptions of God that he so vigorously attacks. Part of the decisive Christological basis for Barth's central claims on constancy is found in this exegetical excursus. For example, Barth's theological exegesis of Phil 2 provides a key basis for Barth's claim that, despite sinful human opposition to God, "God has befriended and continually befriends fallen creation" (515; 579). This exegesis also shows us how God is both perfectly free (free to become what he is not, without ceasing to be who he is) and perfectly loving (loving as the God who humbles himself in order to seek and establish fellowship with sinners).

Our second question concerns in what sense Barth's theological interpretation of Phil 2:5–11 can be regarded as a "proper" exegesis of the verbal sense of Scripture. In other words, did Barth really get the theological judgments (not necessarily the concepts or terminology) that he makes here from "exegesis" (i.e., from the biblical text), or

---

[89]. This is the conclusion of his main argument in the excursus. Barth follows this with an important appendix in parentheses about the "practical significance" of Phil 2:5ff., especially regarding 2:1–4.

are they rather the product of his own creative "eisegesis" (i.e., reading into the text)? This is a crucial question for assessing Barth's degree of adherence to the Reformation's scripture principle. It is also extraordinarily difficult to answer. That said, we offer the following tentative comments.

Barth's theological claims about the self-humiliation of the constant God are not the straightforward result of an exegesis of Phil 2 alone, taken in isolation from other texts. Rather, Barth's exposition assumes a whole group of specific claims about matters such as the nature of the person of Christ, Christ's relation to the Father, and about the nature of the revelation by which we know these things. These Christological claims cannot be simply extracted from Philippians 2—even if they find a degree of support there—but require a certain "ruled reading" of the canon of Scripture as a whole.[90] If Barth's exposition is to be called exegesis, then it must be regarded as *canonical* exegesis—exegesis not of an individual text in isolation, but of that text in the context of other biblical texts. When Barth is interpreting Phil 2, he is tacitly assuming certain exegetical conclusions about a whole host of other texts and their contexts. To a large extent this is true of all exegesis, even that of the "historical-critics," but it is of more obvious significance in an avowedly "theological" exegesis such as Barth's.

With these observations in mind, it would seem that the conclusions that Barth reaches regarding God's constancy are generally the result of *legitimate but indirect relations* between (a) Scripture as a whole and (b) Barth's dogmatic practice. At this point, we can note three typical features of such indirect relations. First, they are typically "Christocentric" in character, offering an overall "construal" or "ruled reading" of scripture that has its centre in the person and work of Christ, even in the case of passages where no direct reference to Christ is made (e.g., in the Old Testament passages regarding divine repentance discussed above). Second, the indirect relation between Scripture and dogmatics is frequently mediated by *tradition* (e.g., the Chalcedonian creed and subsequent reflection on it clearly influenced Barth's understanding of Phil 2). We do not have a situation in which "Barth and his Bible" produce dogmatic conclusions on their own, in

---

90. Other dogmatic or doctrinal claims, such as the Nicene *homoousion*, may be regarded more naturally as results of the theological exegesis of Phil 2 and related passages (see Yeago, "New Testament and Nicene Dogma").

a kind of hermeneutical vacuum. Rather, we have a situation in which Barth was guided by and immersed in Christian traditions of exegesis and doctrine. Third, such mediating tradition, however, is ever-changing and always open to a process whereby engagement with Scripture exercises an abiding critical and constructive pressure upon tradition and its dogmatic results (e.g., Barth was able to critique certain understandings of Chalcedon and move beyond them).[91] Thus, some of the traditions that Barth inherits and shapes—themselves often being traditions of biblical interpretation—arise out of the biblical text and are constantly open to the Scripture as their ultimate "norming norm." The next subsection will explore the indirect relations between Scripture and doctrine more fully.

Themes and Patterns: An Excursus on "Salvation History"

We observed above that a third form of Barth's theological exegesis is one in which Barth makes primary reference, not to particular biblical texts, but rather to larger biblical themes or patterns. In this subsection, we highlight such indirect functions of Scripture within another excursus that Barth placed within his treatment of constancy.

In this excursus, Barth highlights the "peculiar characteristics" of the biblical "history of salvation" (*Heilsgeschichte*) as a clear manifestation that there is "a special act of God" that stands over against the act of creation considered in itself (cf. 506–12; 569–76). This gives Barth an opportunity to speak about God's constancy from the point of view all of God's gracious works *ad extra*.[92]

---

91. See McCormack, "Barths Grundsätzlicher Chalcedonismus"? We could also note here that Barth's exposition of Phil 2 constitutes an implicit but significant critique of the traditional Protestant orthodox view of the two states of Christ. The traditional view regards the humiliation and glory as more or less consecutive states or stages in Christ's action. Barth, by contrast, regards them as two aspects that coexist simultaneously over the whole course of the history of Jesus (on the noetic level, there is a consecutive element for Barth: transition from veiling to unveiling). For Barth's fuller treatment of these matters, see IV/1, §59. Cf. Berkouwer, *Triumph of Grace*, 297–397 (especially 316f. on Phil 2 and the "two states") for an insightful exposition and critique of Barth's view. See also Hunsinger, *Disruptive Grace*, 141f.

92. Herbert Hartwell says that despite the standard English translation "history of salvation," *Heilsgeschichte* actually "embraces . . . God's entire gracious dealing with man from eternity to eternity" (*Theology of Karl Barth*, 38 n. 45).

Although Barth refers to particular biblical texts relatively frequently in this excursus,[93] he usually does so basically to *illustrate* larger biblical patterns of *Heilsgeschichte*.[94] He does not discuss any one passage in detail. Rather, Barth focuses on the main "acts of God" in history, namely, creation (including preservation), reconciliation (covenant and atonement) and redemption (eschatology). He particularly attends to the relationships that exist between these acts in an effort to show the nature of God's constancy.[95]

God's constancy is evident in his unchanging gracious disposition towards creation expressed in one covenant with humanity that Jesus Christ fulfils.[96] We will show at the end of this subsection that this gracious way of relating to humanity is rooted in God's eternal decision to elect humanity in Christ. But for now we need only to note that, since God's constancy is not an inflexible concept of immutability, Barth is also concerned to speak of the genuine "newness" of the divine acts of reconciliation and redemption over against creation. Thus, there is a kind of dialectic between two perspectives on God's gracious relationship to humanity: (1) God's way of relating to humanity construed as a single act (which expresses the unchanging stability of God's works) and (2) God's way of relating to humanity construed as a narrative plot marked by a series of distinct, new acts (which expresses the free and unpredictable vitality of God's ways).[97]

Barth unfolds the flexible constancy of God in relation to *Heilsgeschichte* in five key stages. In these five stages, Barth speaks of the relationship between God and the human creature *in progressively more specific terms*.

---

93. He refers to particular verses eighteen times in the excursus, eleven times in his treatment of prayer (510ff.; 574ff.).

94. Kelsey overstates when he says: "The identification of biblical narrative with *Heilsgeschichte* is expressly rejected by Barth" (*Proving Doctrine*, 50). That said, Kelsey's over-generalization does point to the cautions that Barth sometimes raises about "salvation history" construed *in a certain way* (cf. *CD* I/2, 12f.).

95. Barth later speaks of reconciliation, or the "covenant fulfilled in the atonement," as the "center" of the Christian message and the doctrine of creation and doctrine of the last things as the "circumference" of that message (*CD* IV/1, 3).

96. See *CD* IV/1, 22–43.

97. See Hunsinger's similar analysis of "two temporal perspectives" involved in Barth's doctrine of the Holy Spirit (*Disruptive Grace*, 173ff.).

1. First, Barth speaks of the fact that, after the fall, God begins to have *special relations* with humanity, rather than merely general relations with humanity as part of creation (see 507; 570). God remains "the Creator and Preserver of the whole world . . . But as such reveals Himself and acts in this new reality" (507; 570). Barth regards this new post-lapsarian working of God as representing an advance over the work of God in creation alone.

   > God is [now] more living, because more definite, than the God of Gen 1–2. And He has turned more intimately to the creature than before. *Something other and greater than creation has taken place.* It is so much greater that the dangerous saying is forced to our lips: *felix culpa, quae talem et tantum meruit redemptorem.* And in this different and greater thing we see nothing but the glory of the Creator and creation, forfeited by us and now *for the first time revealed.* (507; 570; emphasis added)[98]

   Barth will return to this idea of the "happy sin" as he continues his exposition.[99] In the kind of dialectical language evident in the above quote (e.g., the dialectic of newness/continuity), Barth speaks of the relationship between God's work of creation and his work of reconciliation in *Heilsgeschichte*.

2. Second, Barth states that "the special act of God in this new work consists in the fact that in these dealings God does not disdain to enter into a kind of partnership [*ein Art Partnerschaft*] with man" (507; 570). In other words, God's relationship with humanity is, more concretely, a *personal* I-Thou relationship and thus a *covenant* relationship (although Barth does not employ these terms here). Barth continues, "In Genesis 1–2 it is only God who speaks," but "from Genesis 3 there is a human reply" (507; 570f.). Barth appeals to Abraham's intercession for Sodom (Gen 18:20ff.), Jacob's wrestling with the angel of the Lord (Gen 32:33ff.), and the "picture of God in the parable of the unjust judge" (Luke 18:1ff.) as illustrations of this theme of human partnership with God and response to God (507; 571). Barth speaks of God as being willing to enter into a "confrontation [*Gegenüber*]" with humans. In that

---

98. Barth cites the Latin phrase (concerning a "happy fault" or "happy sin") from the *Roman Missal*, liturgy for the Saturday before Easter Day (507; 570).

99. See Ford, *Barth and God's Story*, 161.

confrontation, human freedom, even when it is misused, "is taken seriously."

> In the one course [*einen Zug*] of the divine action there is not only the divine predestination [*Vorherbestimmung*], but also a human self-determination [*Selbst-bestimmung*]; not only the divine faithfulness [*Treue*] but also human faith [*Glauben*]; not only God's command and promise, but also the question of obedience and trust. (508; 571)

In this one course of action, then, "God's freedom . . . includes the freedom of the creature." God's special act (or course of action) in *Heilsgeschichte* thus as emerges as a *gracious* work of God, which again leads Barth to make reference to the *felix culpa*.[100]

3. According to Barth, the peculiar characteristics of God's work of salvation appear thirdly in "the fact that from the very outset and in all its stages, the history of salvation is based on a choice [*Auswahl*]." That choice is the choice of God to communicate and have partnership with "specific men who are marked out . . . by God himself" (508; 571). Barth mentions Abel, Noah, Abraham, Isaac, and Jacob as examples of such "special children of God" whom God chose as partners (508; 572). There is a *biblical pattern* of "continual selection and separation in Israel. . . and even within the Church itself." Such *election* does not contradict the universal scope of God's grace and reconciliation.[101] Rather, "it is just in this way" of election of particular people that God "wills that all men will be saved" (I Tim 2:4). The triumph and sheer gratuity of the grace by which God wills to save humanity would not be evident "if the relation between God and all men were uniform" (508; 571). And again, in God's free election of particular people, God has not become other than the one He is. He remains the God who *constantly* loves in freedom. God's free election is another manifestation of the special work of God in history that surpasses the work of creation but also reveals the true nature of creation (see 508; 572).

---

100. Barth's concern to affirm both the supreme divine freedom and a derivative—but corresponding—human freedom is related to his rejection of the misunderstandings of the God-world relation found in both monism and dualism (see above).

101. Barth's quotes Matt 5:45 and 1 Tim 2:4 to highlight this point.

4. Fourth, Barth highlights the *miraculous* character of God's second or saving work. He says the following of this second work: its "occurrence, acceptance by men and its effect on them are always accompanied by the sign of the miraculous" (509; 572). Barth adds that although God's reconciling work occurs in "the sphere and context" of creation, "it is on each occasion something *completely new*." It follows other events, but it does not follow *from* them. By means of "interruption and annulment" God's saving *Heilsgeschichte* establishes a "*new continuity*" with the created order that precedes it.[102]

For Barth, the miraculous work of God does not speak so much of an "ontic" or "ontological" disruption of the created order (and hence standing in tension with God's "other" work of creation), but is construed primarily in "noetic" or "revelational" terms. So he says: "Again, miracle is simply the revelation of the divine glory otherwise hidden from us, on the strength of which we can believe and honour Him elsewhere as Creator and Lord" (509; 573). Whether or not this is a proper reading of Scripture, this interpretation of miracle allows Barth to maintain more easily the conviction that God remains constant in all his actions. Barth again allows his particular reading of the scriptural witness to indirectly authorize his doctrinal conclusions regarding divine constancy.

5. Fifth, and finally, Barth makes the point, to which he has alluded before, that "creation itself gains new depth and perspective" in the revelation of God that is constituted by the new act of God in reconciliation (509; 573). All creation is seen in the light of the "distinction and connection between the reconciliation which is to be received here and now in faith and the redemption which is to be *revealed* one day beyond" (509; 573; emphasis added). Here, Barth first brings into focus the eschatological dimension of salvation history. Again, Barth regards what is new about this "eschatological work" of God in a primarily noetic or epistemo-

---

102. In this context, Barth employs the nature/grace distinction in his own distinctive way. "Grace is the secret behind nature, the hidden meaning of nature" (509; 572). Again, he says, "there is in nature more than nature" and "Nature becomes the theatre of grace, and grace is manifested as Lordship over nature, and therefore in freedom over against it."

logical way, which allows it to be part of God's one unified act of salvation, which, in turn clearly preserves God's constancy. Thus, Barth says that the distinction between reconciliation ("the now") and redemption ("the not yet") is most correctly stated as the distinction between:

> this life and this world [i] in the form and manner in which they are known to us here, and [ii] in the form and manner of their perfection in which they are known to God alone, but will one day be known to us also hereafter; that is, in the form and manner of the kingdom of God which will then be manifested and seen absolutely, exclusively, and *without any contradiction*. (509; 573; bracketed numerals and emphasis added)

As such, creation is not abolished by this new work of reconciliation, and reconciliation is not abolished by redemption.[103] Rather, the principle is that earlier works of God gain "new depth and perspective" through the subsequent works. As such, creation, reconciliation, and redemption are actions within the one central act of God *ad extra*, that is, the act in which God elects to be and is *pro nobis* (for us) as the One who loves in freedom. As such, we encounter the implicit dialectic between the single-act perspective and the multiple-act perspective in Barth's view of God's relationship to creation and its history (see above).

This concludes our exposition of Barth's survey of "history of salvation" in its five "modes" or "moments." This exposition attests to the indirect authorizing function of Scripture over Barth's doctrine of God's constancy. Barth offers a particular narrative construal of the Bible that grounds and confirms his view that God is marked by a flexible constancy in his works *ad extra*. This view, in turn, is indirectly a reason for saying that God is constant *ad intra* (for Barth believes that God's being-in-act *ad extra* are a true revelation of God's being-in-act *ad intra*). We now turn to some further comments about the Christocentric character of Barth's construal of salvation history and how this relates to his use of Scripture.

We observed at the end of the previous subsection on Philippians 2 that Barth's indirect way of authorizing his doctrine of God is typi-

---

103. The revelation of God in reconciliation in turn gives birth to a "living hope" (1 Pet 1:3) that expectantly awaits the final revelation of God (510; 573). In this sense, Barth can speak of the fact that "God is our coming Redeemer" as "a special element in God's constant life" and must be recognized as such by the believer.

cally Christocentric in one way or another.[104] Sometimes, as with Barth's treatment of the biblical texts and patterns regarding God's repentance, the Christocentrism is indirect or implicit. This is again the case here; Barth nowhere names the name of Jesus Christ in his treatment of salvation history in this excursus. However, the implicit or tacit presence of a Christocentric perspective is again evident, and this time more strongly than it was above. As Barth clarifies in this main text after his excursus on salvation history, God's constancy in the "history of salvation" is manifested most clearly in the single act of God in Christ (512ff.; 576ff.).[105] This single act is mysteriously present in five specific "acts" we explained above. These various works of God—whether in past, present, or future—can only be "anticipations" or "repetitions" of what God does in the single work or act of Christ in history.

Thus, Barth's Christocentrism itself is related to the single-act and multiple-act dialectic that we noted above. The paradoxical "logic" of this dialectic can be illuminated by what Hunsinger calls the pattern of "dialectical inclusion." In this "Trinitarian" conceptual pattern, frequent in Barth's doctrine of God, the "whole is understood to be included in the part without rendering the other parts superfluous."[106] In this case, the whole or single act of God's grace in Christ is included in each one of the diverse acts (e.g., creation, reconciliation, and redemption) in a way that does not render the other acts superfluous. On one level, the distinct acts of creation, reconciliation, and redemption each play a distinct special role even though on another level each is simply a "repetition" of the same single act of God's grace towards humanity in Christ. Since God's being is in act, God's Trinitarian being is in a parallel way marked by both simplicity and diversity, by constancy and change.

Underlying the "whole act" or "single act" perspective is God's single eternal decision to elect humanity in Christ. In this way Christological election can be understood as the essential presupposition of or beginning of all God's gracious, covenantal acts *ad extra*, not to mention

---

104. Barth gives eloquent testimony to his own understanding of Christocentrism in a brief excursus earlier in II/1 (320).

105. "The meaning and secret of the creation and preservation of the world is revealed in the history of salvation. But the meaning and secret of the history of salvation itself is Jesus Christ" (512; 576).

106. Hunsinger, *How to Read Karl Barth*, 86; cf. 56; 107ff. and *Disruptive Grace*, 174f.

shaping the contours of God's being-in-act.[107] Accordingly, Barth concludes his discussion of constancy with an excursus that opposes the abstract, non-Christological understanding of God's immutable will as a *decretum absolutum* (519-22; 583-87). In this excursus, Barth shows how the Reformed scholastics tended to ignore the concrete context of the passages about God's will that they cited to support their view. Above all they failed to see how God's will toward creation is united in and determined by Jesus Christ.

We conclude this section with an observation about Barth's Christocentrism that applies to his whole account of divine constancy, not only the account of salvation history he gives within it. Since Scripture is the primary source for Barth's understanding of who Christ is, Barth critiques the theological tradition of classical immutability primarily on the basis of the testimony of Scripture as he understands it. Likewise, it is Scripture, even more than the Christological dogmas of the Christian tradition, that is ultimately the primary determining norm behind his development of a Christocentric doctrine of God's constancy as an alternative to the classical doctrine.

Excursus: Barth and Dorner

We conclude this chapter with an excursus on the theological relationship that exists between Barth and the German theologian and doctrinal historian Isaak August Dorner (1809-1884)[108] especially as it bears upon Barth's doctrine of constancy. Near the beginning of his treatment of divine constancy, Barth comments, "Those who know his essay will recognize as they read this subsection how much I owe to Dorner's inspiration" (493; 554).[109] Barth refers here to "Dorner's great essay" on

---

107. McCormack (*Karl Barth's Critically Realistic Dialectic Theology*, 460ff.) argues that Barth's Christological view of election has a determining effect on Barth's account of the Being of God in II/1, even though he had not yet written II/2, where this Christological view is developed.

108. Note that Dorner's name can be abbreviated either J. A. Dorner (German) or I. A. Dorner (English).

109. The essay to which Barth refers is "Über die richtige Fassung des dogmatishen Begriffs der Unveränderlichkeit Gottes," which first appeared in three subsequent issues of the *Jahrbuch für deutsche Theologie* in the years 1856-1858 and was later included in Dorner's *Gesammelte Schriften aus dem Gebeit der systematischen Theologie*, 1883. An English translation of this essay, with an introduction, has recently been provided by Robert R. Williams and Claude Welch under the title *Divine Immutability—a Critical Consideration*.

divine immutability in which, Barth says, Dorner understood the immutable God as the triune God who is living in himself and "has made this clear in a way that is illuminating for the whole doctrine of God." In this case, Barth clearly recognizes Dorner's influence upon him, although this recognition is not always present with respect to other areas in which Dorner may have influenced him.

Two articles by Robert Sherman (1997) and Matthias Gockel (2000) respectively have explored this question of how much Barth does in fact owe to Dorner with respect to divine immutability or constancy.[110] Earlier, both Jürgen Moltmann and Wolfhart Pannenberg had said that Dorner influenced Barth to speak of three "modes of being" rather than three "persons."[111]

In the remainder of this excursus, we will not attempt to complete the daunting historical task of distinguishing between that which is a genuine "influence" of Dorner upon Barth and that which is merely an accidental correspondence or similarity between them. However we resolve this question, there are clearly many strong similarities between Barth and Dorner, including several to which other scholars have not yet attended.

In what follows, we wish to provide an introductory survey of various "points of contact" between Barth and Dorner, some showing striking similarity and others showing contrast. We will focus on those points of contact relevant to our thesis topic, namely, those which bear upon either the "doctrine of God" or upon "theological method." Part of the evidence will be drawn from secondary sources and part will

---

110. Both Sherman and Gockel came independently to the conclusion that Dorner provides a historical and theological link between the doctrines of God provided by Schleiermacher and Barth, although they understand the nature of this link somewhat differently. Although Gockel's article was published several years after Sherman's, Gockel notes in a footnote that Sherman's article was submitted for publication *after* the completion of his (Gockel's) study ("On the Way from Schleiermacher to Barth," 491, n. 4). For the most part, Sherman follows Williams's view of the relationship between Schleiermacher, Dorner, and Barth, while Gockel does not (see Williams, "I. A. Dorner: The Ethical Immutability of God" and his introduction to Dorner, *Divine Immutability*). See also the additional secondary literature, both English and German, cited by Sherman and Gockel.

111. See Moltmann (*Trinity and the Kingdom*, 139, 241f.) and Pannenberg ("Subjecktivität Gottes und der Trinitätslehre," 99f. and *Systematic Theology*, 295ff.). These authors refer to Dorner's treatment of the Trinity in his *System der christlichen Glaubenslehre* (the English Translation is found in *System of Christian Doctrine*, 433ff.). Barth makes no explicit reference to Dorner in his treatment of the Trinity in I/1.

be drawn from our own research. In this survey we will distinguish three kinds of evidence: (1) evidence from Barth's explicit references to Dorner, (2) evidence from "literary correspondences" between Barth and Dorner, and (3) evidence from more general similarities of thought or method.

First, Barth makes explicit references to Dorner on several occasions. In his *Protestant Theology in the Nineteenth Century*, Barth gives a largely positive interpretation of Dorner,[112] but makes no reference to his treatment of immutability.[113] In his prolegomena volumes to CD Barth cites Dorner several times. In these references (which bear more directly upon Dorner's theological method), Barth groups Dorner together with other nineteenth-century theologians and evaluates him in a largely negative light.[114] For one thing, Barth believes that Dorner and his contemporaries are "too much impelled by a mere acceptance of the achievements of contemporary philosophy,"[115] which in Dorner's case is primarily German idealism.[116] But in his doctrine of God, Barth's comments are positive, both within his general treatment of the perfections in §29[117] and in relation to divine constancy in §31 (as cited above). We will explore the nature and causes of these divergent evaluations below.

Second, there are what we can call "literary correspondences" between Dorner and Barth. With respect to divine constancy, many of these correspondences (e.g., similar phrasing, similar scriptural references, etc.) are surveyed well by Sherman.[118] We have also noted some of additional correspondences in Barth's doctrine of divine unity (see chapter 4). In general, it appears that these correspondences provide

---

112. Barth, *Protestant Theology in the Nineteenth Century*, 563–73.

113. This may be because Barth had not yet read Dorner's essay. The lectures on the nineteenth century (on which *Protestant Theology in the Nineteenth Century* was based) were given in 1932–1933 and II/1 was published in 1939 (see Barth, *Protestant Theology in the Nineteenth Century*, xii and Sherman, "Isaak August Dorner on Divine Immutability," 393f.).

114. See I/1, 276; I/2, 615f. and 830.

115. I/1, 276.

116. On Dorner's relationship to Schelling and idealist philosophy in general (Hegel, Fichte, etc.), see R. F. Brown, "Schelling and Dorner on Divine Immutability," 237–49.

117. Barth cites Dorner earlier in his doctrine of God (II/1, 330; 371f.) for resisting nominalism along with a couple of his contemporaries.

118. "Isaak August Dorner on Divine Immutability," 393–96.

evidence that Barth was influenced by Dorner in ways beyond what his explicit comments or citations verify.

Third, there are general similarities or correspondences between the ideas or approaches of Dorner and Barth. For example, both of them attempt to develop a "flexible," "personal," and largely "non-substantialist" conception of immutability that allows God to relate to the changing world in a way that is constant, faithful, and reliable. However, they develop these ideas in different ways. Dorner has a concept of "ethical immutability" in which "the ethical" (as a roughly Kantian category) creates a kind of continuity between God and humanity, and thus between God and the world.[119] Rather than being marked by such a specific conception of God's ethical immutability, Barth rather places a greater emphasis on God's personal freedom and transcendence in relation to the world.[120] In fact, Dorner appears to arrive at the three modes of being from a conception of God's ethical essence by means of a Hegelian logical derivation,[121] which, at least on the face of it, is quite opposed to Barth's particularism and actualism.[122] Despite these differences, Dorner frequently displays a concern to ground his theological judgments in Scripture, much as Barth does.[123]

How can we summarize this diverse evidence in order to offer a concise comparison of Barth and Dorner? With respect to the doctrine of God, it is clear that important elements of Barth's critique of and alternative to classical immutability were already taken up by Dorner, even though Barth also makes a distinctive contribution that goes beyond Dorner. Dorner made a clear break from the classical view and recovered something of a more biblical view of God's immutability or constancy. Barth develops these biblical features further, with an emphasis on God's freedom. Dorner displays a more a specifically ethical conception of God influenced by modern anthropocentrism and idealism (e.g., Kant, Schleiermacher, Hegel, and Schelling). That Barth is not

---

119. See Williams, "I. A. Dorner: The Ethical Immutability of God"; cf. Gockel, "On the Way from Schleiermacher to Barth," 505.

120. See Sherman, "Isaak August Dorner on Divine Immutability," 398 and Gockel, "On the Way from Schleiermacher to Barth," 505f.

121. See Dorner, *Divine Immutability*, 171f.; cf. Gockel, "On the Way from Schleiermacher to Barth," 503f.

122. See Sherman, "Isaak August Dorner on Divine Immutability," 397f., 400f.

123. See ibid., 389, 396.

entirely free from such influences, however, is evident in his conceiving of God along the idealistic lines of an absolute self-identical Subject.[124] The lingering question is whether or not Barth's use of modern conceptuality, albeit a use less heavy-handed than Dorner's, is genuinely subordinate to the revelation attested in Scripture.[125]

This last question leads to the further question of how we should compare the theological methods of Dorner and Barth. Specifically, how do they compare in their use of Scripture, tradition, and reason? Dorner's own statement of his theological method is perhaps clearest in his *System of Christian Doctrine*, first published in German in 1879–80. There it is clear that Christian faith is the basic postulate and source of dogmatics or Christian doctrine.[126] Dorner believed that dogmatics proceeded from this basis in faith by means of both "science" [*Wissenschaft*] (which relates to the use of reason) and "religion" (which includes the use of church tradition and Scripture).[127] Although Dorner believed that faith involved objective knowledge of God's reality,[128] this starting point is still too anthropocentric for Barth, who wished to begin with the Word of God itself.[129] Further, Barth would regard Dorner's uncritical theological use of general concepts like "science" and "religion" as highly problematic, even though he might recognize that Dorner aimed to be sensitive to the particularities of revelation.

---

124. See Moltmann, *Trinity and the Kingdom*, 139ff., and Pannenberg, *Systematic Theology*, 295ff. See also our related comments and citations in the initial part of chapter 3 on Barth's view of the Trinity.

125. We could develop this question as follows. To what extent does Barth's doctrine of constancy, despite its self-proclaimed biblical roots, still derive from this modern philosophical heritage? If we accept that no theologian can entirely escape having a philosophy or philosophical influences (see Barth's own affirmation of this in *CD* I/2, 727–36), could we say that Barth's particular employment of Idealist and modern philosophy happens to be *more consistent with the Bible* on divine constancy than the "classical" philosophical heritage was? That is, does it represent as positive theological use of "reason" that actually improves one's ability to read and interpret the biblical texts and gives one more insight into them?

126. Dorner, *A System of Christian Doctrine*, 31–187.

127. Dorner, *Divine Immutability*, 130f.; see Sherman, "Isaak August Dorner on Divine Immutability," 389f.

128. See Barth, *Protestant Theology in the Nineteenth Century*, 264f., where he stresses Dorner's improvement over Schleiermacher on this point.

129. See Pannenberg's helpful reflections on these matters (*Systematic Theology*, 43ff. and 126ff.).

The two theologians differing uses of Scripture, tradition, and reason are marked by both similarities and differences. Though he understands Scripture mainly as an expression of the faith of the primitive church, Dorner shows a high degree of reverence for Scripture. In fact, in his comments on "dogmatic method," Dorner says that faith "has by Scripture to continually approve itself as Christian."[130] Again in a way similar to Barth, Dorner also displays respect for the theological traditions (creeds and confessions) of the Church, although they are always subordinate to Scripture.[131] The methodological differences between Barth and Dorner are most clear with respect to their uses of reason. Although Dorner presents critiques of figures like Schleiermacher, Hegel, and Schelling, he also appropriates much from them, showing himself to be very much a man of his time. Accordingly, he is apt to refer to the ideas colored by the culture of his day as expressions of "the universal consciousness of God" or "the common reason of man."[132] Although Barth is by no means exempt from such intellectual influences (not least in relationship to Dorner), he is more careful to subordinate philosophical ideas and concepts to revelation. This is evident in Barth's typical avoidance of general concepts of human experience, religion, or reason such as those that marked Dorner's work.

In conclusion, despite his explicit and implicit reservations about Dorner, Barth regards Dorner as having risen above most of his contemporaries in his capacity to articulate the unique reality of God. Barth's doctrine of God bears the undeniable mark of Dorner's legacy. The precise character of his influence on Barth will no doubt be the subject of future studies.

---

130. Dorner, *A System of Christian Doctrine*, 170; cf. 175f.
131. Ibid., 175ff.
132. Ibid., 170.

6

Barth's Doctrine of Divine Eternity

IN THIS CHAPTER WE WILL EXAMINE BARTH'S ACCOUNT OF ETERNITY in *CD* II/1. This chapter is structured according to the same three-fold pattern we employed in chapters 4 and 5: (1) Barth's presentation and critique of classical views, (2) Barth's alternative view, and (3) the role of Scripture in Barth's argument.

Despite its similar structure, three factors will distinguish our expository analysis in this chapter from our considerations of divine unity and constancy in the last two chapters. First, Barth's view of eternity and the connected issue of God's relation to time has been the subject of a great deal of secondary literature, which contrasts sharply with the relative dearth of material on his views of God's simplicity or constancy. We will therefore give relatively more attention to the description and evaluation of such literature in this chapter. Second, even more than his accounts of God's simplicity or constancy, Barth's view of eternity is marked by a great deal of complexity. This complexity has led to a great deal of interpretative confusion, aspects of which we will expose and resolve below. Third, the question of God's eternity and its relation to time is discussed much more frequently than either simplicity or constancy in other volumes of *CD*. Thus, this chapter relates more easily to the larger themes and issues of *CD*.[1] That said, this chapter treats

---

1. George Hunsinger says the following about Barth's unique views of time and eternity: "No topic in Barth interpretation is more in need of clarification, and none more requires working with the *Church Dogmatics* as a whole, than this one" (*How to Read Karl Barth*, 14). The following parts of *CD* offer the most extensive discussions of time and eternity: I/1, §11("Eternal Son"); I/2, §14 ("Time of Revelation"); II/1, §31.3 ("Eternity and Glory," our focus in this chapter) and III/2, §47 ("Man in his Time"). Roberts, "Karl Barth's Doctrine of Time," and Colwell, *Actuality and Provisionality*, consider all of these passages (and others) relatively comprehensively.

in detail only the relevant section on eternity in volume II/1 (608–40; 685–722).[2]

Barth's Presentation and Critique of Classical Views of Timeless Eternity

Accounts of God's Eternity in Distinction from Earthly Time

After some introductory remarks on what eternity is, Barth turns to an exposition of one aspect of eternity, that aspect which distinguishes it from time. In an excursus, Barth cites three classical theologians who represent the patristic, medieval, and Protestant orthodox periods respectively (608; 686). Barth quotes two passages from Augustine, which can be translated as follows:

> Eternity is the very substance of God, who contains nothing changeable; there, nothing is past, as though it no longer existed; nothing is future, as though it did not yet exist. There, there is nothing except "is."[3]
>
> He was, because he never was not; he will be, because he will never not be; he is, because he always is.[4]

Then, Barth quotes the following passage from Anselm:

> So it is not the case that yesterday you were and tomorrow you will be; rather, yesterday, today, and tomorrow you *are*. In fact, it is not even the case that yesterday, today, and tomorrow you *are*. Rather, you are simply out of time altogether. But you, although nothing exists without you, do not exist in a place or a time; rather, all things exist in you. For nothing contains you, but you contain all things.[5]

---

2. In this chapter, as with the previous two chapters, we follow the practice of referring to Barth's work by means of abbreviated citations in parentheses in the main text. The number or numbers listed before the semicolon refer to a page or pages from the English Translation in *CD*, and the number or numbers listed after the semicolon refer to a page or pages from the German *KD*.

3. Augustine *Enarr. in Ps.* (on Ps 101:2, 10), as cited by Barth in Latin in *CD* II/1, 608; *KD*, 686. Unless otherwise noted, English translations from the Latin in this chapter are provided by Harry M. Hine of School of Latin and Greek, University of St. Andrews, Scotland.

4. Augustine, *Joann. Tract.* 99, as cited by Barth on 608; 686.

5. *Proslogion* 19, as cited by Barth 608; 686. Translation from *Anselm of Canterbury*, 112.

Finally, Barth cites the definition of eternity given by one of his favorite Reformed scholastics, Amandus Polanus.

> The eternity of God is the essential property of God, through which it is indicated that God is not bounded by any time and has neither any beginning in time nor any end of existence, but is earlier than every time and later than every end, and, absolutely without succession, always exists in his entirety at the same moment.[6]

At this stage in his argument, Barth cites these passages without significant criticism, letting them stand as a traditional testimony that confirms the primary biblical testimony to the "clear antithesis" that exists between the eternity of the Creator and the time of the creature (608; 686).

Later in his argument, however, Barth gives a mixed review to the affirmations on eternity offered by these classical writers. On the one hand, the perspective on eternity represented by Augustine, Anselm, and Polanus is found wanting because it expresses only part of the truth of God's eternity—namely, eternity in its "negative" aspect, its distinction from time. But on the other hand, this "part-truth of the concept of eternity in Augustine and Anselm" is an important part-truth, for it shows the irreversible priority, freedom, and transcendence of the eternity of God in relation to time (614f.; 693).

The Classic Boethian Definition of Eternity and Its Interpretative Legacy

Another classical writer, the sixth-century philosopher-theologian Boethius, offers a definition of eternity that "goes farther and deeper than the statements of Augustine and Anselm, which are far too occupied with the confrontation between eternity and time" (610; 688). For Boethius, "Eternity is the total, simultaneous, and perfect possession of interminable life."[7] This definition, as Barth interprets it, captures well the "positive quality of eternity" that allows the biblical writers to speak

---

6. Polanus, *Synt. Theol. Chr.*, 1609. col. 928, as cited by Barth on 608; 686.

7. Boethius, *De Consolatio Philosophiae*, 5.6; translation from Hunsinger, *Disruptive Grace*, 199.

of God as possessing "years and days." As such, the definition is capable of speaking of a view of eternity that includes time.[8]

Barth notes, however, that "although later this statement of Boethius was constantly quoted as authoritative it was never properly exploited" (610f.; 688). He continues, "We can see this clearly in its defense by Thomas Aquinas, which is obviously only partially convinced and certainly only partially convincing."[9] Indeed, Barth refers to a statement that Boethius makes elsewhere (cited by Aquinas) that resists the positive potential of his own definition: "The flowing instant (*nunc fluens*) produces time and the abiding instant (*nunc stans*) eternity."[10] For Barth, "it is not sufficient to contrast [eternity] as the *nunc stans* with the *nunc fluens* of time" (611; 689).[11] Rather, "The interpretation of *aeternitas* by the *possessio vitae* and the *possessio vitae* by the *nunc* ["the instant," "the now"] is correct." For Barth,

> [T]he concept of the divine *nunc* must not exclude the time prior to and after the "now," the past and the future, nor may it exclude the *fluere* [the flowing]. On the contrary, it must include it no less than the *stare* [the static]. Eternity is the *nunc* that is not subject to the distinctions between the past, present, and future. But again, it is not subject to the abolition of these distinctions. The usual way of treating the concept of eternity in theological tradition leads to the dangerous position that there appears to be no eternity if there is no time . . . and that there appears to be no knowledge of eternity except through time, in the form of a negation of the concept of time: *in cognitionem aeternitatis oportet nos venire per tempus*. (611; 689)

The Latin phrase in the last line of this quotation presents a kind of methodological rule provided by Aquinas. It can be translated: "we can only come to know eternity by way of time."[12] This rule arguably stands in opposition to Barth's rule that the divine Subject must give content

---

8. Placher notes, "'life' seems to be an obviously temporal category," even though it speaks of a different kind of life (God's life) and thus a "different kind of time" (*Narratives of a Vulnerable God*, 31).

9. Barth refers to Aquinas' *Summa Theologiae*, Ia, 10 (esp. article 1).

10. Boethius *De Trin.* 4, as cited in Aquinas, *Summa Theologiae*, 1a, 10, 2 (Blackfriars 2:139).

11. See Hunsinger *Disruptive Grace*, 186ff., on this traditional distinction between the two senses of "now" (*nunc*).

12. *Summa Theologiae*, 1a, 10, 1 (Blackfriars 2:135).

to the predicates of God, for they are the perfections of this Subject alone. As we have seen in earlier chapters, Barth's methodological particularism runs up against the abstract, a priori conceptions of God that result from conceiving of God as the opposite or contrast to the created order.[13] Accordingly, Barth states:

> [W]e know eternity primarily and properly [*eigentlich*], not by the negation of the concept of time, but by the knowledge of God as the *possessor interminabilis vitae* [possessor of interminable or unlimited life]. It is He who is the *nunc*, the pure present. He would be this even if there were no such thing as time. He is this before and beyond all time and equally before and beyond all non-temporality [*Nicht-Zeitlichkeit*]... *The theological concept of eternity must be set from the Babylonian captivity of an abstract opposite to the concept of time.*[14]

Classical Contributions Towards a View of Eternity that Includes Time

According to Barth, however, classical writers like Aquinas were sometimes able to break out of their captivity to an abstract, negative view of eternity. Thus, Barth cites with approbation Aquinas' statement: "Verbs of different tenses are used of God, not as though he varied from present to past to future, but because his eternity comprehends (*includit*) all phases of time (*omnia tempora*)."[15] For Aquinas to speak of such "inclusion" of temporality within eternity, Barth thinks, "clearly denotes a positive relation to time that is the special possession of eternity" (613; 691). But Aquinas only hints at this positive relation between time and eternity—a relation of which Barth says "must be brought into greater prominence than in the older theology." The older theologians were aware of "this positive meaning of the concept of eternity," denoting it

---

13. See Camfield, *Reformation Old and New*, 70, and Gunton, *Becoming and Being*, 2ff.

14. II/1, 611; 689; italics in last sentence added. The distinction between the two senses of eternity here is parallel to the primary (positive) and secondary (negative) senses of divine freedom in general (see our discussion of §28.3 in chapter 3).

15. *Summa Theologiae*, 1a, 10, 2 (Blackfriars 2:141). Barth also cites several other passages from Aquinas in this context (612; 691). E.g., Barth quotes without criticism Aquinas' distinction between eternity (as defined by Boethius) and time (as defined by Aristotle) as follows: "eternity is an instantaneous whole [*totum simul*], whilst in time there is before and after" (*Summa Theologiae*, 1a, 10, 4 [Blackfriars 2:145]).

by the term *sempiternitas*, but they did not give it the stress it deserves. "For, rightly understood, the statement that God is eternal tells us what God is, not what He is not." Barth's positive comments on Aquinas are thus qualified by Barth's disapproval of the weight Aquinas gave to the *via negativa* and to the related methodological rule that we must learn of eternity only on the basis of time.[16]

Barth can also cite Polanus with qualified approbation. Barth quotes the following statement of Polanus on the ordering of the Father, Son, and Spirit within God's eternity: "This principle of order is not excluded by eternity, nor is it opposed to eternity" (see 615; 694).[17] According to Barth, Polanus is surely correct to say that this Trinitarian 'principle of order' is not excluded from eternity. But then Barth critiques Polanus' tendency to fall prey to the contrastive, negative logic of much of the classical tradition: "But it is not enough to distinguish this *principium ordinis* [the principle of order] . . . from the *principium temporis* [the temporal principle]," for "this *principium ordinis* is clearly identical with a *principium temporis* in God himself" (615; 694). What this means for Barth will be clarified below, but at this point it suffices for us simply to show that Barth was intentionally qualifying the classical tradition here. Again, Barth desires to develop a view of God's eternity that is still more *inclusive* of time than the classical theologians allowed. Boethius, Aquinas, and Polanus occasionally make affirmations that moved in this direction, but they do not go far enough.

In addition, Barth cites a passage from Augustine as a precedent for the view that eternity includes a genuine, but unique, kind of temporality within it. Augustine writes: "For the years of God are not one thing and God himself another thing, but the eternity of God is the years of God."[18] This is significant for Barth because Augustine here allows God as the self-revealing Subject to determine what eternity means, rather than taking an a priori view of eternity and making God fit into it. Accordingly, Augustine's statement suggests that the theologian should accept the biblical affirmations of God's temporality as saying something about the nature of God's eternity rather than being

---

16. See our comments on Barth's rejection of the *via negativa* in our subsection on "The Perfections of Love and Freedom" in chapter 3.

17. Polanus, *Syntagma Theologiae Christianae*, 1609, col. 929, as quoted by Barth (615; 694). Translation provided by Harry M. Hine and modified by the author.

18. Augustine *Enarr. in Ps.* 101:2,10, as quoted by Barth (638; 720).

merely instances of figurative anthropomorphism. As we will see later in the chapter, this is an important dimension of the view that Barth wishes to develop.

Barth's Alternative View of Eternity

We now take up the difficult task of summarizing Barth's complex alternative to the classical views of eternity. Barth's view incorporates something of these classical views, yet also moves beyond them.[19] While this section focuses primarily on giving our own exposition of the main features of Barth's view, we will also engage and evaluate relevant secondary literature that is helpful in the exposition.[20]

Barth's "Trinitarian" View of Eternity: Introduction and Formal Summary

In keeping with what we observed in the context of Barth's views of divine simplicity and constancy, we begin with George Hunsinger's observation that, in Barth's work, the traditional conception of eternity is "subjected to radical reinterpretation according to christological and trinitarian modes of thought," even if this is not always made explicit.[21] Specifically, Hunsinger speaks of the "perichoretic multidimensionality" and a "patterned complexity" of Barth's view of eternity, which resists reductionistic explanations and criticisms.[22] In an essay

---

19. George Hunsinger comments, "although Barth stands mainly in the tradition of Augustine, Boethius and Anselm, he modifies that tradition in order to appropriate what is valid in Hegel" (*Disruptive Grace*, 188). While we agree that Barth's view involves a conjunction of such pre-modern and modern elements, it is not always clear that Barth stands "mainly" in the pre-modern classical tradition, nor that the modern aspects of his view ought to be associated specifically or directly with Hegel.

20. The relevant works of Hunsinger (*How to Read Karl Barth* and especially the chapter "*Mysterium Trinitatis*: Karl Barth's Conception of Eternity," in *Disruptive Grace*, 186–209) are perhaps the most helpful for the task of *understanding* Barth's distinctive view of eternity correctly. We will largely avoid discussion of how we should *evaluate* Barth's view of eternity, although much of the secondary literature on Barth's account of eternity has been concerned with this.

21. Hunsinger, *How to Read Karl Barth*, 14. Hunsinger shows how a recognition of this point helps to overcome the charge that Barth's theology is "monistic" especially when such charges are prompted by Barth's "objectivism" (14ff.).

22. Hunsinger, *How to Read Karl Barth*, 291. Hunsinger continues, "Barth holds, christocentrically, (1) a thoroughly perichoretic view of eternity, (2) a thoroughly eschatological view of history, and (3) a thoroughly Chalcedonian view of the relation

entitled "Mysterium Trinitatis: Karl Barth's Conception of Eternity,"[23] Hunsinger offers a Trinitarian (and also Christological) exposition of Barth's account of the divine perfection of eternity in II/1. According to Hunsinger,

> Barth makes perhaps the first sustained attempt in history to reformulate eternity's mystery in fully trinitarian terms. The mystery of eternity becomes in effect a subtopic in the mystery of the Trinity. Eternity holds no perplexities that cannot be stated in trinitarian terms, and the Trinity has no formal aspects irrelevant to the question of eternity, so that the form of the Trinity and the form of eternity coincide.[24]

Robert Jenson and Richard Roberts had already referred to the Trinitarian character of Barth's view of eternity before Hunsinger.[25] But neither Jenson nor Roberts appears to have taken this point sufficiently into account in their actual exposition of Barth's view.[26]

We will devote the remainder of this subsection to a survey of Barth's view of eternity—a survey that focuses on its Trinitarian "formal aspects," as Hunsinger calls them. (We will treat the detailed Trinitarian and Christological content of Barth's view of eternity later.) Hunsinger observes that there are three irreducible formal aspects or "forms" of Barth's account of eternity. They are: (1) eternity as "pure duration" [*reine Dauer*] (2) eternity as "beginning, middle, and end,"[27] and (3) eternity as the "simultaneity [*Gleichzeitigkeit*] of beginning, middle, and

---

between them, such that within the Chalcedonian framework all aspects of historicity are ultimately *aufgehoben* by eternity" (my numerals in parentheses). See Hunsinger's explanation of the Hegelian pattern of *Aufhebung* in Barth (85f.). Hunsinger's later work (*Disruptive Grace*, 186–209) shows that the perichoretic nature of Barth's view of eternity (mentioned here) is only one of its several Trinitarian features.

23. Hunsinger, *Disruptive Grace*, 186–209.

24. Ibid., 189f.; emphasis added.

25. E.g., Jenson, *God after God*, 128; Roberts, "Karl Barth's Doctrine of Time," 106f., and 134f.

26. Regarding Roberts, Hunsinger comments: "In his severe criticism of Barth's conception, ... Roberts fails almost entirely to take its trinitarian structure into account. ... Much of Roberts' exasperation can perhaps be traced to this oversight" (*Disruptive Grace*, 197). In our view, the primary source for Roberts' exasperation with Barth lies in convictions about theological method, which are very different from Barth's.

27. Some variations of this "form 2" of eternity are "beginning, succession [*Folge*] and end" (608, 611; 685, 689) or "origin, movement and goal" (*Ursprung, Bewegung und Ziel*) (612; 690).

end" or simply "simultaneity" (608; 685). We may identify the presence of three forms of eternity in the following excerpt from Barth's opening discussion of eternity in II/1.

> God's eternity ... is the sovereignty and majesty of His love in so far as this has and is itself pure duration [form 1]. The being is eternal in whose duration [form 1] beginning, succession and end [form 2] are not three but one, not separate as a first, as second, and a third occasion, but one simultaneous occasion [form 3] as beginning, middle, and end. Eternity is the simultaneity of beginning, middle, and end [form 3], and to that extent is pure duration [form 1]. Eternity is God in the sense in which in Himself and in all things God is simultaneous [form 3], i.e., beginning and middle as well as end [form 2], without separation, distance, or contradiction. (608; 685f.)

Hunsinger then points out that these three aspects (or temporal forms) of eternity roughly correspond to three aspects of Trinitarian doctrine—not to the three persons, but to three Trinitarian concepts or terms and to the theological judgments that lay behind them.[28] The following table offers an overview of these conceptual correspondences.

The Trinity and Eternity[29]

Category	A [form 1]	B [form 2]	C
Traditional Trinitarian Terms	One "being" or "essence" (*ousia*)	Three "persons" or "modes of being" (*hypostases*)	"Interpenetration" or "mutual indwelling" (*perichoresis*)
Relations of God's "Self"	God as self-identical	God as self-differentiated	God as self-unified
Correlative "Forms" of Eternity	Eternity as "pure duration" [form 1]	Eternity as "beginning, middle, and end" [form 2]	Eternity as "simultaneity" [form 3]

28. Hunsinger, *Disruptive Grace*, 197f.

29. This chart is an attempt to summarize and organize relevant comments of Hunsinger's (*Disruptive Grace*, especially 190, 196). Hunsinger also notes other correspondences, but these are not pertinent to our purposes.

The essential soundness of these Trinitarian correlations will be tested in the course of our exposition. We will also observe other possible Trinitarian (and Christological) formal features in Barth's account of eternity.

At this point, we may raise several important questions. Does Barth really speak of all three of these forms of eternity, and, if so, does he do so with equal emphasis on each? In other words, does Barth reduce any one of the three forms of eternity to any one of the others? Or is the Trinitarian structure that Hunsinger speaks of an imposition on Barth's view? Also, does Barth's own Trinitarian doctrine itself involve a kind of reductionism, which in some way is reproduced here in his account of eternity?

Although we will not develop answers to these questions at length, these critical questions will remain in the background of our exposition in the remainder of the chapter. For now, we can simply note that previous commentators have indirectly charged Barth with what we are here calling "reductionism," of emphasizing only one or two rather than three forms of eternity to the detriment of others. For example, Richard Roberts appears to regard form 1 (pure duration) and form 3 (simultaneity) as more or less equivalent in Barth and does not perceive the presence of form 2 (beginning, middle/succession, and end) in Barth.[30] As such, Roberts believes Barth's view of eternity is reducible to at most two formal aspects, and in effect he reduces these to one—to a Boethian concept of "pure duration."[31] This is representative of a general tendency of many interpreters and critics of Barth to see a tendency in his view of eternity to swallow up the real temporal distinctions of beginning, middle, and end—and hence the significance of "history" for God.[32] The question that then arises is whether Barth's view is, after all, actually

---

30. Roberts, "Karl Barth's Doctrine of Time."

31. And here one might wish to go farther, by linking this analysis with the critique that others have made of Barth's doctrine of the Trinity (see the first section of chapter 3). Most importantly, one could speak of a "reduction" to pure duration that corresponds to a "semi-modalist" reduction of the three *hypostases* to the one *ousia* of God. Without due attention to the *hypostases*, *perichoresis* is likewise trivialized and reduced to God's simple *ousia*. Although Hunsinger would resist these charges, including the charge of "modalism," he does say that Barth gives a "logical and perhaps ontological precedence" to the divine *ousia* (Hunsinger, *Disruptive Grace*, 191).

32. For example, see Gunton, *Becoming and Being* and Moltmann, *Theology of Hope*.

decisively different from the classical view of eternity as timelessness, a-temporality, or non-temporality.

Eternity as Non-temporality: "Classical" Features of Barth's View of Eternity

As we now turn to the actual content of Barth's view of eternity, we begin where Barth begins: namely, with the more or less "classical" features of his view. Since we have alluded to several of these features in the first section of this chapter, we may be relatively brief.

In essence, the classical features of Barth's view of eternity are those that emphasize the distinction between eternity and time, and thus argue that in some sense God is a-temporal or timeless. This emphasis appears in the opening part of Barth's discussion of eternity. In this context, Barth makes the following claims.

> Eternity is not, therefore, time, although time is certainly God's creation or, more correctly, a form of His creation. Time is distinguished from eternity by the fact that in it beginning, middle, and end are distinct and even opposed as past, present, and future. Eternity is just the duration which is lacking to time, as can be seen clearly at the middle point of time, in the temporal present and in its relationship to the past and the future. Eternity has and is the duration which is lacking to time. It has and is simultaneity. (608; 686)

This passage creates the impression that Barth is defining eternity by contrasting it to time, the very tendency that he critiqued in Aquinas and that he persistently rejects as a manifestation of "natural theology" in the classical tradition.[33] Is it possible to define eternity as "just the duration which is lacking to time," and at the same time to escape this charge? Barth's apparent "Babylonian captivity" to a view of eternity as "an abstract opposite of time" appears to be confirmed in his strong words against the possibility of construing eternity as "everlastingness."

> Eternity is not, then, an infinite extension of time both backwards and forwards. *Time can have nothing to do with God.* The infinity of its extension cannot help it. For even and especially in this extension there is the separation and distance and con-

---

33. Because of this passage and other similar ones, Douglas Farrow charges Barth with natural theology in which eternity is defined in opposition to time (*Ascension and Ecclesia*, 291ff.).

tradition that mark it as time and distinguish it from eternity as the creature from the Creator. It is quite correct, as in the older theology, to understand the idea of eternity and therefore God himself first of all in this clear antithesis. In the sense mentioned, it is in fact non-temporality. (608; 686; emphasis added)

Whether Barth is actually falling prey to a classical kind of natural theology here depends on two important questions. (1) What does Barth mean by "time" in the context of affirmations such as, "time can have nothing to do with God"? (2) Does Barth come to his views on eternity's distinction from time on the basis of a priori conceptions of time and eternity or on the basis of a posteriori reflection (*Nachdenken*) on God's self-revelation as it is attested in Scripture? While we will not be able to resolve these questions decisively, we can offer some initial observations.

On the first question of what Barth means by "time" in the context his affirmations of eternity as non-temporality, the above-cited passages give us some clarification. Here, Barth refers to time as:

i. a form of God's creation and as such a "creature"

ii. a reality in which "beginning, middle, and end are distinct and even opposed"

iii. a reality that lacks duration and simultaneity

iv. a reality that is marked by (potentially infinite) extension [*verlängerte*].

Clearly, then, Barth is speaking of time in a specific sense, of time as it is found within creation.[34] Although Barth does not make it explicit, he is not referring to time or temporality in all of its possible senses here, some of which prove more amenable to being positively included within eternity (see below). Barth is referring to eternity in a *particular* (rather than general or all-inclusive) sense in this context: "*In the sense mentioned*, it [i.e., eternity] is in fact non-temporality" (608; 686; emphasis added).[35]

---

34. One of the difficulties in understanding Barth's view of time and eternity is that he uses these terms in many different senses (see our treatment of the four different senses of time in Barth's work above). Also, it is an open question whether Barth is referring to fallen creation (see his references to "fallen time" in I/2, §14), or to creation and created time in the present context (see Hunsinger *Disruptive Grace*, 204f.).

35. In a later passage, Barth says, "If in this triune being and essence of God there is nothing that *we call* time, that does not justify us in saying that time is *simply excluded*

The second question of the methodological basis for Barth's view of eternity as non-temporality or a-temporality cannot be answered on the basis of the passages cited so far. At this point we need only observe that even when Barth defines eternity as "just the duration which is lacking to [in] time" he may not be starting with an a priori conception of time and then negating it to arrive at a general conception of eternity as timelessness. Rather, it is certainly possible that Barth begins with "empirical" reflection on revelation and only then arrives at a view of eternity that *just so happened* to involve a contrast with time as a form of creation. Whether this is actually what Barth was doing will need to be considered in the course of our discussion. This, in turn, will determine whether Barth abides by his own methodological standards, particularly by his rejection of natural theology.

We will see that Barth's dialectical view of eternity includes a strong affirmation of both: (a) the transcendence of God's eternity in relation to time as a "form" or feature of creation and (b) the existence of a kind of temporality within God. The classical theologians occasionally moved towards affirming both sides of this dialectic (see above), but they did not go far enough with respect to God's real temporality.

Eternity as God's Unique Temporality: Ad Intra *and* Ad Extra

Eternity is not simply non-temporality; it is also what we could call God's unique temporality. As such, eternity has not only a negative relationship to time (608–10; 685–88), but also a positive relationship to time. The vast majority of Barth's exposition of eternity discusses the positive relationship of God to time (610–40; 688–722). We would misunderstand Barth if we thought that he was contradicting himself when he speaks of God as both a-temporal and temporal. Rather, we will see that Barth uses eternity and time in a variety of ways, and that various senses of these terms operate at different levels of meaning. For example, Barth could say that God is non-temporally temporal, when "non-temporally" means "not marked by time as a limited form of creation" and when "temporal" means "marked by temporality as it is found in God's unique life."

---

in God, or that his essence is simply the negation of time. On the contrary, . . . God has and is himself time" (615; 693f.).

The positive sense in which God is temporal begins to emerge in Barth's interpretation and use of the Boethian definition of eternity. Hunsinger observes that "what Barth does with this definition, in effect, is to relocate it within an explicit doctrine of the Trinity."[36] If we read between the lines of Hunsinger's exposition, we can make several points about Barth's use of this definition—points that move from the explicit, to the clearly implicit, to the possibly implicit. (1) The definition explicitly refers to eternity as simultaneity (form 3; "*simultaneous . . . possession*"). This relates, Hunsinger thinks, to the Triune *perichoresis* (see chart on "The Trinity and Eternity" above). (2) The definition clearly implies "pure duration" (form 1)[37] in its concept of "*interminable* life" and possibly in its concepts of totality and perfection. Both of these ideas are, in turn, connected with God's self-identical *ousia*.[38] (3) Finally, the Boethian definition, at least in Barth's view can be seen to imply eternity as beginning, middle, and end (form 2). The reason is that simultaneity, totality, and even duration appear to *presuppose* or *imply* some kind of succession of distinct temporal moments—some kind of beginning, middle, and end—even as simultaneity, totality and duration also qualify these distinct temporal moments as, in another sense, united with each other without separation or opposition.[39] This

---

36. Hunsinger *Disruptive Grace,* 199f. In a later passage where he is not explicitly discussing Boethius, Barth says: "A correct understanding of the positive side of the concept of eternity . . . is gained only when we are clear that we are speaking about the eternity of the Triune God" (615; 693), a point that he goes on to expound in ways that confirm Hunsinger's Trinitarian interpretative thesis.

37. Roberts rightly speaks of how Barth's concept of pure duration "stems from the informing of the Boethian *totum simul* by the Trinitarian impulse" ("Karl Barth's Doctrine of Time," 116).

38. Hunsinger says that "Totality, perfection and possession . . . correlate with the simplicity, singularity and sovereignty of the trintarian *ousia*" (*Disruptive Grace,* 199). Regarding "interminability," he says, "The definition states not merely that the divine life is endless or unlimited, but that it cannot possibly terminate . . . Therefore, the definition of eternity does not depend on the negation of time" (199f.).

39. Hunsinger states the point with caution: "The ideas of simultaneity and totality . . . seem to imply certain distinctions not found in the Boethian definition. From a Trinitarian standpoint, at least as Barth carries it through, they can be taken to imply temporal distinctions that correlate with the trinitarian *hypostases*" (*Disruptive Grace,* 200). As God's self-*uniting* movement, *perichoresis* presupposes three distinct *hypostases* that can nonetheless indwell each other (*Disruptive Grace,* 190). So also *simultaneity* would require beginning, middle, and end as distinct realities that can nonetheless indwell each other.

third point, like the second, is not explicit in the Boethian definition, but expresses how Barth may have appropriated the definition. Barth's appropriation would not contradict Boethius, but rather fill out his meaning in the light of Barth's own understanding of God as the living, Trinitarian God.

What, then, does Barth mean when he speaks of God's eternity as a kind of "temporality"? Colin Gunton refers to "God's eminent temporality," and John Colwell to the "authentic temporality of God's eternity."[40] Alan Padgett is close to the mark when he says that, for Barth, "eternity is the fullness of time without the defects of succession."[41] But what is time without the defects of succession? Rather than attempting to capture this divine time through a general definition, Barth's approach is to say that it is the unique time of God that is revealed in Jesus Christ.[42] Accordingly, Barth undertakes lengthy meditations on the scriptural narratives about Jesus in other parts of *CD*, especially on the forty days between his resurrection and ascension, in order to "define" this uniquely "real" time of God.[43] In his exposition of eternity in II/1, the Christological dimensions of Barth's view of eternity are smaller in scope and detail, but are still important. We can summarize such Christological dimensions by stating that the time of God revealed in Jesus, unlike "our time" (the time humans ordinarily experience), is not marked by any tension between the past, present, and future, or between beginning, middle, and end. Rather, Christ's time embodies these distinctions in a way that is marked by continuous "duration" and harmonious "simultaneity."

---

40. Gunton, *Becoming and Being*, 177ff. and Colwell, *Actuality and Provisionality*, 31ff.; cf. 131ff. Colwell's terminology seems slightly preferable to Gunton's for two reasons (1) Barth himself uses the term "authentic temporality" (III/2, 437), and (2) Gunton's "eminent temporality" has the connotation of the classical method of the *via eminentiae*, which Barth rejected (see II/1, 347 and our comments in chapter 3). That said, Barth himself uses terms that suggest something like eminent temporality, as when he asserts that "God . . . is supremely temporal" (*CD* III/2, 437).

41. Padgett, *God, Eternity, and the Nature of Time*, 143. However, we disagree with Padgett's claim that this implies that Barth's view of God's time lacks "process" or the "past-present-future distinction." If Barth were strictly consistent, this might be the case, but he is "dialectical" instead. Thus, Padgett neglects the presence of "form 2" of eternity in Barth's work.

42. See Placher *Narratives of a Vulnerable God*, 35–40 for a fine exposition of how Jesus Christ reveals "God's time" in Barth's view.

43. See especially III/2, §47, 440ff. Cf. Ford, *Barth and God's Story*, 142–46.

At this stage in our argument, we need to pause to clarify the main senses that Barth gives to the word "time" and to explain how these are related to the distinction between God *ad intra* and God *ad extra*. Even an appreciative interpreter of Barth like Hunsinger concedes that Barth lacks clarity on such matters.[44] With some reading between the lines of Barth's treatment of eternity in II/1, §31.3, we can understand Barth to be employing at least four distinct but inter-related concepts or senses of "time." The first two have to do with God's time (and therefore our particular concern) and the latter two with human time.

- *Time A*: God's own "time" *ad intra*, the "order and succession" and "inner movement" of God's eternal Triune being independent of a relationship to creation (615; 693f.).[45] This concept can also be spoken of as God's "eternity," as "absolute time" and sometimes as "readiness for time" (618ff.; 696ff.).

- *Time B*: God's time for us *ad extra*, "the time for us, the time of revelation, the time of Jesus Christ" (611f.; 689f.).[46] This concept of time can also be referred to as "real time" (613; 691),[47] as redeemed time (cf. 617f.; 696) or as another form of God's "readiness for time."

- *Time C*: Created time, or time as a non-eternal "form of creation" (608; 686).[48]

---

44. Hunsinger, *Disruptive Grace*, 189 and 200.

45. We recall from our discussion above Barth's comment in reference to a passage in Polanus in which Barth says that "this *principium ordinis*" of the eternal immanent Trinity "is clearly identical with a *principium temporis* in God himself" (615; 694). This "temporal principle" appears to refer in the first instance to Time A, a time God has independently of his relationship to the created order. "Time A" is what Hunsinger speaks of as "God eternal becoming" and associates with the dynamic of *perichorisis* (ibid., 200); it is also what A. Torrance calls God's "non-temporal 'becoming'" (ibid., 85).

46. See ibid., 201f.

47. Cf. I/2, §47, 47 and passim.

48. See the treatment of created time in I/2, 45ff., where Barth stresses that we do not have any access to such created time, since we live only in the realm of "fallen time" (Time D) that has become "revelation time" (Time B). If Hunsinger is correct that such created time, being marked by imperfection of transitoriness and division, stands in need of the eternal God's "healing" even without sin's corruption (*Disruptive Grace*, 204f.), then this is a speculative issue on which Barth does not appear to comment directly. See Barth's related language about "raising" created time to a form of his eternal being (616; 694 and see also Cullmann, *Christ and Time*, 63f.).

- *Time D*: Fallen time, "our time," or the "lost time" of human experience.[49]

We may make five observations about these four conceptions of time and their inter-relationships. First, Barth is not contradicting himself when he says that God is both timeless and temporal. God is timeless in the sense of being free from and sovereign "over" Time C and Time D. God is temporal insofar as God includes time—in its various meanings—within himself. (God does include even Time C and 4 in himself in a sense—not inherently, but by a voluntary act in which he overcomes their deficiencies christologically).

Second, Barth can refer to both Time A and Time B as "God's time" or even "eternity," and thus he does not always clearly distinguish when he is referring to God's being in itself (*ad intra*) and in relation to the world (*ad extra*).[50] Indeed, it appears that both Time A and Time B can be regarded as a "prototype" of Time C, or created time. But several passages (including those cited in our list above) show that Barth does wish to make a distinction between Time A and Time B, and that he regards the former as the ultimate "basis" (and hence prototype) of the latter.

Third, the distinction between Time A and Time B does not imply that Time B is simply not eternal, for God has *eternally* determined himself (in election) to create and redeem the world in Christ. Moreover, this eternal determination of God can be regarded not only as *ad extra*, but in some sense *ad intra*. This does not deny the distinction between Time A and Time B, but it shows that they are inseparably united with each other.[51]

---

49. Barth does not appear to refer directly to the concept of fallen time or sinful time in the section we are expounding in II/1, but he does imply it (e.g., he refers to the "rectification" of time on 618; 696). He refers to "Time D" explicitly under the rubric of "our time" in I/2, §47, 45 and passim.

50. For example, both Time A and Time B seem to be present in Barth's exposition of God's temporality in terms of pre-temporality, supra-temporality, and post-temporality (see below). The ambiguity between Time A and Time B may have to do with the ambiguity in Barth surrounding whether God's being is constituted by or expressed by his decisions and acts (again, see McCormack, "Grace and Being").

51. See Colwell for a generally accurate and insightful explanation of Barth's view of the distinction and close relation between God *ad intra* (the immanent Trinity) and God *ad extra* (the economic Trinity) (*Actuality and Provisionality*, 195–230). Jenson also recognizes that Barth draws both a distinction and an "analogy" between the Time A and Time B. He regards this aspect of Barth's thought as ambiguous and problematic (*God after God*, 152–55).

Fourth, Time C and Time D both refer to human time (and more broadly to the time of the created order), and thus, like Time A and Time B, are not always carefully distinguished from each other. But fortunately, this distinction is not crucial to understanding Barth's view of eternity.

Fifth and finally, we observe that, against some commentators, an accurate description of Barth's view of eternity does not require that we ascribe to Barth a specific philosophical view of the nature of time.[52] In fact, Barth's approach, with its typically ad hoc use of philosophy, does not lend itself to such an interpretation. While Barth may have certain ontological tendencies regarding the nature of time, he does not wish to bring premature closure to philosophical issues on which revelation does not speak decisively.

The Christological Features of Barth's View of Eternity

We have seen that God's eternity involves both a unique kind of divine non-temporality (in relation to Time C and Time D) and a unique divine temporality (in relation to Time A and Time B). In many ways, the heart of Barth's view of eternity is Time B, the "revelation time" that manifests what Time A (God's "inner" eternal Triune being) is like. Indeed, Time B also reveals that the positive relationship between the eternal God and time extends not only to God's own time (Time A and Time B), but also to creaturely time (Time C and even Time D). For in God's time *pro nobis* in Jesus Christ, God includes creaturely time within eternity, i.e., within his own time (Time B and even Time A). As God does so, he heals and transforms created-fallen time, all without making it any less creaturely. (This is similar to what we have observed in regard to God's simplicity and constancy in their respective relations

---

52. There are two main views of time in contemporary philosophical debate, the "stasis view" (or "four dimensionalism") and the process view (or "temporalism") (see Padgett, *God, Eternity and the Nature of Time*). Padgett ascribes to Barth a qualified version of the "stasis" view, shared by certain classical writers such as Aquinas (*God, Eternity and the Nature of Time*, 143ff.). See also Roberts, "Karl Barth's Doctrine of Time," 134 and 115, where he speaks of the affinity between Barth and a recent proponent of the stasis view, J. M. E. McTaggart. Barth's view of eternity and time seems to share elements of both of these views of time, perhaps incoherently; his view cannot be easily reduced to one or the other. This is consistent with his "philosophical eclecticism" and his view that systematic consistency is not possible in theology.

to the created realities of multiplicity and movement/change.⁵³) Even at this point, there is no need to regard Barth as contradictory, since God is still a-temporal in the sense that God's redeems fallen created time as the Lord over our time and who overcomes the defects of time rather than being captive to them.

Given Barth's Christocentric inclinations, it will come as no surprise that Barth construes this time (Time B) in thoroughly Christological terms. As Barth puts it,

> [God] does have time for us, the time of revelation, the time of Jesus Christ, and therefore the time of His patience, our lifetime, time for repentance and faith. But it really is He Himself who has time for us. He himself *is* time for us. For His revelation as Jesus Christ is really God Himself. (611f.; 689f.)

To be Christocentric is, for Barth, to be Trinitarian, for the person and work of Jesus Christ reveals the eternal Triune God, for the revelation in Jesus Christ is a work *of* the eternal Triune God (see chapter 4). Further, the *christological inclusion* of creaturely time within eternity is "modeled" after a particular understanding of the "hypostatic union" of the divine and human natures within Christ's *hypostasis*—a union, which involves the inclusion of the human within the divine *hypostasis*.⁵⁴ This Christological inclusion is marked by two distinct formal or "grammatical" patterns in addition to the "Trinitarian pattern" and other Trinitarian features that we have been exploring above, namely: (1) The Chalcedonian pattern, and (2) the Hegelian-*Aufhebung* pattern. In the remainder of our discussion in this subsection, we will apply these two patterns (identified by George Hunsinger as formal features of Barth's theology) to the concrete Christological content of Barth's view of eternity.⁵⁵

---

53. Barth makes this connection explicit in his account of eternity: "We have seen again and again that God is alive. His unity does not exclude but includes multiplicity and His constancy movement" (612; 690).

54. Barth states, "The Word spoken from eternity raises the time into which it is uttered (without dissolving it as time), up into His own eternity, as now His own time" (*CD* I/2, 52). See Dalferth, "Karl Barth's Eschatological Realism," 28ff.

55. Hunsinger speaks of only the Trinitarian and Chalcedonian patterns in his treatment of divine eternity (*Disruptive Grace*, 202). However, he earlier identifies the Hegelian-*Aufhebung* pattern as a third, distinct formal pattern in Barth's theology as a whole (*How to Read Karl Barth*, 85f.). In our view, aspects of this third pattern are implicit in Barth's treatment of eternity. In fact, this Hegelian pattern informs the

Above we noted that classical theologians like Aquinas and Polanus had affirmed, to a limited extent, that eternity includes time within it, even though their primary emphasis was on God's timelessness. Barth, by contrast, gives primary attention to God's voluntary inclusion of creaturely time within eternity and secondary attention to God's timelessness (see 613ff.; 691ff.). The positive affirmation of God's voluntary inclusion of creaturely time within eternity finds its basis[56] in God's own eternal temporality. Barth develops a theme that classical writers like Aquinas and Polanus did not develop satisfactorily, namely, that *Jesus Christ is the mediator between eternity and time*, so that the latter is included in and transformed by the former. In the incarnation, eternity and time enjoy a positive relation of "real fellowship" with each other (616; 694).[57] It is with this basic fact that we must start in our a posteriori reflection (*Nachdenken*) on eternity.

> The fact that the Word became flesh undoubtedly means that, without ceasing to be eternity, in its very power as eternity, eternity *became* time. What happened in Jesus Christ is not simply that God gives us time, our created time ... In Jesus Christ, it comes about that God *takes time to Himself*, that He Himself, the eternal one, *becomes temporal*, that He is present to us in the form of our existence and our own world, not simply embracing our time and ruling it, but submitting himself to it, and permitting created time to become and be the form of His eternity. (616; 694; emphasis added)

But what does Barth mean when he says that, in the incarnation, God permits *created* time (Time C) to "become and be the form of His eternity"? Although Barth does make it explicit here, the answer to this question is best found in Barth's Christocentric view of God's election—that for Barth, we recall, is a part of the doctrine of God.[58] Accordingly, we can answer that created time is the form of God's eternity in the sense that God eternally elects Jesus Christ as the one in

---

structures of Barth's doctrines of unity and constancy as well (see the Appendix to this book).

56. God's time for us, his readiness for time, is the basis and prototype for our time as both created and redeemed (612; 690). See Hunsinger *Disruptive Grace*, 200ff.

57. See ibid., 202.

58. See Gunton, "Karl Barth's Doctrine of Election," Colwell, *Actuality and Provisionality*, 183–230 and McCormack, "Grace and Being" and "Barths Grundsätzlicher Chalcedonismus."

whom and through whom God will relate to the world. Insofar as Jesus Christ is human, he lives in created time. Further, Jesus Christ is eternally elected as the *God-man*, not as the divine Logos without flesh (the *logos asarkos*). Therefore, the created time that is a form of the human nature of Jesus Christ is eternally the form of God's eternity. This does not mean that created time (Time C) is the *only* temporal form of God's eternity. Rather, Barth's discussion, as we have seen, implies that God has prior forms of eternity that are properly his own (Time A and Time B), and that these are what account for God's *readiness* for created time. That is, God's own "time" independent of creation (especially Time A) accounts for God's capacity to take this Time C that is not his own and to make it his own. According to a transcendental argument, we could say that Time A and Time B are the conditions of the possibility of God's taking Time C into himself. But we would not know about God's own inherent forms of temporality in any way except by God's decision to reveal himself to us in the form of *our* time. This is an eternal decision that implies the inclusion of the form of our time in God's eternal being, in Jesus Christ.

The nature of the real fellowship and unity between creaturely time and eternity in Jesus Christ is clarified by describing it in terms of the Chalcedonian pattern it manifests. Like Christ's divine and human natures, eternity and time are united to each other ("without separation or division"), yet they remain differentiated ("without confusion or change"). Thus, the Christological act that includes creaturely time within God's eternity does not make this time any less creaturely,[59] nor does it make God's eternity any less divine (see the above quotation from Barth). The last feature of the Chalcedonian pattern of relationship between eternity and time is its "asymmetry," i.e., the clear and irreversible precedence of divine eternity (and thus divine time) over human time.[60] In Jesus Christ, then, eternity and time are related to each

---

59. "Yet even in God's fellowship with His creature, this eternity belongs exclusively to God. In its fellowship with God the creature is permitted to taste it in one way or another, but it does not on that account itself become God and therefore eternal" (609; 687).

60. In a couple of polemical excurses within his treatment of the perfection of eternity, Barth makes this irreversible asymmetry abundantly clear. Barth points out that "the statement that God co-exists with our time cannot be reversed," first with respect to certain trends in modern Catholic theology (614f.; 692f.) and then with respect to Ritschl's Neo-Protestantism (618f.; 697f.). Time does not have any inherent potentiality for eternity, nor is it co-eternal (cf. Hunsinger, *Disruptive Grace*, 204).

other in unity, differentiation, and asymmetry, and thus according to a Chalcedonian pattern.[61] This pattern is evident in two main features of the work of God in Christ, the entry of eternity into time (the downward vector, or *anhypostatic* movement) and the elevation of time into eternity (the upward vector, or *enhypostatic* movement).[62]

In Jesus we come to see that God's eternity is not such that God "must set it over against our time" nor "that God is prevented from causing [our time] to be His own garment and even His own body" (616; 695). Hence, the name of Jesus "is the refutation of the idea of a God who is only timeless." Since the eternal God actually became time, making our time his own, then God's eternity must include this possibility, "the potentiality of time" (617; 696f.). God becomes our time by a free decision, and likewise always maintains his sovereign freedom over our time. God's work does not leave our time "as it is."

> He masters time. He re-creates it and heals its wounds, the fleetingness of the present, and the separation of the past and the future from one another and from the present . . . Real created time acquires in Jesus Christ and in every act of faith in Him the character and stamp of eternity, and life in it acquires the special characteristic of eternal life. The God who does this and therefore can do it is obviously in himself both timeless and temporal. He is timeless in that the defects of time . . . are alien to him and disappear. . . . He is temporal in that our time with its defects is not so alien to Him that He cannot take it to Himself by his grace, mercy, and patience, Himself rectifying and healing it and lifting it up to the time of eternal life. This power exercised in Jesus Christ consists in His [i.e., God's] triune being. (617f.; 696)

Barth's description of the healing and redemption of our created and fallen time is characterized by a Hegelian pattern of *Aufhebung*, which complements the Chalcedonian pattern by drawing attention to other features of the saving work of God in Christ. This *Aufhebung* pattern involves three ordered aspects: affirmation, cancellation, and reconstitution on a higher plane. Thus, there is affirmation in God's gracious entry into our time for our sakes in the incarnation and in his

---

61. See Hunsinger, *How to Read Karl Barth*, 85f. and *Disruptive Grace*, 202f. See also the Appendix to this book for further comment.

62. See Hunsinger *Disruptive Grace*, 203ff., and A. Torrance, *Persons in Communion*, 103.

consequent inclusion of our time in eternity, where he preserves created time without abolishing it. Yet insofar as our time is fallen and corrupted by sin it is cancelled and done away with, as is especially evident in the atoning work of Christ on the cross. Finally, our time is reconstituted within the higher plane of eternal life, in which it acquires, as Barth says, "the character and stamp of eternity." This re-constitution of our time corresponds to and is accomplished above all in the resurrection of Christ and in the believer's union with Christ in his resurrection, for in this event the unity of the divine and human is at its apex, but without dissolving the distinction between the two (consistent with the Chalcedonian pattern).

Although this concludes our focused discussion of the Christological features of Barth's view of eternity, these features will continue be relevant to the remainder of our chapter. Barth's view of eternity as a whole is both Christocentric and Trinitarian and is thus grounded in Christocentric and Trinitarian forms of theological biblical interpretation.

Eternity as the Three Forms of Temporality: Their Distinction and Unity

In this last subsection of our overview of Barth's account of the divine perfection of eternity, we turn to Barth's discussion of eternity under the rubric of three forms of divine temporality: pre-temporality, supra-temporality, and post-temporality. In terms of volume, this discussion takes up most of the second half of Barth's account of eternity in II/1 (619–38; 698–720). In content, it emphasizes God's real but distinctive temporality, and God's positive but free relation to our time. In form, it is Trinitarian (three modes of one temporal being that are perichoretically inter-related), and it is so in a Christological way. Christ is the central figure in all three forms of divine temporality (pre-, supra-, and post-temporality) and human temporality (past, present, and future). All the various forms of eternity (the three forms of eternity discussed above), time (the four concepts of time described above), and temporality (the three forms discussed in this subsection) converge in Jesus Christ, the "centre of time" (629; 709) and the mediator of time and eternity.[63]

---

63. Cf. Col 1:17: "In him all things hold together" (cf. II/2, 98f.).

Before we summarize Barth's three forms of temporality, we may consider how these three forms relate to the analytical distinctions we have used above. (1) These three forms are not to be confused with the three forms of eternity that Hunsinger believes are implicit in Barth (see above).[64] Rather, Barth's three forms of temporality correspond as a whole to what Hunsinger calls Barth's *second* form of eternity, namely, the form in which eternity is seen as "beginning, middle, and end" or a similar threefold order of succession. The other two forms of eternity that Hunsinger identifies (i.e., "pure duration" and "simultaneity") are present in Barth's discussion of the three forms of temporality, but do not have the primary focus. (2) Barth's discussion of the three forms of divine temporality expounds upon the nature of God's eternity/time (Time A and Time B), rather than human time (Time C and Time D). As such, the overall focus is on the concrete expression of God's readiness for our time in his works *ad extra* (Time B). Yet Barth never forgets the ultimate basis of this readiness (as a free and voluntary readiness) in God's internal temporality/eternity (Time A; see especially his exposition of God's pre-temporality and post-temporality).[65]

Barth begins his discussion of the three forms of temporality with an introduction that offers at least two reasons why it is important to speak of God's eternity in terms of pre-temporality, supra-temporality, and post-temporality (619ff.; 698ff.). First, Barth says that to speak of eternity in these terms is to speak *biblically*, and Barth's assumption (as we have seen consistently in this book) is that he ought to follow the Bible's example in his dogmatics (see our section on Barth's use of the Bible below). The scriptural witness to God's Word speaks of eternity in temporal terms, yet does so in a way that also speaks of the eternal God's unqualified superiority to and freedom over our time. "He precedes its [i.e., time's] beginning, He accompanies its duration [*Dauer*], and He exists after its end." "This," Barth says, "is the concrete form of eternity as readiness for time" (619; 698). Second, Barth believes that "a great deal depends" on God being, quite literally, "before, above, and after all things" (620; 699). "Without God's complete temporality the

---

64. To avoid confusion, we typically refer to Barth's explicit categories as three forms of *temporality* and Hunsinger's categories as three forms of *eternity*, even though both sets of categories actually describe different forms of *both* God's temporality *and* eternity (since God's eternity is temporal and his temporality is eternal).

65. The following passage confirms the latter point: eternity "is itself temporal, and would be so *even if no time existed apart from it*" (620; 698; emphasis added).

content of the Christian message has no shape." Without a definite temporal shape, the gospel message becomes either a "human monologue" indistinguishable from a timeless myth or dream, or a proclamation that consists only of "inarticulate mumbling." Against such errors, Barth wishes to express that God's eternity surrounds and encompasses our time on all sides.

Barth considers the three forms of divine temporality in order. We need only summarize these briefly, especially since we will discuss aspects of them in relation to Barth's use of Scripture below.

First, "God is pre-temporal [*vorzeitlich*]," which "means that His existence precedes ours and that of all things" (621; 700). Taken in its literal sense, this speaks the profound truth that God is not dependent on creation or created time for self-fulfillment. This is crucial for the affirmation that eternity is a perfection of the divine *freedom*. God is free in relation to the world and its time, because there is a "pre-time" (an aspect of Time A and Time B), a "time before time" (before Time C and Time D, that is) (622; 701). In this pre-time of God, "everything . . . was decided and determined, everything that is in time." This prior determination of the whole of God's work *ad extra* (creation, reconciliation, and redemption) has "its centre in Jesus Christ."[66] Again, "To say that everything is predestined . . . is just the same as to say simply that everything is determined in Jesus Christ." God's Christocentric time for us (Time B), reveals the essentially Trinitarian shape of God's eternal temporality (especially Time A).[67]

Second, "God is supra-temporal [*überzeitlich*]" (623; 702). Barth believes that this word itself is "not adequate to express what has to be expressed here," which includes something like "co-temporal" or "in-temporal." Here especially "we have to do with the positive relationship of eternity to time." This relationship consists "in the fact that eternity faithfully accompanies time on high" or, more precisely, "it causes itself to be accompanied by time."[68] This supra-temporal accompaniment implies that in God's eternity, our time, our present, is no longer "separated

---

66. Clearly Barth has here incorporated into II/1 the decisive motif of Christological election, before his extensive exposition of it in II/2 (see McCormack, *Karl Barth's Critically Realistic Dialectic Theology*, 461).

67. "[T]his pre-time is the pure time [*die reine Zeit*] of the Father and the Son in the fellowship of the Holy Spirit" (622; 701).

68. Barth adds that all our markers of temporal succession (hours, years, epochs) "are all [embraced] in eternity like the arms of its mother" (623; 703).

from its beginning and end" (623; 702). Thus, supra-temporality cannot be construed simply as God's "perpendicular connection with each moment of time," but also in horizontal connection with the "divine before and after" (624; 703). But God surely is connected with the present, with the now, and this is the emphasis of supra-temporality. "Eternity did not cease when time began [only] to begin again when time ceases" (624; 704). This supra-temporality of God makes it possible for him to love us in freedom in the midst of our time, in the midst of its process of unfolding. Again, Barth unfolds this supra-temporality in a Christocentric manner. Christ is "the centre [*Mitte*] of time" (629; 709) in whom there is a decisive and momentous turning from past to the future, or, in biblical terms, from the old age to the new (626ff.; 705ff.).

Third, "God is post-temporal [*nachzeitlich*]" (629; 709). Completing the idea that eternity embraces time, God's post-temporality consists in the view that our time moves towards the goal of the eternal God, to a future in which God will be revealed as "all in all." Humanity, which was elected and is reconciled, will one day be "redeemed." In the "time" of post-temporality, God exists in "His Sabbath rest after the completion of all His works, the execution of all His will *ad extra*" (630; 710). "God is the Last as he was the First." This means that God is the "God of all hope" (631; 711). Indeed, although it is hidden to us now, God already is the Last *ad intra* (i.e., "in himself"). In the post-temporality yet to come, all that God is will be fully revealed to us (630f.; 710f.).[69]

Following his exposition of each of the three distinct forms of temporality, Barth offers a lengthy excursus about how there "can be no basic rivalry [*Konkurrenz*]" between them (631–38; 711–19).[70] "They are not played off one another." Barth then proceeds to give an account of how, in the history of theology, each form of divine temporality has at some time been over-emphasized to the exclusion of the others. The Reformers of the sixteenth century showed a "dangerous one-sidedness" in favor of pre-temporality, which led to a kind of hopelessness or gloom in their theologies (631f.; 712). The Neo-Protestants of the

---

69. We recall our discussion of salvation history within our discussion of the role of Scripture in Barth's account of divine constancy (chapter 5), where we saw that Barth regarded eschatological redemption as primarily bringing about a noetic change in us (via full revelation) rather than an ontic change in God or in our relationship to him.

70. To use Hunsinger's terminology, Barth moves from the second form of eternity (as "beginning, middle, and end") to the third form ("simultaneity," understood along the lines of *perichoresis*). See above.

eighteenth and nineteenth centuries showed an even more serious over-emphasis, this time on God's supra-temporality to the neglect of the "before" and "after" (632f.; 713). This reaction against the Reformers led to a secularization of God's eternity that turned it into a kind of "religious" anthropocentrism. Finally, at the end of the nineteenth century and the beginning of the twentieth century, there was a reaction against the previous over-emphasis on supra-temporality in the form of a new and excessive preoccupation with post-temporality (633–37; 713–18). Within his account of this recent overemphasis on post-temporality, Barth criticizes his own earlier work in the *Epistle to the Romans* (second edition).[71] Barth now realizes clearly that the errors of previous centuries "are not overcome by suppressing the element of truth which lay at the basis of the errors" (637; 719). Instead, "they can be overcome only by seeing and establishing the truth in the context from which it should not be separated." This means that our view of eternity must involve equal emphasis on each of the three forms of God's temporality or eternity—i.e., on God's time for us as beginning, middle, and end. For all three forms are "equally God's eternity and therefore the living God himself" (638; 720).

This last point is unfolded in the concluding section of Barth's account of the perfection of eternity (638–40; 720–22). Here Barth emphasizes several points similar to those we have identified in his accounts of God's simplicity and constancy. God, the unique Subject, must define eternity, the predicate. The nature of God's eternity as it is revealed *ad extra* is the nature of God's eternity *ad intra*. Since the Christian knowledge of eternity has to do with the living, self-revealing God, it is not a matter of speculation, but of obedience to the revelation of God attested in Scripture.

Barth also uses the concluding pages of his account of eternity to highlight some Trinitarian patterns in this account. First, Barth draws attention to the real distinctness and real order of the three forms of temporality or eternity.

---

71. See Barth, *Romans*, 6th ed. Barth's self-criticism is moderate, since he believes that much of what he said then was necessary at the time, though incomplete with hindsight. For example, he says that his earlier interpretation of Rom 13:11f. had paid attention only to matters "at the periphery" of the passage, and had missed its central and distinctive feature: that is "the teleology which it ascribes to time as it moves towards its real end" (635; 716). See Moltmann's critique of Barth's early eschatology (e.g., *Theology of Hope*, 57f.).

> Once we are clear that eternity is the living God Himself, it is impossible to look on eternity as a uniform grey sea before, above, and after time ... Eternity is really beginning, really middle, and really end, because it is really the living God. There really is in it, then, direction [*Richtung*], and a direction which is irreversible. There really is in it an origin and goal and a way from the one to the other. Therefore there is no uniformity in it. Its forms are not to be exchanged or confused. (639; 721)[72]

Barth summarizes his understanding of the basis of the eternal God's real temporal distinctions by saying that "God *lives* eternally," and as the living God he is neither uniform nor without temporal form.

Second, Barth draws attention to the real unity, *perichoresis*, or "mutual indwelling and interworking of the three forms of eternity" (640; 721f.).[73] Whether or not we follow Hunsinger in consistently associating this perichoretic feature of Barth's view of God's temporality or eternity with "simultaneity," it is clearly an important feature of Barth's account of God's eternity. Barth sums up his understanding of the basis of unity of the temporal forms of eternity by repeating the statement he had made above but with a different emphasis: "*God* lives eternally." The eternal God lives as the single undivided subject even in all of his self-distinctions. As the next section will confirm, to speak of God as "living" is one expression of the biblical roots of Barth's account of eternity.

The Role of Scripture in Barth's Account of Eternity

Introduction to the Role of Scripture in Barth's Treatment of Eternity

As with his treatment of divine simplicity, Barth's treatment of divine eternity does not include an extended exegesis of any one scriptural passage.[74] Instead, Barth's engagement with Scripture here again falls into two main categories: the "catena" form (citation or quotation of a group

---

72. Barth goes on to say that, while there is a kind of "symmetry" between the three forms of divine temporality, this symmetry is not to be reduced to geometrical formulae or illustrations (like the sphere or the point). The reason is that the asymmetrical and "irreversible direction" of eternity is not found in them (639f.; 721).

73. Barth here uses the phrase "three forms of eternity" here to refer to what he more usually calls "three forms of divine temporality."

74. His treatment of constancy, by contrast, includes an extended treatment of Phil 2:5–11 (see chapter 5).

of passages with little comment on them) and the "thematic" form (with or without the citation of text or group of texts associated with it). These two forms of scriptural usage are inter-related. Biblical-theological themes typically provide the basis for grouping certain scriptural texts together, and biblical texts often provide either the grounds for or illustrations of the themes.

We will now examine several biblical themes (or motifs or patterns) and will consider Barth's citation and discussions of various biblical texts (usually in catenae or groups) in the context of these themes. In looking at the function of Scripture in Barth's account of eternity, we will strive to determine to what extent and in what way Scripture is the basis of Barth's theological proposals regarding eternity.

The Minor Theme: Eternity as God's Freedom Over Our Time

As we have seen above, Barth begins his treatment of divine eternity by stating how eternity is distinct from and contrasted with earthly time, and, as such is "non-temporality." Immediately following his quotations of Augustine, Anselm, and Polanus (see the first section of this chapter), Barth says: "From the witness of the biblical passages (especially in Deutero-Isaiah and Revelation), the older theology recalled the definitions in which God is spoken of as "the first and the last," as Alpha and Omega" (608; 686). This recalls how Barth regards the biblical witness to God as *commensurable* with both the "older theology" of the classical theologians and his own theology (see the subsection on "commensurability" in the latter part of chapter 4). Barth does not cite any of the biblical passages that include the "definitions" of God as the first and the last or the Alpha and Omega,[75] but he does quote a group of three passages related to these: Isa 43:10, Ps 90:2–4, and Ps 102:25ff. Psalm 90:2–4 is the only passage on which Barth offers any interpretative comments. This passage reads:

> Before the mountains were brought forth, or ever you had formed the earth and the world, from everlasting to everlasting you are God. You turn us back to dust, and say, "Turn back, you mortals." For a thousand years in your sight are like yesterday when it is past, or like a watch in the night. (Ps 90: 2–4; NRSV)

---

75. Barth has in mind passages like Isa 41:4, 44:6, 48:12, Rev 1:8 and 1:17.

Following his quotation of verse 2, Barth comments,

> The final duplication, "from everlasting to everlasting," which is so common in both Old and New Testaments,[76] may be regarded as particularly significant. It can be taken to mean from duration to duration, that is, in pure duration [*in reiner Dauer*]. This is how God exists in distinction from us who exist from one time to another, but never in pure duration. In light of this we can understand the continuation of the passage. (609; 686)[77]

Barth here takes a biblical stock phrase to be semantically equivalent to, and hence fully commensurable with, one of his own theological definitions of eternity, i.e., "pure duration." To use David Yeago's distinction again (as we have done in previous chapters), we could say that the scriptural writers use one set of *conceptual terms* to make basically the same *judgment* about the eternal God that he (Barth) wishes to make using a different set of *conceptual terms*.[78] As such, the biblical phrase and Barth's theological phrase have the capacity to illuminate the meaning of each other. "Everlasting to everlasting" ensures that "pure duration" does not take on an a priori philosophical meaning foreign to that of the biblical text. In turn, the more abstract term "pure duration" has the capacity (at its best) to relate "everlasting to everlasting" to a wider range of related conceptual terms (especially in theology) that share essentially the same theological judgment about God.[79]

In another excursus, Barth develops a similar point in the context of developing the biblical-theological motif of God's freedom over time,

---

76. In the Old Testament, Barth has in mind passages like 1 Chr 16:36, Neh 9:5, Ps 41:12, Ps 103:17 and Ps 106: 48. It is not clear what New Testament passages he has in mind, although they would likely include 1 Tim 1:17, which speaks of God as the "king of ages" and uses the phrase "glory forever and ever" (literally "to the ages of the ages").

77. Barth then quotes Ps 90:3–4 and cites 2 Pet 3:8 for comparison.

78. Yeago, "New Testament and Nicene Dogma," 159ff. (see our comments in chapter 2).

79. A similar conceptual relationship of mutual-illumination and equivalency of theological judgment between Barth's "pure duration" and biblical phraseology is implicit with respect to the other passages that Barth quotes. For example, the Psalmist says to God, "you endure" and "you are the same and your years have no end," which he contrasts with the transience of even the least transient created things, "the foundation of the earth, and the heavens" (Ps 102:25ff.). For God to endure and to be the same over time surely relates closely to what Barth means by "pure duration."

and thus we shift from the catena form to the thematic form of Barth's Scripture usage. "Whenever Holy Scripture speaks of God as eternal it stresses his freedom" (609; 687). By "freedom" Barth here means basically what he does by the term elsewhere. God's freedom is that aspect of God that separates him from all created things precisely so that God might surround and be "utterly present" to humanity in "complete power over him" (609f.; 687).

Barth sometimes seems to accord eternity a special place among the perfections of God's freedom. For example, he says, "Eternity is the source of the deity of God in so far as it consists in His freedom, independence, and lordship" (610; 687). This is congruent with Barth's attempt to regard eternity as what we might call the Bible's "leading ontological concept," as the biblical alternative to "Being," the leading ontological concept in Greek philosophy and in most classical theology. Barth states the point as follows:

> At the very place at which the later theology fell under the influence of Greek philosophy and made the concept of being predominant, the Bible speaks of the eternal God. According to the Bible, it is not being as such, but that which endures, duration itself, which is divine... Being does not include eternity, but eternity includes being. The genuineness of being is examined ... and tested by eternity. It is being or non-being according to its relation to eternity. (610; 687f.)

At first glance, Barth in this passage appears to align the Bible, and hence his theology, with a particular revisionist ontological perspective that stands against other ontological perspectives.[80] If this is so, the question arises whether this is a case of "eisegesis"—i.e., a case in which Barth reads an a priori viewpoint (a natural theology or a philosophy) into rather than out of the Bible.

What is the nature of the "implied ontological component"[81] in Barth's doctrine of eternity? In Barth's view, God's self-revelation has priority *over* all such a priori ontological views, and his doctrine of

---

80. See Jenson, "Karl Barth."

81. Richard Muller speaks of "an implied ontological component" in Barth's doctrine of constancy ("Incarnation, Immutability, and the Case for Classical Theism," 27). Barth's own comments sometimes suggest that he sees eternity as ontologically prior to God's constancy. For example, he calls eternity "the principle [*Prinzip*] of divine constancy," stating that "the reason why he is free to be constant is that time has no power over him" (609; 687).

eternity is an attempt to follow that revelation, especially in its witness to God's freedom. Barth does not disavow the use of ontological schemes altogether, but only rules out the inappropriate imposition of such schemes upon revelation. In our judgment, the dialectical nature of Barth's doctrine of eternity (God being both above time and engaged in time) prevents Barth from *systematically* imposing a specific ontology on the testimony of revelation to God's eternity. This does not mean that he does not occasionally fall prey to "ontological imposition" in a non-systematic, ad hoc sense. Insofar as this is true, Barth is open to the dangers of eisegesis or natural theology.[82] In any case, the fundamental character of Barth's dialectical, revelation-based theological method is structured so as to minimize these dangers.

At the least, Barth appears to improve on the method of the classical theologians in this regard. The classical accounts of eternity highlighted the biblical theme of God's sovereignty, supremacy, and incomparability by drawing attention to how God's eternity is different from our time. But insofar as their concepts of eternity showed the influence of the Hellenistic concept of being, it was seen simply as "the negation of time" or "abstract opposite of the concept of the time." Thus, the classical accounts were not faithful to the other features of the scriptural witness to God's eternity that involved a more positive relation to temporality. Barth's dialectical, non-reductionistic approach *also* aims to stress these aspects of the biblical witness, yet without neglecting the negative aspect of God's eternity.

The Major Theme: Divine Eternity as God's Positive Relation to Time

Barth argues that the true "negative" sense of eternity as "duration without separation between beginning, succession, and end" is true only against the background of the decisive and positive characteristic that as true [*echte*] duration, the duration of God Himself is "*the* beginning, succession, and end" (610; 688).[83] How is this claim grounded in Scripture?

---

82. As noted above, this may be the case when Barth says that "eternity is just the duration that is lacking to time" (608; see above). See Farrow, *Ascension and Ecclesia*, 291ff.

83. This claim is consistent with Barth's statement of the positive and negative sides of divine freedom in general in II/1, §28.3; see our comments on this in chapter 3.

According to Barth, "in distinction from the concept of eternity that later dominated the Church, *the Bible is interested primarily, if not exclusively, in this primary and positive quality of eternity*" (610; 688; emphasis mine).[84] Barth supports generalization about the Bible's thematic content by means of an argument about the meaning of biblical terms for eternity. "By the terms *'ôlām* and *aiōn* the Bible understands a space of time fixed by God, and eternity is generally ascribed to God under the categories of beginning, succession, and end."[85] Barth, continues, "The biblical writers do not hesitate to speak of God's years and days, or to describe these as eternal."[86] The biblical writers' use of such "temporal" terms to speak of God's eternity is not "to be explained as naïve, Semitic realism," but is "incomparably more profound" than an abstract conception of eternity as merely "non-temporality." In some real and proper sense, God has freedom and power over our years and days both because he is their origin and because he possesses them *a se* or "in Himself" (i.e., Time A). According to Barth, this "positive quality of eternity" is "finely expressed" in the classic definition of Boethius, as long as it is not interpreted (as it was by the scholastics) so as to make eternity secondary to being.

In a later excursus, Barth refers to a specific biblical phrase that speaks of the positive concept of eternity. Having already spoken of eternity as God's own unique temporality (Time A), Barth now begins to speak of God's time for us (Time B), which is God's positive relationship to our time (Time C). In this context he says,

> It is because God is the eternal One that Psalm 31:15 is to be taken literally [*wörtlich*]: "My times are in thy hands." God's hands, the workings of His omnipotence, are not themselves

---

84. For Barth to say "if not exclusively" seems to be a rhetorical over-statement in the light of what we have observed above about the "minor theme" of Barth's view of eternity.

85. Here and elsewhere, we are using the standard contemporary forms of transliteration for Hebrew and Greek terms, which sometimes differ from Barth's own usage.

86. The passages that Barth's quoted earlier (as noted in the previous section on the "minor theme") express well what Barth has in mind here. Psalm 90:2 employs the Hebrew term for "eternity" (*'ôlām*). Barth translated the term as *Ewigkeit* (*KD*, 686) but we used the term "everlasting" (as did the translator of *CD* and the NRSV), a term that does not have the "a-temporal" connotation that "eternity" can have in English. That said, we recall, that Barth does not regard God's *Ewigkeit* as the "infinite extension of time" (608; 686; see the beginning section of this chapter), which is the main sense of "everlasting" in English.

timeless but supremely temporal, so that our time can be really in them, and can be not merely apparent but real [*wirkliche*] time ... [T]he eternal God co-exists with the time created by Him. (613f.; 692)

Although Barth does not make the link explicit, this text's reference to our times being *in* God's hands is an example of the biblical basis for Barth's conception of the *inclusion* of our time within God's eternity—i.e., within God's eternity as the "workings of His omnipotence" that are "supremely temporal" (Time B).

This positive relationship between divine eternity and human time, prefigured in the Old Testament, is established and revealed definitively in Jesus Christ. The biblical testimony to Jesus Christ and his incarnation constitutes another biblical motif or theme that Barth unfolds as the basis for his view of eternity. Barth does not explicitly refer to any biblical texts in expounding this motif, although he does quote part of John 1:14 ("the Word became flesh") without reference to its chapter and verse (616; 694). Barth uses this biblical statement as a kind of basic theological fact or axiom, a statement so basic that it needs no explanation, let alone defense. Thus, Barth can say: "The fact that the Word became flesh undoubtedly means that, without ceasing to be eternity... eternity became time."

Barth's lack of exegetical comment on John 1:14 here does not mean that Barth regards such exegesis as unimportant, for he engages in this exegetical task elsewhere in *CD*.[87] Rather, this is an example of a two-fold phenomenon that is important for understanding the biblical basis of Barth's view of eternity and indeed of his doctrine of God as a whole. That is,

1. Barth often does not spell out the exegetical basis for a given biblical-theological claim in the context in which he is "using" that claim. He often uses such claims as "premises" in macro-arguments for other biblical-theological claims, rather than as "conclusions" to exegetical micro-arguments (see chapter 2).

2. When Barth does not spell out the exegetical basis in the immediate context, he often has done so *somewhere else* in *CD*.

---

87. E.g., I/1, 401. Barth cites John 1:14 seven times in I/1 alone.

Another example of this phenomenon is implicit in further claims Barth makes about the significance of the incarnation for our understanding of eternity. When God becomes man,

> **This does not mean that He ... ceases to be who He is** in His superiority. But while He is still this, *He humbles himself* and lifts us up by becoming one of us *like us in all things*. ... He raises time to a form of His own eternal being. For our being, as created human being, has this form [i.e., temporal form], and He could not assume our being ... without taking time also and **concealing and revealing** his eternal being in it. His own time, eternity, **is not so precious to him** ... that he must set it over against our time. ... **No contraction or diminution of deity takes place.** (616; 695; italics and bold type added)

We may make two observations about this passage. (1) The two italicized phrases are biblical allusions or "echoes," whether or not they are intentional ones. The first alludes to Phil 2:8 and draws attention to the whole of Phil 2:6–11, which appears to be in the background of Barth's comments here. The second alludes to Heb 2:17a,[88] which can be seen as a parallel passage to the passage in Phil 2. (2) The phrases in bold type highlight terminology that is similar or identical to the terminology that Barth used in his exegesis of Phil 2:6–11 in the context of his treatment of divine constancy.[89] Taken together, these two observations show that *Barth's theological conclusions regarding incarnation and eternity are more firmly rooted in the theological use of Scripture than might first appear.* Several theological points that Barth takes for granted here (e.g., that it is God who is humbling himself in Christ; or that this humiliation ought to be understood under the rubric of concealment and revelation) are given an explicit and extended exegetical basis elsewhere in *CD*. This confirms the main argument of our book as a whole, namely, that Barth's unceasing attention to and engagement with Scripture is decisive in determining and supporting his theological conclusions regarding God's perfections, often in places where this might not be apparent on the "surface" of a given section of *CD*.

---

88. "Therefore he had to become like his brothers and sisters in every respect...." (NRSV).

89. *CD* II/1, 515–18; see our relevant comments in chapter 5. See also *CD* IV/1, 186–92.

The Biblical Basis of the Three Forms of God's Temporality

Introduction to the Three Forms of Temporality

Barth's account of the three forms of temporality is central to the biblical foundations of his account of eternity in its positive relationship to time. So long as we guard against misuses in which eternity is read in the light of our time, "the temporality of eternity may be described in detail as the pre-temporality, supra-temporality, and post-temporality of eternity" (619; 698). He continues, "With these terms we return to the direct proximity of the biblical outlook." Why do these terms or concepts stand in unmediated nearness to the biblical outlook? The answer is that these terms speak of God's eternity in temporal terms—*in positive relationship to* time—and this is exactly how the Bible typically speaks of God's eternity. Again, this is not a sign of the Bible's "naivety." Rather, it points to the profound awareness of the biblical outlook that eternity is both distinct from (our) time, and yet related to it. Specifically, we would argue that, for Barth, the Bible uses its own conceptual terms to affirm that the eternal God is before, above, and after our time.[90] This is no mere "figure of speech," but is a "serious and divine truth" (620; 699). God really is "He who was, and is, and is to come."[91] This statement tells us the truth about "God himself." Neither it nor its temporal language is to be taken "figuratively" [*bildlich*] or "metaphorically" [*uneigentlich*] (620; 699). Barth explains what this implies in a passage that is instructive for understanding his view of the relationship between Scripture and theology in this context.

> It is quite impossible to deny to God's eternity the possession of preparedness [*Bereitshaft*, or "readiness"] for time. It is for this reason that this is true and the concepts of pre-temporality, supra-temporality and post-temporality are legitimate: *because they simply spell out and analyse* what the Christian message guarantees [or "assures us," *versichert*] to be the Word of God and therefore the truth. This message cannot be proclaimed nor believed as the truth without the proclaiming and believing of these statements about God. They are not simply inferences from the Gospel. . . . they are elements of the Gospel itself.

---

90. This is what Barth calls the "concrete form of eternity as readiness for time" (619; 698; see above).

91. Barth quotes this phrase from Rev 1:4 (and elsewhere in Revelation) twice here (620; 699), yet without giving the scriptural reference.

> The Gospel itself and as such cannot be spoken without these statements being made and this understanding of God's eternity *forcing itself upon us*—not indirectly [*mittelbar*], as a scholastic parergon, but directly [*unmittelbar*], because the Gospel must either remain unproclaimed or be spoken in the form of these statements. (621; 700; emphasis mine)

To paraphrase, Barth believes that the three forms of temporality are strongly authorized by Scripture, because they offer what Frei called a conceptual analysis or redescription of aspects of the gospel message; they "spell out and analyze" essential elements of God's Word. These basic statements about God's "temporal" eternity (i.e., that God is before, above, and after our time) are not only inferences from the gospel but integral elements of its form. As such, the scripturally-attested gospel "forces us" to speak of God's eternity in a particular (three-fold) way.[92]

We can explain the scriptural authorization of Barth's three forms of divine temporality by employing, once again, the distinction between judgments and conceptual terms. Barth is best interpreted as saying that certain theological judgments, stated by both Scripture and himself in different ways, are "statements" necessary and essential to the gospel's form. As such, Barth regards his own conceptual terms (i.e., pre-temporality, supra-temporality, and post-temporality) as legitimate means of expressing these essential judgments. Although Barth's rhetorical overstatement may lead us to think otherwise, it is the judgments that "force themselves upon us," not the particular conceptual forms that Barth or even Scripture uses to express them. Thus, Barth's three forms of temporality are merely "legitimate," not "necessary" or "essential." They are Barth's best (yet provisional) attempt to affirm, spell out, and analyze more basic theological judgments—judgments that are in some sense an aspect of the divine Word of truth. Moreover, Barth first encounters and comes to believe in these judgments or statements about God's time and eternity "directly" through God's "speaking to him" in the course of his reading of Scripture, and thus in the form of Scripture's presentation of the gospel in its own conceptual terms. We cannot discern by rational

---

92. As we noted in chapter 2, what Barth here calls "direct" could still be seen as a case of "indirect authorization" in our usage. The "Word" encounters us in the "words" and this can be seen as both direct and indirect on different levels. In this case, Barth associates an "indirect" relationship between the Bible and theology specifically with an inappropriate scholastic mode of inference (quite different than our typical use of "indirect").

analysis precisely where the divinely authorized theological judgments end and where the relative and provisional linguistic forms begin. But Barth would say that this ambiguity is an inescapable feature of the mystery of theological God-talk in the face of revelation.

The preceding observations help us to understand what Barth means when he says: "Without God's complete temporality the content of the Christian message *has no shape*" (620; 699). The gospel has a three-fold temporal shape or form. We will now examine how Barth expounds upon this with a view to uncovering how Barth concretely authorizes it through his use of Scripture. Barth intends his survey of the three forms of temporality to remind us of "two aspects," namely, (i) "that the truth of God's Word depends on" the truth of the statements (i.e., theological judgments) about God's temporality, and (ii) "that they themselves are based on and preserved by the truth of God's Word" (621; 700). As we look briefly at the function of Scripture in each of the three forms of temporality, we must keep in mind this mutual dependence between (a) the basic theological statements implied in speaking of the three forms of temporality and (b) the truth or message of God's Word.

Scripture and God's Pre-temporality

In regards to the pre-temporality of God, we already noted above that God regards this "pre-time" (*Vorzeit*) in a Christocentric manner. Accordingly, Barth states: "If we understand eternity as pre-time . . . we have to recognize that eternity itself bears the name of Jesus Christ" (622; 701). Immediately following this statement, Barth quotes three New Testament passages as "relevant in this connection": John 8:58, Eph 1:4f, and I Pet 1:18f. The first text in this catena is Jesus' statement: "Before Abraham was, I am." The latter two texts speak of the election and reconciliation of humanity that is accomplished in Christ and from eternity. Eph 1:4 figures prominently in Barth's account of Christological election in *CD* volume II/2, which provides fuller exegetical substantiation for what Barth argues here.[93] Barth follows his

---

93. Barth cites Eph 1:4f. ten times in II/2 and discusses it extensively (see Cunningham, *What is Theological Exegesis?*). Barth's exegesis in II/2 provides the fuller biblical basis for what he says here and in similar passages in II/1 (see our comments above). If McCormack (especially in *Karl Barth's Critically Realistic Dialectic Theology*) is correct about the decisive significance of Christological election for Barth's theology

quotation of these three passages with this comment: "Note how in all these and similar passages the eternal presence of God over and in time [i.e., supra-temporality] is established by reference to a pre-time in which time, and with it the existence of man and its renewal, is foreseen and determined" (622; 702). For Barth, the scriptural witness to God's eternity as "before time" (in Christ) is unmistakable and is inextricable from its witness to the other aspects of God's temporality. Specifically, God's pre-time reality establishes God's supra-time reality.

Scripture and God's Supra-temporality

Scripture figures even more prominently in Barth's account of God's supra (*über*)-temporality. In the course of a lengthy excursus, Barth quotes and comments on three Scripture passages that deal with God's supra-temporality from the perspective of the incarnation and especially the birth of Christ. We will examine Barth's treatment of each of these three passages in turn.

(1) First, Barth quotes the message of the angels in Luke 2:14: "Glory to God in the highest and on earth peace, good will toward men" (as translated on 623f.). Barth states:

> This is the most accurate description of God's supra-temporality. For these words declare that, since God is in the highest over [*über*] the earth, and all glory belongs and is due to the One who is there, there is peace on [*auf*] earth, there is not to be any lack of security on earth, that is, among the men to whom this God who dwells in the highest has turned His good will... It is as He is supra-temporal... that He exercises and interprets His freedom in our favour... that He wills to be not only God, but God among and for the men of His good will, and that He creates for the glory proper to Him in the highest a *complement* on earth in the peace which is guaranteed to us to magnify His glory and to be thankful to Him. It is in this way that God knows and wills all things. (624; 703; emphasis added)

Here Barth is in interested in drawing out one text's witness to the positive relationship or correspondence between the eternal God and the peace among humans that is made possible by God's grace in the

---

from the writing of II/1 onwards (and we have no reason to doubt this judgment), then the exegetical underpinnings of Barth's doctrine of Christological election confirm our view that Scripture is decisive for his doctrine of God as a whole in II/1 and indeed for his theology in the remainder of *CD*.

birth of Christ. Later in the excursus, Barth notes: "The angel's message in Lk 2:14 ... does not proclaim a general truth" (625; 705). Rather, he says, "it proclaims the fulfillment of the promise to Israel and the basis and meaning of the Church—the birth of Christ." This helps Barth to establish his point that the God-given significance of history in general derives from the special significance of the particular history of Israel, of the Church, and above all, of Jesus Christ. This confirms that God's pre-temporal election determines God's supra-temporal way of relating to the world and its unfolding history. The birth of Christ marks the beginning of the special time the incarnation, the central time that gives meaning to all earthly time.

(2) A second passage Barth quotes and discusses in his account of supra-temporality is Psalm 2:6-7, which reads: "'I have set my king on Zion, my holy hill.' I will tell of the decree of the Lord: He said to me, 'You are my son; *today* I have begotten you ...'" (NRSV; emphasis added). For Barth, the "today" in this text refers to "the temporal present" in which the messianic king is set up or installed on Zion, "which is contemporary with the *nunc aeternitas*," and is thus "eternal time" (625; 705). Barth believes this text speaks of a human "now" ("today," the present) that is "contemporary" with the eternal divine "now," and therefore speaks of "eternal time," time that is a part of eternity. Such theological exegesis is Christocentric, since Barth believes that the ultimate referent to the "my king" in this passage is Christ. On this point, Barth follows both the New Testament (see Heb 1:5) and the "older theology." But it is subtle Christocentrism. As such, Barth follows Calvin in departing from the tendency of the older, pre-critical theology to regard the text as referring directly to the eternal Son in contrast to the earthly Jesus.

> Calvin rightly perceived that this *hodie* ["today"] cannot mean eternity so that the begetting cannot be the eternal begetting of the Son by the Father. But this makes it all the more certain that what is meant is the appearing of the Messiah King *in time*. And in this appearance, as Calvin says, eternity is revealed, or, we should now say more specifically, the supra-temporality of God *as His presence in time*. (625f.; 705)[94]

---

94. Barth refers to Calvin's comments in *C. R.* [*Corpus Reformatum*], 31, 46f. Harry M. Hine translates Calvin's comments as follows: "As for the fact that God pronounces that he has begotten him, this ought to be referred to the sense or knowledge of humans. ... And so the adverb 'today' marks the time of that declaration, because after it became known that the king had been divinely created, he went forth as though recently begotten by God."

Indeed, Barth states: "In this appearing [of Christ] time and all times have their direct meaning in relation to God ... From it there is in all times and for all times that peace on earth for men of good will" (626; 705).

(3) In his account of supra-temporality, Barth also quotes a classic New Testament passage about Christ's (first) advent, namely John 1:9f. This text speaks of Jesus Christ as the "true light, which lights every man" and is "coming into the world." It goes on to speak of this one, the light, as (a) the creator of the world and yet not known by the world; (b) as one not received by "his own" and yet received by those (through faith) to whom he gave the power to become sons of God. Barth comments on this text with this illuminating reflection on the incarnation:

> This occurrence [Geschehen] is the concrete form [Gestalt] to which we must hold fast in relation to God's supra-temporality ... Because, in this occurrence, eternity assumes the form of a temporal present, all time, without ceasing to be time, is no more empty [leere] time, or without eternity. *It has become new. This means that in and with this present, eternity creates in time real past and real future, distinguishes between them, and is itself the bridge and way from the one to the other. Jesus Christ is this way.* (626; 705; emphasis added)

Barth develops this motif of Jesus Christ as the way from the past to the future in terms of a wide ranging biblical-theological reflection. As the "hidden centre of time" (626; 705), Christ is the one in whom God accomplishes a decisive "turning" [Wende] from the "old age" (or sphere) of sin and death to the "new age" (or sphere) of righteousness and life (see 626–29; 706–9). This exposition of a complex biblical-thematic pattern involves reference to many features of the biblical witness, sometimes with and sometimes without the citation of specific passages. Barth offers a rule for interpreting the relevant biblical material and life seen in light of it: in Christ, human existence is moving out of the old age or sphere (it is made genuinely "past" and thus is passing away) and into the new age or sphere, the genuine future (see 626f.; 706f.). This view stands in contrast to "a heathen view of the two spheres" in which there are the "timeless, objective spheres" that are caught in an "endless repetition" or "endless dialectic" (626; 706 and 628; 707). Thus, "the past is that from which we are set free" by Christ, and "the future is that for which we are set free by Him" (628; 798). Barth includes a discussion of the practical consequences of this delivering work of Christ in relation to our view of the past and the future. He quotes and comments on Ps 103:2 and Phil 3:13 in discussing how we should look at the past (628; 708), and alludes to Jesus' admonition not to worry (Matt 6:25–34; Luke 12:22–30) in relation to how we should look at the future (628f.; 708f.).

Scripture and God's Post-temporality

Third and finally, we look at Barth's use of Scripture in his treatment of God's post-temporality. In this relatively short treatment (629ff.; 709ff.), Barth does not include an exegetical or historical excursus and does not treat Scripture in any detail here. However, he does refer in the main text to how God will one day be "all in all," a phrase taken from 1 Cor 15:28 (630; 710). In this day of the eschatological future, all things will find their ultimate destiny in God and under his final judgment. Barth's distinctive "revelatory" view of eschatology is evident when he says that in the future lies the "*revelation* of the kingdom of God," the revelation of the kingdom of God about which we can *already* say that "He is all in all" (630; 710).[95] Barth also refers to scriptural passages and themes indirectly in his treatment of God's post-temporality, as when he alludes to Gen 2:2f. in his reference to God's final "Sabbath rest after the completion of all His works" (630; 710).

In the last part of his treatment of eternity, Barth spells out how there is "no basic rivalry" between the three forms of temporality (631; 711; see 2.4 above). There Barth employs Rom 11:36 as a leading passage and uses it as a rubric for referring to the distinction and unity of the three forms of God's temporality: "For *from* him and *through* him and *to* him are all things" (NRSV). Barth comments: "coming as it does at the end of Rom 9–11," Paul's adoption of this phrase[96] "surely points

---

95. Barth continues, "It is only in its revelation that the kingdom of God is post-temporal and therefore lies in the future. Already pre-temporally God was, and supra-temporally God is, all and all without reservation or reduction" (630; 710f.). It is not clear that this is what 1 Cor 15:28 or similar passages actually teach when read in context.

96. After quoting the "adopted" phrase in Greek, Barth adds in parentheses: "and there may be a verbal connection with certain ideas found in the mystery religions" (631; 711). This points out how Barth is not averse to making "higher-critical" observations about the historical origins of the text or its content, though here (as typically elsewhere) the observation does not affect his theological interpretation of the text in its final form.

to the fact that … in the same love and freedom, God is the One and all, the beginning, middle, and the end, the One who was and is and is to come, at perfect peace within himself" (631; 711f.). This concludes our survey of some of the ways in which Barth employs Scripture as a basis for his view of the three forms of divine temporality and the relationship that exists between them.

Concluding Reflections on Scripture in Barth's Doctrine of Eternity

In Barth's doctrine of eternity, as in other aspects of his doctrine of God, it is sometimes difficult to know how to characterize Barth's use of Scripture. Insofar as it verges on exegesis, it is surely not the kind of exegesis typical of academic biblical studies in the twentieth century. In addition, Barth develops the relationship between the text and theological conclusion in various ways that resist facile generalizations. Also, the various practices that we refer to as Barth's engagement with Scripture, interpretation of Scripture, or use of Scripture are practices that could often simultaneously be placed under the rubrics of Barth's use of tradition or use of reason. As we have also seen with respect to his treatment of divine unity and constancy, Barth weaves the three strands of the threefold cord so tightly together that they are often difficult to distinguish from each other.

But it is possible to make some observations that illuminate the nature of Barth's complex use of Scripture within his account of divine eternity and his doctrine of God as a whole. These observations concern the question of whether Barth avoids the related dangers of "eisegesis" and "natural theology." This question has been raised a number of times in this book, and once again we cannot escape the great difficulties involved in answering this question. Rival understandings of the nature of scriptural normativity and the criteria of exegesis yield rival answers.

One way of probing the question of whether Barth falls into eisegesis is to consider one of Barth's sympathetic critics, in this case the New Testament scholar Oscar Cullmann. Cullmann offers an "internal" critique of Barth's doctrine of eternity—i.e., criticism that agrees with Barth's methodological principle that theology should strive to be biblical and to avoid the imposition of foreign ideas and convictions upon the Bible.[97] In the forward to his influential book *Christ and Time*,[98] Cullmann compares his own view to Barth's.

> I am united with [Barth] in recognizing the strictly Christocentric character of the New Testament theology to which he in his *Dogmatik* gives so powerful an expression. When I here demonstrate that his conception of time, in which I see the last but quite momentous remnant of the influence of philosophy upon his exposition of the Bible, is incompatible with Primitive Christianity, I believe that thereby I am carrying out his Christocentric program on the field of New Testament exposition and by means of exegetical methods.[99]

Cullmann is clearly happy with Barth's "Christocentric program," but he believes that Barth allows a philosophy incompatible with the primitive Christianity of the New Testament to influence his biblical exposition. In a related passage, Cullmann finds in Barth "the last traces of a philosophical and non-biblical statement of the relation of time and eternity."[100] Yet, he commends Barth for "treating the problem of time *as a whole*," thus avoiding a one-sided treatment of it that focuses on only one of the three forms of temporality.

What kind of "philosophy" does Cullmann believe has influenced Barth's view of eternity and how eternity relates to time? The philosophy Cullmann has in mind is "Platonism."[101] Cullmann describes the relevant aspect of Platonic thought as follows:

> For Greek thinking in its Platonic formulation there exists between time and eternity a qualitative difference, which is not completely expressed by speaking of a distinction between limited and unlimited duration of time. For Plato, eternity is

---

97. See Hunsinger's description of the difference between internal and external critique (*Disruptive Grace*, 10).

98. Cullmann, *Christ and Time*. (The 1946 German edition was published only a few years after the publication of Barth's treatment of eternity in *KD* II/1).

99. Ibid., xiii. The kind of "influence of philosophy" that Cullmann wishes to speak of would probably fall under Barth's category of natural theology, rather than being merely "terminological."

100. Ibid., 60. He is commenting on Barth's treatment of the three forms of divine temporality (*CD* II/1, 621ff. and *KD* II/1, 698ff.).

101. See the similar conclusion reached by Moltmann (e.g., *Coming of God*, 18; see our comments in chapter 2) and the pertinent reflections of Gunton (*Becoming and Being*, 182ff.).

not endlessly extended time, but something quite different; it is timelessness.[102]

Barth's claim that "eternity is not ... an infinite extension of time both backwards and forwards" (608; 686) is designed to reinforce precisely the kind of qualitative distinction between time and eternity that Cullmann ascribes to Platonic thinking. Barth stresses that eternity is not simply "timelessness" (as Cullmann recognizes), but he also consistently says eternity is more than everlasting time.[103] Cullmann, by contrast, says that what the Bible calls eternity is simply the "unending duration" of linear time under God's direction, "the endless succession of the ages."[104]

Does Barth really come to his view primarily on the basis of Scripture? Or, as Cullmann thinks, does he read a Platonic view of eternity into Scripture? At times it does seem that Barth's theological claims about God's eternity, especially when he speaks of eternity as "non-temporality," involve quasi-classical (perhaps Platonic) philosophical assumptions that are not sufficiently governed by the concrete particularities of Scripture.[105] In such cases, Barth's views on eternity's distinction from time are not entirely based on a posteriori reflection (*Nachdenken*) on God's self-revelation as it is attested in Scripture. However, we could say much the same thing about Cullmann's views of time and eternity. His view that eternity is everlasting time does not simply arise from "objective" exegesis, but involves certain assumptions about reality (ontology) and the proper methodological relationship of Scripture to theology and philosophy.[106] Thus, the views of both Barth

---

102. Cullmann, *Christ and Time*, 61.
103. Ibid., 62ff.
104. Ibid., 62.
105. See our references to Douglas Farrow's criticism of Barth above.
106. Indeed, there is some reason to think that Cullmann's view of time is closer to a "modern progressivist" view of time than a "Christian" or biblical view of time (see Bauckham and Hart, "The Shape of Time," 46ff.). We can also observe that part of the contrast between Cullmann and Barth on time and eternity owes to the fact that they are writing in different genres. Cullmann is doing "New Testament exposition" (similar to what Barth calls "biblical theology"), whereas Barth is doing dogmatic theology. The former genre tends to eschew all use of philosophy (although Cullmann's attempt indicates that this may not be entirely possible), while the latter, as Barth saw it, is free to make use of philosophical discourse and concepts on an ad hoc basis (see chapter 2, in the subsection called "The difference between dogmatic and biblical theology").

and Cullmann are best seen as different possible ways of interpreting the totality of what Scripture has to say about the matters of time and eternity, ways that both involve a limited form of "eisegesis"[107] or perhaps even "natural theology."[108] Each view has its own strengths and weaknesses. Cullmann's view arguably has the advantage of simplicity, coherence, and proximity to the "letter" of the New Testament. Barth's dialectical perspective, while it may be less coherent and more difficult to grasp, is perhaps more sensitive to the "spirit" of Scripture, which testifies to God in his unique mysteriousness—a mysteriousness that we would expect to strain or even burst ordinary human concepts of time and eternity. Cullmann and Barth are both striving to be biblical, but are speaking about matters that the Bible's explicit statements do not clearly resolve. On the basis of a combination of direct and indirect authorization (Cullmann stressing the former and Barth the latter), they reach differing doctrines of eternity. As such, they are able to critique each other's errors and excesses and help their readers to identify where "eisegesis" may hide under the guise of a noble attempt to be biblical.

---

107. See Barth's comments on the inevitability of some degree of "eisegesis" in theology (I/1, 106).

108. Here we are not referring to a comprehensive or intentional natural theology, but simply to the inadvertent intervention of non-revealed (non-biblical or non-Christological) ideas or convictions into theology on specific points or occasions.

7

Conclusion

IN THIS FINAL CHAPTER, WE WILL DRAW TOGETHER THE VARIOUS strands of our argument and reflect on its significance. We will do so in two sections, the first offering a summary of our argument and the second some concluding observations.

A Summary of the Argument

By reflecting on our thesis statement (initially offered in the concluding section of chapter 1), we will now summarize the heart of our argument, which is principally concerned with the nature of Barth's theological method.[1] We recall that this thesis-statement is composed of the following two sentences.

1. In Barth's doctrines of God's unity, constancy, and eternity, Scripture functions as the authoritative source and basis for theological critique and construction, and tradition and reason are functionally subordinate to Scripture.

2. Yet, in this process of redescribing the biblical testimony to God, Barth employs a predominantly indirect way of relating Scripture and theological proposals, a way that allows tradition and reason to play important mediatory roles.

In light of the expository analysis given in chapters 4–6, we can now offer the following reflections on what this thesis statement means and implies.

---

1. Again, by Barth's theological method, we refer broadly to his way of doing theology, as it is evident primarily from his practice and secondarily from his programmatic or theoretical comments.

The first sentence in the thesis statement affirms the functional priority of Scripture over tradition and reason in Barth's method. This functional priority is evident in both the critical and the constructive aspects of Barth's dogmatic theology. With respect to the former, Barth's multifaceted use of Scripture[2] typically forms the primary and decisive basis for his critique of certain classical conceptions of divine simplicity, immutability, and a-temporal eternity. With respect to the later, Barth "redescribes God" primarily by means of redescribing the scriptural witness to God and thus provides an alternative to the faulty classical and modern doctrines of God that he critiques. Thus, with only occasional exceptions, Scripture functions in Barth's doctrine of God with the priority we would expect given his theoretical comments (see chapter 2). Rather than functioning with independent authority, tradition and reason function positively only in the hermeneutical task of interpreting and responding obediently to revelation and its scriptural witness.

The second sentence in the thesis statement clarifies the character of Scripture's functioning in Barth's work by saying that it is "predominantly indirect." That is, most of the claims Barth makes in his doctrines of divine perfections are not supported directly or independently through exegesis of scriptural proof texts (as might be the case for "biblical theology" as opposed to "dogmatics"). The second sentence of the thesis statement also affirms that, although Scripture has priority both in functional authority and in its capacity to explain Barth's method as a whole, tradition and reason retain a ubiquitous and significant presence alongside Scripture within Barth's unified theological practice. The indirect relationship between Scripture and a given doctrinal proposal is mediated in various ways by tradition and reason. Tradition does so either positively as a guide for the proper interpretation and use of Scripture, or negatively as a foil that displays Scripture's capacity to critique tradition. Reason mediates Scripture and theological conclusions by enabling the theologian to form concepts, judgments, and inferences that express obedience to the truths of revelation. Thus, the "three-fold

2. The multifaceted character of Barth's use of Scripture can be profitably described in terms of the five features that mark Barth's method as a whole (see relevant sections of chapter 2 and chapter 3). To review, Barth's theology is: (1) reverent, (2) Christocentric, (3) textually-based, (4) ecclesial, and (5) creative. See Pokrifka-Joe, "Appropriating Karl Barth's Use of Scripture," for a much fuller exposition of the five features in relation to Barth's use of Scripture.

cord" of Scripture, tradition, and reason enables Barth to redescribe God on the basis of a redescription of the biblical testimony to his self-revelation.

Concluding Observations

The Unifying Center of Barth's Method

The unity of Barth's theology has been construed in different ways by different scholars. Barth's own comments suggest that it is unwise to look for a stable unifying conceptual center to his dogmatic theology. Such a center would imply that Barth's theology is in *Church Dogmatics* is a closed system, something that Barth consistently strove to avoid.[3] A more promising suggestion, and one that Barth himself offered, is that his dogmatics is "Christocentric" in concentration and determination.[4] As such, his dogmatics is united around the person of Christ as the living Lord. This Christocentrism has been emphasized and is generally accepted in Barth scholarship.[5]

But Christocentrism is only one way of understanding the character and unity of Barth's theology, and it bears consideration whether other ways might complement the picture that Christocentrism provides. In this book we have argued that Barth's interpretation and use of Scripture provides just such an illuminating way of explaining the character and unity of Barth's theology, especially in relation to the method Barth actually employs to reach his dogmatic conclusions. In the words of Francis Watson, "Barth's biblical interpretation is . . . the foundation and principle of coherence of his entire project" in *Church Dogmatics*.[6] It would not be appropriate to regard biblical interpretation or usage as the *only* foundation or principle of coherence of Barth's *CD*, as Watson's comment might suggest. However, it is both appropriate and necessary to complement reference to Barth's

---

3. See our comments on Barth's rejection of the model of a system for dogmatics in chapter 2. See also the critical comments of Steven Sykes suggesting that Barth actually falls into a kind of Christological system in which incarnational doctrine prematurely predetermines Barth's interpretation of Scripture (*Karl Barth*, 41f., 47ff.; cf. Pugh, *The Anselmic Shift*, 139ff., 151f., 160f.).

4. See II/1, 320 and Barth, *How I Changed My Mind*, 43.

5. E.g., Hunsinger, *How to Read Karl Barth*, 225–33 and McCormack, *Karl Barth's Critically Realistic Dialectic Theology*, 453ff.

6. Watson, "The Bible," 57 (see our comments on Watson in chapter 1).

Christocentric concentration with significant attention to the scriptural concentration of Barth's theological method. This point is not only supported by a number of Barth's theoretical comments, but is more importantly supported by close attention to how Scripture functions in Barth's actual dogmatic practice. When we were faced with the task of explaining what method actually lead Barth to reach the conclusions he did about the doctrine of God, we found repeatedly that that Barth reached those conclusions by reflecting on Scripture and using it in a wide variety of direct and indirect ways.

Although our findings in this book have found little emphasis in previous Barth scholarship, these findings are not particularly surprising. All Barth scholars agree that Barth is consistently preoccupied with revelation in his theology. Christocentrism is one expression of this point. But since Scripture is the primary and only direct witness of God's Christological self-revelation, it is only natural that Barth's theology will also be consistently preoccupied with the interpretation and use of Scripture. Revelation is mediated. It is mediated to humanity primary through the testimony of Scripture and secondarily through tradition and reason that help to explicate that scriptural witness. It is strange, then, that while interpreters of Barth universally recognize the importance of revelation for Barth, few have emphasized adequately how this concern for revelation is concretely manifested in a thoroughgoing and unrelenting engagement with Scripture.

But we have also seen that Barth's concrete methodological practice is concerned with more than engagement with Scripture, at least if this engagement is understood narrowly as exegesis of specific biblical passages. Recognizing this, we have spoken of the roles of tradition and reason in his method in mediating Scripture and doctrine, such that doctrine is indirectly authorized by Scripture. But even here, we found that tradition and reason typically functioned in ways that either aided or were accountable to the interpretation and use of Scripture. Therefore, the functions of tradition and reason in Barth's work, as important as they are, are best and most accurately understood when we examine them in the context of the more basic function of Scripture in his work.

Indeed, every significant feature of Barth's theological method (e.g., its a posteriori character, its particularism, its opposition to natural theology, etc.) can be illuminated by understanding it as an aspect of Barth's interpretation and use of Scripture, including his Christocentrism.[7] Moreover, these diverse methodological features are linked together as necessary aspects of the practice of (Christocentric) theological biblical interpretation. The concrete features of Barth's way of doing theology can be fruitfully illuminated by putting them into the framework of the reverent use of Scripture, which includes roles for tradition and reason within it.

Theological Method and Divine Action

Making such a strong claim for the significance of Barth's engagement with Scripture in his theology is only tenable when one speaks of the free and gracious power of the Word of God and the Holy Spirit as they are active in Scripture and in the theologian. Barth consistently stressed that scriptural interpretation and use cannot be seen as a purely immanent human endeavor.[8] In this respect, a faithful interpretation of Barth must regard basic Christian doctrines about God and his relationship to sinful humanity as prior to claims about "theological method."[9] This is one important contribution of the dominant scholarly emphasis on Barth's substantive, soteriological Christocentrism. But again, we wish to provide a corresponding and complementary concentration on the concrete scholarly and spiritual practices and disciplines involved in Barth's scripturally-focused method. As such, we concentrate on an aspect of the "human side" of the divine-human relationship, namely the faithful human response to God's gracious initiative that is, or at least should be, expressed in dogmatic theology. But the "divine side" should not be forgotten. Barth regarded God's decisive and ongoing self-revelatory action as the primary presupposition and basis of all legitimate human theologizing and all human hermeneutical activity in relation to Scripture.[10] God's reconciliation and revelation is what

---

7. Strictly speaking, this observation is limited to the scope of our examination, namely Barth's doctrine of God in II/1, and especially his doctrines of unity, constancy and eternity—although it may well apply more generally.

8. In this respect, the use of Scripture itself finds its "divine" center and foundation not in itself, but in an "extrinsic" or "referential" foundation and center: the God revealed over and over in the revelatory action of Jesus Christ (see Watson, "Bible," 57f.).

9. Bruce McCormack frequently speaks of the priority of material decisions over shifts in method in Barth's method (e.g., *Karl Barth's Critically Realistic Dialectic Theology*, 19f. and 438).

10. See Webster, *Barth's Ethics*, 31f.

makes possible a theology that is anything more than sinful human self-projection—the religious self-projection that Barth thought Ludwig Feuerbach so accurately depicted. Barth believed that unaided human reasoning was unable to speak of God rightly, but, because of revelation, the theologian can speak of God and can do so without speculation.[11] Thus, the theologian tries to redescribe or reinterpret what God says and reveals about himself, rather than constructing a portrait of God out of his own mind or even out of the mind of the Church—both of which Barth regarded as plainly fallible. In all the human activities of the "hermeneutic of obedience," the theologian must constantly hope and pray for the ongoing self-revelatory action of God without which these activities are empty and unable to make real reference to the mysterious reality of God.[12] Barth aims, together with his church community, to be guided, confronted, and animated by the presence and ongoing word and work of the true and living God. In this "hermeneutical situation," Barth's hermeneutical theology weaves together the strands of the "three-fold cord" in an effort to respond in faith and obedience to the Triune God of grace.[13]

The Significance of this Study and Some Unanswered Questions

This study is significant for a number of reasons, many of which we have already indicated.[14] Here we need only to recall some of the most important reasons, all of which relate to Barth's use of Scripture. Barth scholars have recently noticed the importance of several of Barth's overlooked exegetical writings, especially several of commentaries.[15] A

---

11. In developing the idea of theology that assiduously avoids "speculation," Barth joins the ranks of both Calvin and Schleiermacher in different respects.

12. See Sykes, *Karl Barth*, 45. Barth makes some helpful comments along these lines in conversation with John Godsey. Reflecting on his view that no human activity (even theology) can "make room for revelation," Barth nonetheless says that we can and must *pray* for God's revelatory activity (Godsey, *Karl Barth's Table Talk*, 95).

13. For further comments on the "hermeneutical situation" as it is framed by distinctively Christian doctrine, see Webster, "Hermeneutics in Modern Theology."

14. See especially the opening section of chapter 1 called "Barth's Theological Method."

15. See the comments of John Webster (*Disruptive Grace*, 13f.) and the introductions in the new English edition of Barth's commentary on Philippians (*Epistle to the Philippians*).

number of worthy scholars have already examined Barth's exegesis in his *CD*, concentrating on his exegetical excurses.[16] Yet no scholar has examined comprehensively the role of Scripture within Barth's *CD*, or even in a section of *CD*. In particular, scholars have neglected the indirect role that Scripture has in supporting and authorizing many of the main dogmatic claims that Barth makes in his work—often without explicit citations of specific texts. With respect to one section of *CD*, Barth's doctrine of God in II/1, this study bridges the gap between the concern for Barth's interpretation of Scripture and concern for the main contours of his dogmatic claims.

There are a number of unanswered questions that future research on Barth could pursue. First, there is the question of *consistency*, of whether what we have found about Barth's method in selected portions of II/1 would hold true with respect to other parts of *CD*. We have indicated some reasons why it would be likely for the scriptural priority evident in Barth's method II/1 to be all the more evident in other parts of *CD*,[17] but such a claim would need to be tested. Future studies could also consider the degree to which Barth's theological method remained consistent, not only in the various volumes of *CD*, but in all of his writings throughout the various stages of his intellectual development. Comparisons of his method of scripture usage between his early exegetical works (i.e., commentaries) and his later dogmatic works would be particularly illuminating.

Second, there is the question of *evaluation*, of whether the various aspects of Barth's method are right or wrong, helpful or unhelpful. We have raised such critical questions occasionally throughout the book, and have made observations relevant to them. But it has been outside our purview to develop definitive or thorough answers to such evaluative questions. For example, we have been somewhat ambiguous about the extent to which Barth's use of Scripture sometimes involves improper "eisegesis." Future studies could also consider whether Barth's emphasis on Scripture causes him to underestimate the methodological

---

16. See the works surveyed in the section entitled "The Role of Scripture in Barth's Theology" in chapter 1.

17. The nature of Barth's doctrine of God in II/1, involves less exegesis and requires a greater emphasis on *indirect* scriptural authorization—and thus greater stress on the mediating roles of tradition and reason—than most other doctrines in his *CD* (see our comments in chapter 1, in the subsection entitled, "The Strategy of this Book in Relation to Previous Studies").

contributions of tradition, reason, or other factors such as "experience" or "culture."

Third, there is the question of *constructive appropriation*. We have not considered how Barth's method could be appropriated in a critical and constructive way within contemporary theology. Future studies could take up the question of what contemporary theology can learn from Barth in the areas of his doctrine of God or his theological method.

Our hope is that this study has laid a stable foundation for potential future studies by providing a sound and illuminating interpretation of Barth's biblically-focused theological method in a select portion of his work.

Appendix

The Shared Formal Structure of Barth's Doctrines of Divine Unity, Constancy, and Eternity

IN THIS APPENDIX, WE WISH TO DRAW OUT CERTAIN SHARED ASPECTS OF the formal structure of Barth's accounts of unity, constancy and eternity, the "leading" perfections of divine freedom, as these were understood in chapters 4–6.

Barth's accounts of divine unity, constancy and eternity share a common formal structure. Although Barth does not make this structure explicit, the following pattern seems implicit in his account. Each of these three perfections stand in a particular dialectical relationship with what we might call its "correlate" or "opposite."[1] Barth understands God's unity (simplicity) to be in a dialectical relationship with multiplicity, constancy with movement or change, and eternity with time. In each case, the relationship is "dialectical" in a specific sense: it involves both an element of *identity* (or inclusion or unity) between the perfection and its correlate and an element a *distinction* (or exclusion, contrast or opposition) between the perfection and its correlate.[2] Also, implicit in these three pairs of dialectical relationships is an element of *asymmetry*, in which the divine perfection proper (unity, constancy or eternity) has a kind of ontological priority over its correlate (multiplicity, movement/change or time/temporality).

This dialectical structure of identity-distinction-asymmetry in Barth's doctrine of God is an example of what George Hunsinger calls

---

1. Although we did not have occasion to stress it in this book, a similar point could be made of some other divine perfections. For example, we could suggest that Barth's conception of omnipresence exists in a dialectic with (determinate) space.

2. In this respect, Barth's work manifests something like the Hegelian principle of the identity of opposites, particularly in the relationship between the thesis and the antithesis in his dialectic (see Stace, *Philosophy of Hegel*, 96f.; cf. 106f.).

the "Chalcedonian" formal pattern in Barth's *CD* (see our comments in chapter 6).³ While the dialectical relationships involved are too complex and ambiguous to be pure examples of this pattern, the basic elements of the pattern are clear. In correspondence to the pattern we described above, the Chalcedonian formulation teaches that the divine and human natures of Christ are united ("without separation or division"), distinct ("without confusion or change") and asymmetrical (the implicit "precedence of the divine over the human nature of Jesus Christ").⁴ For example, divine constancy and divine change (what Barth called "holy mutability") are united with each other, yet are distinct realities in which constancy takes a certain precedence over change. In more dynamic terms, just as God, in and through the person of Christ, *includes* humanity within the divine identity, without denying that humanity, so also God in his constancy *includes* change within his constant identity, rather than strictly excluding or opposing it.⁵ A similar point could be made with respect to unity and eternity and their respective "opposites."⁶

---

3. Hunsinger, *How to Read Karl Barth*, 85.

4. Ibid. Here, Hunsinger describes the asymmetry as "unqualified *conceptual* precedence" of the divine over the human nature of Christ. This conceptual precedence seems rooted in a more basic ontological precedence. Perhaps Hunsinger would agree.

5. The language and conceptuality of Christological inclusion is evident at many places in Barth's work (see Dalferth, "Karl Barth's Eschatological Realism").

6. The points made in this paragraph about the Chalcedonian pattern are clarified by Hans Frei's comments on the logic of the Chalcedonian affirmation within Christian self description. Within the Chalcedonian "conceptual redescription" of features of the gospel stories, the categories of person and nature "both function logically as descriptions of the unitary subject to whom they are ascribed" (*Types of Christian Theology*, 125). He continues, "The logic, I suggest, of the formula is that of a subject-predicate description, rather than that of a substance-accident description." He notes that this does not imply a subject-predicate ontology, which did not appear in earnest until Hegel. We would suggest that, in Barth, both the subject-predicate logic and a parallel (quasi-Hegelian) ontology are at work. This is in keeping with Barth's "realism" (in a sense stronger than Frei's) in which the biblical witness and its logic genuinely refers to external reality, which in this case is the reality of God and Christ. The subject-predicate ascriptive logic thus points to the God who can be described in a rudimentary personalist-actualist theological ontology. Strictly speaking, then, Barth does not uphold the classical Chalcedonian two natures doctrine, in the sense of a substantialist ontology (see Farrow, *Ascension and Ecclesia*, and McCormack, "Grace and Being," 108f. and "Barths Grundsätzlicher Chalcedonismus?").

The following passage from Barth's account of eternity brings out this formal dialectical, Chalcedonian pattern that runs through Barth's doctrine of God.

> We have seen again and again that God is alive. His unity does not exclude but includes multiplicity and His constancy movement. And God does not first create multiplicity and movement, but He is one and simple, He is constant, in such a way that all multiplicity and movement have their prototype and pre-existence in Himself. Time, too, pre-exists in this way in Him, in His eternity... The form of creation[7] is the being of God for a reality distinct from Himself. (612; 690)

Since the tension in the relationship between the divine perfections and their correlates are not resolved in a higher synthesis,[8] there is an element of ambiguity in this relationship. Multiplicity, movement and time are ambiguously properties *both* of God (and so are unified with the perfections of unity, constancy and eternity) *and* of the created order (and so are distinguished from the three perfections). Put differently, multiplicity, movement and time are both (1) realities that are included in prototypical form within God's unity, constancy and eternity, and (2) realities that are part of creation or forms of creation. Ambiguity arises in Barth's account of divine perfections in part because Barth believes that a reverent response to the biblical testimony to God's revelation requires a dialectical combination of both of these emphases. That is, Barth resists a priori tendencies to define God *either* in basic continuity with the created order or in total contrast to it.

---

7. By "the form of creation" Barth here refers to time. In the same context, Barth also refers to space as another aspect of the form of creation. Space finds its prototype in God's omnipresence (*CD* II/1, 464f.), even as time finds its prototype in eternity.

8. In this respect Barth's dialectic here is different from Hegel's. There is no "third term," no synthesis of the thesis and antithesis. As such, the opposites that form the two sides of his dialectic remain in an unresolved tension with each other. This is typical of Barth's use of dialectic (as in the dialectic between love and freedom) and is indicative of his Trinitarian and Chalcedonian thought-patterns.

Bibliography

Anselm. *Anselm of Canterbury.* Vol. 1, *Monologion, Proslogion, Debate with Gaunilo, and a Meditation on Human Redemption.* Edited and translated by Jaspar Hopkins and Herbert Richardson. London: SCM, 1974.

Aquinas, Thomas. *Summa Theologiae: Latin Text with English Translation, Notes, Appendice, and Glossaries.* 61 vols. Blackfriars edition. New York: McGraw-Hill, 1964–1981.

Augustine. *City of God.* In *Nicene and Post-Nicene Fathers.* The First Series. Vol. 2. Edited by Philip Schaff. Grand Rapids: Eerdmans, 1977.

Bächli, Otto. *Das Alte Testament in der kirchlichen Dogmatic von Karl Barth.* Neukirchen, Vlyun: Neukirchener, 1987.

Balthasar, Hans Urs von. *The Theology of Karl Barth.* Translated by John Drury. Garden City, NY: Doubleday-Anchor, 1971. Originally published as *Karl Barth: Darstellung and Deutung siener Theology.* Colonge: Jacob Henger, 1951.

Barr, James. *Biblical Faith and Natural Theology.* Oxford: Clarendon, 1993.

Barth, Karl. "The Christian Understanding of Revelation." In *Against the Steam: Shorter Post-War Writings.* London: SCM, 1954.

———. *Church Dogmatics.* 13 vols. Translated by Geoffrey Bromiley. Edinburgh: T. & T. Clark, 1956–75. Originally published as *Die kirckliche Dogmatik.* Munich: Kaiser, 1932, and Zürich: Evangelischer, 1938–1965.

———. *Credo.* Translated by J. Strathhearn McNab. London: Hodder & Stoughton, 1936.

———. *Epistle to the Philippians.* 40th anniversary ed. Introductions by Bruce McCormack and Francis Watson. Louisville: Westminster John Knox, 2002.

———. *The Epistle to the Romans.* 6th ed. Translated by Edwyn C. Hoskyns. Oxford: Oxford University Press, 1933.

———. *Fides Quaerens Intellectum: Anselm's Proof of the Existence of God in the Context of his Theological Scheme.* Translated by I. W. Robertson. London: SCM, 1960.

———. *The Göttingen Dogmatics: Instruction in the Christian Religion.* Vol. 1. Edited by Hannelotte Reiffen. Translated by Geoffrey W. Bromiley. Grand Rapids: Eerdmans, 1991.

———. *How I Changed My Mind.* Edinburgh: Saint Andrew, 1969.

———. *Protestant Theology in the Nineteenth Century: Its Background and History.* Grand Rapids: Eerdmans, 2002.

———. *The Theology of Schleiermacher.* Translated by Geoffrey Bromiley. Grand Rapids: Eerdmans, 1982.

———. *The Word of God and the Word of Man.* Translated by Douglas Horton. New York: Harper & Row, 1957.

Barth, Karl, and Emil Brunner. *Natural Theology*. Translated by Peter Fraenkel. London: Centenary, 1946.

Bauckham, Richard. *God Crucified: Monotheism and Christology in the New Testament*. Grand Rapids: Eerdmans, 1998.

Bauckham, Richard, and Trevor Hart. "The Shape of Time." In *The Future as God's Gift: Explorations in Christian Eschatology*, edited by David Fergusson and Marcel Sarot, 41–72. Edinburgh: T. & T. Clark, 2000.

Baxter, Christina Ann. "The Movement from Exegesis to Dogmatics in the Theology of Karl Barth, with Special Reference to Romans, Philippians and *Church Dogmatics*." PhD diss., Durham University, 1981.

———. "The Nature and Place of Scripture in the *Church Dogmatics*." In *Theology beyond Christendom*, edited by John Thompson. Allison Park, PA: Pickwick, 1986.

Bengel, John Albert. *Bengel's New Testament Commentary*. 2 vols. Translated by Charlton T. Lewis and Marvin R. Vincent. Grand Rapids: Kregel, 1971.

Bowman, Donna. "Barth and Whitehead on Divine Self-Determination." *Encounter* 60 (1999) 441–62.

Bradshaw, Timothy. *Trinity and Ontology: A Comparative Study of the Theologies of Karl Barth and Wolfhart Pannenberg*. Edinburgh: Rutherford, 1989.

Bromiley, G. W. *Barth-Bultmann Letters 1922–1966*. Edinburgh: T. & T. Clark, 1982.

———. *Introduction to Karl Barth*. Grand Rapids: Eerdmans, 1979.

———. *A Late Friendship: The Letters of Karl Barth and Carl Zuckamayer*. Grand Rapids: Eerdmans, 1982.

Brown, Robert McAfee. *Scripture and Tradition in the Theology of Karl Barth*. Pittsburgh: Duquesne University Press, 1965.

Brown, Robert F. "On God's Ontic and Noetic Absoluteness: A Critique of Barth." *Scottish Journal of Theology* 33 (1980) 533–49.

———. "Schelling and Dorner on Divine Immutability." *Journal of the American Academy of Religion* 53 (1985) 237–49.

Büttner, Matthias. *Das Alte Testament als erster Teil der christlichen Bibel: zur Frage nach theologischer Auslegung und "Mitte" im Kontext der Theologie Karl Barths*. Gütersloh: Kaiser, 2002.

Calvin, John. *Institutes of the Christian Religion*. 2 vols. Edited by J. T. McNeill. Translated by Ford Lewis Battles. Philadelphia: Westminster, 1960.

Camfield, F. W., editor. *Reformation Old and New*. London: Lutterworth, 1947.

Childs, Brevard. "Toward Recovering Theological Exegesis." *Pro Ecclesia* 6 (1997) 16–26.

Chisholm, Roderick M. *The Foundations of Knowing*. Minneapolis: University of Minnesota Press, 1982.

Clark, Gordon H. *Karl Barth's Theological Method*. Philadelphia: Presbyterian & Reformed, 1963.

Clark, Tony. *Divine Revelation and Human Practice: Responsive and Imaginative Participation*. Eugene, OR: Cascade, 2008.

Cobb, John B. *Living Options in Protestant Theology: A Survey of Methods*. Lanham, MD: University Press of America, 1986.

Cole, Graham A. "Towards a New Metaphysic of the Exodus." *Reformed Theological Review* 42 (1983) 75–84.

Colwell, John E. *Actuality and Provisionality: Eternity and Election in the Theology of Karl Barth*. Edinburgh: Rutherford House, 1989.

Crawford, Robert G. "The Theological Method of Karl Barth." *Scottish Journal of Theology* 25 (1972) 320–26.

Cross, Terry L. *Dialectic in Karl Barth's Doctrine of God*. New York: Lang, 2001.

Cullmann, Oscar. *Christ and Time*. Philadelphia: Westminster, 1951.

Cunningham, Mary Kathleen. *What is Theological Exegesis? Interpretation and Use of Scripture in Barth's Doctrine of Election*. Valley Forge, PA: Trinity, 1995.

Currie, Thomas W. "Being in Act: Ontology and Epistemology in Karl Barth's Doctrine of God." PhD thesis, University of Edinburgh, 1976.

―――. "The Being and Act of God." In *Theology beyond Christendom*, edited by John Thompson, 1–12. Allison Park, PA: Pickwick, 1986.

Dalferth, Ingof U. "Karl Barth's Eschatological Realism." In *Karl Barth: Centenary Essays*, edited by S. W. Sykes, 14–45. Cambridge: Cambridge University Press, 1989.

Daveney, Sheila Greeve. *Divine Power: A Study of Karl Barth and Charles Hartshorne*. Philadelphia: Fortress, 1986.

Dean, Eric. "Relation between Scripture and Tradition: Theoretical Statements by Calvin and Barth." *Encounter* 23 (1962) 277–91.

Demson, David E. *Hans Frei and Karl Barth: Different Ways of Reading Scripture*. Grand Rapids: Eerdmans, 1997.

Dorner, Isaak August. *Divine Immutability: A Critical Reconsideration*. Translated by Robert R. Williams and Claude Welch. Minneapolis: Fortress, 1994.

―――. *A System of Christian Doctrine*. 4 vols. Rev. ed. Translated by Alfred Cave. Edinburgh: T. & T. Clark, 1897.

Dorrien, Gary. *The Barthian Revolt in Modern Theology: Theology without Weapons*. Louisville: Westminster John Knox, 2000.

Duke, James O., and Robert F. Streetman, editors. *Barth and Schleiermacher: Beyond the Impasse*. Philadelphia: Fortress, 1988.

Farrow, Douglas. *Ascension and Ecclesia*. Edinburgh: T. & T. Clark, 1999.

―――. "Karl Barth on the Ascension: An Appreciation and a Critique." *International Journal of Systematic Theology* 1 (2000) 127–50.

Fiddes, Paul S. *The Creative Suffering of God*. Oxford: Clarendon, 1992.

Ford, David F. "Barth's Interpretation of the Bible." In *Karl Barth: Studies of His Theological Method*, edited by S. W. Sykes, 55–87. Oxford: Clarendon, 1979.

―――. *Barth and God's Story: Biblical Narrative and the Theological Method of Karl Barth in the Church Dogmatics*. New York: Lang, 1981.

Frame, John M. *The Doctrine of the Knowledge of God*. Phillipsburg, NJ: Presbyterian and Reformed Publishing, 1987.

Frei, Hans W. *The Eclipse of Biblical Narrative*. New Haven: Yale University Press, 1974.

―――. *The Identity of Jesus Christ: The Hermeneutic Bases of Dogmatic Theology*. Philadelphia: Fortress, 1982.

―――. "The 'Literal Reading' of Biblical Narrative in the Christian Tradition: Does It Stretch or Will It Break?" In *The Bible and the Narrative Tradition*, edited by Frank McConnell, 36–77. Oxford: Oxford University Press, 1986.

―――. *Types of Christian Theology*. Edited by George Hunsinger and William C. Placher. London: Yale University Press, 1992.

Gilkey, Langdon. "A Theology in Process: Schubert Ogden's Developing Theology." *Interpretation* 21 (1967) 447–59.

Gockel, Matthias. "On the Way from Schleiermacher to Barth: A Critical Reappraisal of Isaak August Dorner's Essay on Divine Immutability." *Scottish Journal of Theology* 53 (2000) 490–510.

Godsey, John D. *Karl Barth's Table Talk*. Edinburgh: Oliver & Boyd, 1963.

Green, Joel B. "Scripture and Theology: Failed Experiments, Fresh Perspectives." *Interpretation* 56 (2002) 5–20.

Greene-McCreight, Katherine. *Ad Litteram: How Augustine, Calvin and Barth Read the Plain Sense of Genesis 1–3*. New York: Lang, 1999.

Gunton, Colin E. *Becoming and Being: The Doctrine of God in Charles Hartshorne and Karl Barth*. Oxford: Oxford University Press, 1978.

———. *Christ and Creation*. Grand Rapids: Eerdmans, 1992.

———. "Karl Barth's Doctrine of Election as Part of His Doctrine of God." *Journal of Theological Studies* 25 (1974) 381–92.

———. *The One, the Three and the Many: God, Creation and the Culture of Modernity*. Cambridge: Cambridge University Press, 1994.

———. "Salvation." In *The Cambridge Companion to Karl Barth*, edited by John Webster, 143–58. Cambridge: Cambridge University Press, 2000.

Hart, Trevor A. "Living with Diversity: Scripture, Tradition and the Present." Occasional Paper, Scholarly Engagement with Anglican Doctrine, Occasional, 2000.

———. *Regarding Karl Barth: Essays Toward a Reading of his Theology*. Carlisle, UK: Paternoster, 1999.

———. "Spirit of the Age or Spirit of Truth? Identifying the Holy Spirit." Unpublished Paper, 1999.

Hartwell, Herbert. *The Theology of Karl Barth: An Introduction*. Philadelphia: Westminster, 1964.

Haupert, Thomas J. "Faith in Search of Certainty: Karl Barth's Method in Dogmatics and Apologetics." PhD thesis, University of Edinburgh, 1977.

Hendry, George S. "The Freedom of God in the Theology of Karl Barth." *Scottish Journal of Theology* 31 (1978) 229–44.

———. "The Transcendental Method in the Theology of Karl Barth." *Scottish Journal of Theology* 37 (1984) 213–27.

Heppe, Heinrich. *Reformed Dogmatics*. Translated by G. T. Thompson. London: Allen & Unwin, 1950.

Holder, Rodney. "Karl Barth and the Legitimacy of Natural Theology." *Themelios* 26:3 (2001) 22–37.

Hunsinger, George. *Disruptive Grace: Studies in the Theology of Karl Barth*. Grand Rapids: Eerdmans, 2000.

———. *How to Read Karl Barth: The Shape of His Theology*. Oxford: Oxford University Press, 1991.

Jenson, Robert W. *God after God: God of the Past and God of the Future in the Work of Karl Barth*. Indianapolis, IN: Bobbs-Merrill, 1969.

———. "Karl Barth." In *The Modern Theologians*, edited by David F. Ford, 21–36. Oxford: Blackwell, 1997.

Jersild, Paul. "Natural Theology and the Doctrine of God in Albrecht Ritschl and Karl Barth." *Lutheran Quarterly* 14 (1962) 239–57.

Johnson, William Stacy. "Barth and Beyond." *Christian Century* 118 (2001) 16-20.
———. *The Mystery of God: Karl Barth and the Postmodern Foundations of Theology.* Louisville: Westminster John Knox, 1997.
Jüngel, Eberhard. *The Doctrine of the Trinity: God's Being Is in Becoming.* Translated by Horton Harris. Grand Rapids: Eerdmans, 1976.
———. *Karl Barth, a Theological Legacy.* Translated by Garrett E. Paul. Philadelphia: Westminster, 1986.
Kelsey, David H. *Proving Doctrine: The Uses of Scripture in Modern Theology.* Harrisburg, PA: Trinity, 1999. Formerly published as *The Uses of Scripture in Recent Theology.* Philadelphia: Fortress, 1975.
Kirchstein, Helmut. *Der souveräne Gott und die Heilige Schrift: Einfürung in die biblische Hemeneutik Karl Barths.* Aachen: Shaker, 1998.
Leftow, Brian. "God, Concepts of." In *The Routledge Encyclopedia of Philosophy,* edited by Edward Craig, 4:93-102. London: Routledge, 1998.
Leslie, Benjamin C. *Trinitarian Hermenutics: The Hermeuntical Significance of Karl Barth's Doctrine of the Trinity.* New York: Lang, 1991.
Lindbeck, George A. *The Nature of Doctrine: Religion and Theology in a Postliberal Age.* Philadelphia: Westminster, 1984.
MacIntyre, Alasdair. *Three Rival Traditions of Moral Inquiry: Encyclopaedia, Genealogy, and Tradition.* London: Duckworth, 1990.
———. *Whose Justice? Which Rationality?* Notre Dame, IN: University of Notre Dame Press, 1988.
Macquarrie, John. *Principles of Christian Theology.* London: SCM, 1966.
———. *Twentieth Century Religious Thought.* New York: Harper & Row, 1963.
Marquardt, F. W. "Exegese und Dogmatik in Karl Barths Theologie." In *Die kirchliche Dogmatik: Registerband,* edited by Wolfgang Erk and Marcel Pfänder, 649-76. Zürich: EVZ, 1970.
McCormack, Bruce L. "Barths Grundsätzlicher Chalcedonismus?" *Zeitschrift für dialektische Theologie* 18 (2002) 138-73. Later published in slightly revised form in Bruce L. McCormack, "Karl Barth's Historicized Christology: Just How 'Chalcedonian' Is It?" In *Orthodox and Modern: Studies in the Theology of Karl Barth,* 201-33. Grand Rapids: Baker Academic, 2008.
———. "Grace and Being: The Role of God's Gracious Election in Karl Barth's Theological Ontology." In *Cambridge Companion to Karl Barth,* edited by John Webster, 92-110. Cambridge: Cambridge University Press, 2000.
———. "Historical Criticism and Dogmatic Interest in Karl Barth's Theological Exegesis of the New Testament." In *Biblical Hermeneutics in Historical Perspective,* edited by M. S. Burrows and Paul Rorem, 322-38. Grand Rapids: Eerdmans, 1991.
———. *Karl Barth's Critically Realistic Dialectic Theology: Its Genesis and Development 1909-1936.* Oxford: Clarendon, 1995.
McDowell, John C. "A Response to Rodney Holder on Barth on Natural Theology." *Themelios* 27 (2002) 32-44.
McGlasson, Paul C. *Jesus and Judas.* Atlanta: Scholars, 1991.
McGrath, Alister E. *The Genesis of Doctrine: A Study in the Foundations of Doctrinal Criticism.* Oxford: Blackwell, 1990.
Meijering, E. P. *Von den Kirchenvatern zu Karl Barth: Das Altkirchlichen Dogma in der "Kirchlichen Dogmatik."* Amsterdam: Gieben, 1993.

Molnar, Paul D. *Divine Freedom and the Immanent Trinity*. Edinburgh: T. & T. Clark, 2002.

———. "The Function of the Immanent Trinity in the Theology of Karl Barth: Implications for Today." *Scottish Journal of Theology* 42 (1989) 367–99.

———. "Toward a Contemporary Doctrine of the Immanent Trinity: Karl Barth and the Present Discussion." *Scottish Journal of Theology* 49 (1996) 311–57.

Moltmann, Jürgen. *The Coming of God: Christian Eschatology*. Translated by Margaret Kohl. Minneapolis: Fortress, 1996.

———. *Crucified God: The Cross of Christ as the Foundation and Criticism of Christian Theology*. Translated by R. A. Wilson and John Bowden. New York: Harper & Row, 1974.

———. *Theology of Hope: On the Ground and the Implications of a Christian Eschatology*. Translated by James W. Leitch. New York: Harper & Row, 1967.

———. *The Trinity and the Kingdom: The Doctrine of God*. Translated by Margaret Kohl. San Francisco: Harper & Row, 1981.

Muller, Richard A. "Incarnation, Immutability, and the Case for Classical Theism." *Westminster Theological Journal* 45 (1983) 22–40.

Owen, H. P. *Concepts of Deity*. New York: Herder & Herder, 1971.

Padgett, Alan G. *God, Eternity and the Nature of Time*. New York: St. Martin's, 1992.

Pannenberg, Wolfhart. "The Appropriation of the Philosophical Conception of God as a Dogmatic Problem of Early Christian Theology." In *Basic Questions in Theology*, translated by G. H. Kehm, 2:119–83. Philadelphia: Fortress, 1971.

———. "Die Subjecktivität Gottes und die Trinitätslehre: Ein Beitrag zur Beiziehung zwischen Karl Barth und der Philosophie Hegels." In *Grundfragen systematicher Theologie: Gesammelte Aufsätze*, 2:96–111. Göttingen: Vandenhoeck & Ruprecht, 1980.

———. *Systematic Theology*. 3 vols. Translated by Geoffrey W. Bromiley. Grand Rapids: Eerdmans, 1991–1998.

———, editor. *Revelation as History*. London: SPCK, 1968.

Placher, William C. *Domestication of Transcendence*. Louisville: Westminster John Knox, 1996.

———. *Narratives of a Vulnerable God*. Louisville: Westminster John Knox, 1994.

Plantinga, Alvin, and Nicholas Wolterstorff, editors. *Faith and Rationality*. Notre Dame, University of Notre Dame Press, 1983.

Pokrifka-Joe, Todd. "Appropriating Karl Barth's Use of Scripture in Contemporary Theology." Unpublished paper, 2001. Online: http://www.luthersem.edu/ctrf/Papers/2001_Pokrifka-Joe.htm.

Poythress, Vern S. *Symphonic Theology: The Validity of Multiple Perspectives in Theology*. Grand Rapids: Zondervan, 1987.

Provence, Thomas E. "The Hermeneutics of Karl Barth." PhD diss., Fuller Theological Seminary, 1980.

Pugh, Jeffrey C. *The Anselmic Shift: Christology and Method in Karl Barth's Theology*. New York: Lang, 1990.

Rahner, Karl. "Scripture and Tradition." In *Sacramentum Mundi: An Encylopedia of Theology*, edited by Karl Rahner et al., 6:56. London: Burns & Oates, 1970.

Ramm, Bernard. *After Fundamentalism: The Future of Evangelical Theology*. San Francisco: Harper & Row, 1983.

———. "Karl Barth and T. S. Eliot on Tradition." In *Church, Word and Spirit: Historical and Theological Essays in Honor of Geoffrey W. Bromiley Bradley*, edited by James E. Bradley and Richard A. Muller, 241–61. Grand Rapids: Eerdmans, 1987.

Ricoeur, Paul. *Oneself as Another*. Chicago: University of Chicago Press, 1992.

Rogers, Eugene F. *Thomas Aquinas and Karl Barth: Sacred Doctrine and the Natural Knowledge of God*. Notre Dame, IN: University of Notre Dame Press, 1996.

Roberts, Richard. "Karl Barth's Doctrine of Time." In *Karl Barth: Studies of His Theological Method*, edited by S. W. Sykes, 89–146. Oxford: Clarendon, 1979.

Sauter, Gerhard. *Eschatological Rationality: Theological Issues in Focus*. Grand Rapids: Baker, 1996.

Scalise, Charles J. "Canonical Hermeneutics: Childs and Barth." *Scottish Journal of Theology* 47 (1994) 61–88.

Schleiermacher, Friedrich. *The Christian Faith*. Edinburgh: T. & T. Clark, 1928.

Schlichting, Wolfhart. *Biblische Denkform in der Dogmatik: Die Vorbildlichkeit des biblischen Denkens für die Methode der "kirchliche Dogmatik" Karl Barths*. Zurich: Theologicher, 1971.

Schwöbel, Christoph. "Theology." In *The Cambridge Companion to Karl Barth*, edited by John Webster, 17–36. Cambridge: Cambridge University Press, 2000.

Sherman, Robert. "Isaak August Dorner on Divine Immutability: A Missing Link between Schleiermacher and Barth." *Journal of Religion* 77 (1997) 380–402.

Smend, Rudolph. "Nachkritische Schriftauslegung." In *Parrhesia: Karl Barth Zum achtzigsten Geburtstag*, edited by E. Busch, J. Fangmeier, and M. Geiger, 215–37. Zurich: EVZ, 1966.

Smith, Steven G. "Karl Barth and Fideism: A Reconsideration." *Anglican Theological Review* 66 (1984) 64–78.

Soulen, R. Kendall. "*YHWH* the Triune God." *Modern Theology* 15 (1999) 25–54.

Stace, W. T. *The Philosophy of Hegel: A Systematic Exposition*. New York: Dover, 1955.

Stead, Christopher. *Divine Substance*. Oxford: Oxford University Press, 1977.

Strauson, P. F. *Individuals: An Essay in Descriptive Metaphysics*. New York: Routledge, 1959.

Sykes, Steven W. "Barth on the Centre of Theology." In *Karl Barth: Studies of His Theological Method*, edited by Steven W. Sykes, 17–54. Oxford: Clarendon, 1979.

———, editor. *Karl Barth: Studies of His Theological Method*. Oxford: Clarendon, 1979.

Tanner, Kathryn. "Creation and Providence." In *The Cambridge Companion to Karl Barth*, edited by John Webster, 111–26. Cambridge: Cambridge University Press, 2000.

Torrance, Alan J. *Persons in Communion: An Essay on Trinitarian Description and Human Participation*. T. & T. Clark, 1996.

———. "The Trinity." In *The Cambridge Companion to Karl Barth*, edited by John Webster, 72–91. Cambridge: Cambridge University Press, 2000.

Torrance, Thomas F. *The Christian Doctrine of God: One Being Three Persons*. Edinburgh: T. & T. Clark, 1996.

———. *Divine Meaning: Studies in Patristic Hermeneutics*. Edinburgh: T. & T. Clark, 1995.

———. *Karl Barth: An Introduction to His Early Theology, 1910–1931*. London: SCM, 1962.

———. *Karl Barth: Biblical and Evangelical Theologian.* Edinburgh: T. & T. Clark, 1990.

———. *The Trinitarian Faith.* Edinburgh: T. & T. Clark, 1988.

Toulmin, Stephen. *The Uses of Argument.* Cambridge: Cambridge University Press, 1964.

Trowitzsch, Michael, editor. *Karl Barths Schriftauslegung.* Tübingen: Mohr/Siebeck, 1996.

Van Hoozer, Kevin J. "The Voice and the Actor: A Dramatic Proposal about the Ministry and Minstrelsy of Theology." In *Evangelical Futures: A Conversation on Theological Method*, edited by John G. Stackhouse Jr., 61–106. Downers Grove, IL: InterVarsity, 2000.

Van Niekerk, Erasmus. "The Biblical Conceptual Form in Barth's Church Dogmatics." *Theologia Evangelica* 22 (1989) 13–23.

Vischer, Wilhelm. *The Witness of the Old Testament to Christ.* Translated by A. B. Crabtree. London: Lutterworth, 1949.

Wallace, Mark. *The Second Naïveté: Barth, Ricoeur and the New Yale Theology.* Macon, GA: Mercer University Press, 1990.

Watson, G. W. "Karl Barth and St Anselm's Theological Programme." *Scottish Journal of Theology* 30 (1977) 31–45.

Watson, Francis. "The Bible." In *The Cambridge Companion to Karl Barth*, edited by John Webster, 57–71. Cambridge: Cambridge University Press, 2000.

———. *Text and Truth.* Grand Rapids: Eerdmans, 1997.

———. *Text, Church and World.* Grand Rapids: Eerdmans, 1994.

Webster, John. *Barth's Ethics of Reconciliation.* Cambridge: Cambridge University Press, 1995.

———. "Hermeneutics in Modern Theology: Some Doctrinal Reflections." *Scottish Journal of Theology* 51 (1998) 307–41.

———, editor. *The Cambridge Companion to Karl Barth.* Cambridge: Cambridge University Press, 2000.

Welker, Michael. "Barth's Theology and Process Theology." *Theology Today* 43 (1986) 383–97.

Wharton, James A. "Karl Barth as an Exegete and His Influence on Biblical Interpretation." *Union Seminary Quarterly Review* 28 (1972) 5–13.

Williams, Robert R. "I. A. Dorner: The Ethical Immutability of God." *Journal of the American Academy of Religion* 54 (1986) 721–38.

Wolterstorff, Nicholas. *Divine Discourse: Philosophical Reflections on the Claim that God Speaks.* Cambridge: Cambridge University Press, 1995.

———. "Divine Simplicity." In *Our Knowledge of God*, edited by Kelly J. Clark, 133–50. Boston: Kluwer Academic, 1992.

Wood, Charles M. *The Formation of Christian Understanding: An Essay in Theological Hermeneutics.* Philadelphia: Westminster, 1981.

Work, Telford. *Living and Active: Scripture in the Economy of Salvation.* Grand Rapids: Eerdmanns, 2002.

Yeago, David S. "The New Testament and Nicene Dogma: A Contribution to Theological Exegesis." *Pro Ecclesia* 3 (1994) 152–64.

Young, Frances M. *Biblical Exegesis and the Formation of Christian Culture.* Cambridge: Cambridge University Press, 1997.

Index of Names

Anselm, 24, 31–32, 81, 83, 88, 94, 106, 139, 141, 144, 160, 162–64, 169, 178, 249–50, 254, 276

Aquinas, Thomas, 25, 75, 80–81, 83, 119, 156, 160, 163, 165, 169, 172–73, 178, 192, 198, 251–53, 258, 265, 267

Augustine, 23, 26, 80–81, 86–87, 162–64, 197, 203, 206, 249–50, 253–54, 276

Bächli, Otto, 17–20, 57, 65
Balthasar, Hans Urs von., 11, 34, 36, 50
Barr, James, 11, 51
Bauckham, Richard, 190, 221, 292
Baxter, Christina Ann, 6, 13–17, 19–21, 56–57, 103
Bengel, John Albert, 77, 85–87
Bowman, Donna, 129
Bradshaw, Timothy, 34, 38, 118
Bromiley, G. W., 35, 55, 59, 86, 117, 222
Brown, Robert McAfee, 5
Brown, Robert F., 137, 244
Brunner, Emil, 51, 200
Büttner, Matthias, 23

Calvin, John, 23, 75, 79, 84, 85, 160, 165, 287, 299
Camfield, F. W., 39, 166, 203, 211, 252
Childs, Brevard, 12, 67, 104
Chisholm, Roderick M., 100
Clark, Gordon H., 2, 29, 46, 136, 176
Clark, Tony, 7, 34, 37, 109
Cobb, John B., 9
Cole, Graham A., 177, 205
Colwell, John E., 118–19, 137, 248, 262, 264, 267
Crawford, Robert G., 2
Cross, Terry L., 36, 127, 145–47, 150, 169–70, 179

Cullmann, Oscar, 263, 290–93
Cunningham, Mary Kathleen, 21, 22, 285
Currie, Thomas W., 39–41, 145

Dalferth, Ingof U., 92, 129, 266, 304
Davaney, Sheila Greeve, 39
Dean, Eric, 5, 73
Demson, David E., 23
Dorner, Isaak August, 34, 83, 129, 183, 185, 203, 205, 210, 242–47
Dorrien, Gary, 3, 4, 34, 50, 84
Duke, James O., 34

Farrow, Douglas, 258, 279, 304
Fiddes, Paul S., 129
Ford, David, 2, 6, 14–17, 20–21, 56–57, 98, 105–6, 149, 157, 160, 172, 221, 228, 237, 262
Frame, John M., 88, 101
Frei, Hans W., 16, 20, 23, 35, 53, 69, 85–86, 95–98, 119, 158, 183, 192, 195, 221, 284, 304

Gilkey, Langdon, 81
Gockel, Matthias, 34, 243, 245
Godsey, John D., 28, 50, 77, 299
Green, Joel B., 14
Greene-McCreight, Katherine E., 13, 23, 53, 85
Gunton, Colin E., 24–26, 30, 34, 38–39, 50–51, 80, 88–89, 97, 107, 111, 119–20, 122, 125, 141, 167, 171, 202, 206, 216, 252, 257, 262, 267, 291

Hart, Trevor A., 51, 84, 90, 117, 119, 133, 166, 218–19, 292
Hartwell, Herbert, 9, 30, 34, 51, 235
Haupert, Thomas J., 28

Hendry, George S., 34, 100–101, 135, 184
Heppe, Heinrich, 86–87, 156, 204
Holder, Rodney, 29–30
Hunsinger, George, 3–4, 8, 30, 32–33, 35, 37, 39, 67, 79, 84, 88–92, 94–97, 101, 111, 122, 125, 128, 131, 137, 144, 147, 167, 171, 173–75, 177, 179, 193–95, 205, 221, 235–36, 241, 248, 250–51, 254–57, 259, 261, 263, 266–69, 271, 273, 275, 291, 296, 303–4

Jenson, Robert W., 25, 38, 41, 96, 105, 158, 255, 264, 278
Jersild, Paul, 34
Johnson, William Stacy, 39, 50, 100, 124, 130, 150
Jüngel, Eberhard, 8, 38, 64, 110, 112, 119, 126, 130, 206–7, 209, 211

Kelsey, David H., 7, 11–14, 16, 54, 66, 69, 98, 102, 130, 221, 236
Kirchstein, Helmut, 23

Leftow, Brian, 81, 156
Leslie, Benjamin C., 27–28, 34, 35, 38, 51, 73, 110, 117, 120
Lindbeck, George A., 96, 97

MacIntyre, Alasdair, 33, 90, 191
MacQuarrie, John, 30, 88, 90
Marquardt, F. W., 8, 22
McCormack, Bruce L., 6, 24–25, 34, 36–39, 52, 84, 88–90, 94, 100, 103, 105, 107, 121–22, 125, 144, 209–11, 232, 235, 242, 264, 267, 272, 285, 296, 298, 304
McDowell, John C., 30
McGlasson, Paul C., 6, 19–21, 36, 79, 96, 184, 190, 192, 195
McGrath, Alister E., 192
Meijering, E. P., 27, 82
Molnar, Paul D., 120
Moltmann, Jürgen, 25, 34, 118, 243, 246, 257, 274, 291
Muller, Richard A., 201–2, 278

Owen, H. P., 80, 82

Padgett, Alan G., 163, 262, 265
Pannenberg, Wolfhart, 93, 112, 118, 243, 246
Placher, William C., 81, 83, 167, 251, 262
Plantinga, Alvin, 50
Pokrifka-Joe, Todd, 106, 295
Poythress, Vern S., 176
Provence, Thomas E., 8
Pugh, Jeffrey C., 24, 88, 296

Rahner, Karl, 78
Ramm, Bernard, 2, 9
Ricoeur, Paul, 130, 178, 182–83, 205, 212–19, 221
Rogers, Eugene F., 25, 173
Roberts, Richard, 30, 248, 255, 257, 261, 265

Sauter, Gerhard, 43
Scalise, Charles J., 104
Schleiermacher, Friedrich, 26, 34, 83–84, 129, 165, 168, 202, 243, 245–47, 299
Schlichtling, Wolfhart, 10–11, 13–14, 18
Schwöbel, Christoph, 33, 101
Sherman, Robert, 34, 185, 243–46
Smend, Rudolph, 8, 22–23
Smith, Steven G., 30–32, 89–90
Soulen, R. Kendall, 114
Stace, W. T., 303
Stead, Christopher, 159, 162
Strauson, P. F., 158
Streetman, Robert F., 34
Sykes, Steven W., 2, 38, 92, 118, 296, 299

Tanner, Kathryn, 167, 208
Torrance, Alan J., 38, 50, 63, 89, 95, 101, 110, 118–19, 125, 217, 263, 269
Torrance, Thomas F., 6, 13, 26–27, 30–31, 37–38, 43, 46, 51, 92, 106, 119, 206, 220
Toulmin, Stephen, 98

Trowitzsch, Michael, 22-23
Van Hoozer, Kevin J., 12-13, 67
Van Niekerk, Erasmus, 11
Vischer, Wilhelm, 104

Wallace, Mark, 8
Watson, G. W., 24
Watson, Francis, 9, 53, 59, 71-72, 296, 298
Webster, John, 39, 84, 96-97, 158, 160, 298-99

Welker, Michael, 25, 34
Wharton, James A., 22
Williams, Robert R., 242-43, 245
Wolterstorff, Nicholas, 50, 54, 156, 161, 162, 191, 192
Wood, Charles M., 54
Work, Telford, 12

Yeago, David S., 67, 114, 194, 198, 210, 234, 277
Young, Frances M., 13

www.ingramcontent.com/pod-product-compliance
Lightning Source LLC
Chambersburg PA
CBHW050619300426
44112CB00012B/1570